Book Project

Schools of Hope

Douglas H. Heath

Schools of Hope

Developing Mind
and Character
in Today's Youth

Conrow Publishing House

Published by Conrow Publishing House
P.O. Box 1411, Bryn Mawr, PA 19010
www.conrowpub.com

Printed in the United States of American
by Thomson-Shore, Inc., Dexter, Michigan

Library of Congress Catalog Card Number: 99-094613

ISBN: 0-9641727-5-5 (paper)

First Soft Cover Edition

With appreciation for their inspiration

Friends Council on Education
Haverford College
Model High School, Bloomfield Hills
Monteux School for Conductors and
Orchestra Musicians
Proctor Academy

Contents

ix

Preface

Schools of Hope seeks to resurrect the historic, liberally educating vision of <u>arete</u>, or <u>all-around human excellence</u>, as the <u>only proper and realistic goal for preparing today's students for their future.</u> I ground that vision on a validated model of healthy growth and then draw out its implications for creating schools of hope—schools that educate for character (interpersonal skills and ethical values) and self-command, not just for excellence of mind. The model provides a systematic rationale for the whats, whys, and hows of educating today's youth for their rapidly changing and increasingly interdependent and incoherent world.

Current national educational goals, such as expecting today's students to win the international mathematics sweepstakes by the year 2000, neither inspire students to work harder nor invigorate teachers' calling to their profession. Desirable, certainly. Appropriate for students' futures, barely. Attainable, no.

What must we do to inspire students to work harder and invigorate teachers' calling? We must understand

- What students and teachers *themselves* <u>feel and think about their schools and each other</u>
- How the society and schools that we have created over these past several decades have made today's students less educable if we maintain the same type of schooling

- The principal strengths that students really need to succeed and flourish as adults in the twenty-first century
- How students and teachers psychologically mature and become liberally educated
- The intrinsic *systemic* character of schools and the kind of education necessary to nurture students' and teachers' calling to learning and teaching

We must understand how to create schools of hope.

A former secretary of education, legislators, business leaders, and reformers claim that schools must "radically" change to achieve even the limited national goals now on the country's agenda. The proposed "radical" changes—longer school days and years, increased choice, restructuring, experimental schools—will not, I predict, make much lasting difference. They might if we deepened our understanding of today's students, teachers, and schools and took the really radical step of asking and answering the central questions: how do we grow healthily, and how can we create schools that more effectively nurture such growth?

The probable continuing slow pace of school improvements, the deep hurt and despair of so many youth, the continuing disparagement of our many caring and dedicated teachers, and the erosion of our communal and national ideals compel me to provoke you with a different perspective about how to create schools that inspire hope rather than confirm despair.

Background of the Book

Because the issues that concern schooling are so central to a community's health and are so complex and far-reaching in their implications, I have severely disciplined myself to focus on the search for and construction of the ideal. Thus, I do not discuss political and economic issues, such as the federal role in education or bilingual education, or more specific curricular topics, such as the scientific information that every student should know. For the book's purposes, I view, for example, mastering liberal arts courses, such as geometry and history, as a means to achieving the liberally educating outcomes, such as imagination, curiosity, love of learning, and self-educating skills, that students need for their future.

I have relied on data that I have collected for many years from primarily independent and suburban public schools recognized for their excellence by state and national agencies. My data confirm one U.S. secretary of education's comment: most students, not just African-Americans and Hispanics, are not doing as well as they could.

My work with urban and rural schools tells me that their vulnerable and neglected youth desperately need the small schools of hope that I describe. Such schools could become the focal point for regenerating communities and encouraging more parental support.

Because the American public middle and high schools have been found most wanting by critics, I target them primarily; I rely on data about and select many of my examples from the adolescent years. This emphasis should not be misunderstood. I am also writing about becoming educated in elementary schools as well as in colleges and graduate schools. If I had had more space and you unlimited patience, I could have illustrated and supported my observations and conclusions more thoroughly.

I ground my judgments and proposals on thirty-five years of researching the healthy growth of exemplars of success and wellbeing in the United States and abroad, thirty of those years also consulting with and studying more than nine hundred schools and colleges. I have simultaneously collected information about the changing personalities of youth, their and their teachers' morale, the ethos of their schools, and the effects of schools and their causes.

My early findings about maturing, which I reported in *Explorations of Maturity* (1965) and *Growing Up in College* (1968), led to their application and integration with my consulting work with schools and colleges in *Humanizing Schools: New Directions, New Decisions* (1971). *Maturity and Competence: A Transcultural View* (1976) confirmed the generality of my model of maturity through studies of Catholic Italians and Muslim Turks. *Fulfilling Lives: Paths to Maturity and Success* (1991), based on a comprehensive longitudinal study of seventeen-year-old men growing into middle age and of their spouses, identified the strengths necessary to fulfill our principal adult roles. It also identified the familial, school, and adolescent and adult personality contributors to success, virtue, and well-being. These books, especially *Fulfilling Lives*, provide the foundation for understanding human excellence, the ideal that frames this book.

Overview of the Contents

Part One of the book speaks for students and teachers whose expressions of their feelings and beliefs about each other and their schools have not been really heard by legislative reformers. Chapters One through Three propose that students' personalities—their minds, characters, and selves—have changed in ways that make them less educable in the kinds of schools their parents attended. Chapter Four examines the causes of their altered educability in order to identify guidelines for reorganizing schools. Chapter Five documents why single-minded valuing of academic excellence above all else betrays education's historic goal of arete and so undermines its own achievement. These chapters should interest any person concerned about today's youth and how they need to be raised and educated to grow healthily.

Part Two begins to reconstruct education's vision of human excellence. Chapter Six summarizes the research identifying the strengths that youth need to adapt to the demands of the twenty-first century. It proposes a validated model of healthy growth or maturing that comprehends education's historic goals and predicts adult success and well-being. Chapters Seven through Nine describe the typology of human excellence: the maturing of mind, of character's interpersonal skills and ethical values, and of self. They integrate philosophers' and educators' views with research on the effects of schooling to define human excellence. These more technical and research-based chapters should be of special interest to faculties, school improvement committees, and leaders seeking a comprehensive developmental model of their outcomes.

Part Three relies on the model of maturing to suggest ways in which we can reconstruct schools, their curriculum, and their classrooms. Chapter Ten describes four schools of hope that illustrate how students' educability can be altered to achieve excellence.

Chapter Eleven analyzes those schools of hope and proposes twenty principles for creating schools that educate for maturity or human excellence. The creation of a school of hope inevitably depends on adults for whom their work is a calling—not just a job. Chapter Twelve shows how the principles of maturing can be applied to nurture a faculty's calling and hence the members' educability for change. Chapters Thirteen through Fifteen then use the model of maturing and its principles to illustrate how to create the curriculum and classroom necessary to educate mind, character, and self. These "how-to" chapters speak most directly to practicing professionals. They illustrate by example how professionals can create a school climate and teach their liberal arts curriculum to produce liberally educating outcomes to enhance academic mastery. Chapter Sixteen summarizes the practical steps necessary to create schools of hope. I want to provoke legislators and other leaders responsible for educational policies to reconsider their priorities and mandates, some of which actually undermine improvement of our schools and achievement of their goals.

Acknowledgments

My search to understand the ideal of arete has been aided by innumerable schools and people. I dedicate the book to the Friends Council on Education—the umbrella organization of Quaker schools—which for thirty years has been a source of inspiration and faithful support, and to four exemplars of schools of hope that meet the needs of today's changing youth. Proctor Academy's experiential focus prefigures the path that schools must take if they are to educate successfully many of today's youth. Bloomfield Hills' Model High School's adventurous and exploratory efforts to create an interpersonally humane and self-educating learning environment show us just how educable students can become when provided a developmentally appropriate learning setting. Haverford College's historic success in integrating its Quaker values with expectations of academic excellence could speak, I believe, to youths' needs for an ideal of human excellence and hope. The Monteux School for Conductors and Orchestra Musicians tells us how great teachers use their discipline to teach for human excellence. I am indebted to

Proctor's David Fowler, Bloomfield Hills' Gary Doyle and Cindy Boughner, in particular, and the Monteux School's Maestro Charles Bruck and Nancie Monteux-Barendse for their inspiration and permission to share their schools with you. Each illumines another facet of the meaning of excellence.

I am also indebted to a long, long procession of philosophers, researchers, educators, and students who have taught me what I have learned. *Schools of Hope* falls squarely within the philosophical tradition of John Dewey and the views of contemporary educational leaders Ernest Boyer, John Goodlad, Theodore Sizer, Phillip Schlechty, and Thomas Sergiovanni, among a host of others.

The book has been critiqued by teachers, public and independent departmental and school heads, regional and national heads of educational organizations, and faculty development consultants, among others. I am most grateful to them for their perspectives. The stringent and careful critiques by Michael Murray, Charles Abelman, and Thomas Read resulted in major changes in the book. The probing comments of Cindy Boughner and Gary Doyle, affirming comments and suggestions by Gale Erlandson, Linda Farr, Joyce Fouts, Julie Frame-Hansen, Lesley Iura, David Mallery, Dwight Raulston, Robert Smith, and others, and tutelage about Montessori by David Kahn have strengthened the book. I am also grateful to the editors and staff of Jossey-Bass for their care in preparing the book for publication.

Emily Kingham faithfully prepared the massive amounts of information from thousands of students and teachers for analysis. My wife loyally supported without complaint my research and consultations, which have taken me away from our home and family for more months than I care to count.

Haverford, Pennsylvania   Douglas H. Heath
December 1993

The Author

Douglas H. Heath is professor emeritus in the Psychology Department at Haverford College. He received his B.A. degree (1949) from Amherst College in psychology and his M.A. (1952) and Ph.D. (1954) degrees from Harvard University in clinical psychology.

Heath lectures and consults worldwide, presenting the findings of his research and their implications for creating more effective and healthy organizations to youth, educational, religious, and business groups. He has recently been developing measures of educational outcomes such as ethical values and psychological maturity to assess how adolescents mature from the ninth through the twelfth grade. He has been a National Science Foundation Fellow and a Fulbright Scholar. The results and implications of his research have been reported in numerous books and journal articles.

Schools of Hope

PART ONE

The Challenge
of Educating Today's Youth

Chapter 1

Minds:
More Vulnerable
and Less Educable

A clear understanding of a problem prefigures its lines of solution.

—Margaret Mead

Experienced teachers don't doubt that youths' personalities have been changing noticeably since the mid 1950s. They believe that their students are less educable for the ways they have been taught to teach them. What have they observed about students' changing personalities?

Dorothy Cohen, a consultant to hundreds of nursery schools, told me she had heard the same theme over and over. She quoted one teacher as saying of her four-year-olds, "They flit or they can't seem to stay with anything for very long. My children today prefer the stapler to the paste, which is harder to manage. And they will not stay with a project when several steps are involved that take longer than a few minutes." Cohen was not emphasizing that children are learning how to adjust to a technological stapler society; she meant that they are not learning how to persist when frustrated, regardless of the tool or problem with which they work.

Janet Healy, who has also worked as a consultant with innumerable teachers, reports that they claim that students' minds are changing. One of the comments that she has heard from experienced teachers (as I have) is "Ten years ago I gave students materials and they were able to figure out the experiment. Now I have

3

to walk them through the activities step by step. I don't do as much science because of their frustration level."[1]

A southern dean of students at a private school wrote me, "In many ways, students seem to me to be considerably less able to formulate plans, implement ideas and carry out collaborative projects without significant adult supervision, and this need for more adult-input is considerably greater than it was . . . fifteen years ago. Yearbook, student government, long term research projects, school newspapers . . . seem more difficult to bring to successful completion."

Since the sixties, I have asked experienced teachers to identify how students' strengths and limitations have changed in ways that affect their ability to achieve their classroom goals. Teachers here and abroad speak the same words. In California, where most every new change begins, teachers from an exemplary suburban school identified the following:

Strengths	*Limitations*
Are more exposed to rich and varied experiences	Need to be entertained; are more easily bored
Hold adults in less awe, so are less inhibited and more honest in expressing feelings when around them	Operate more within a "pragmatic moral parameter"
	Are extremely competitive to get good grades
Are less easily manipulated	Won't work on what they are not interested in
Have a stronger sense of fairness	Are more materialistic
Are flexible, able to accept new ideas	Lack a strong will
	Are covertly racist and sexist
Are poised and self-confident	Have a "false maturity"
Are potentially as intellectually capable	Are less able to concentrate for long periods of time

If something happens in Kansas, America's heartland, surely it must have already happened elsewhere. Kansans believe that. But they are not as far behind as they believe. Faculty from ten Kansas colleges agreed about their students' strengths and limitations:

Strengths	*Limitations*
Desire to communicate	Are passive; their motto is "Do
Are freer to challenge	it unto me"
Show occasional flashes of	Have less intrinsic motivation
idealism	"No longer chase ideas for the
Are more strongly motivated for	fun of it"
practical and materialistic	Have more pragmatic concern
goals	about money
Are more demanding of the	Are unwilling to take risks; fear
faculty	failure
Are creative when released	Are outwardly carefree but in-
Have more varied cultural	wardly tense and are more
experience	sensitive about acceptance
	Have increased lack of self-
	discipline, seen in poor man-
	agement of time

Because researchers have not systematically studied most of these changes, we lack firm evidence that today's youth really differ from earlier ones. But is it not reasonable to assume that changing environments, technologies, and familial and cultural values shape the generations somewhat differently? Indian youth driving water buffalo to a local water hole and American adolescents driving their cars to McDonald's develop different minds, characters, and identities. Might not the dramatic increase in divorces and single-parent families of the past three decades alter children's personalities? What happens to the eight-year-old boy who asked me who his parents would be next year?

Some documented evidence, however, confirms teachers' intuitions that students' personalities have in fact been changing, possibly as a result of our rapid and bewildering familial, technological, and societal changes. Increases in suicide, violence, sexual activity, adolescent pregnancies, and drug and alcohol use suggest that more fundamental personality changes are at work. Might not our societal preoccupation with these troubling visible changes be obscuring their underlying personality roots? As a result, might we be misdirecting our remedial efforts and squandering scarce resources? Might insisting that all youth adjust to traditional schooling only aggravate its unhealthy effects? Requiring apathetic students to stay in school longer and take more academic courses may just aggravate their boredom. Boredom contributes to dropping out physically or psychically and to thrill-seeking violent, sexual, and drug behavior.

Evidence about our changing minds comes from the ceaseless drumbeats of declines in students' academic skills and achievement. The evidence seems to be unassailable: high percentages of students read far below grade level and do not write clearly or logically; achievement and scholastic aptitude test scores have declined; smaller percentages of college students continue work in mathematics and science; and on and on.[2] Sparse evidence suggests that the long-term decline in mental competence may be bottoming out and that some reforms are beginning to "take." However, in the words of one researcher, "a long climb over many years will be required to attain the previous high levels"; others question the reliability of the test results; some dispute that the reforms have increased test scores.[3]

Let us not quibble about how accurately the drumbeats have been signaling such visible and measurable changes. Instead, let us search for hints about underlying personality changes that may make youth more vulnerable to stress and impaired functioning. I turn to the beliefs of teachers and students who are closest to today's youth as well as to students' beliefs about themselves. After all, what we *believe* to be true is the reality to which we react. When different persons working with youth of different ages in different parts of the country share the same belief, then what they believe probably has some validity.

Furthermore, if we believe that students are distractible and think more descriptively and less analytically, then we will react to them as if they couldn't concentrate and think actively. If we believe we are stupid, then we will not try to learn. Our beliefs then do become self-fulfilling prophecies. Politicians know this truth. Before Gorbachev resigned as president of the former Soviet Union, a Russian politician who was asked whether Gorbachev had any power left replied, "It is the perception of power, not power itself, that makes the difference."

Margaret Mead wisely told us that if we clearly understood our problems, their lines of solution would be prefigured. Might not a decade of frenetic but fruitless efforts to figure out how to improve our schools suggest that we have not yet clearly understood today's students, teachers, and schools? For example, consider legislators' seemingly worthwhile proposal to lengthen the school day and year—a proposal made by outsiders, not insiders, to the schools. Without an understanding of what students—and teachers—daily face in their classrooms, their proposal is doomed to fail, unless schools alter their goals and teachers change how they teach. Students who believe school to be irredeemably boring will note every sign that confirms that, downplay or ignore those that don't, resist becoming involved or excited, put down the involved "nerds" to confirm their own view, and react even more stubbornly. Teachers are not aware of just how boring school is to students. Fifty-six percent of college-bound public high school students—but only 11 percent of their teachers—believe that school is boring. Not until teachers understand students' "reality" will they be willing to teach differently.[4]

Understanding Teachers' and Students' Views

We now have one way to discover quickly, simply, objectively, and cheaply what another's reality is. We can provide teachers and students with a large number of traits and values (typically 150), such as "academic," "excellence," and "well-informed." They rapidly check every word they believe describes, for example, their typical student, school, or faculty, or themselves; they also circle every word they don't check but wish that they could have checked.[5] Collating and ordering a faculty's checks for each word provides its collective portrait of its typical student; its combined number of circles portrays its collective frustration about or hopes for them.[6]

Two decades of collecting such information from hundreds of schools of all types in the United States and abroad have produced very stable norms for faculty and students from independent schools and a select group of suburban public schools, including some nationally recognized as exemplary.[7] I have less reliable results from urban, rural, and multinational American schools throughout the Middle East and Asia as well as diverse colleges and universities. Their results, however, confirm that the beliefs I describe about students' personalities are widespread, especially for deprived urban minority youth. They prefigure a quite different path to enhancing student academic achievement than has yet to be thoughtfully considered.

Mind's Increasing Need for External Structure

A fundamental change altering our minds is our increasing need for stimulation and structures to initiate, direct, organize, and stabilize our personalities. Students' shorter attention spans demand that teachers be entertainers with the wit of Bill Cosby. Students' lack of persistence when the going gets tough forces teachers to be drill sergeants. Their wandering minds challenge teachers to be step-by-step programmers. Four pieces of evidence support the idea that many students need more structure and direction nowadays. Decreased strength of will, undeveloped academic coping skills, and impoverished imagination predispose many, though certainly not all, to boredom. While these traits may not be characteristic of a majority of youth, a substantial minority who don't have strong wills, for example, can disrupt classrooms and interfere with other students' maturing.

① *Decreased Willpower*

What are some signs of a strong will? They include inhibiting impulses when we are tempted; tolerating frustration, even pain, when we are blocked from getting what we want; and resisting distractions and persisting even when the steps to what we want are tedious, even boring.

In *Fateful Choices*, Fred Hechinger summarizes extensive survey data and other information that tell us that since the mid 1950s, more young people live less-restrained lives. They do not inhibit their impulses and tolerate frustrations as strenuously. They explore risk-taking alternatives more impulsively. The adolescent suicide rate has tripled since the mid 1950s, doubling since 1968, when it was the fifth most frequent cause of their deaths. Now it is the third most frequent cause, following accidents and homicides, some of which are probably disguised suicides, particularly for black males.[8]

American adolescents are <u>more prone now than forty years ago to act out aggressively when frustrated.</u> Court and prison statistics document a thirty-fold increase in teenage arrests since 1950, including a disturbing increase in more violent crimes, such as homicide.[9] In 1987, an estimated 135,000 boys daily brought a gun to school. A 1991 survey of 11,631 high school students found that 20 percent brought lethal weapons, 5 percent of which were guns, to school.[10]

Dramatic changes in resisting sexual temptation have also been well documented. During the 1920s, 84 percent of males (but only 31 percent of females) reported having had premarital sexual relations. The percentage of males has increased until now about 95 percent report not being virgins when they marry. Since the 1960s, women's premarital sexual activity has dramatically increased. When surveyed several years ago, 41 percent of women aged thirty-five to forty-four said that they were *not* virgins before marriage; that number has doubled in the past twenty years for eighteen- to twenty-four-year-old women. Eighty-one percent today have had premarital sexual relations. In 1970 4.6 percent but in 1988 about 25.6 percent of fifteen-year-old girls had had sexual relations.[11]

<u>Decreased inhibition about sex and its increased cultural acceptance can be seen in the striking increase in the rate of out-of-wedlock pregnancies</u> since the mid fifties, especially among white as well as younger teenage girls.[12] The rate may only now be slowing down. Societal attitudes have also become more accepting of premarital pregnancy; they no longer provide a bulwark supporting either abstinence or disapproval of the consequences of unprotected sex. <u>Unwed mothers no longer lose status among their peers.</u> They don't have to leave town and hide in a Florence Crittenden home or with a distant relative; they can continue their schooling until term.

<u>Finally, widespread use of drugs has continued since the sixties,</u> though its pattern and the type of drug have varied. <u>Alcohol remains the most widely used drug;</u> the rate of adolescent alcohol-

ism has also been increasing, even for pubertal children. In 1990, 39 percent of high school seniors said they had been drunk within the previous two weeks.[13]

    Such profound changes in how adolescents control their impulses reflect an underlying lessening of willpower that directly undermines academic achievement in the classroom. Table 1.1 maps the percentages of public and independent high school faculties who describe their typical students as having traits that are characteristic of weak willpower. These are teachers whose students achieve well and plan to go to college—not those whose students do poorly, give up, and drop out. (Keep in mind that I report the judgments of teachers, not the percentages of students who may lack strong wills.) Table 1.1 also includes the self-descriptions of students in one state's most exemplary high school, which I call Prestige. Students' self-descriptions generally agree with others' judgments of them within fifteen to twenty percentage points.

Table 1.1. Teachers' and Students' Judgments of Students' Willpower.

	High school teachers' views (%)		Prestige students' self-descriptions (%)
Trait	Public	Independent	
Self-centered	60	55	13
Demanding	52	52	40
Impatient	49	38	48
Impulsive	49	34	25
Distractible	47	38	30
Aggressive	39	39	50
Average:	49	43	34

    Note that about 49 percent of high school teachers in public schools and 43 percent of those in independent schools believe that their students show signs of weak willpower; 34 percent of Prestige's students believe this about themselves and this does not mean that the rest of them believe that their typical peers (or they themselves) have stronger wills. Surely being self-disciplined means having command of oneself or a strong will; only 11 percent of public and 14 percent of independent high school teachers believe that their typical student has such self-control. A national survey sponsored by Metropolitan Life Insurance confirms these findings: "The majority of teachers feel their students are not paying attention most of the time . . . about one-third of the students said that they paid attention all of the time."[14]

Students generally agree with their faculties: only 25 percent of public and 30 percent of independent school students attribute self-control to their peers. Only a third of Prestige's exemplary students believe that they themselves are self-disciplined; 30 percent actually wish they had better control of themselves, which leaves about another third who apparently do not care. They neither describe themselves as nor wish they were more self-disciplined.

Although these findings scarcely need interpretation to those who work with today's youth, two implications need to be highlighted. The first is that children who are impulsively distractible, impatiently self-centered, and aggressively demanding are frequently diagnosed as having a neurological or emotional problem. Susan has a "learning disability"; Gary is "hyperactive"; Brian has a "minimal brain impairment"; Bill is an "acting-out psychopath"; Jane has an "attention deficit disorder"; Bruce is "emotionally disturbed." As early as nursery school, experienced teachers report increasingly more children like Susan, Gary, and Bruce.

National mental health surveys now confirm teachers' beliefs that they have substantial numbers of children who are not educable for traditional forms of teaching. The 1988 National Health Interview survey reported that 20 percent of today's children are educationally impaired; the authors believed that they had underestimated the actual number.[15] Our society infused with drugs, tobacco, chemicals, lead, nutritionless junk food, and parentlessness may be impairing some children's brains. More than four million have been formally diagnosed as having neurological impairments to their abilities to inhibit their impulses or integrate well their visual and motor skills for learning.[16]

So while 20 percent or more of today's students may not be very educable for a variety of diagnostic reasons, such labels may disguise a more troubling fact. Recall that 45 to 50 percent of teachers judge students not to show signs of self-discipline or strong wills. A more pervasive change may be occurring that is *not* attributable to neurological impairment or emotional upset alone. The

20 percent of children who are impaired may be the disruptive and exaggerated manifestations of a more widespread personality change that we may too quickly label as a diagnosable brain disorder. The troubling consequence is that our technical labels can provide teachers the excuse to refer increasingly more students to remedial professionals so that they can continue to teach the way they have always taught. We must be wary that we do not define a cultural problem—that is, a socialization, and so, at its root, an educational problem—as a more intractable neurological or emotional disorder for which we don't have to be responsible.

The second implication of these findings is that we will fail to teach our students higher-order thinking skills if we don't first teach them willpower. We begin to learn to think when faced with a problem whose solution is not immediately available. We must learn to inhibit our immediate impulsive reactions and tolerate the frustration of uncertainty while learning how to think through alternatives. If we demand quick, simplistic solutions and cannot persist when faced with a difficult task, we will simply not learn to speak, write, and think clearly and logically. Adolescents who as four-year-olds were unable to endure frustration have lower Scholastic Aptitude Test scores and are less academically as well as socially competent than those who were.[17]

What might be some teaching strategies to teach willpower? Nursery school teachers should provide paste but not staplers to teach old-fashioned persistence. Elementary school teachers need to teach their students how to wait, be silent, and reflect in the presence of a frustrating problem. Montessorian teachers have shown us that even four-year-olds can remain silently attentive for many minutes at a time. Middle, high school, and college teachers must stop impatiently answering their own questions. They should tolerate first a minute, then three or even five minutes of class silence. Students need such silences during which to learn how to order their own minds before collectively working with other students to think through a problem.

We need a curriculum that enables students to secure command of their own minds so they do not have to depend upon external stimulation and direction. We first need to ressurrect old-fashioned virtues such as inhibition, tolerance of frustration, patience, and persistence as curricular goals. Then we must *self-consciously* educate for them from kindergarten on. To ignore educating willpower is to risk converting the goal of acquiring higher-order thinking skills into another transient and failed educational "fad."

② *Undeveloped Academic Coping Skills*

The second of the four pieces of evidence suggesting that students depend more on external direction and control nowadays is the widespread agreement that few possess the skills necessary to use their minds effectively. The decades' declining SAT scores have provoked anguished concern and numerous explanations. Experts claim that the decline cannot be fully accounted for by the increased number of minority students and larger percentages of heterogeneously talented students taking the tests. No agreement yet exists about other reasons for the decline in scores and the failure of efforts to improve them [18]

The decline may reflect other changes in our minds not yet clearly identified. I doubt that today's students are less smart than previous ones. Rather, they may be developing a different pattern of talents as a result of adapting to their changing society, a pattern that we have not yet learned how to measure.

I am reminded how plastic our minds are each time I take the terrifying kamikazi taxi ride from Calcutta's airport to my hotel. A decade ago, an Indian boy may have sleepily herded water buffalo on the Ganges plain. Today the same youth may expertly race a taxi at seventy kilometers an hour, weaving in and out of heavy traffic, racing in the wrong lane toward an oncoming taxi only to swerve at the last moment, never scraping a fender, and, when I dare open my eyes, not hitting, by my quick counts, the fifteen water buffalo wandering in the middle of the main road or running over the twenty-two children and elderly Indians walking along it that my Western logic said he should have.

American youth have also been learning different types of skills to get along in their emerging future. Like what? Greater awareness and knowledge of differences among peoples. "Street smarts" and hustling skills necessary to survive in unfamiliar situations. Psychological mindedness or perceptiveness that far surpasses that of most adults. When I ask middle schoolers why they put each other down, they reply with insights that I never could have summoned at their age. Listen to adolescents talk about adults and be appalled by how well they see through us. A history professor said of his freshmen, "If I can stay fired-up, they usually do; if I seem bored or burned-out, they pick it up *immediately*." Apart from ethical reasons, I urge adults *never* to manipulate or deceive today's children. More likely than we knew when their age, they will know our deception.

Let's grant that many are developing a different pattern of intellectual strengths that we have not yet learned how to measure. But why are they not using their abstract verbal and quantitative talents more effectively? Table 1.2 suggests one reason why test scores have declined. Increasingly more youth have a less firm, disciplined control of the skills necessary to *use* their potential imaginative and abstract abilities effectively. The table is roughly ordered in terms of the steps necessary to complete a task, such as homework. Clearly, few teachers believe that their typical students know how to use their talents efficiently, and only a minority of exemplary students describe themselves as skilled in academically coping with their work. Do not think that even seniors who have high grade averages can set goals for themselves, manage time effectively, memorize efficiently, and prepare for exams. Many don't, as they ruefully discover when faced with a demanding college course.

**Table 1.2. Teachers' and Students' Judgments
of Students' Academic Coping Skills.**

	High school teachers' views (%)		Prestige students' self-descriptions (%)
Coping skills	Public	Independent	
Anticipating consequences	17	18	48
Planning ahead	11	9	41
Taking the initiative	9	17	17
Scheduling self	19	24	19
Being efficient	11	19	36
Being thorough	5	6	20
Completing plans	15	16	40
Average:	12	16	32

Let's put some flesh on some of Table 1.2's bare-boned skeleton of the skills necessary to approach one's work. Only small percentages of teachers and students agree that today's youth have good work skills, compelling evidence of why Americans fail in their international competitive races. We don't value such personality traits. The Japanese do, and they excel in them.

Planning Ahead. A student told me, "I would really like to take your course, but I am scared to."

"Scared? Why?"

"Because you're known to not accept late papers."

"But you would have eight weeks' warning when it was due. Besides, it's only a small one."

"Yeah. I know. But I don't trust myself to get it done on time."

Taking the Initiative. Initiative is a critical academic competence, but few teachers believe that today's students show it. Sadly, only 17 percent of Prestige's capable students believe they have initiative. Perhaps few students ever have had it. Carl Jung, a brilliant psychoanalyst, claimed that he failed algebra because he didn't know what X meant in an equation. He hadn't tried to find out—or been encouraged to.

A professor wrote, "Only when I have adult students or foreign exchange students do they stay after class to ask questions and come for help. Otherwise, the freshmen ask me only about their grades. This is what makes teaching such an onerous job." Kindergarten children brim with initiative. What do we do, or not do, that suppresses or even snuffs it out in so many?

Though few apparently believe that students show initiative in their schools does not mean they cannot when provided a learning environment that encourages it to flourish. Concerned about how to develop just such an environment, the leaders and school board of Bloomfield Hills, Michigan, have sponsored a small experimental school, called the Model High School (MHS), charged with implementing the educational principles of Theodore Sizer of Brown University.[19] Its students have great freedom to learn how to educate themselves to achieve clearly defined competencies and initiate their own assessment procedures, including public demonstrations and assessments by outside experts. That 43 percent of its faculty believe that its students show initiative tells us that schools can do much better than they do now to encourage its blossoming.

Self-Scheduling to Achieve One's Goals. Another coping skill not widely seen in students is the ability to set goals and then schedule or organize their time and energy to achieve them. Some college faculties, even in Kansas, now require entering freshmen to take a course to learn how to set daily goals, plan successive subgoals, and schedule their time. We need to teach students from early elementary school on how to make a list each night of what they wish to accomplish the next day. We then must teach them how to monitor their own progress in setting goals for themselves and efficiently working to achieve those goals.

Thoroughness. Apparently the word *thorough* has become a foreign—really Japanese—idea. It is slipping out of our everyday vocabulary. Thoroughness requires a commitment to perfectionism— which some pejoratively relabel today as "compulsive." Though only 20 percent of Prestige's capable students think they are thorough, that 34 percent call themselves perfectionists reassures me that excellence may still live, even if it may not be consistently implemented. Thoroughness also requires persistence, single-mindedness, and dedication. However, national surveys tell us that the typical high school senior spends only forty-five minutes to an hour a day on homework[20] and reads fewer than ten pages a day either in school or for homework.[21] High school students claim that they study only when they expect to be tested the next day, probably the reason teachers quiz their students so frequently.

Every one of the skills necessary to use one's talents effectively can be taught, beginning in kindergarten. We can no longer assume that coping skills just develop naturally or are predictable consequences of growing up in contemporary American society. To do so is to condemn millions of youngsters to ignorance of the full measure of their minds' potentials.[22]

(3) *Impoverished Imaginal Life*

The third of the four lines of evidence that support the idea that today's youth need more external input and structure comes from observations about changes in their imagination.

Children who can't inhibit their impulses are less likely to develop their imaginations than are those who can. Imagination is vitally important because it provides the resources for playfully anticipating and planning alternative ways of satisfying one's needs. As imagination is a precursor to mind's further development, an impoverished imagination limits the maturation of skills such as taking others' viewpoints and thus of empathy, analytical and relational thinking, judgment, and creativity.

Some elementary school teachers who value imaginative play tell me students can be as imaginative as they have ever been. However, Table 1.3, which lists the strengths necessary for or correlative with imagination, suggests that too many teachers tell us otherwise for us to be able to deny that some impoverishment of our inner lives is occurring. Although the majority of public and independent school teachers do not view their students as notably imaginative, students predictably feel differently about themselves. I say "predictably" because adolescence is an inward-turning, moody, and self-preoccupying time to re-create oneself; emotion-infused daydreams become confused with creativity, which requires highly dis-

Table 1.3. Teachers' and Students' Judgments
of Students' Imaginative Traits.

	High school teachers' views (%)		Prestige students' self-descriptions (%)
Traits	Public	Independent	
Playfulness	32	41	55
Creativity	26	38	60
Artistic ability	24	34	35
Imagination	22	31	52
Deep interests	9	14	55
Reflectiveness	6	10	19
Average:	20	28	46

ciplined communicative, artistic, and reflective skills to blossom
fully. Only a minority of capable students, however, think of
themselves as either artistic or reflective.

Implica-
tions for
Kgn.

One of the most important imaginative traits is playfulness.
Play is children's most natural medium through which to nourish
and express imagination. But teachers in the United States and
abroad tell me that children are losing their "natural" ability to
play symbolically. An elementary school faculty argued for an hour
about why its children no longer played in a large sand pile in the
schoolyard. Eventually, one young brash but down-to-earth teacher
suggested that they ask the children why—a most empirical way to
find an answer. Guess what the children said? They did not say, as
one teacher had claimed they would, "We'd get dirty," or what
another had suggested, "Cats play there!" The children said that
there was nothing to do there. They had no cars or houses with
which to play. Noting that their children were not playing as imaginatively as they used to, some Israeli teachers told me that they had

Example

identified imagination's component symbolic skills and were now
teaching their children how to play imaginally.

Boarding school teachers now complain that weekends drag
even more for students who themselves complain that there is
"nothing to do," except to smoke pot, drink beer, and "party,"
which typically means listening to music, dancing, and possibly
having sex—if my dictionary accurately describes *party*'s contemporary meaning. Adolescents don't seem to play or spontaneously
generate their own games as frequently as they used to. They need
more structured programming to be able to participate. Dads have
become indispensable to keeping the Little League game going for
nine innings.

Whether from the head of an art department in North Carolina, an English teacher in Rhode Island, or a first-grade teacher in
Pennsylvania, I hear that students are not imagining as fancifully
as they used to. Though art is very popular with today's students,
teachers report that students prefer to draw abstract designs, TV
monsters, and other nonhuman figures. A twenty-year veteran said
of her first-grade children, "They are so violent; they are so aggressive with each other, even the girls. They don't play as creatively as
they used to. And they get bored so easily. If nothing is going on

for several minutes, they'll come up to me and say, 'I'm bored. What should I do now?' "

Other signs that may indicate imagination's impoverishment are an inability to tolerate silence, a lack of reflectiveness and deep self-sustaining interests, and a compulsive addiction to computer games, afternoon soap operas, and other TV programs. Addiction to noise blocks out access to our inner imaginal lives. As my youngest daughter told me when I asked why she wanted a stereo deck in the car, "Because it is too quiet in the car; I get lonely."

Sony has made a fortune from our inability to tolerate silence. Just as we adults need a Walkman when we jog, so our children need their stereos going full blast to be able to concentrate. Study hall supervisors, librarians, and parents don't yet understand the role that noise plays in the life of today's youth—and how it overwhelms and so drains our imagination.

A vivid and rich reflective inner life can buffer us from the persistent intrusiveness of our noisy and seductive society. I have long advocated that we teach children from kindergarten through twelfth grade yoga, meditation, and other inward-listening skills by which to live more harmoniously with their bodies and inner silence. By securing access to and articulating their less conscious dreams and thoughts, they will know and trust themselves better, develop more self-control, and so live more sanely in our kaleidoscopic world. Persons who have such skills do not need to turn to drugs to initiate their inner "trips."

Sugg.

(4) *Predisposition to Boredom*

Inability to control our impulses, immature skills for coping with work's demands, and impoverished imaginations predispose us to depend upon external controls and continued stimulation. We become predisposed to be bored earlier in our lives and more readily— the fourth type of evidence supporting the idea that we no longer depend as much on our own resources.

Boring is students' most frequently used word to describe their schools. Recall the first-grade teacher who reported that today's six- and seven-year-olds believe school to be boring. Another elementary school teacher reported that her students said at the end of a class discussion about explorers and their travels, "You know, Mrs. James, it's not fair. There is nothing left to discover. They did it all." The 1988 National Longitudinal Survey of 24,599 eighth-graders in about a thousand schools found that "half . . . reported that they were bored in school at least half of the time, and many go to class unprepared."[23] Minnesota's public school students identify boredom as their principal complaint about their schools.[24] I know of public schools in which more than 90 percent of the students believe school to be boring. And their dropout rates reflect it. One-third of college students report that they are bored.[25]

If students believe that school is boring, then they come to school each morning expecting it to be. Unfortunately, schools too often confirm their students' expectations.[26] The supervisors of two of Connecticut's wealthiest public schools each followed a randomly selected student's schedule for a day; each found it too painful to continue after the fourth period because the classes were so repetitively similar. Teachers who shadow a student through a school day report two major reactions: boredom and emotional exhaustion, due in part to the day's fragmentation. On-site inspectors of one of Britain's most exemplary secondary schools report similar results. Classes were "dull and unimaginative with 'too much reliance on textbooks.' . . . As pupils grow older, they say less and less in class."[27] What is it like then to be a student in such schools day in and day out for months and years?

School does *not* have to bore today's youth. While more independent high school students (28 percent) are bored with school than their teachers might wish, they are consistently less bored than similarly affluent, bright, college-bound public school students (56 percent). Even 33 percent of students in independent schools though only 19 percent of those in public schools describe their schools as intellectually exciting. The students of Bloomfield Hills' Model High School also tell us that public schools don't have to bore them. Only 8 percent rated MHS as boring; 70 percent even claimed that MHS was intellectually exciting.

Teachers apparently are not bored by their schools—at least not enough to want to change what they do. Only 11 percent of public and 6 percent of independent school teachers describe their schools (classrooms?) as boring and dull. Lack of compelling mo-tivation to improve their schools is the most critical teacher-related reason why school reform is failing, according to the U.S. Depart-ment of Education.[28] "Boredom is the students' problem. Not mine. They have to learn how to cope with it themselves," said one ex-asperated teacher when learning how many students were bored in his school.

On the other hand, and somewhat paradoxically, the major-ity of teachers agree with their students that their high schools are not intellectually exciting places. Only 29 percent of teachers in public high schools and 40 percent of those in independent high schools believe that their schools are intellectually stimulating. About a third of both even wish that their own schools were more exciting. Distressingly, I have not yet found a single school in which the majority of teachers describe their colleagues as enthu-siastic and intellectually stimulating. Two-thirds of the teachers in one reputedly excellent school actually wished that they themselves could become more intellectually excited persons.

Boredom provokes numerous effects. It is a measure of how quickly we humans can adjust. We learn how to adjust very quickly to novelty, which then becomes routine. This has always been the case. Whether it is going to the Roman circuses to watch the glad-iators kill each other or lions kill Christians, or going to mass to watch the weekly pageantry, or participating in the saturnalia of a Mardi Gras or Walpurgis Night, or getting stinking drunk each Saturday night, or gambling at Atlantic City or Macau, or fighting in the Persian Gulf, or stirring up trouble in the boys' bathroom, we seek excitement and impulsive release to bring some emotional balance to our humdrum, occasionally dreary lives.

But today the pursuit of excitement and novelty is a driving compulsion for many young people as well as adults. We seek more and more frequent, intense, and varied excitement. It takes more raw violence on TV today than yesterday to arouse our interest. Even X-rated porn videos become boring after the first fifteen min-utes. Publishers tell me to keep a book to no more than several hundred pages; reviewers say to include more stories and examples because we can no longer sustain concentrated attention when reading about ideas. We avoid the drill and practice of hard work when it becomes tedious and loses its novelty. To avoid boredom, we shift from one job, spouse, or lover to another. Some youth even seek violence and flirt with death, as with suicide.

Boredom also can sap one's motivation to learn—the second of the two principal reasons that school reform is failing, according to the U.S. Department of Education.[29]

Boredom is painful, especially to those raised on excessive stimulation and cultural beliefs that one should not be bored. This pain can compel us to avoid it. It is students' major reason for dropping out of school, say 37 percent of high school dropouts.[30] It is the major reason students identify for dropping out of college.[31]

Boredom undermines students' morale, which predicts not only dropping out but also a host of other behaviors.[32] Compared to students who have high morale, students who are very dissatisfied with school get poorer grades, participate less frequently in cocurricular activities, work more hours for money during the school year, and use drugs and alcohol more frequently. In one strong academic school, 41 percent more low-morale than high-morale students viewed their school as boring, 34 percent more viewed it as dull, 42 percent more found it unexciting intellectually, and 29 percent more saw it as unenthusiastic. No wonder the school had a high dropout rate. Its teachers needed to understand more empathically why their low-morale students were so bored and found school so unexciting. Boredom is not solely a student's responsibility; it is also the responsibility of schools and teachers.

So how do teachers teach children in a society that exhausts novelty so early? A teacher of seventh-grade science in rural Maine wearily told me when I asked, "Keep pressing on to new topics but circle back and back to previous ones." Others resignedly tell me, "Become a comedian." Others look forward to interactive technology as the "magic bullet." But aren't these strategies only palliatives? As we have seen, predisposition to boredom results from reduced strength of will, undeveloped academic coping skills, and impoverished imagination.

What steps must schools therefore take to increase students' educability to learn how to adapt to their future?

Implications for Schools of Students' Changing Minds

What will students' emerging future be like? Since the present pre-figures the probable evolving future, what reasonable assumptions can be made about it? Expanding knowledge and technology will continue to produce *rapid change* and increasing *complexity* and *interdependence* in our relationships and institutions. Traditional sources of our identities, such as status, political and religious ideol-ogies, work, and even gender, no longer organize and give meaning to us as firmly and coherently as they have in the past—at least in the United States.[33] So greater *instability* or fluidity in self-definition and *incoherence* in beliefs will become even more pro-nounced. Given such a future, how should schools respond to stu-dents' changing minds?

Educating to Strengthen Willpower and Academic Coping Skills

A more complex and interdependent future will demand that youth be able to select from and organize a vastly increased amount of information and evaluate alternative solutions for complicated eco-logical, economic, and political issues. To understand their chang-ing world, they will have to know how to analyze diverse peoples' perspectives on problems. And as citizens and workers, they will have to keep informed about changing events and knowledge. They must want to and know how to be their own self-educating teachers. However, neither will such high-level skills be mastered nor will current curricular reforms succeed if students do not have the un-derlying self-management skills that futurists and reformers have assumed they already have—but which many do not.

Educators should reexamine their curriculum to identify the competencies it assumes that students need. So obvious; so ne-glected. Especially by university curricular consultants unfamiliar with current students' inadequate self-management and self-teaching skills. No curricular reform should be considered that fails to consider the underlying developmental readiness of today's stu-dents. Teachers need to be more astute diagnosticians about why

students are not learning. They must more self-consciously implement teaching strategies that extend their students' ability to
concentrate, persist, tolerate frustration and anxiety, initiate, and
plan and organize their time, among other basic self-directing and
self-educating strengths.

Enriching Students' Inner Lives by
Educating Imagination and Reflection

An extraordinarily seductive and harassing society empties youth of
their inner resources to know and depend on themselves. Increasing
dependence on technology's absorbing wonders risks replacing
imagination. Ceaseless noise and compulsive activity crowd out
reflection.

Compared to earlier generations, today's youth's knowledge
about and vocabularies for describing their outer world may be
more richly diverse. As test scores demonstrate, however, their
knowledge about it is not as accurate and precise as it should be.
But they are at least more aware that their world, including the
heavens, is far more complicated and complex than my generation
had any inkling of. Just imagine the reaction of a youth who might
have seen "Star Trek" 's Enterprise and Mr. Data, the rational com-
puterized android, in 1938. Technologies and their languages that
give access to and represent such complexity will make them more
aware and understanding of their outer world.

But students' access to, understanding of, and creative use of
their inner world under their own control is seriously underdeveloped. Does not their need for stimulation and novelty, even reliance
on drugs, tell us that? As we continue to technologize and rationalize students' minds, we risk estranging them from what enriches and
gives meaning to living: their inner worlds' godlike and demonic
dreams and impulses, myths, aesthetics, the compelling mysteries of
religion, the imagination of the humanities as well as of science.

Educators must continue to develop students' skills to represent their increasingly complex outer world, especially the knowledge that science and the power that its technology provide.
Students need much greater control of their communication skills
to adapt well to an information-organized and interdependent

world. However, educators must always keep the whole student in the forefront of curricular reform. They should not neglect students' inner world. They should teach a richer variety of mind's skills, especially skills such as imagination, reflection, intuition, and induction, as well as the vocabulary of the humanities. They provide the access to the sources of creativity, meaning, and vitality that enable students to be what "Star Trek" 's Mr. Data longs to be: a human being who feels, cries, laughs, jokes, and loves.

to teach !

Building Actively Organizing Minds

To make sense of and effectively use the future's overwhelming amount of information, some of it contradictory, students must have actively selecting, organizing, and judging minds. Too many faculty tell me that today's youth think too descriptively and simplistically and resist the *active* relational and problem-solving types of thinking that math and science, for example, require. Their minds are like the textbooks on which they passively depend for selecting and organizing and the multiple-choice tests on which they depend for telling them what is important to know. Passivity breeds boredom. Few teachers report school to be boring. Why? Because they are the ones who are actively and ceaselessly involved, selecting, organizing, evaluating, as well as responsibly initiating, anticipating, planning, scheduling, managing, talking, and adapting to ongoing real-life issues, problems, and conflicts. Educators need to create schools in which students are teachers.

Today's youth are somewhat like us adults. But that is not good enough for their future. Given the complexity of the world they are inheriting, they must be more mentally mature. And given their world's increasing personal and global political and economic interdependencies, they will have to develop not just more mature minds but also more mature characters. How have their interpersonal skills and values been changing?

Chapter 2

Characters:
Riskier Relationships
and Uncertain Values

Teachers who have worked with young people for several decades believe that more have troubled relationships and confused values nowadays than did in earlier times. The perceptive professor in Kansas noted that students are more "outwardly carefree, inwardly tense, and very sensitive about acceptance." The Southern dean believed them to be "less able to . . . carry out collaborative projects without significant adult supervision." A New England teacher bemoaned his students' "lack of respect for others." A midwestern superintendent sought help for his middle school students. "They have become so cruel to each other they are driving kids out of school."

National statistics describe increased rates of premarital sex, out-of-wedlock pregnancy, divorce, and child and wife abuse. Might they reflect underlying changes in our interpersonal skills and values that we have not clearly understood?

Youth's Changing Interpersonal Relationships

Increased Sensitivity About Acceptance

Teachers more frequently describe their children as "fragile," "easily hurt," and "vulnerable" nowadays than in the past. Some feel that they have to be nurturing parents more than exacting teachers. More youth are much too sensitive to signs of disapproval, lack of respect for their opinions, and rejection. Not yet sure of who they are and what they are to become, youngsters are understandably most sensitive to what others think of them. When studying the causes of adult success, I found that not feeling accepted and loved or feeling rejected by one's parents was a powerful predictor of later adult failure and poor mental health.

Less buffered than their predecessors by strong and stable families, communities, work, and religious traditions, a distressing number of young people have not developed the interpersonal skills necessary to learn well in their classrooms. One articulate student taught me how sensitive some can be and how it can affect their work. His letter at the end of a course said that he had been excitedly involved its first weeks. But because I had "ignored" an important question that he had asked, he had stopped participating. I had been too preoccupied to discover why.

Table 2.1 reports students' current views of their peers' interpersonal relationships and Prestige's students' of their own. How well would you learn if you were a student in their schools?

I must elaborate on the table before drawing out its implications. Adolescents thrusting toward independence typically think that they don't need others' approval. However, 50 percent of their teachers think otherwise. It is also predictably human to think better of oneself than of others, as the Prestige students do about, for

Table 2.1. Youths' Views of Their Interpersonal Relationships.

| Traits of Peers | High school students' views (%) | | Prestige students' self-descriptions (%) |
	Public	Independent	
Being competitive	77	75	54
Being casual	63	55	74
Defensiveness	60	47	48
Aggressiveness	58	50	50
Being sarcastic	57	47	47
Being critical of each other	56	58	29
Putting each other down	47	35	6
Needing approval	33	29	25
Feeling for others	29	35	73
Being genuine	26	25	53

example, feeling for others. That almost half know they act defensively, not genuinely, with their peers tells us how uneasy their relationships can be. Apparently, it is more acceptable to think that one is sarcastic, particularly if spiced with TV sitcom humor, than to believe that one criticizes and puts down others. Put-downs are too hostile an attack to be an approved part of one's self-concept.

A few examples may clarify Table 2.1's bare statistics. First-graders routinely call each other stupid, dummy, and sissy. Older ones call each other nerd, wimp, faggot, queer, asshole. When I asked the midwestern superintendent's seventh-grade girls what word hurt them most, they immediately agreed *slut*. Ninety-five percent of suburban Detroit's West Middle School's children reported being verbally abused and cursed at by their peers.[1] A national survey of high school students concluded that sexual harassment had "reached 'epidemic' proportions. . . . Sixty-five percent of the boys and 52 percent of the girls admitted to sexually harassing other students."[2]

Many adults don't understand how painful children's relationships are and so fail to try to alter them. More than twice as many of Table 2.1's students as their teachers believed that their classmates were sarcastic. When studying fifteen multicultural junior high schools in Saudi Arabia, I found that 48 percent of the students but only 14 percent of their teachers viewed the typical student as sarcastic—a huge 34 percent difference.

Research consistently identifies the quality of our relationships as critical to healthy growth. How might you act as an eighth-grader in a coed independent school known as an academic "pressure cooker"? More than two-thirds of such students described each other as putting each other down and as competitive, able to say no, critical of and sarcastically humorous to each other, talkative, not afraid to complain, amusing, defensive, demanding, aggressive, and masculine.

Even more poignantly, what kind of relationships did these eighth-graders wish they had? When at least a third wish their peers had such traits, enough frustration and discontent exist to merit paying attention to their wishes. An average of 41 percent wished that their peers were, in declining order of importance, able to feel for others, considerate, open, accepting, caring, loving, sensitive, and understanding. Only an average of 23 percent of seventh- and eighth-graders in independent schools but 36 percent of the midwestern public school girls hurt by the word *slut* wished that their middle school peers had such interpersonal traits.

I have consistently found that excessively competitive academic schools risk creating immature interpersonal effects. Teachers single-mindedly committed to academic excellence may unwittingly create an ethos that suppresses interpersonal maturation, especially of middle school children. These children are just beginning to learn how to create intimacy relationships that require empathy and caring for others. A failure to value such skills or to provide youth with opportunities to develop them may limit their future ability to reach out to and maturely love another.

Some critics reply, "Children have always put down and been cruel to each other." Perhaps. But might not TV's nightly verbal mayhem make sarcasm a more acceptable way of relating to others and so have increased it in frequency as well as intensity? If so, then we must examine more carefully how students interpret such potentially hurtful comments, particularly since so many are so sensitive to signs of disapproval. Table 2.1 tells us that they become warily defensive. Fewer than a third—and even fewer of their teachers—believe that their peers are genuine, open, and trusting or empathic, sympathetic, and understanding.

How do students protect themselves in their potentially threatening relationships? Ask middle schoolers about how their wariness about being hurt by others, including sarcastic teachers, affects their learning. They fear making mistakes, standing out, taking risks in the classroom, and, especially for boys, becoming too involved in and enthusiastic about learning. It's safer not to learn than to risk peers' scornful put-downs—a major cause, so some researchers report, of adolescent black males' resistance to schooling.[3]

The Kansas professor's comment that students are "outwardly carefree but inwardly tense and are more sensitive about acceptance" suggests that youth have learned not to let others know that their put-downs have struck home. Play the role of being outwardly carefree, casual, and laid-back and roll with the verbal punch—a role that 69 percent of pubertal children and the majority of high school students believe that their peers play.

The game's next step is to retaliate. When attacked, the victim is expected to react aggressively, to retaliate with a humorously disguised though even more sarcastic put-down. This game can be healthily, even affectionately and warmly playful, when its rules are understood and its participants are not overly sensitive friends. The game, however, sets up a potentially harmful Catch-22 conflict for those who, alert to rejection, take the put-down personally. Few of us are sufficiently sure of and comfortable with ourselves, or well armored, to be protected all the time from such slights or intended hurts, as playful as they may be. By appearing to be casual and invulnerable and escalating our sarcastic rejoinder, we risk eliciting others' competitive efforts to retaliate jokingly with a more intensely hurtful put-down. As John Lennon and Paul McCartney warned us in "Hey Jude," such cool behavior makes our world "a little colder." Is not the world "a little colder" for more youth these days?

Decreased Empathy

Chapter One suggested that today's youth are more psychologically minded and perceptive than their predecessors. Heightened awareness of and sensitivity to others can increase empathic understanding of others and their feelings. Empathy is a valuable and necessary skill for success in most adult roles. To be empathic requires accessibility to our own feelings as well as being nondefensively open to the cues that others may give about theirs. Empathy also requires that we be aware of what those cues express, even unconsciously, and of what we feel as a consequence. Uptight, rigid persons who are afraid of their depressed, lonely, or angry feelings will not be able to feel, recognize, and understand such feelings in others. An empathic man can feelingly understand why modern women fume about not getting equal pay for equal work. An empathic white person can feel the fury that Hispanics suffer when discriminated against. An empathic teacher can feel the hurt of the kid who, ignored by her mother and rejected by her father, goes home every day to a lonely house to be absorbed by TV soaps and believes that her boyfriend's sexual advances mean that he loves her.

But when our sensitivity is defensively used to protect *our-*

selves from being hurt, we become overly alert to only those cues that affect *us*. We become self-centeredly preoccupied by our own feelings rather than open and sensitive to how others may be feeling. Hypersensitivity exaggerates even the slightest of hurts as signs of rejection, as with the student whom I had inadvertently ignored. Recall that 60 percent of public high school teachers, as well as 53 percent of their students, view today's adolescents as self-centered.

So despite the potential of their increased sensitivity to make them a more empathic generation than previous ones, the Catch-22 effects of their interpersonal style actually decrease their opportunity to nurture that potential. Why? As perceptive as many young people are, they misread the defensive reactions of others to their casual, laid-back, sarcastic, bantering style. Since their "victims" cannot admit that they have been hurt, they don't learn that their brilliant rapier thrusts were taken seriously instead of playfully. They do not get the cues to learn about or feel vicariously the effects of their comments. We just have not raised and educated youth to use their sensitivity to understand empathically how others feel.

Effects of Increased Sensitivity and Decreased Empathy on Boys' Maturing

The prominently published research about society's and schools' unhealthy effects on pubertal girls has alerted us to how subtly gender roles affect their educability. However, such studies have ignored their unhealthy effects on boys.[4] A typical boy's relationships bespeak American society's confusion about its goals for healthy other-centered maturing, largely because we don't know what to do about his emerging sexuality. Though ignored, it has manifold effects on his schooling, friendships, relationships with girls, and future adult success and well-being. (Chapter Three focuses on how girls' ideas about themselves affect their educability.)

Puberty's Physiological Effects on Boys' Interpersonal Maturation

Let's compare prepubertal fifth-grade boys with pubertal eighth-grade boys to understand how unhealthily American society deals with their emerging sexuality. An elementary school's library I visited had a corner filled with tens of woolly teddy bears. When the fifth-graders pressed in, who rushed to the corner to grab, cuddle, and talk to the two or three teddy bears in their arms? Not one girl. They had no chance to compete for the bears. Would eighth-grade boys race to grab the teddy bears? Never, middle school teachers tell me. Why? Where do such deeply human needs to give and receive affection, to touch and be touched, go when lust begins to seep into affections?

What do we know about testosterone-driven pubertal boys? Very high aggressive energy levels! More middle than high school teachers consistently describe these boys as aggressive and energetic. Both boys and girls agree; boys are just more rambunctious. They are restlessly exploring, intrusive, itchily charged but very affectionately responsive, diffusely arousable creatures. Their changing hormones upset their former ways of relating, making them very educable for developing more mature ways of getting along with others—if adults learn to help them how.

Pubertal boys can be very sexually responsive. In his revealing book *Male Sexuality*, about the meanings of maleness, Richard Handy, a lawyer exploring the effects of surgically caused impotence, resurrects his early pubertal meanings of his lost erections and their effects on his interpersonal maturing.[5] Testosterone-aroused boys are physiologically programmed to channel excitement and tension into spontaneous erections, as when closely dancing with a girl, roughhousing, or even going to the blackboard to solve a math problem. Handy traces adolescent males' need to control their emotions in part to their not having full control over the embarrassingly visible arousal of their emerging maleness.

Relations with other boys used to be safer than they are now. Aroused erections caused by mutual roughhousing, wrestling, and other playful forms of physical contact used to be bemusedly explored, frequently mutually; they were not questioned as signs of gayness. So pre-TV boys used to learn about sexuality through their playfully affectionate relationships with other males—one reason psychologists used to call puberty the time for forming "homosexual chumships."

Changing Emotional Meanings of Pubertal Sexuality

The advent of mass media and entertainment have projected into youth's awareness adult values about sexuality. While puberty's onset occurs earlier now than fifty years ago, its sexual meanings have accelerated by a light year. They flood youth's awareness; sexual innuendos such as "eat me," "you suck," and "m —— f ——," as well as words such as *slut, queer, faggot, butch,* and *gay,* are rampant. These pejorative terms are the derisive currency of put-downs and verbal sadism, increasingly even for pre-pubertal boys and girls. Such derogatory sexualized language and its casual use can create four potentially unhealthy effects on youth not sure of their own affections that can adversely affect their educability in the classroom.

Confusion About Sexual Identity. Puberty has become a much more self conscious period of sexual change for American youth. Boys are now more aware of adult meanings of what a real male is supposed to act like. But nowadays to have an erection in the presence of another boy, whether due to roughhousing, physical contact, or the arousal of affection, risks one's being labeled by others or by oneself as "queer."

Being called a fag, for whatever reason, can precipitate compensatory macho efforts to deny to others and oneself such an identity. Some vulnerable boys panic and react with violent outbursts to "prove" their "maleness." Peter, a bright thirteen-year-old seventh-grader, was going "whacko," according to his principal. He had been a warm, cheerful, and enthusiastic school citizen. But within a month he had become mulishly defiant. His grades had plummeted. More disruptively, he wildly lashed out at and scuffled with other boys in the corridors. He was tight as a clam when asked about his behavior by his worried principal and parents. Before requiring that he get psychiatric help, the principal asked a counselor to see him. Out tumbled Peter's story and his hurt. The other guys had been calling him fag. He was showing everyone that he wasn't. Once he understood the "game," he calmed down and his work improved. How many other vulnerable kids have been similarly hurt and have not been reached by any adult? Male adolescent suicide is more frequently caused by conflict over one's emerging sexual identity than adults are aware of.

Constriction and Suppression of Emotionality. A second effect of adults' confused values about sexuality that have prematurely penetrated American boys' awareness is their generalized equation of emotionality with homosexuality. Nowadays, a boy who is too openly sensitive, too sentimental, too excitable, even too enthusiastic or too affectionately demonstrative—except when on the athletic field or at a rock concert—risks being called faggot. A boy who reaches out to reassuringly or even affectionately touch another— unless disguising it as a punch—may be labeled homo. The head of a boys' school told me how his football players ingeniously resolve their emotional Catch-22 "teddy bear" dilemma. After affectionately putting an arm around another, they unambiguously and vigorously whack him. Imagine the raucous reaction of seventh-grade boys when I told them how Nepalese and Turkish males walk down the streets of Kathmandu and Istanbul with their arms around each other or holding hands. Yet, just two years earlier, the boys had cuddled teddy bears.

Table 2.2 illustrates how boys suppress their emotionality and interpersonal strengths. It reports how Prestige's high school

Table 2.2. Prestige Boys' and Girls' Ratings of Their Own Interpersonal Strengths.

Interpersonal traits	Boys (%)	Girls (%)
Feelings for others	57	84
Cheerfulness	57	85
Being loving	52	79
Being trusting	49	71
Openness	43	65
Sincerity	43	67
Giving	42	76
Genuineness	41	62
Joyfulness	41	66
Sympathy	35	72
Expressiveness	30	49
Warmth	30	61
Being personal	24	44
Being natural	18	55

boys and girls describe their own interpersonal emotions and strengths. The table orders the traits in terms of the decreasing percentage of boys who believe that they possess them. The differences between boys and girls revealed in the table are most telling— really chilling. The majority of boys believe that they have only three of the fourteen interpersonal strengths: feeling for others, cheerfulness, and loving. The majority of girls believe that they have twelve. That fewer boys than girls see themselves as open, expressive, natural, and genuine suggests that boys know they are estranged from emotional sources of vitality that would result in more fulfilling relationships.[6]

Such male-female differences can have serious consequences, not just for boys' schooling but also for their future adult success. Forty percent of public high school teachers view their students as apathetic. Why? Of the several reasons, one is that boys risk being labeled a fag if they are too emotionally involved in—even excited, let alone passionate, about—an idea or project. Control by suppression and withdrawal, muted interest, and diffident coolness produce dead classrooms. Only when emotion is sanctioned by dramatics and music, released by the rare teachers portrayed in movies such as *Conrack* and *Dead Poet's Society*, discovered when aiding a younger child, or evoked on an athletic turf do boys get in touch with their sources of vitality.

Boys who manage to keep their feelings alive know they must hide them. A seventh-grade boy wrote a letter to his teacher thanking him for helping him through some difficult moments. He concluded by requesting, "Please don't tell anyone about this letter."

Chapter Six will describe how critical the interpersonal qualities listed in Table 2.2 are to a boy's future marital, parental, and sexual success as well as to his ethical behavior and well-being. Failure to raise boys more healthily contributes to communal ethical and familial disintegration.

Dilution of Male-Male Friendships. American boys also now know that adults distrust too close male friendships. They confuse affection with sexuality. Two "chums" who hang around with each other too frequently, playfully lean on, hug, or even wrestle with each other *not* aggressively enough, or tell each other that they like each other risk thinking of themselves or being labeled by others as gay.

How do boys adjust to these confusions? Unsure about their own affectionate needs and sexual orientation, they shy away from too close and self-disclosing friendships.[7] They quash any overt sign of affection and its distantly related emotions of tenderness, warmth, and appreciation. One man plaintively told me that he had never learned how to tell another male that he liked him and wanted to be his friend. Boys go further to hide their edginess about their "teddy bear" needs. They disguise them by hitting out physically or by verbally putting others down with sexual witticisms, calling others what they fear in themselves, and withdrawing from too intense emotional friendships with other males—permanently so in the United States. Their warmer, caring, and affectionate impulses, consigned to their emotional underground, emerge only much later in safer relationships, such as with their own children.[8]

Premature Sexualization of Relationships with Girls. The fourth effect of our cultural confusion about the meaning of maleness is to encourage boys to seek out girls to test their emerging sexuality. After I had given a talk to high school military cadets, a fourteen-year-old cadet furtively took me aside to tearfully ask, "Is it all right not to have sex with girls until I marry? The guys are calling me queer." That the United States has one of the highest rates of out-of-wedlock teenage pregnancy in the world suggests that sex must have some very special meanings to its boys that are not shared by boys in other cultures who are less confused about their maleness. It is not surprising that the number of middle school boys reporting having had sex has markedly increased in the past decade.

Boys' early sexualization of their relationships can block their healthy growth. They may fail to integrate their sexual responsiveness with affection and the communicative skills necessary to have a loving mature intimate relationship with another in the future. Don't males' increased violence and sexualized relationships with girls tell us something most important? American males have too few channels through which to express the richness of their interpersonal needs. Slapping a woman's rear, punching her or putting a headlock on her, and date-raping or sexually possessing her are predictable "abuses" in a society that so constricts its males' healthy interpersonal growth.

Not understanding the changing meanings of boys' relationships, schools have not provided as healthy learning environments as they could. A boys' school implementing its mission to "make men" by requiring its boys, even first-graders, to participate in tackle football sought advice about its low faculty and student morale. When I arrived, the head expressed puzzlement about why two-thirds of the seniors had volunteered to work with a nearby Boys Club. I knew why. They had been stretched too far out of psychic shape. The boys, as well as the faculty, had described the students as excessively macho. But 55 percent of the seniors wished that their peers were more "loving." Working with younger boys in a "masculine" way enabled them to grow more wholly and so more healthily.

Such are some of the potential emotionally damaging effects of adults' confusion, mediated in part by the names we call others, about the meaning of maleness. By failing to question our values about gender roles and their effects on students' educability, we have failed to create as healthy schools as today's youth need. How else have youth's changing values affected their educability?

Youth's Changing Values

I have heard no voices nor read any studies that claim that the ethical climate of the United States' educational, political, business, and religious institutions has improved within the past several decades. Rather, critics charge that communal ethical expectations have fragmented and behavior has deteriorated. In the 1980s, 65 percent of Americans believed that the country's ethical climate had declined. The greatest decline had apparently occurred in those under fifty years of age. For example, 41 percent of executives under fifty but only 24 percent of those over fifty reported cheating on their income taxes.[9] Or need I call the limitless roll of ethically bankrupt exemplars whom alert youth learn about from the mass media: universities padding their overhead charges for grants; politicians billing taxpayers for their notorious junkets; business leaders lying and stealing; religious evangelists bribing secretaries not to reveal their sexual fall from grace; and on and on?

Growing up with such immoral exemplars must affect the maturing of youth's values and consciences. Their clamorous questioning of long-cherished values about what the good life should be has been especially troubling to moralistic guardians of the true paths to salvation. The theme is not new. Humans have always chafed under God's discipline. TV's thundering Sunday evangelists evoke images of their vividly illustrious mentors, the Puritan divines, who similarly accused our ancestors of "atheism, sodomy, blasphemy, murder, whoredom, adultery, witchcraft, buggery . . . all of these things stirring within thee . . . like a nest of snakes. [You are] stained dunghills, bogs of filth, lumps of lewdness, slough and slime."[10] They would add nowadays, "pickled alcoholics, fried cocaine addicts, wicked child abusers, slothful welfare recipients, profligate yuppies, and corrupt savings and loan bankers."

The eternal drama of temptation's conflict with conscience takes different forms in each generation. Comments from teachers again provide glimmers of a deeper understanding of what temptation and conscience mean to today's youth. Scarcely a faculty member has failed to note that today's students are more outspokenly critical of authority than previous ones. Not just California teachers believe that students are more morally pragmatic and seemingly insensitive to transcendent and spiritual values. Teachers in many other regions of the country believe that. Paradoxically, adolescents appear to be more committed than previous generations of adolescents to an ethic based on fairness and equality of opportunity that bolsters their much less judgmental attitude about diverse styles of living.

Surveys about youth's changing values confirm teachers' views. Since the early 1900s, their religious activities and beliefs have become increasingly secularized. They less frequently attend church, pray, and read their Bibles. Fewer now believe in hell, the devil, an afterlife, or the existence of one true religion.[11] The same trends are occurring in other countries. About 10 to 15 percent fewer Irish Catholic students believe in God, heaven, and the devil than did in 1975.[12]

Since the end of World War II, researchers have extensively

documented how other American values have been changing. I cite only a few of numerous examples that affect students' school behavior and achievement. Between 1945 and 1953, college students valued self-indulgence and sensuous enjoyment fifth among other values; nowadays, they value them first.[13] One researcher claims that they have become more me-oriented, more competitive to get everything that they can before "the *Titanic* goes under," more interested in material success, and more consumer-oriented.[14]

George Gallup's surveys complement these. He compared the values of different age groups in 1955 with those of the same age groups in 1980 to questions such as "I have enjoyed work so much I have had a hard time putting it down." In 1955, 44 percent of persons younger than thirty agreed, whereas in 1980, only 26 percent did; of those thirty to forty-nine, 51 percent agreed in 1955 but only 32 percent in 1980. Erosion was less for those aged fifty or over.[15]

Alexander Astin has studied the values of several hundred thousand entering college freshmen each year for about two decades. Since their pyrotechnic flashes of idealism in the sixties, students (and their parents) have become progressively more centered on their materialistic welfare. The percentage of college freshmen preparing to serve others or seeking a world view or philosophical ideal consistently declined for years until recently. Competitive success, status, and an economic "security blanket" are now the dominant reasons for going to college.[16] Students major in fields, such as economics, that they believe will guarantee them a job, even though large numbers admit that they are not intrinsically interested in such fields. To make the big buck, to become an *instant* millionaire, is the impatient obsession of many of our brightest youth. And they guilelessly admit that they are self-centered and want to live the good life now. A *Wall Street Journal* poll of the children of Fortune 500 company executives reported that they wanted to live like their parents but didn't want to work as hard. It is not surprising, therefore, that charities report that the young adults of the 1980s have not contributed at the rate of previous generations[17] or that few wish to become teachers.[18]

A decade-long study of the declining achievement of eleventh-graders in Illinois concluded that decreases in student "thirst for knowledge" and "will to achieve," particularly in mathematics and natural science, were the principal culprits.[19] Student interest in scientific research, though not engineering, has declined since 1966.[20]

How shall we make sense of such changes and their implications for schools? The worldwide repudiation of moral authorities, abetted by the mass media since the 1960s, has undermined the power of imposed moral proscriptions for controlling our behavior. The consequences have been both baleful and hopeful. The baleful ones are increased ethical uncertainty, distressing amorality, and the erosion of commitment to the values that sustain academic motivation. Both baleful and hopeful is the boundless experimentation to fashion more self-fulfilling ways of growing healthily and living together. The hopeful effect is the resurgence of self-righting or balancing tendencies to moderate the individualistic extremes that liberation from oppression always produces. We are in a necessary but fitful transition to a more mature national conscience that better balances self-fulfillment and adjustment to communal needs for *all* of our people.

Repudiation of Moral Authority

The key question to ask about the modern conscience is "Who now decides what is right, true, or good?" Whom do youth respect? Traditional authorities no longer automatically command respect and obedience for increasingly more Americans. No longer does role or position, whether of president, Supreme Court justice, labor boss, principal, teacher, or even parent, guarantee respect and acknowledged acceptance of authority.[21] The dethronement of traditional moral authority goes far beyond American shores. Within the past decades, Turkish fathers, who had had control for as long as they lived of their sons' every major decision, have been forced to relinquish their power. Tokyo's youth increasingly challenge their monolithic cultural values. Even that symbol of righteous authority the pope has been loudly harangued by feminist nuns, revolutionizing Central American priests, contraceptive-using American Catholics, and the obstreperous Dutch. Seventy-five percent of American Catholic youth no longer believe that the pope is infallible. Sixty percent say the church should be more democratic. Whereas 72 percent of youthful Catholics agreed in 1969 with the pope that premarital sex was morally wrong, only 33 percent agreed by 1987.[22] No longer can males arbitrarily tell females what is best for them. Questioning of political authorities is occurring worldwide, from Nepal to Eastern Europe.

A central meaning of the American tumult of the sixties was the shift of moral authority from externalized symbols of conscience to each individual's feeling about what was best for his or her own fulfillment. Fulfillment is interpreted by many to mean "If it feels good, do it."

The confrontational rebellion against authority has retreated quite far from its height in the late sixties and seventies. However, the disposition to repudiate moralistic authorities' efforts to arbitrarily reimpose their consciences on others is very much alive. Authority's exhortations, warnings, and prohibitory laws have not noticeably suppressed drug, sexual, and other fleshly temptations. Anyone who understands the evolving American character knows that the Supreme Court's refusal to strike down Georgia's prohibition of oral and anal sex in the privacy of one's bedroom is not going to change one whit the behavior of anyone. We know a profound moral revolution has occurred when one of America's most conservative columnists, James Kilpatrick, chided the Court that "homosexuals ought to have the same right to privacy in Georgia that the court long ago guaranteed to heterosexuals in New Haven."[23] Even the very decent but conservative adults of Maine decisively rejected the efforts of moralistic arbiters to take away their *Playboys* in a 1986 referendum.

Today, those who wish to influence the morals and values of young people have to earn such a right. As one teacher returning to the classroom after a several-year absence wrote, "I'm sitting here trying to figure out exactly why I had left teaching. I left with a bitter taste in my mouth. Where were the students who were so eager to learn just a few short years ago? Where was the respect for teachers or, for that matter, for a fellow human being? I grew up loving school, eager to please, eager to learn. I respected my teachers. But now when I walk into the classroom, I feel I am there to earn their respect." The predisposition to assert one's *own* values is not confined to adolescents; it has become rooted in elementary school children as well. Seventy-six percent of elementary compared to 72 percent of high school faculty say today's children are not afraid to complain, one of their traits about which teachers agreed most frequently.

As long as proscriptive "authorities" held conscience captive, developing a more mature conscience—that is, one that is aware of its values, genuinely other-centered, integrated with one's actions and not just on Sundays, enduringly principled and centered, and emotionally owned as one's own for which one is responsible—was impossible.

Increasing Ethical Uncertainty

The repudiation of traditional authorities has created an anarchical ethical vacuum. Many now justify an "anything goes" moral stance on the basis of "it feels good to me"; they also tend to consign moral lapses to someone else's responsibility. A business leader explained away a 1986 Wall Street insiders' trading scandal by claiming, "Well, they were young and hadn't yet learned the right way of doing business!" A cynic might add, "so they wouldn't get caught." I would ask, "If young adults responsible for millions of dollars of other people's money should not be held accountable for their acts, why should we parents and grandparents—anyone, for that matter?"

To take the ethical pulse of today's youth, carefully study Table 2.3. It describes high school teachers' and their students' view of youth's ethical behavior as well as Prestige High School's students' view of their own. It tells us how perilous our ethical tone has become. Do the table's implications trouble you as much as they do me? They blatantly tell us that no ethical trait is seen by a majority of teachers or students as describing their typical student or peer. Recall the survey results about the increased preeminence of self-indulgent and materialistic goals and decreased altruistic commitments and the California teachers' observations of covert racism and sexism. Furthermore, a survey of California high school students found that the majority cheated, knew that other students also cheated, and weren't upset that they did. These findings were

Table 2.3. Teachers' and Students' Judgments of Students' Ethical Values.

| Ethical value | Public high schools (%) | | Independent high schools (%) | | Prestige students' self-descriptions (%) |
	Teachers	Students	Teachers	Students	
Caring	43	40	46	46	83
Honesty	33	30	49	41	71
Fairness	30	31	32	30	53
Idealism	26	26	28	30	27
Integrity	15	14	31	20	26
Strong convictions	12	19	17	18	21
Courage	8	33	13	27	42
Deep ethical sense	6	14	8	14	42

accentuated in the state's most competitive academic schools—the type of schools that Table 2.3 describes.[24]

Remember that the table describes perceptions. What we *believe* other people and ourselves are like can be a more powerful determinant of how we respond than what they or we may *actually* be like. If teachers and students don't think students are honest or idealistic, they will act as if they weren't. If we believe that most people cheat on their income tax, we may be more inclined also to cheat unless our honesty is engrained in our character.

Much as I would like to yield to Panglossian idealism, I cannot blithely explain away and deny the table's disturbing implications. First, it shows too widespread consensus about the value immaturity of youth.

Second, while some apologists say that students don't know what words such as *integrity* mean, I reply, "Well, that's why I believe liberal education's vision of arete has been forgotten. Don't even our most academic schools sensitize their students to character's vocabulary?"

Third, yes, teachers' and students' perceptions are only one way to assess others' ethical behavior. My studies of similar traits of adults showed that others' judgments of our public ethical behavior agrees only moderately with our private assessment of it. We believe we are more ethical than others may believe.[25] Yet a majority of Prestige's students describe themselves as ethical on only three traits; they agree quite well with others' views about contemporary students' lack of idealism, strength of convictions, and moral sense.

Fourth, some argue that youthful behavior never approaches others' expectations or hopes. Most parents say, "My child is not like that. Those teachers and students are describing other kids; besides, they are too critical and use only a few students' behavior to describe their typical student or friends." Surveys of parents do show that they believe that their children are very ethical—almost angelically so. The parents may be right, but they may not be the most unbiased of observers. The real test of children's character is how they act outside their watchful homes.

Finally, Table 2.3 supports the U.S. Department of Education's belief that students have lost a sense of the ideal for themselves. True, youth are neurologically programmed to be idealists. Their maturing ability to foresee and plan alternative futures can be a source of "revolutionary" ideals. Chinese, Thai, and South Korean students who have fought for democratic freedoms demonstrate that. Youthful ideals have upset numerous governments. But maturely stabilized ideals lead to commitments for more than a month or two of "occasional flashes of idealism" noted by Chapter One's Kansan professors.

Unable, then, to dismiss the table's collective portrait of how youth appear publicly, I then explored their hopes for their peers and themselves. Has their commitment to education's values, such as honesty, integrity, fairness, and courage to defend truth, been diluted? Has that dilution eroded their motivation to become educated? Are the virtues associated with the search for truth irrelevant to youth today? Has America lost its historical Puritan vision of striving for character perfection?

Decreasing Commitment to Academic Values

For answers to these questions about our commitment to academic virtues, I first turn to one of America's foremost academic schools, which I call Premier. Its alumni occupy major positions of political and economic power. I then examine students' and teachers' commitment to academic values in public and independent schools.

How can students' commitment to virtue be assessed? Commitment means more than just assent or belief; it means emotional ownership, conviction, dedication. More than our rational beliefs, our spontaneously organized ones are the crucibles from which sustained passion, ideals, and commitments draw their energy. Premier's students completed the Word Check List, which assesses such emotionally felt rather than considered beliefs by urging respondents not to hesitate when describing and expressing their wishes for their peers, for example, but to impulsively complete the instrument as quickly as possible. By combining the percentage of students' descriptions of their peers for each value with that of their wishes for them, we can identify the remaining percentage for whom the value in question is irrelevant, certainly not salient enough to have responded to one way or another.

Except for caring, the majority of Premier's juniors and seniors—some of our country's future leaders—did not describe their peers as honest, fair, ethically concerned persons of integrity. More disturbing, no more than 26 percent wished that they were. For example, only 6 percent believed that their peers had a deep ethical or moral sense; only 16 percent more wished that they did. Or symptomatic of the loss of commitment to ideals, only 14 percent saw their peers as idealistic; only 6 percent more wished that they were, leaving 80 percent for whom idealism was irrelevant.

I had to confront their faculty: "What is our future when 78 percent of our potential leaders don't care about having a deep ethical sense or 54 percent about being honest? Are you producing contented intellectual sociopaths, not confronted with and made aware of the purposes for which the power—the knowledge and skills—you are giving them should be used?"

Dismayingly, Premier's results do not differ very much from those of other leading public and independent schools, whose teachers' and students' views of and wishes for their students and peers were remarkably similar to each other. Fifty-two percent of public and 50 percent of independent school teachers neither believed that their students had integrity nor wished that they had. Sixty-two percent of public and 67 percent of independent high school students believed that idealism was not typical of their peers and did not wish that it were. That faculty and students from varied schools in different regions of the country respond so similarly attests to the reliability of the results.

The majority of teachers and students are unreservedly committed only to honesty and caring; teachers are possibly committed to a strong moral sense. That the majority of faculty, as well as students, apparently believe that other values, such as integrity, fairness, courage, idealism, and strong convictions, are irrelevant is sobering. The results scarcely reassure us about the future ethical behavior of today's students, at least in strongly academically oriented schools. Or about the current vitality of our liberal education tradition? Or about the future health of our communities and nation?

Furthermore, students do not have high expectations for their own ethical growth. They are either content with their character or find its virtues irrelevant. They too express no commitment to the same values for themselves that their teachers and peers also believe to be irrelevant. While more than 80 percent of Prestige's boys and girls, for example, are committed to values such as honesty and caring, less than a majority value fairness, courage, depth of moral sense, or integrity or believe that having strong idealistic convictions is important. Prestige's students are not exceptional. Their ethical commitment is generally similar to that of other students in other regions of the country.

Boys, however, tend to be less committed to ethical values than girls. Why? Because males have not developed the other-centered interpersonal skills that underlie ethical values? Yes. My studies of adults found that virtue is rooted in typically feminine interpersonal skills, such as those that Table 2.2 shows distinguish Prestige's girls from its boys. Almost 20 percent more of Prestige's boys than its girls, for example, reported that having a strong moral sense was irrelevant to them.

What implications do these findings have for educators? Educating boys for character outcomes may be a more daunting challenge than so educating girls; we could at least rely on girls' nurturing interpersonal skills to support our efforts. Another implication is that securing contemporary youth's ownership for some values as proper educational goals will likely provoke considerable resistance by both sexes, as well as by high school faculty—unless they become convinced that virtue pays off in more pragmatic ways, which my research finds that it actually does.[26]

Where are those young people and adults with a committed vision to an ideal of what they could be? You might say that if I had comparable data from twenty or thirty years ago, I would find a similar pattern of results. Most experienced teachers would disagree. Schools and colleges that have seen the erosion of their honor codes and increased incidence of cheating, stealing, drinking, harassment, and even gang rapes would also disagree. Even if there has been no change in our values over the past several decades, youth's lack of emotional commitment to an ethical ideal does not provide much reason to rejoice today.

Religious adults tell me that I would find more ethically sensitized people in religiously oriented schools. Possibly. Religious people are generally more virtuous than others, though one does not have to be religious to be virtuous.[27] However, Prestige High School drew students from a religious region of the country.

We cannot too complacently assume that religious schools necessarily attract and/or produce ethical people. In one well-known midwestern fundamentalist college, 60 percent of the faculty but a scarcely visible 15 percent of the students believed the typical student to be deeply ethical. Clearly, more was going on (or perhaps not going on!) than the faculty was aware of. In a southern Bible Belt college in which more than two-thirds of both faculty and students agreed that the college *and* the typical student were conservatively religious, a bare majority of faculty and students could agree that only two of the ethical values—honesty and caring—described the typical student. For 59 percent of the students, integrity was even irrelevant.

There are, however, both secular and religious institutions whose ethical ethos and concerned student bodies are obvious. And there are institutions, such as some Quaker schools and colleges I have studied, that have been known for years to have influential ethically concerned climates. Studies of Haverford College's alumni, for example, showed that the college had powerfully altered their consciences; it had permanently sensitized them to feel that they should be committed to honesty, compassion, integrity, and courage. Such institutions have historically stood for a deeply principled way of life, sought to be consistently faithful to such a vision, and created specific institutional ways to encourage the development of such values.[28]

An Emerging Principled Conscience?

Probably no sector of our national personality has been so affected by the social and technological whirlwinds of recent decades as have our values. We are immersed in a transitional epochal moment of change, marked by uncertainty, incoherence, and doubt. Transitional times are moments of potentially great growth—or collapse. They shake us up, make us question our values, and prod us to explore other alternatives and try out other ways of living. The less mature fall along the wayside; the more mature resiliently move ahead to create a way of life that is healthier for themselves and more adaptive to their future.

Where might we be going in the future? To what will we commit ourselves?

I now defend the hypothesis that we are reaching the nadir of self-centered amorality. Our naturally given self-righting potential is beginning to rouse itself from decades of slumber to spur us to lay the cornerstone on which a more principled mature conscience can be built. I speak out of my understanding of healthy growth and findings about the psychic worth of virtue. No firm evidence exists to justify my optimistic crystal-ball gazing.

Youth's repudiation of the right of moralistic authorities to tell them what they should and should not do occurred for several reasons. The most important was that such prescriptions, frequently parochial, collided with the healthy growth of too many oppressed Americans' desires to evolve a more just ethic.

Conscience used to mean a list of specific do's and don't's. It is fitfully inching toward meaning principled attitudes about how to relate to others. Many young people no longer listen to authorities that proscribe specific personal behaviors, such as whom to have sex or live with, that affect only themselves or willing partners. What do violate their emerging ethic are authorities who, while condemning such behavior, hypocritically trample on what increasingly more believe to be fundamental universal ethical principles. Like what? Respect for those whose life-styles and beliefs differ from one's own. Equal justice for all. Life-preserving, more peaceful ways of resolving disputes. Respect for our planet's environmental integrity.

Consider the increasing commitment to our historical American values of fairness and equality of opportunity that is reshaping our meaning of justice. In the sixties, could we have tolerated Archie Bunker's offensive racism, sexism, and every other -ism on TV? No. In the seventies and the reruns in the nineties? Yes. We could laugh at him and at what we had once been. A national consensus had emerged since. Such prejudice violated a more universal principle of equality and fairness. Of course, racism and sexism still exist, as the California faculty said of its students and the 1992 Los Angeles riots told us. But still, who could have predicted in Archie Bunker's day that gays would feel secure enough to mount their massive Gay Rights march in Washington in 1993?

The large percentage of students who neither see nor wish to see such virtues as fairness in their peers also warns us that virtue must ceaselessly be defended. But the direction of our collective moral evolution has been set, codified in our laws, and embedded in our national conscience. When such prejudice occurs nowadays, more often than not it occurs with guilt. Before, we were either unaware of or felt guiltless about our prejudice.

Or consider the commitment to self-fulfillment. To create a way of life that nurtures and integrates one's needs and strengths means that each has to have an opportunity to do just that. Jerry Falwell, the eighties leader of the moralistic minority (misnamed the Moral Majority), would not have been widely viewed by youth in the fifties as a Christian hypocrite if he had defended South Africa's system of apartheid then. In the mid eighties, he was.

The ethical cornerstone now being laid for a more principled conscience is the commitment to the personhood of *all* people, not just those like ourselves. Our wandering youngsters have met—if not personally, at least imaginally on television—Iranians, Germans, and Mexicans. More are beginning to identify with human beings, not just with southerners, Americans, or whites. Younger people are beginning to marry interracially and internationally more frequently. (The number of such couples has doubled since

1980 to 1,200,000.) They are beginning to talk more about being a person than about being an American or a Thai. Such an evolution in our self-identities portends a future dilution of an *unthinking* allegiance to one's country of birth. We are beginning to think of ourselves as members of an interdependent global village.

Implications for the Future

Tumultuous transitional moments aren't favorable times from which to wrest a perspective about what character the future will demand. You may quarrel, even strenuously, with my judgments about youth's interpersonal and value strengths and the paths that they need to take to adapt to the twenty-first century's imperatives. But at least let us think more deliberately and thoughtfully about the character for which we need to educate, rather than ignore it as we have been doing.

Greater Ethical Awareness and Sensitivity

The leading edge of youth's maturation is their increased aware-ness, particularly of their relationships and value choices. Growing up in a psychologically sophisticated society and novelty-searching mass media culture has encouraged their perceptivity and psycho-logical mindedness. This is one of the principal changes that a national survey of adults reported occurred between 1957 and 1976. [29] What adult secrets and blemishes, even curse words, are left for even sixteen-year-olds to discover? Many have a more subtle interper-sonal vocabulary today than I had in the censorious and naive thir-ties and forties. Surely these are important skills and information necessary for living in an interdependent world that will require more sophisticated understanding about human possibilities for good and evil.

Today's youth are not as bound by proscriptive values as their grandparents were. They are freer to self-consciously question the reasons for their choices and to explore alternative life-styles and so make potentially more honest choices. Some are more aware of their potential complexity and consequences, such as the unhealthy effects of drugs, nuclear power, and ozone depletion. But too many still do not know enough about such issues, including their own sexuality, to make as informed choices as they need to make. They have a long way to go to become as ethically aware and sensitive as well as intellectually honest as they will need to be.

Educators must learn how to create schools that integrate more value-centered issues with their curricula if students are to become more ethically sensitive persons.

More Other-Centered Skills and Values

Young people may be more accepting and tolerant of others who differ from themselves than previous generations were. More of them casually accept sexual, ethnic, social class, and religious differences. But tolerance is not caring and empathy, the two other-centered but underdeveloped strengths most needed in the future. They are two of the principal adhesives that hold together marriages, families, and communities, which will become even more vulnerable in the future to society's fragmenting forces. A healthy country requires stable, caring families and communities for the mental health of its children and adults.

Perceptive commentators about the American character believe that raising boys to be independent, self-sufficient, rugged macho males must now be moderated. Our exaggerated self centered individualism has devalued and suppressed the maturation of other-centered strengths. Caring and empathy are necessary to create and sustain not only the egalitarian, interdependent personal relationships but also the cohesive communal values that a potentially incoherent and unstable future will require.[30] Such values that transcend differences that have historically divided peoples prepare youth to be at home in a diversely interdependent world.

Educators need to create learning environments in which students—especially boys—learn to care and work *for* as well as *with* others, and so develop empathy. Males are not ready to create the sustained mutuality and cooperative relationships that females expect and that stable communities must have.[31]

Idealistic Goals and Commitment to the Community

Many youth lack a value gyrostabilizer for adapting to the future's uncertainties. Having rejected the more secure but moralistic proscriptions that integrated previous generations' values, many youth, "ideal-less" about their future, have become preoccupied with enjoying only today's pleasures. However, lives bereft of ideals and commitments are lives empty of meaning and hope. The absence of strong value commitments makes vocations, marriages, and friendships fleeting and eventually unfulfilling.

The endangered and contentious world of the future also needs people who care for its welfare and devote their lives to an ideal of what our small planetary community could become. Where are the schools that witness to altruistic ideals and educate for the other-centered values and skills necessary if we are to be effective stewards of an increasingly fragile planet? Where are the schools that encourage their students to develop their own meanings and goals that organize and purposefully steer behavior, even at the sacrifice of immediate enjoyments?

Only one realistic path is open for us: educate youth to form their own humane meanings guided by liberal education's historical values, such as honesty, compassion, and integrity. It is more imperative than ever before that educators find ways to create schools of hope that prod and enable students to begin creating their own goals.

How our minds and characters mature affects and is influenced in turn by who and what we think we are. Our sense of self organizes and regulates our actions. We can so value growth itself and secure such control over its processes that we become autonomous agents of our maturing. We can transcend the barriers and limitations of the biological, familial, school, peer, and other societal forces more than many of us have thought. The key is our sense of self. How has our changing society affected the maturing of our views of and command of ourselves?

Chapter 3

Selves:
Wavering Self-Confidence
and Faltering Self-Command

Self-confidence, self-esteem, and self-command result from years of learning who one is and what one can and cannot do well. While the roots of a mature sense of self are numerous, acquiring compe tence in a *variety* of activities, not just one or two, is the most important way to develop a realistically firm self-confidence. Competence teaches us trust in, we might say, our generic ability to cope and adapt successfully. Avoiding tests of our competence because we anticipate failure means that we don't discover potential strengths and their limits. Fearing to risk in turn restricts further the compass of our self-confidence and limits our educability. As we become progressively more aware of what we can and cannot do well, we learn what we realistically dare risk—or must avoid. We no longer need a parent or teacher to approve or to warn us. Our growing competence frees us from depending on its affirmation by others— a sign of maturing self-autonomy.

It is more difficult nowadays to develop such a confident and strong sense of self. Mind's and character's confluent changes roil, mix up, unsettle our ideas of who we are and our feelings of being in control of ourselves and our destinies. Much of what used to ground our sense of self and make our future predictable we now doubt. We can no longer take for granted what women and men are to be, or that we can have an uncomplicated relationship with the opposite sex, or that we will stay married long enough to celebrate a golden anniversary, or that we will have lifelong security with the

company, an improving living standard, children who will do better than we, and eternal life.

Transitional times such as the present undermine self-
confidence, particularly for the vulnerable, including young people
whose evolving identities are buttressed by only spotty records of
competence and success. Feeble self-confidence saps mature command of ourselves. Yet our future's continued uncertainty and instability demand more self-conscious command of our maturing
than ever before.

The Weakening Trust in Self

Experienced elementary school teachers talk more frequently nowadays about their students' self-doubt, lack of confidence, and "fragility." The phrases differ, but the message is the same. Recall the
California teachers who talked of their students' "false maturity"
and the Kansas professors who cited their students' "fear of failure"
and unwillingness to take risks. I have heard teachers from New
England to Louisiana also claim that their capable students today
are more afraid of failure and less willing to take risks than former
ones. I, too, found my own students more unwilling to take risks,
such as enrolling in courses they might not do well in, because they
didn't trust themselves, for example, to complete their papers on
time. Good evidence does not exist to firmly assert that this distrust
is more widespread nowadays. However, we can examine today's
students' principal strengths on which self-confidence and self-
esteem are built.

Strengths of Typical Students

Trust and confidence in one's strengths, their availability and reliability, are essential to being a successful adult.[1] To build a strong
and confident sense of self, youth must know what their strengths
are. I have mentioned their awareness of and tolerance for different
people and life-styles, their perceptivity, and their hustling skills.
What other strengths do their teachers and peers believe they have?
At least two-thirds of both public and independent high school
teachers believe that their students are capable, friendly, social, com-

petitive and talkative. Their students generally agree that their peers resemble their teachers' portrait. They also describe themselves similarly.

Using the less stringent criterion of at least 50 percent faculty agreement, students would also be judged to be casual, unafraid to complain (a sign of potential autonomy), cooperative, good-natured, cheerful, academic, and fun. Remember that these are the perceived strengths of favored students attending good suburban and independent high schools.

What does this portrait tell us? Teachers and students agree quite well about privileged youth's core strengths. They are typical American teenagers who are capable, delightfully talkative, socially gregarious, and cheerful people who are enjoyable to be around; their competitiveness is balanced by cooperativeness.

The portrait is disturbing, however. Where are mind's coping and character's interpersonal skills and ethical values that the students' future will demand? Why don't teachers and students identify specific academic-related strengths? The portrait does not tell us whether students' academic potential is realized in achievement, which is ultimately the source of trust and confidence in mind's capabilities. So let us compare high school teachers' and students' descriptions of students' academic-related strengths and Prestige's students' views of their similar strengths. Table 3.1 shows that teachers and students in public and independent schools generally agree with each other about their students' and peers' academic strengths. However, the *majority* identify distressingly few strengths. They do not believe that students have the motivation or academic achievement that could ground self-trust and a healthy self-confidence. Public school students are not believed to be highly motivated to work hard and achieve academically. The results are consistent with other findings, such as the minimal amount of time they spend on their homework.

Compared to public school teachers and students, independent school teachers and students judge their typical students to be stronger academically than public school students, especially in their motivation to work hard. Almost twice as many public as independent school teachers believe, for example, that their students are apathetic, 40 versus 22 percent. Given similar parental socioeco-

Table 3.1. Teachers' and Students' Judgments of Students' Academic Strengths.

	Teachers (%)		Students (%)		Prestige students'
	Public	Independent	Public	Independent	self-descriptions (%)
Motivational strengths					
Ambition	41	57	55	63	62
Being hardworking	28	56	43	58	61
Dedication	16	25	31	38	52
Intellectual excitement	8	21	17	23	24
Achievement strengths					
Clear thinking	19	25	30	42	58
Being well informed	19	24	30	35	38
Excellence	15	21	27	30	29
Being intellectually rigorous	8	13	13	23	14

nomic and educational backgrounds, these noticeable differences raise a provocative question: why may highly regarded public high schools not be creating as motivating learning environments for today's students? Chapters Four and Sixteen suggest reasons that have major public policy implications.

Table 3.1 is troubling for other reasons. Note the large discrepancy, for example, between the number of Prestige students who work hard and the number who are intellectually excited. Forty percent of Prestige's students are bored with school; 61 percent call their teachers boring. Are college-bound students compulsively working for extrinsic rewards, such as good grades and test scores, rather than intrinsic ones, such as joy of learning? The table also provokes other questions: Why is students' achievement not more commensurate with their ambition and hard work? Is schooling not "taking" because they learn only to pass tomorrow's quiz? Are students just playing the game of becoming educated? If so, how does conforming to the rules about how to "get ahead" affect a youth's self-trust and self-confidence?

Wavering Self-Confidence

What about youth's confidence in themselves? Not many teachers and students view today's typical student as self-confident; nor do many students feel self-confident. Only 21 percent of public and 28 percent of independent school teachers, though about 40 percent of students, describe the typical student as self-confident. Actually 39 percent of public and 24 percent of independent school teachers believe that their students *lack* self-confidence.

More important, how confident are students in themselves? Only a minority—about the same percentage as their teachers—think of themselves as self-confident. Perhaps because they know they are part of an exceptional group of students, 40 percent of Prestige High School's students feel confident about themselves, though 22 percent explicitly say that they lacked confidence.

Do boys and girls differ in their self-confidence? The evidence is equivocal; the answer depends on how we measure it. For example, a national survey by the American Association of University Women (AAUW) asked students how good they were "at a lot of things," their measure of self-confidence. Though progressively fewer boys and girls answered "Always true" from the fourth through the tenth grade, more boys agreed than girls for every grade level. By tenth grade, 42 percent of the boys but only 23 percent of the girls reported high self-confidence. The girls' more precipitous decline was associated with their growing doubts about their math ability.[2]

Other studies report contradictory results. Presumably, students who are confident about their competence will report less anxiety about its demonstration. However, college males and females do not differ in math anxiety.[3] When I studied the self-confidence of boys at Hardwick, a boys' school, I found that they agreed with their teachers' judgments. Only 26 percent felt self-confident; 24 percent lacked confidence in themselves. The remaining 50 percent felt neither way.

The fairer conclusion is probably that the majority of today's adolescents, regardless of their sex and how we measure their confidence, do not feel highly confident about themselves.

Diminishing Self-Esteem

Self-esteem has become an educator's catchword and lack of self-esteem a favored explanation for why children, especially girls and minority students, do not do well on achievement tests. If girls are happy about the way they are, like themselves, and don't wish to be someone else (three of AAUW's five indices of self-esteem), then, so educators assume, they'll have the confidence to do well in subjects such as math.

While self-esteem and self-confidence can reinforce each other, they are not equivalent. I can feel good about myself and not wish I were different but lack confidence that I can do many things that I wish I could do well, such as solving math problems or dropping a tree where I want it to fall. Conversely, my study of adult women identified a number who confidently and most competently fulfilled their roles as wives, mothers, and community participants but who had such low self-esteem that they had sought psychotherapy. One woman felt that she was an empty eggshell; another said that she was a good mother and wife but didn't know who she was. How could she have good self-esteem if she didn't know who she was?

Self-esteem, even confidence, does not necessarily lead to competence. Harold Stevenson, researching minority and transcultural differences in achievement, found that black and Hispanic children feel better about their reading and math abilities than white children but achieve less well. He believes that to bolster their students' self-esteem, teachers overly praise them and so create a false belief about how competent they are. Compared to comparable Chinese children, American children like math as well and believe they are very competent but actually achieve significantly less.[4]

Given these complicated qualifications, what do we know about students' self-esteem? It declines progressively from fourth to tenth grade, again noticeably more for girls than for boys from puberty on. The AAUW's survey reports that only 29 percent of tenth-grade girls but 46 percent of tenth-grade boys say they are happy with themselves, one index of high self-esteem. Girls' self-esteem is more closely related to feeling good about their physical appearance and pride in their academic work; boys' self-esteem is associated with feeling good about their sports ability.[5] Carol Gilligan suggests that girls' esteem plummets in their early pubertal years because they repress their own "voices" to become "nice" girls.[6]

When I index self-esteem by the number of positive traits students use to describe themselves, I find that high school students are generally much more positive about themselves than they are about their peers. But what troubles me is that few wish they were different. In fact, so few wish to "improve" themselves that I have wondered whether Americans have lost an ideal of personality perfection or the drive to achieve it. The U.S. Department of Education also believes that students' lack of commitment to an ideal for their own growth is the major student-related reason for the failure of their test scores to improve.[7] Why don't boys and, especially, girls have more positive beliefs in themselves?

A Shifting Foundation to a Strong Sense of Self

The roots of our adult success go deeply into our personalities. At the core of our identities are our views of ourselves as females and males, our earliest and most stable foundations on which to construct our personal self-concepts and good feelings about ourselves. Any threat to these foundations can be traumatic. Historically and still today, in the United States and many other countries, to really insult a man, you challenge his manhood. The tests and symbols of manly honor are numerous: fathering many children, especially sons; duels; tournaments; Rose Bowls; the National Rifle Association; Rambo; James Bond; Desert Storm. Ironically, some contemporary males who are uncertain about their own maleness have turned to a poet, Robert Bly, to defend their honor as iron men and warriors; he tells them it is okay to be a male. Doubted and challenged; defended and vindicated!

No societal change has more threatened the historical meaning of maleness than the changing identity of women. Why? Because maleness and femaleness define each other reciprocally. Men formerly learned to protect women, who needed to be cared for; women formerly yielded to men, who needed to assert. Changing some meanings of femaleness inevitably changes some meanings of maleness. And that is painfully unsettling. When I tell middle-aged male audiences that research shows that androgynous females and males are more successful and happy than singularly feminine females and macho males, some become restless, even angry.

The irrepressible human urge toward wholeness, for that is what maturing leads to, is clearly seen in the rapidity with which women's identity has been evolving. The changing meaning of femaleness has been rushing ahead at the speed of a Mount Rainier avalanche; that of maleness at the speed of Alaska's Hubbard glacier. No other revolution in our collective image of ourselves has been so rapid, intense, and widespread.[8]

The centuries-old view that women should be accommodating homemakers and mothers had by the sixties become too maladaptive and suppressive of their urge to wholeness. Though the feminist movement had been preparing us for such a revolutionary change for decades, the reintegration and consolidation of its values precipitously occurred within only a few years. In 1969, 49 percent of entering college women agreed that "A woman's career is as important as that of her husband"; in 1973, just four years later, an astounding 81 percent agreed. In 1969, 17 percent agreed that "A husband and wife should share equally in all household and child-rearing tasks," but in 1973, 43 percent agreed.[9] Young men have shown similar though less marked changes in their values.[10] These are remarkable shifts in the cornerstones of our identities.

How much do our ideas about maleness and femaleness affect our educability? A great deal for some youth. Males, particularly blue-collar or black and Latino (but not Asian) boys, are not supposed to do well in school, so many don't when they could; boys who do well are slighted, are put down, and, unless they are on the football team, risk being suspected of lacking "balls."

Females also confront an ambiguous message about their femaleness and achievement. They are supposed to do well, but not too well. In her inaugural presidential address to the American Association for the Advancement of Science, Sheila Widnall cited evidence about the lower percentage of women than men completing graduate work in mathematics and science. Why don't proportionately as many women as men complete their Ph.D. degrees?[11]

Only since the mid eighties have researchers begun to ask how femaleness affects educability.[12] My studies of adolescent girls' morale and women's healthy growth question some currently popular ideas about their development and its relationship to achievement. What sense do you make of these facts? What implications do they have for educating girls—and boys?

> Fact 1: Girls consistently enjoy school more than boys do. From fifth grade on, girls report being more satisfied than boys with an increasing number of school-related factors, such as the teaching of their teachers, their relationships with other students, and the amount of freedom that school provides. Boys are not reliably more satisfied than

girls with any of thirty different factors related to being a
student. [13]

Fact 2: Girls consistently get better academic grades than
boys throughout school and college. [14]

Fact 3: Girls have lower self-esteem than boys; it markedly
declines in puberty. [15]

Fact 4: Boys do better than girls on national aptitude and
achievement tests. Boys have done so much better than
girls on quantitative SAT tests that Julian Stanley, the
principal researcher on pubertal SAT aptitudes, has
claimed that genetics accounts for such differences. [16]
However, in recent years, the gap between the sexes' scores
has been closing. [17]

Fact 5: A girl's adolescent personality does not predict well
her adult well-being or success; a boy's does. Studies of
adolescent girls cannot be generalized to adult women's
healthy growth. [18]

Fact 6: Adult males and females mature similarly; when freed
from the confines of their traditional sex roles, both develop stronger, more autonomous selves. Psychology does
not need two different models for female and for male
healthy growth. [19]

Tentative fact: Adolescent girls mature more psychologically
from ninth to twelfth grade in emotionally cold girls'
schools than in warm girls' schools or either warm or cold
coed independent schools. [20]

How does your explanation compare with mine? For centuries, girls have been raised to organize their identities around their
relationships. Their self-esteem has depended, therefore, on how
well they fulfilled their relational obligations; that is, ensured their
children's and husbands' success and well-being.

The consequences for their healthy growth and achievement
have been momentous. They develop the skills to accommodate,
nurture, please, "be nice," and conform to others' expectations,
often at the expense of discovering their own talents and integrating
them into a more stable and autonomous sense of self. (One middle-
aged woman insightfully told me, "All I am is a collection of roles
put together by a committee.") They feel good about themselves if

they are pleasingly attractive to others and get good grades for their parents and teachers. What they learn is more contingent on their relationships with their teachers than on their intrinsic interests. We might say that what they learn is more a part of their role than of their selves. They therefore don't do as well on impersonal national tests. Their adolescent personality does not predict their future well-being because they have been estranged from their "real" selves. They mature more when *not* rewarded for playing their traditional feminine role; too developed feminine interpersonal skills distort healthy growth and block the development of more typically masculine coping skills. So they mature more in cold learning environments that demand that they grow androgynously. Intensive study of successful men's and women's personalities, reported in *Fulfilling Lives,* supports this interpretation.

If my hypothesis approaches truth, then its implications for enabling girls to develop a stronger sense of self should be clear. The analysis of boys in Chapter Two implied that they need to develop typically feminine interpersonal skills. Similarly, we should raise girls to develop more typically masculine strengths, though not in ways that derogate or suppress their other-centered ones. We should raise them to take a position not to please us but to discover what they believe—to assert, argue, debate, follow their interests, compete, affirm their own worth.

To ignore the fact that youth's ideas of maleness and femaleness so powerfully affect their educability condemns them to a failure to command and fulfill their academic promise as well as to become successful and happy adults.

Faltering Self-Command

When interviewed about how he had changed during his four years at Harvard, a senior said that he had become more in command of himself. "I'd never believed I could do things, that I had any power, I mean power over myself, and over effecting any change that I thought was right."[21] To gain command of mind's talents and character's strengths and so over oneself is the best way to prepare for the future's uncertain dangers and opportunities.

Too many signs suggest that many youth today cannot make their minds and characters work for their own growth. The previous chapters have told us that: we see increasing *addiction* to alcohol, drugs, sex, aggression, TV, computer games, even staplers. Fewer than 15 percent of high school faculty members and 30 percent of their students believe that today's youth can control or discipline themselves well; only 37 percent of Prestige's exemplary students thought of themselves as self-disciplined.

The most practical test of how well a school has educated its students is not their transitory achievement test scores but their enhanced and enduring ability to teach themselves and others. Table 3.2 maps the judgments of teachers and students about contemporary students' self-reliance, self-motivation, and self-teaching strengths. It tells us that both public and independent school teachers and students believe that their schools are failing.

Let's not quibble at this point about the table's specific figures (they may be off by five or ten percentage points). Or claim that students don't know what *autonomous* or *self-reliant* means (they may not, but surely their teachers do). Or argue that the table grossly underestimates the percentage of students who actually are self-reliant, self-motivated, and self-teaching, if not when in school at least when outside it. (I believe that this may be true, but no one has yet sought the evidence.) Keep in mind that the table portrays teachers' and students' beliefs about students and peers as well as Prestige's capable students' ideas about themselves as self-teachers.

Table 3.2. Teachers' and Students' Views of Students as Self-Teachers.

Strengths needed to be self-teaching	Teachers (%)		Students (%)		Prestige students' self-descriptions (%)
	Public	Independent	Public	Independent	
Self-reliance					
Autonomy	11	9	8	12	7
Independence	18	24	39	48	62
Self-reliance	11	16	25	26	40
Self-motivation					
Curiosity	24	37	42	41	53
Initiation	9	17	17	20	16
Self-motivation	9	17	30	30	40
Self-teaching					
Self-confidence	21	28	41	41	40
Self-discipline	11	14	25	30	37
Self-education	5	7	20	23	31

Also, don't forget that reality is in the eye of the beholder, and it is the reality that we see to which we react. If you doubt the validity of the table's figures for the school you know well, dare to go to its sand pile and discover just what its teachers and students actually believe about each other and themselves when working there.

The message seems clear. The majority of teachers and students do not believe their typical students or peers to be teachers of themselves—that is, in command of their own minds and characters. Even the majority of Prestige's students don't believe they have most of the strengths necessary to educate themselves. I repeat again. The table portrays students of schools whose students score high on aptitude and achievement tests, receive national honor awards, and have high college-acceptance rates. Despite these measurable signs of excellence, their faculties themselves judge that they have failed to prepare their students to become self-reliant, self-motivated, and self-teaching American Jeffersons, Franklins, Emersons, and Lincolns.

Table 3.2 tells us what teachers and students judge to be so; it does not tell us whether they believe that securing command of oneself is a valued commitment or an irrelevant goal. Just how *emotionally committed* are faculty and students to a vision of student self-empowerment or of students becoming teachers of themselves? With few exceptions, both public and independent high school teachers *and* students remarkably agree. They generally do not vary by more than ten percentage points from each other in judging students as not being more self-educating or wishing that they were. Their message is disturbingly clear. Neither teachers nor students emotionally value students becoming self-teachers. For example, only about 40 percent of teachers and students view typical students as being self-educating or wish that they were. Fifty-seven percent of Prestige's capable students neither viewed themselves as self-educating nor wished that they were.

You may be incredulous and tempted to dismiss such findings. How is it possible that so few teachers emotionally value curiosity, initiative, even self-confidence, or teach in ways to encourage them? Or that 45 percent of Prestige's hardworking and ambitious students don't think that they are curious or wish to be? Or that fewer than half value autonomy, initiative, or self-reliance?

If we put our preconceptions aside and visited actual high

school classes in every region of the country, we would sadly discover what typically goes on: teachers assuming responsibility for students' learning, using mind-crippling textbooks, assigning pages to read, talking 85 percent of the time, working hard to entertain their students, reviewing the textbook, directing students moment by moment, giving daily or weekly quizzes, providing science lab books to follow, and racing through their lesson plans to complete the syllabus by the end of the semester. Do these pedagogical crutches really empower students to be self-teachers?

No, they do not, if the test of their empowerment is freedom to be responsible for their own education. Some experimental schools of the late sixties and seventies collapsed because they naively assumed that their students could educate themselves when freed from such teacher-directed activities. The MHS faculty also provided such freedom. Its new students, attracted to but unprepared for the responsibility such freedom provided, listlessly moped for weeks wondering what they should be doing. Some angrily blamed their faculty for not telling them what to do and complained that they were not "teaching" them. Eventually, the faculty's clear expectations, available guidance, varied resources, group activities, and demands for accountability provided the bridge to more autonomous growth.

More upsetting is that of the hundreds of schools and colleges about which I have similar information, only five faculties (three of them Montessori) and not one student group have been emotionally committed to or valued most of the strengths of a competent self-teacher that schools could encourage.

Nor do faculties themselves see their colleagues modeling self-teaching. I do not have as good information about public as I do about independent school teachers. But the majority of the latter do not view their colleagues as curious, self-confident, self-motivated, and self-educating or as demonstrating any other attributes of a self-teacher. Nor do the majority of students view their teachers as self-educating people.

In our pursuit of higher and higher test scores and advanced placement scores, we have lost our historical liberally educating vision of preparing students to be responsible citizens in command of themselves. Does not a democratic form of government require citizens who are curious, initiating, self-motivated, and self-educating, among other strengths? What eventually happens to a democracy when its people do not educate themselves to be informed citizens? What happens when only "16 percent of young people say they have a 'great deal' of interest in current events, politics or government,"[22] and not many more than that vote?

Self-Maturation for the Future

The maturation of the self depends on the maturation of mind and character. We don't accurately know ourselves if we are not reflective. We don't develop a strong sense of self if we block off our assertive or interpersonal strengths. We don't secure command of ourselves if we indulge our every whim and appetite. How do students need to grow if they are to become the mature persons they will need to be in the twenty-first century?

Developing an Empathic
Understanding of Gender Roles

Compared to their parents at their age, today's youth have better reflective tools, greater breadth of knowledge, and more diverse interpersonal experiences to enable them to understand themselves better. Prior to the women's movement, girls unreflectively accepted their accommodative feminine role. Their first doll and doll house told them they were to be mothers. School and college were where to "find a man," not to search for an identity, career, even meaning. Their *prescribed* "role" did not incite the self-exploration that boys had to engage in to create their individual identities. Nowadays, girls cannot escape society's provocations to understand their femaleness more accurately and create their selves more self-consciously.

Though boys are better prepared to explore their vocational world, the historical source of their identities, they are not as well prepared to understand how their maleness limits their ability to fulfill well their future familial roles. You may object to what Handy,[23] more, I think, than Bly, has taught us. Men's understanding of the subtle and pervasive meanings of their maleness and its effects on their relationships lags far behind women's understanding of their femaleness and its effects.

Women, frustrated by the thinness of their relationships with men, will prod to close that gap. Not understanding the meanings of maleness to men will gnaw at their patience. They need to understand why males need to control, if not suppress, their emotionality and dominate them and why men feel more alive while playfully hugging and wrestling with their young "teddy bear" sons.

Men, unaware of maleness's personal meanings to themselves, will continue to be mystified by women's prodding perplexity about them and why they need to understand and communicate with females in the way females understand and communicate with each other. However, I anticipate that such empathic understanding will come very slowly. The sexes' future relationships will continue for many years to be as stormy for most as it has been since Eve and Adam.

Educators should help assist students to learn empathically about their own and the opposite sex's maleness and femaleness. They need to create nonjudgmental and reflective opportunities for each sex to share what its gender means to each and how it affects how each acts. Everyone needs to become more sensitive to the unconscious sexist behaviors that feminists have identified in the classroom that limit everyone's educability.

Encouraging the Development
of Androgynous Self-Concepts

Youth now verge on expanding the circumference of their core identities beyond being just American white Anglo-Saxon Protestants, Brooklyn East European Jews, or expatriate southern blacks. While such parochial sources of identity will continue to fuel inspiration and vitality, a more tightly interdependent world will compel us to identify with and care more for those who differ from us.

Similarly, males and females are beginning to grow beyond their stereotypical gender roles. Though those roles are also sources of meaning and vitality, research confirms what feminists have claimed. Men and women who share the stereotypical strengths of the opposite sex are more adaptable, successful, healthy, and happy than those who don't.[24] More androgynous women will free men from being held hostage to their historical image as *the* provider; more androgynous men will free women from being held in bondage to their idea as *the* nurturer. Their androgyny may open up a shared path to supporting each other in ways that further more healthy selves.

However, each sex experiences different conflicts in integrating its own undeveloped strengths of the opposite sex into its self-image. A woman's biology reinforces her historical identity as a nurturer that bonds her to and prepares her to care for her child. Though more free nowadays of cultural restrictions, women's conflict between their biologically based nurturing and their achieving and autonomous potentials will stubbornly resist resolution for many. Few career women I studied had created a fulfilling resolution.

Boys confront a different conflict. Undersocialized in other-centered interpersonal skills, they will stumble badly in their future familial relationships if they remain captive to their testosterone, which in its way prepares them to be aggressive, dominant, competitive, and self-sufficient. Culturally hardening a macho self-concept risks casting out empathy, caring, understanding, and affection from one's self-image. Not until American males cease equating sensitivity, empathy, and emotionality with gayness will they be free to develop a more humane and adaptive self-image.

Educators need to create school and classroom climates that value the stereotypical strengths of each sex. Girls should be encouraged to assert themselves, compete, and explore their athletic, economic, and political communities. They need typical Outward Bound experiences to test their autonomy and ability to survive.

Boys should be taught to be expressive, empathic, caring, and cooperative. They need art, singing, drama, and tutorial experiences with kids. They really need more teddy-bear "Inward Bound" experiences to learn the language of their feelings and so grow more wholly.

Educating for Autonomy and Self-Command

Genuine command of our self depends on getting our self together and testing how well our provisional identity fits our interests, talents, and values. Nowadays, creating a coherent self is not an achievement for youth, even young adults, to complete. It takes a lot more experience, hard personal work, and varied tests to discover for what we are suited and with whom we can continue to grow. Healthy self-command depends on having an integrated, stable, and strong sense of self whose worth has been tested in a rich range of situations over which one feels some control.

The transition from rigidly culturally defined gender roles to more self-defined ones provides the freedom to create a more genuinely coherent self. How maturely are youth using such freedom? Not very. Following the herd stampeding into materialistic corrals, rushing into jobs rather than laboriously creating callings, depending on alcohol and drugs to be free and uninhibited, and substituting transitory sexual for faithful intimacy relationships suggest that many are a long way from maturely "getting their acts together."

Historically, growth in autonomy has been more conflictual for women. The revolutionary significance and irreversible effect of the women's movement have been freeing their self-concept from men's control. Research shows that their movement's principal effects have been to encourage them to develop more aware, stable, and autonomous self-concepts. [25]

Historically, American males have been expected to be autonomous, dominant, and in command. But such a self concept is now obsolescent and unhealthy—obsolescent because it ignores males' teddy-bear needs; unhealthy because research shows that emotionally healthy males are cooperative, warm, lovable, and sensitive to others' needs. [26] A fourth-grade boy's poem reveals its obsolescence: "I'm a space man riding in space alone . . . circling around the moon seeing every distant star." Too emotionally self-sufficient, males have *not* been raised to write poems about "riding in space with my copilot and space children . . . circling around the moon seeing every distant star."

How can educators create schools to enable healthy autonomy and self-command? They must believe in and do not underestimate students' ability to be responsibly independent. When freed of the suppressive effects of the traditional school and given measured responsibility, American youngsters can be quite independent entrepreneurs. They seek work; they hustle; they wander the world.

What do teenagers want? When asked to identify what one change would make schooling more relevant to their lives, they most frequently reply that they want school to help them become more independent by teaching them how to help themselves and develop coping skills.[27] When they have been educated *appropriately*, I have seen seven- and eight-year-olds as well as adolescents, such as Bloomfield Hills MHS's students, blossom into much stronger self-determining persons.

Have the changes in youth's personalities provoked you, as they have me, to ask why? What can we learn from the past decades' familial, school, and other sociocultural changes about why their educability may have changed? As Margaret Mead suggested, might not a clearer understanding of the whys prefigure how we might reconstruct our schools and society to produce more mature youth?

Chapter 4

Why Youth
Have Become Less Educable

I learned just how complex the causes of personality change are from intensive studies of how institutions affect healthy growth.[1] Studies of how Haverford College's freshmen, for example, grew into seniors unequivocally demonstrated three insights about the causes of personality change.[2] First, each effect of the college could be traced to several different causes. Maturation in interpersonal skills was affected by, among other determinants, roommates, type of student the college admitted, and a freshman English course. The potential effect of one of a school's programs is more likely to become a permanent attribute of its students' personality if it is supported by similar effects of its other values and programs. The supportive *patterning* of the values of family, peers, and school is more crucial than any one cause's effects. We will fail to improve our schools if we blame one isolated change, such as the advent of television or mothers entering the work force, for the complicated changes that I have identified.

Second, each of the numerous attributes of Haverford College's learning environment, such as its intellectual atmosphere and its honor system, produced a variety of personality changes. There is no one-to-one predictable maturing (or immaturing) effect of a specific educational intervention. Making available a computer-based algebra program may increase some eighth-graders' test scores, accuracy, and interest. But it may also strengthen feelings of anonymity and distance from the teacher and, for some computer-

71

jock boys, addiction to technology as a source of power. Awareness of its varied effects can alert teachers to integrate the program with ways of learning that educe collaborative and empathic growth as well as mastery of algebra.

Third, the effect of any cultural or school innovation depends on the maturity and other personality attributes of the individuals affected. While viewing TV may contribute to some children's distractibility, it may not have the same effect on those who have more stable cognitive skills.

Failure to understand these lessons produces costly and foolish proposals for improving our schools and holding them accountable. Only if an innovation is *consistently* supported by other institutional values, teacher commitment, altered teaching strategies, and student receptivity will it likely affect maturation and take hold. No curricular fad, such as reorganizing math sequences, will magically increase test scores if it ignores a school's systemic character.

I do not have as reliable evidence to support my speculations about the causes of youth's changing personality here than I had for those in the previous chapters. Researchers have not *comprehensively* studied the effects of television or parental divorce on youth. Nor have they determined whether they have had delayed healthy or unhealthy effects over long periods of time. Although the chapter's topic could be a book itself, I limit its purposes to two: to illustrate, even though only sketchily, how complex the societal and other causes of personality change are and then to begin to identify how schools must be reconstructed to remedy their own and counterbalance other causes' unhealthy effects on youth.

Dependence on Stimulation

Chapter One told us that increased dependence on external sources of stimulation betrays a lack of willpower, coping skills, and imaginative resources, which, in turn, predisposes us to boredom. Increased dependence on and need for stimulation are caused by several mutually reinforcing events: the emergence of self-fulfillment as a primary value that increased affluence encourages, the advent of television's sound bites and thirty-minute instant gratifications, and inappropriate educational activities.

The Triumph of Self-Fulfillment over Adjustment

The emergence of self-fulfillment as a predominant American value has produced momentous changes in our national personality.[3] Consider that until the mid sixties, our culture's underlying organizing and directing values came primarily from our Puritan legacy: self-discipline, self-abnegation, self-improvement, hard work as the road to salvation, belief in the inevitability of progress, accommodation to external authority that controlled our consciences, wariness about pleasurable indulgences (with sporadic revolts, as during the swinging twenties and Prohibition days), and visions of tomorrow's heavenly rewards for today's good behavior.

Strong wills, as moralists have told us frail humans for centuries, are forged by learning how to resist temptation. But beginning with Adam and Eve, and in the post–World War II era with the publication of the Kinsey report, the pill, and drugs, we have found increasingly clever ways to make temptation respectable. Some examples? Consider every moralist's nemesis: sex. Kinsey and psychologists reassured conflicted and guilty youth who had been fruitlessly trying to inhibit the temptation to masturbate that they were not alone and that, in fact, it was okay to give in—without guilt! Now it is culturally expected that we learn how "to pleasure ourselves," even ask and give in on the "first date," and enjoy what were formerly called perversions, still legally proscribed in some states, such as oral and anal sex.

"Self-fulfillment," a respectable technically defined concept in psychology, became the leading value for the youth of the seventies and since. It was loosely misinterpreted and used to rationalize pleasurable indulgence not just of sex but of all kinds of tempting appetites. To be inhibited, uptight, straight, puritanical, virginal was not "in." Conscientious hard workers were called "compulsive," perfectionists and grinds "sick"; greed became "healthy." Self-fulfillment provided at one time the "permission" to explore not just sex but also acid and pot, later heroin, cocaine, and crack. Drugs, including alcohol, are not known to increase attention or concentration, logical thought, or, over time, creative imagination.

Powerful cultural incentives justify self-fulfillment's reign as our primary value. Credit card mania and its associated debt and bankruptcy—formerly socially stigmatized—are now acceptable, even easily excusable. Advertisers, encouraged by governmental policies, ceaselessly urge us to spend and spend today to get what we want, ironically now necessary to have a "healthy" economy. Tax laws do not impel us to scrimp and save, as do the compulsive Japanese, and postpone living the good life today in order to have it thirty years from now. Our leaders have ceaselessly prodded the thrifty, hardworking Japanese to spend their money and really enjoy life a little more today; Japanese youth apparently agree. They are beginning to follow our path. Might not such advice turn out to be our most effective psychological Trojan horse to undo the character that produces their competitive success?

Learning to resist temptation and to work for survival or long-term economic health disciplines willpower. Both affluence and poverty can prevent and undermine the development of a strong will. Affluence provides the means to satisfy needs too readily. Children of affluent families may not learn how to tolerate their frustration long enough to take the time to master the coping skills necessary to adapt. Poverty, when in the presence of nightly TV's visible affluence that creates unrealistically high expectations, dampens the hope of possibly satisfying such needs by one's own effort. Hope is necessary for one to want to inhibit poverty's anger, despair, and resignation long enough to learn more constructive ways of getting what one wants.

It is the optimal balancing of self-fulfillment and adjustment that defines a healthy adaptation, not the persistent dominance of one over the other. Successful adjustment—meeting others' expectations—without personal fulfillment breeds conformity, emptiness, and eventually feelings of futility. Self-fulfillment without adjustment leads to self-centeredness, isolation, and eventually social suicide. Self-fulfillment's preeminence and excesses tell us how unhealthy our former adjustment to our Puritan legacy had become. Hurt women, youth, and ethnic and other minorities have crusaded for the equal opportunity to fulfill themselves. But self-indulgence, not monitored by self-restraint and hard work, undermines adult success and well-being. Self-indulgent youth do not turn out to be vocationally fulfilled. Purposeful and determined ones do.[4]

Self-fulfillment's triumph was aided by its seductive purveyor—visually compelling television—which pictured its attainment as effortless and ecstatic.

Television's Absorption of Experience

Television's entrance into our homes in the fifties decisively and vividly enriched our awareness of the world's every remote corner. It provided shared bonding experiences, it heightened expectations of the good life, and it encouraged dependence on external stimulation for organizing time and activities. Never forget that typical American seventeen-year-olds have watched television for more than 17,000 hours, several thousand hours more for urban youth, and six thousand hours more than they have been in school.[5] Of the many questions such a fact raises, two help us understand why young people may differ from pre-TV generations.

The first is, what are the enduring effects of "Sesame Street"? I pick "Sesame Street" because as TV's most valued educational exemplar, it may unknowingly sow the seeds of harmful effects that don't appear until later. What happens to children when their first "school" experience is so professional, so colorful, so fast-paced, so entertaining? After hundreds of hours of such absorbing and frenetic excitement, what do five- and six-year-olds expect school (life?) to be like? First-grade teachers say their children expect to meet a colorful Big Bird or the Cookie Monster, who will entertain them. School is supposed to be colorful, exciting, and fast-paced.

What might be some of "Sesame Street"'s delayed effects?[6] Might accelerating some children's acquisition of letters and numbers by probably no more than six months affect their subsequent achievement? Possibly. Some research suggests that after several years of schooling, children who had been placed by intellectually pushy mothers in "academic" nursery schools did not score higher than others on reading tests but instead were more negative toward school and less creative.[7] Montessori schools' success in aiding children's growth tells us that rigorously structured, hands-on, self-paced, and individualized learning environments may be what more distractible and impatient students need today. Such environments may more effectively prepare them for schooling, without creating delayed immaturing effects, than may kaleidoscopic, vicarious TV programs or less professionally trained preschool teachers.

Furthermore, might hundreds of hours of "Sesame"-like programs during the most formative cognitive years predispose a first-grader to say, "I'm bored. What should I do now?" Does mind-absorbing TV teach children to be more readily bored by fourth rather than, say, seventh grade? What do 28,000 to 30,000 hours of TV, long yellow bus rides to their consolidated schools, and typically didactic school instruction teach students? To prefer staplers to paste? To passively absorb information? To want shorter sentences, paragraphs, and books to skim? To impatiently tune out when the answers do not come quickly? In the words of Kansas professors, are we learning how to get others "to do it unto" us and not to actively chase "ideas for the joy of it"?

The second question about how TV may have contributed to the personality changes I've described is more important to answer, particularly by working parents who use TV as a baby-sitter: What growing-up experiences do young people *not* get when they watch TV for 17,000 hours—more than *eight* years of most adults' working lives—during their most critical mind- and character-forming years?

Ask children. They can tell you: sleeping, playing with other children and parents, reading and being read to, doing their homework. I would add daydreaming, which is imagination's womb, creating games to entertain oneself when bored, learning how to decide and plan what to do with 17,000 hours, and then practicing the skills of anticipating, planning, initiating, scheduling, and carrying out one's plans. I used such skills when as a child I collected newspapers every Saturday morning to earn my afternoon movie money. Would I have learned such entrepreneurial skills if Pee Wee Herman and cartoons absorbingly entertained me on Saturdays?

Not only thousands of TV hours predispose youth to depend on external sources of stimulation, however. Other monopolizers of youth's life space and time, such as teachers, harden that dependence.

Teachers as Didactic Information Dispensers

Teachers know that students' educability has changed. But they have not clearly articulated how and then appropriately reexamined their curricular goals. They also have not reflectively examined how to achieve them more effectively.[8] Nor have most high school and college teachers altered their medieval mode of teaching. When teachers do not understand how easily bored today's students are, they do not feel impelled to teach differently. We teach like the monks of the University of Bologna, whose students had not yet been taught by books, TV, VCRs, video disks, and computers. We know that lectures are an ineffective mode of instruction.[9] Given that today's students have had thousands of TV hours learning how to depend passively on external stimulation, what is another lecture's real effect? Not the mastery of information or development of a new skill but the entrenchment of the need to be entertained and passively receptive as well as the reinforcement of boredom. Today's didactic information dispensers risk consolidating the very immaturing change that they bemoan: increased dependence on external structure for organizing one's personality.

Guidelines for Reconstructing Schools

If I have accurately identified some principal causes of increased dependence on outside sources of stimulation, then how to improve our schools should be clear. Teachers must involve students much more actively and experientially by minimizing their monkish didactic lectures; they should rely less on dependency-breeding textbooks, workbooks, even TV. They need to develop a curriculum and implement teaching strategies that shape willpower and academic coping skills while teaching reading, history, and the arts. And they should be ceaselessly alert to schoolwide as well as classroom practices that breed and deepen the very dependency behaviors of which they complain.

Increased Sensitivity, Decreased Empathy

Like increased dependence on stimulation, heightened sensitivity to disapproval and reduced empathy have been caused by a number of interwoven societal forces, including those that I have already mentioned.

Cultural Devaluation of Caring

We have a less caring society than formerly in which to learn how to care. City and suburban living separates us from the natural world of animals for whom to be responsible and to care. One-child families, strictly age-segregated schools, societal uneasiness about too close same-sex friendships, and isolation from older generations dilute our relationships. We no longer have the rich emotional opportunities that teach us how to be sensitive to, feel responsible and empathic toward, and care for others who differ from us. Our legal system has even taught us not to be "our brother's keeper." We dare not aid an accident victim or protect a neighbor's child from parental abuse. We might be sued! Our changing society teaches us not only to ignore others but also to take more from them. We learn to give more to ourselves than to others.

When self-fulfillment becomes a dominant value and is interpreted to mean uninhibited self-expression and gratification, then we may more readily ignore what others feel and stumble over or trample on their sensitivities. When television provides hundreds of hours of aggressive and sarcastic witticisms and thousands of incidents of physical violence a year, then some of us may learn how to be sarcastic as well as to get what we want by stomping on others.

Other societal changes make today's children more easily hurt and less empathic. They are just not as protected by the strong ethnic and religious traditions that historically provided the emotional security and bonding experiences that nurtured caring. Nor do children grow up in as personal and caring neighborhoods and schools as they once did. Nor do they have peers whom they believe are caring or empathic, as Chapter Two reported. More distantly, we adults and our leaders are not models of caring to each other; we even object to taxes that deprive us of our pleasures and so ignore the needs of millions of our children. Their world is indeed a colder one.

Decreased Family Intimacy and Stability

Because the family and school occupy so much of a child's emotional life space, they are important crucibles in which to learn how to care, cooperate, and live harmoniously with others. A caring parent who models empathy through his or her understanding of children in many different emotional situations contributes most to a child's interpersonal maturing. Such maturing takes years of spontaneous diverse interactions in which a child learns how his or her parents, and other people as well, feel and react. Children who later succeed as adults had parents who talked openly with each other about their feelings and ideas, who expressly valued caring for and being sensitive to others' needs.[10] The less time that children are in the presence of such caring and empathic adults, the less opportunity they have to learn how to feel how others feel.

The facts about the instability of the American family are well known. Its long-term effects are not. But ask yourself what might happen to the future health of a five-year-old boy or a twelve-year-old girl living through a divorce and then in a single-parent family or a second family of stepbrothers and stepsisters, or of being a latchkey child of one of those 60 percent of American mothers who now work full-time or of typical fathers, who allegedly spend about ten to twenty minutes a day reading to or playing with their children,[11] or of spending seven to eight hours a day when one, two, or three years of age in a day-care center or every day after school alone when six or seven. The limited research done on some of these questions has been neither systematic nor comprehensive enough to identify *honestly* their long-term delayed effects, both healthy and unhealthy.[12]

We do, however, have some sobering clues. A recent survey of 24,599 eighth-graders in more than one thousand public schools identified 20 percent as being at high risk of failing school. Two of the six best predictors of who would fail were "living in a single-parent family . . . and being at home alone without an adult for long periods on weekdays."[13] The 1988 National Health Interview

Survey of Child Health independently also identified 20 percent of
its 17,000 youngsters as having learning or emotional problems, due
in large part to family disruption, single-parent upbringing, and
conflicting divorcing parents.[14] Finally, American children's poorer
math performance than that of other nations' children is apparently
associated more with growing up in poor single-parent families
than with school.[15]

There is one effect of such changes in parent-child relationships that cannot be denied. More children today have much less
opportunity for direct emotional involvement with their mothers
and fathers. They do not have the same kinds of experiences that
previous generations have had by which to learn skills such as caring, cooperation, and empathy. It is a fact that the most frequently
spontaneously mentioned fear of today's children of all ages is that
they will lose a parent.[16] Quite understandable. The model they
have grown up with has been the disappearing parent—and for
children with only one parent, an absent one—possibly a parent
seen as a rejecting one.

The critical question to ask may not be one of those that
parents typically ask, such as "Should I restrict TV viewing for my
six-year-old?" but "What kinds of mothers and fathers and familial
relationships contribute to what kinds of adult outcomes?" Study
of the families of successful adults suggests that just having a parent
around may not be as decisive as having a *loving* mother and father
who *respect* their children's individuality and have *firm expectations* of their behavior. A child might be better off in the long run
not having a parent around who is cold, rejecting, authoritarian, or
too permissive.[17]

Depersonalizing Large Schools

School also affects youth's interpersonal maturing. In the United
States, schools commandeer about 12,000 hours of a youth's
growing-up time. The facts about schools' potential effects on
teachers' and students' relationships are now well established. Little
other educational research has produced such consistent but such
tragically and irresponsibly ignored results. We have known since
the early sixties from excellent studies initiated in Kansas that aban-

doning the small, personal neighborhood school could have numerous potentially unhealthy effects and almost no healthy effects, not even enduring academic ones, on the maturing of students. [18]

Large schools reduce the opportunity for sustained relationships to occur between everyone in the school. Once an elementary school has more than about 200 to 350 students and an upper school 400 to 500 or more, a host of potentially unhealthy effects become noticeable, especially for vulnerable kids. Their interpersonal climate is impersonal and bureaucratic. Teachers don't know other teachers or students as well as do those in smaller schools; they don't talk as frequently about individual students or about curricular issues in faculty meetings; and, like students, they do not know who makes what decisions. Students see their friends less frequently, have less contact with adults other than their teachers, participate much less frequently in extracurricular activities, including athletic teams, have much less opportunity to hold leadership positions, are more aggressive and disorderly, and cheat more frequently. Parents no longer visit the school as frequently or know their children's teachers as well.

John Goodlad's thorough study of public high schools reached similar conclusions. The smallest schools in the sample were better able to solve their problems more effectively. Their atmospheres were more intellectual; their teachers cared more about students; their students and parents, as well as their teachers, were more satisfied with the school. [19]

I have found only one positive educational benefit of a large high school. Its students do better on advanced math achievement tests because the school can provide more math courses. [20] However, computers and telecommunications may make such courses available in the future even to small schools.

Taxpayers and critics argue that big schools are more economical: breaking up a 2,000-student school into no fewer than four schools would be too expensive and reduce the available resources for each school. Not true. The argument is seriously flawed for one never accounted-for reason. Let's put aside their proportionately greater administrative, security, discipline, and busing costs. *Large schools' full long-term educational, psychic, and social costs have never been estimated.* What community has determined even crudely how much its large schools may have contributed to its miseducated and bored students' drug, unemployment, welfare, and prison costs five, ten, and fifteen years after dropping out, if not physically, then psychically?

Presumably, a more mature youth may not be as adversely affected as a less mature one by being in a large, impersonal school. Yet even at the college level, students do not like being treated impersonally. Forty-eight percent (62 percent in research universities) complain that "students are treated like numbers."[21] How can it be otherwise when freshmen, particularly in our large universities, are anonymous numbers sitting in classes of five hundred or more? Empathic youth cannot be mass produced like cars or computers.

Vulnerable children from very fragmented families need a small, stable, caring neighborhood school that their parents know, trust, and support. They need to be "known all of the way around" by the adults in the school. Impersonality does not foster caring or understanding. To be cared for and understood is the first, most necessary experience for one to learn how to feel for and understand others.

I have found that students who have low morale and are potential dropouts view their schools very differently than students of high morale do. Recall the public high school discussed in Chapter One in which 60 percent more low- than high-morale students saw school as boring. What were their next highest differences? More than a third more of the low-morale than the high-morale students consistently saw school as unfriendly, emotionally cold, unfair, self-centered, uncaring, and lonely. I asked the leader of one of Philadelphia's most notorious and violent gangs what had been the most important event in his life that had got him into prison. He instantly said, "When I got to junior high school and found no one cared for me." Curricular programs to reduce dropout rates will fail unless they make schools more caring places in which to grow up. Large schools don't make it easy to know others so as to be able to care.

Americans pay devastating financial and emotional costs because their families and schools do not produce caring citizens. Have we created schools that really prepare today's youth with the interpersonal skills that they need to succeed as workers, family members, and citizens in the twenty-first century? What costs will come due then?

Guidelines for Reconstructing Schools

The societal changes discussed above should make how to reconstruct schools clearer. We must abandon large schools. We must create more safe, caring, and "familylike" places in which to grow up and work. We must reintegrate schools with their neighboring communities to make sustained parental involvement and support possible. Chapter Sixteen suggests ways to create psychologically smaller schools out of large ones, schools in which students can have consistent and prolonged caring contact with the same adults and students for several years. As our society becomes increasingly technological, impersonal, and uncaring, schools must become increasingly more humane, personal, and caring—and therefore smaller.

Diminished Ethical Values

The dilution of commitment to the values that sustain and give meaning to academic excellence and moral lives is also due to a variety of intertwined and mutually reinforcing societal changes, including the ones already mentioned.

As the North Korean, Iraqi, and other dictatorial leaders know full well, whoever controls the information that we get shapes our minds and values. Unfettered mass media, particularly television, have permanently altered our feelings about what is right and good. Just reflect about TV's effects on our feelings about the Vietnam War, or its effects on children who have grown up exposed to many different adults and ways of being raised and relating to others. They have had thousands of hours of learning about alternative value choices with which to confront those imposed by moralistic authorities.

Emergence of self-fulfillment as a salient value also reinforces the traditional American value of individualistic autonomy and the right to make one's own decisions. Adjustment to communal values, such as honesty, compassion, and commitments to others, takes second place when one's own interests are paramount.

Ethical values are rooted in and sustained by caring, empathic, respectful relationships with others. Cultural devaluation of caring saps ethical sensitivity and commitment. Unstable families, indifferent or anonymous neighbors, crooked business leaders, parochially self-serving politicians, money-grasping impersonal physicians, and ambulance-chasing lawyers are not compellingly admirable models of how youth could lead ethical lives. I have asked young people whom they look to as models of ethical integrity. Other than Mother Teresa, I hear only silence.

Today's moral confusion, even anomie, results from a more subtle but, I suspect, very powerful societal change: the weakening for many—and demise for some—of hope for the future.

Because adolescence is the time when mind's maturation enables one to anticipate and imagine an ideal of the future, it has historically been the time of idealism, optimism, and hope. Chapter Two cited evidence that today's adolescents see neither their friends nor themselves as idealistic. Only 30 percent of public high school students and 27 percent of their teachers believe that the typical youth is optimistic. Only 26 percent of Hardwick's high school boys thought of themselves as optimistic; 45 percent of Prestige's students did. For the first time beginning a decade ago, more people under thirty reported being more pessimistic about their society's future than those over thirty reported.[22] Only 50 percent of American high school youth believe that their children will be better off than they.[23] Adolescent suicide betrays a loss of hope in the future. The authors of *A Cry for Help* wrote that the suicidal adolescents that they talked to "groped for words to describe what they felt was a void in their lives—the lack of anything to stand for, of an altruistic goal, of a push to improve the community, the country, the world, or, in two words, 'meaningful values.' "[24]

Why is hope just an inert idea for so many? Again, probably numerous accumulative reasons contribute to such a change.

Heightened Awareness of Planetary and Human Fragility

One environmental onslaught after another unremittingly alerts young people to the fragility of our planet, with seemingly little being done to forestall its death. If you were a German youth, how might you feel seeing the destruction of the Black Forest by acid rain and adults doing little about it? Or a sensitive Brazilian youth seeing the rapacious clearing of the Amazon jungle, whose irreversible global climatic and ecological effects are unknown, and your leaders unconcerned about what they might be? Or aware American youth seeing their country's astronomical debt doubling into the trillions of dollars within the eighties, preventing the necessary investments to forestall the potentially devastating greenhouse effects? Knowing that they must bear its punishing tax burden the rest of their lives, how will they view their parents' unwillingness to moderate their comfortable lives today to lighten their own onerous tax loads in the future and preserve the environmental health of their planet?

Another dramatic scientific novelty since the fifties has become inescapable to every aware child. The advent of nuclear power has created in many a low-level background radiating fear of their annihilation. Be empathetic with today's adolescents and ask yourself, "If I were an adolescent today, how would I live my life differently?"

During the cold war, precocious thirteen-year-old Stevie asked his grandmother, "How old are you?"

She replied, "I am rather elderly."

"You are lucky," which was not quite her view.

"Why?" she asked.

"Because I have only three more years to live. We are going to have a nuclear war."

Another thirteen-year-old boy spontaneously said, "I wish you of the older generation would try to understand my generation. After all, we may be the last generation on earth."

Or consider a youth living within fifty miles of Chernobyl's nuclear explosion who now has to live with the fear of dying prematurely of cancer from its silent radiation—or an American youth living near one of the country's hundred or so nuclear power plants aware that there could be a radiation leak anytime.

Today's youngsters grow up with an emotional reality that I never knew in my childhood and, though I may know it rationally, cannot feel so personally: that all life could vanish in eighteen minutes or a few days or a few months or a few years.

Some skeptics have recoiled at my belief that this is a unique event in the history of children. "Well, humans have always lived under the cloud of the apocalypse. Think of the days of the Black Death." They might now say of AIDS.

"Yes, but then there wasn't the belief that *all* life could be destroyed. And there was still hope. One could still be saved and have eternal life in the Kingdom."

No longer for more and more sensitive young people.

Secularization of Religion's Symbols of Hope

Religion has always been the steward of hope. We waywardly sinful humans have always needed hopeful bribes to be virtuous and live the good life. At the day of judgment, salvation, eternal life, the Kingdom will be our reward. Such religious hopes, which have historically allowed us to accept but also deny the incomprehensible mystery of our own mortality, have been dying in more and more young people. Only 5 percent of both public and independent school teachers and 15 percent of their adolescent students believe the typical youth or peer to be religious. However, higher percentages who live in conservative religious communities, such as 46 percent of Prestige's students, may call themselves religious.

Chapter Two reported that youth have become progressively less committed to traditional religious beliefs and practices, a trend confirmed by other researchers for college-educated youth[25] and by increases in religiously mixed marriages. In 1985, 10 percent of Jews married non-Jews; in 1991, 50 percent married outside their faith.[26] More of today's youth have been raised to not be narrowly sectarian, to distrust mysteries, and to believe that everything is eventually knowable, even the genesis of life itself, and controllable, even the evolution of life itself.[27]

Do we really believe religion's message of hope? For many, God's promise is dying. So how did you answer the question "If you were a youth, how might you live your life differently if you had little hope for your future?" Most adults whom I have asked say "Live for today." And that is just what many young people (and their parents) now do. Get on the fast track. Get what you can quickly. Try every temptation. Enjoy! Now!

The erosion of hope results in a foreshortening of time. We forget our past and deny our future. We seek more immediate pleasures. We hesitate about making long-term commitments, such as marrying or bringing children into such an uncertain world. We no longer devote as much energy to long-term community ideals and projects. Ethical values witness to our ideal of what our relationships and communities should be. When a future is so contingent, ideals waste energy, and ethical values become irrelevant.

Schools as Ethical Wastelands

Educators have not distinguished moralistic attitudes about personal and public issues, such as those about prayer, abortion, or nuclear power plants, from liberal education's universal and intrinsic values, such as honesty and integrity. Fearful of community reaction, they ignore the former and do not vigorously assume responsibility for the latter. Table 4.1, which portrays teachers' and students' views about their schools' ethical climate, tells us that large numbers of students, at least, believe schools to be ethical wastelands. Remember that schools may not be so to an objective extraterrestrial observer. But also remember that what students believe to be so is what influences their behavior.

The majority of both faculty and students apparently don't spontaneously use ethical terms to describe their schools, with the

Table 4.1. Teachers' and Students' Judgments of Their Schools' Ethical Maturity.

Ethical value	Teachers (%)		Students (%)		Prestige students' self-descriptions (%)
	Public	Independent	Public	Independent	
Caring	65	74	35	52	35
Fairness	44	53	30	37	30
Honesty	41	51	31	48	27
Idealism	37	36	25	37	20
Integrity	32	47	16	28	16
Strong convictions	25	40	21	29	12
Deep moral sense	24	38	18	30	15
Courage	16	21	23	18	25

few exceptions of values such as caring, though not even that is cited by public high school students. Possibly because independent schools are smaller and include some religious ones, more of their teachers and students view them as ethical. Their independence, however, apparently does not inspire any greater courage to stand for ideals.

Guidelines for Reconstructing Schools

Schools must become places of hope for all tomorrow, rather than the places of despair for the many that they are today. They must rededicate themselves to their historical liberally educating tradition and its values—the only reasonable, practicable, and hopeful goal for today's students. Only recommitment to human excellence, of which educational excellence is a critical but only one component, will do. It can provide the ideal and so meaning and incentive to youth to begin to work for their own and their communities' betterment. Since ethical values are nurtured by our relationships, smaller, more humane schools will enable teachers to be known by and related to by their students as the caring, ethical, idealistic people that they in fact are. The following chapters begin to lay the conceptual and then the actual foundations of what such a school of hope should be.

Declining Self-Empowerment

Command of oneself depends on a reliable and stable self. The self-confidence and self-esteem that mark a strong sense of self have myriad roots: perhaps biological factors, certainly interpersonal experiences, definitely school, other work, hobbies and interests, and, more overarchingly, cultural values. The more of youth's life space that these influences occupy, the more likely they are to affect them. Parents have been slipping out of a child's life since the end of World War II; TV has taken over a large part of it; peers and their media are more present now from day care on; schools may be ceding some of the psychic space that they used to have to paid work, which takes more of a suburban adolescent's time now and will more in the future as the McDonald's restaurants scratch for more low-paid workers.

By now, you are probably forming your own hypotheses about how television, school size, and other societal changes deprive youth of a vigorous sense of self-empowerment. So I focus here instead on the effects of enhanced expectations of entitlement, disappearing mothers and disappeared fathers, seductive McDonald's, and sterilizing schools on the development of a self-confident and self-reliant self.

Enhanced Expectations of Entitlement

For decades, the circumference of our expectations about the rights and rewards that society owes us has been expanding. The emerging dominance of self-fulfillment over adjustment and the devaluation of other-centeredness on which communal values depend for their sustenance have contributed to such a change. Entitlement's specific expectations vary from Sweden's "cradle to grave" fulfillment of one's needs to England's guarantee of medical care to America's affirmative action and food stamp programs. Although we lag behind some other countries in, for example, our medical and higher educational rights, the psychic effects of entitlement expectations are similar.

Equity and the opportunities that entitlements provide do release talent from the bondage of poverty and ill health. However, such expectations can also drain self-reliance and related self-empowerment skills and attitudes, such as confidence in one's ability to cope. The evidence is anecdotal but pervasive. Swedish youth reputedly do not work hard or stick at boring work because they will be taken care of in any case. Britain's unemployed coal miners get such large benefits that they don't move out of their midland valleys to seek work elsewhere. Maine's clam diggers dig long enough to qualify for unemployment benefits and food stamps during their harsh winters. Supreme Court Justice Clarence Thomas said of his sister, "She gets mad when the mailman is late with her welfare check. That is how dependent she is. What's worse is that now her kids feel entitled to the check too. They have no motivation for doing better or getting out of that situation."[28] Tenure and nondiscrimination laws protect inept teachers from dismissal and can work against motivating them to improve. Safety nets can ensnare some and make them psychological prisoners of their immaturities.

The Disappearing Mother and Disappeared Father

The massive shift of women from the home into the work force and the emergence of two busy, full-time-career parents can rob a child of the early parental experiences that undergird later self-esteem. Surveys show that fathers have not noticeably increased the amount of time spent with their families. Quality time and purchased day-care love cannot substitute for the kind of early parental experiences that most children need to feel good about themselves. "Just an old-fashioned opinion," you may be saying. No—a disciplined hunch based on the familial, child, and adolescent experiences of men and women I have been studying who felt good about themselves during their adult years. Self-esteem is a remarkably stable core of our personality; those who felt very good about themselves when adolescents also reliably felt good about themselves when in their early thirties as well as in their mid forties.

What were the families like who contributed to the self-esteem of their sons over a twenty-five-year period? In contrast to the men of low self-esteem, those of high self-esteem consistently had, among other positive growing up experiences:

> Very favorable family home atmospheres and parents who had accepted and enjoyed being parents
>
> Favorable relationships with both parents, who had not rejected them but valued and encouraged their independence
>
> Close and loving relationships with their mothers
>
> Warm and affectionate fathers who verbally expressed the importance of loving others and who were available and accessible when they needed help
>
> A mother or father who had emphasized the importance of their academic achievement

Obviously, a son's parents strongly contribute to his good feelings about himself, and this effect persists into his adult years.

Middle-aged women who felt good about themselves reported that they also had had very positive childhood homes and mature parents. They had had involved and warm fathers who emphasized the importance of expressing love and care for others; their mothers had had similar expectations.[29]

Regardless of how competent, wayward, tumultuously rambunctious, or petulant children are, they need to feel good about themselves if, as they get older, they are to be able to risk earning their own competence and thus their self-esteem and self-confidence. And where do adolescents begin to become aware of just how competent and successful they will be as adults? In work in their communities and schools.

The Seductive McDonald's

Many more teenagers now work than their parents did as adolescents, and they earn comparatively more. Even more may do so tomorrow as Exxon stations and grocery stores are forced to pay higher wages to get unskilled labor from a diminishing adolescent pool of potential workers. A third of today's tenth-graders work an average fourteen hours a week; 60 percent of twelfth-graders work an average twenty hours a week.[30] My data from the schools with which I am familiar suggest somewhat lower percentages, but the psychic effects are similar.

From where does all of this time come? From hanging out, leisure activities such as hobbies, family life, and school. Students working for money during the school year (excluding those involved in school-organized vocational programs integrated with academic courses) feel more alienated from school than students who are not and are more likely to get into trouble with the law.[31] They miss school more often, spend less time on homework, participate less frequently in cocurricular and community activities, and drink alcohol and use drugs more regularly.[32]

Why do they work? For money. Some, such as those from poor families, work to survive. Fewer than 20 percent work to contribute to their family expenses. Many work, more crassly, to buy the good life and have fun: stereos, alcohol, drugs, and cars. Forty-six percent of boys and 27 percent of girls work to support their cars.[33]

They also work to feel competent and in charge of themselves. If one doesn't feel good about oneself as a student, one can as a guy who hustles and earns a lot of money and has a sports car, even if it is secondhand. So the McDonald's restaurants and Exxon stations of the world provide an alternative route to self-esteem. Developing responsibility, work competencies, and independence can shore up a shaky self-confidence. For males, work could provide an avenue to discovering some of the strengths necessary to fulfill their traditional adult identities, if they had challenging, growth-inducing types of work; for females, work is a way to become more self-reliant, ambitious, and independent of their traditional sex role expectations but with parental approval.[34]

The downside effects of working twenty hours a week at McDonald's during the school year may not appear until later: the failure to develop the kind of strengths that a school and its cocurricular activities potentially can provide—when properly educed. Apart from the allure that a weekly paycheck has for a stapler generation, might not its large numbers working for money during the school year also tell us a more sobering message—that many students have lost confidence that their schools are empowering them with the competence and confidence they need to succeed as adults?

The Sterilizing School

Replacement of small neighborhood schools by mammoth ones combined with the devaluation of human excellence and overvaluation of only a few kinds of academic excellence make schools sterilizing and defeating places for many.

We know that feeling good about school and being a student aids academic achievement, which in turn inspires feeling good about oneself and contributes to adult success. Students who have high morale get better grades, are less likely to drop out, participate more frequently in cocurricular activities, drink alcohol and use drugs less frequently, don't work for money for as many hours during the school year, act more ethically, and have parents who support these activities.[35] Boys who have enjoyed school and have held leadership positions turn out to succeed in most areas of their adult lives. Haverford College's entering students who had high self-esteem had held several leadership positions in high school; freshmen with lower self-esteem tended not to.[36]

The pubertal years are critical to the development of self-confidence and self-empowering skills. They are the years of heightened vulnerability; more self-conscious discovery of one's potentials, particularly for interpersonal relationships; and the birth of enduring interests and commitments. However, student morale precipitously declines from fifth to eighth grade, after which it tends to level off. As Chapter Three reported, boys are more dissatisfied with school than girls at every grade level, and increasingly so during the pubertal years. Though girls' confidence about their mathematical and scientific achievement declines more than boys', they consistently enjoy school more.[37]

Why do boys not like school more? Of the many possible reasons, large middle or junior high schools are dreadfully mismatched with the psychology of pubertal children, especially restlessly intrusive boys.[38] Formal academic curricula traditionally taught by specialists and frequently outpacing students' readiness teach boys more than girls that they are academically incompetent. To appear competent to their peers and feel good about themselves, boys turn to athletics and other acts of bravado. Sadly, consolidating three or four small schools into one elephantine one dilutes the quality of everyone's interpersonal relationships. Consolidation reduces students' opportunities to discover that they can be responsible, self-initiating, and self-confident persons, even if not stellar academic champions. In such schools, a boy must be a superjock to even sit on the one varsity football, basketball, or baseball bench. Only one president or editor comes with the student council or newspaper, not the three or four of several smaller schools.

Americans bemoan their country's inept political and business leadership and lack of economic competitiveness. Misguidedly believing that bigger and bigger schools are better schools, we have reduced opportunities for students to discover and test their own self-empowering and leadership potentials. Naively believing that higher achievement test scores will improve economic competitiveness, we have told students that only their academic grades, not their character, really counts. Each turn of the academic screw snuffs out the confidence of more children and tells them that they are stupid and not going to "make it"—tragically, falsely so for most students, as the next chapters will document.

Christopher Cross, as assistant U.S. secretary of education trying to understand students' low test scores, interpreted studies as showing that American students are "lethargic, bored. . . . They are asking not what can I do to maximize my potential, but what is the least I can do to get out of here and get a ticket—'Is this on the exam? Is this required?' "[39] Is this not the game that society and schools have taught them to play? Today's perceptive students know that the potentials they need to develop for their future far transcend those measured by their test scores. Teachers know this also. Why else have neither emotionally committed themselves to society's one-dimensional definition of excellence?

Guidelines for Reconstructing Schools

Schools must provide opportunities for students to assume more meaningful responsibility for their own growth, not only within but also outside their walls. From their first day in school, students must be expected and taught how to be responsible for the growth of their minds, characters, and selves. Schools must recognize and reward the human excellence that results from valuing students' maturing as whole persons. Overvalued and too limited measures of academic achievement rob students not just of their self-confidence but also of the empowering ideal of human excellence to which to aspire and work to achieve. Until we break the shackles of our national obsession with test scores, we will not be free to create schools and classrooms that come to grips with the changed educability of today's youth. Schools will remain sterilizing and so less effective places than they could be in which to mature; the educational reform movement will continue to stumble and eventually fail.

The next chapter documents the fact that traditional academic measures only feebly predict adult success. By bringing research's perspective about just what academic grades and test scores contribute to adult success and well-being, it prepares the way to begin resurrecting liberal education's ideal of human excellence. It is the only goal, as I document in Chapter Six, that can provide today's students with the minds, characters, and self-empowering attitudes and skills necessary for them to adapt to their future.

Chapter 5

Moving Beyond
Academic Excellence

Since we place so much national emphasis on academic grades and scores on achievement and scholastic aptitude tests, should we not first ask what they predict about a youth's future? If they don't predict much, as is the case, then should we not search more thoughtfully about what it is about schooling that contributes to a youth's future effectiveness?

Schools' Measures of Achievement and Adult Outcomes

Academic Grades as Predictors of Human Excellence

Academic grades are teachers' principal measure of how well their students have mastered their liberal arts courses. Their contribution to adult success and well-being is, however, ambiguous and, in any case, very small.[1] Separating out their effects from those of familial factors, socioeconomic status, and type and quality of school attended poses formidable methodological problems. Obviously, failing courses and dropping out of school can also indicate intellectual and/or character handicaps that can limit subsequent adult success. Failing to learn to read and master practical math and other skills necessary to adjust to society's demands can often limit, even calamitously, success in some areas of life, especially the vocational. But failing to recall when Marco Polo discovered China or the former Soviet name for St. Petersburg or other bits and pieces of information does not adversely affect later success and well-being.

96

Furthermore, hundreds of studies of high school and college grades have examined their contribution to only a few of the rich variety of adult outcomes that describe human excellence, such as citizenship, marital happiness, well-being, and virtue. Fewer than a handful have studied how youth mature far into their adult years to discover what grades contribute to their later success and well-being.

Because the research reported in my book *Fulfilling Lives* reveals why males and females succeed when middle-aged in their principal roles, such as breadwinner, marital partner, and parent, we now have more information about how academic measures may contribute to important adult outcomes. There is no other as comprehensive a study of the academic predictors of as many adult competencies as well as well-being with which to cross-check the validity of the study's findings.[2] So I will shortly also summarize others' results from more focused studies of more intellectually diverse groups.

The college grades of the women and men I studied predicted very little about how they turned out as adults. The women's grades predicted only one outcome fifteen to twenty years later: high-achieving women had been less happy and productive during their early adult years than those who had received lower grades. The men's grades also predicted few outcomes: those who had earned high grades, for example, not surprisingly received more fellowships and honors in graduate and professional schools and published more scholarly books.

Academic grades did not predict who would and would not fulfill their adult roles successfully. By middle age, a former A student was no more likely than a former C student to be maritally happy or have a happy partner, to be more sexually compatible with his or her partner and a better lover, to be a better parent and have more mature children, or to have closer friends. High grades predicted neither vocational fulfillment or income, virtue, physical or mental health, nor happiness. The only adult outcomes that high academic grades predicted were the middle-aged men's *peer* judgments that they were well adapted vocationally and had high leadership potential. Although grades did not predict involvement in one's community, another study found that students who achieved high grades contributed *less* frequently to its welfare.[3]

Though not contributing to adult success, academic grades predicted, ironically, the middle-aged men's personality. When adults, those who had earned high grades in college were judged by their peers to be more purposeful, self-disciplined, reliable, self-acceptant, to be more fully reaching their potential, and to be less easily hurt by others' comments than the men who had earned primarily C's. Since the men's adolescent personality predicted their adult personality quite well, could such strengths have contributed to their achievement of high grades in college? Purposefulness and self-discipline surely must contribute to the effective use of one's talents. And one must indeed have a tough skin to take the criticisms that we teachers who hold students to high expectations ceaselessly inflict. Might these results suggest that today's less self-disciplined and purposeful but more sensitive youth do not have the kind of personality that enables exceptional academic achievement?

Researchers studying more intellectually diverse students have also failed to find that grades contribute much to later success, either directly or indirectly.[4]

Successful Achievement in Similar Academic Areas. Academic grades do predict quite well achievement in next year's courses. Freshman grades predict sophomore grades better than they do senior grades, which in turn predict moderately well early graduate and professional school grades. But they predict achievement much less well the closer one gets to the "real world," such as completing graduate school[5] or medical school. College pre-med grades, as well as medical aptitude tests, only modestly predict students' grades during their first two years of medical school; they predict not one single measure of clinical effectiveness during students' third and fourth years.[6] Actually, 70 percent of those who excelled in their clinical work had *not* done well in their basic science courses.[7]

Vocational Success. College grades only modestly predict an adult's job status and possibly rate of promotion, and do not predict vocational fulfillment, in one's early years.[8] One of the more believable studies reported that grades predicted, though not very impressively, the amount of scientific knowledge retained and number of publications produced early in one's scientific career.[9] But the weight of the evidence now is that academic grades only "marginally," in the words of another reviewer, predict vocational success.[10]

Vocational Eminence and Creativity. What about eminence and distinctively creative contributions? The evidence is mixed and depends upon many factors, including the type of eminence being predicted. One author found that graduates of Oxford and Cambridge who later became eminent British politicians and judges had had "academic records that we would nowadays view as catastrophic." Cynics might be tempted to reply, "That's why the world is in the mess that it is." However, the author claimed that even eminent scientists could not be identified from the level of their university honors.[11]

A study of three hundred of this century's most eminent political, literary, artistic, and scientific figures belies contemporary parental views that not attending college condemns a youngster to eternal failure. Sixty percent of such eminent people had disliked or even flunked out of school; only 50 percent had gone on to college.[12] Singular examples such as Einstein or William Gates, founder of Microsoft and America's wealthiest person, can always be cited to illustrate how school grades don't predict high creativity. However, there is now sufficient evidence for us to conclude that academic grades account for between 5 and 10 percent of why individuals vary in later adult creative achievement, more so in some fields, such as the sciences,[13] than perhaps in others, such as the arts. Clearly, high grades help but are not essential to achieving eminence later in life in many areas. If high academic achievement were essential, how shall we explain why the Japanese have received only five but Americans more than two hundred Nobel prizes for eminent achievement?

Income. Surely people who get good grades at least get higher incomes? Possibly, but the question is so complicated to probe that the available results are quite flimsy and contradictory. How, for example, does one compare the oranges that physicians get and the lemons that professors get? But it is clear that failure to do well in school, even graduate school, does not bar one from earning a lot of money later in life. The one person in my study who had dropped out of tenth grade eventually created her own business; within five years, she grossed more than a million dollars a year. A rigorous critique of the studies examining the contribution of grades to earnings found that at most "about 2.3 percent . . . of the differences in income are explainable by differences in college grades."[14]

Teachers' Judgments and Academic Honors as Predictors of Adult Success

Academic grades do not always reflect the quality of a student's mind. Might the judgments of professors who know most intimately the quality of their seniors' minds predict subsequent adult success? I found that those seniors rated as most intellectually capable did not differ on any measure of adult competence from those rated as less capable. But as adults, they did turn out to be *less* well integrated, stable, and autonomous; to have *less* mature relationships with their colleagues and *less* intimate ones with their spouses; and to be judged by their spouses, friends, and colleagues as desiring power and acting like leaders.

Just as personality strengths may have contributed to the men's high academic grades, so may they have influenced their professors' judgments of their intellectual capability when college seniors. The most intellectually capable seniors were viewed by their peers thirty years later as ambitious, self-disciplined men with strong personalities. Again, might not such strengths have contributed to the fulfillment of their intellectual talent in college? And again, what might these results say about the strengths that today's youth need to do well academically and why many are not fulfilling their talents?

One coveted measure of academic success is a faculty's collective recognition for having excelled academically, such as a Phi Beta Kappa key or honors. The receipt of honors at Haverford College used to require faculty nominations, based in part on academic grades, and then searching oral examinations by multidisciplinary groups of faculty. But recognition for fulfilling its scholarly ideals turned out to be a mixed blessing. Academically honored graduates later published more articles and books than those not so successful, but as adults they were "quite removed psychologically from the practical and realistic problems of the day. Their thought processes were more abstract and conceptual . . . [and] had become significantly less realistic [since graduation]. . . . Their interests had also become less practical and applied. They were less concerned about money; their wives more frequently took the initiative sexually; they seemed to be less involved with their children. . . . [They] were more depressed and less aggressively energetic, though their fantasies were more dominated by aggressive thoughts."[15]

Harvard graduates who received honors for distinctive academic achievement were less happy ten years later than those not graced with such distinction.[16] Upon hearing these results, one university president told me "That sounds like my faculty." I hoped he was being facetious, but I was not sure.

David McClelland, a Harvard researcher of adult achievement, has assessed as thoughtfully as anyone the available findings about academic accomplishments.[17] He claims that it is not an A or C+ average or honors but a college degree that predicts adult outcomes. Schools produce many more liberally educating effects than their grades measure. And because we have not known until now just what qualities contribute to adult success, parents, teachers, and students have exaggerated the contribution that grades and honors make to later life.

Achievement and Aptitude Indices
as Predictors of Adult Success

Much national breast-beating and soul-searching have occurred because American students don't score as well as Japanese or British students on achievement tests. What do such tests predict about future performance? Like academic grades, they predict success in similar courses quite well; they predict academic success the first year of college only moderately well. But do they predict qualities of human excellence?

Consider the English achievement test, which is widely required for admission to college and surely must tap something important about a person. It barely contributed to subsequent college grades and did not predict a single measure of adult competence that I examined; it may predict some other adult outcome that I didn't assess. Clearly, given our obsession with achievement test scores, much more comprehensive study should be done to determine what they may predict about students' futures. They may modestly predict some adult successes, but measures of relevant personality strengths will probably predict even better.

If tests of what we learned in traditional liberal arts courses don't contribute much to adult success, what does better? Scholastic Aptitude Test (SAT) scores that measure the ability to learn and think about abstract ideas that are not tied as closely to specific course content? Apparently not; they do not predict future success, at least for above-average students. McClelland critiqued the research on SAT scores and concluded that scholastic aptitude does not contribute to "actual accomplishments in social leadership, the arts, science, music, writing, and speech and drama."[18]

I too found that average or above-average SAT scores predicted *no* adaptive trait, competence, or other measure of human excellence in adult males. Students who suffer the disgrace of being on the fiftieth percentile in their combined SAT scores can turn out to be just as good spouses, lovers, parents, and citizens or as ethical, healthy, happy, and wealthy adults as those who secretly burst with pride in being on the ninety-second.[19]

However, and more distressing, students with superb SAT scores may even be at risk of failing as adults. The findings shock most people until they reflect about why. So I describe in detail what the men's verbal and then quantitative SAT scores predicted about their success. (The women's school records were not available to secure reliable scores.) Eleventh-grade males who have high *verbal* aptitude scores in contrast to those with average SAT scores may thirty years later

> Be less well-integrated and have lower self-esteem and less accurate self-insight
>
> Be less empathic for other persons
>
> Feel they are not well understood by the person they feel closest to

> Have professional relationships that are tense, distant, and
> conflictual, as rated by themselves and by their colleagues
> who know them most intimately
> Fulfill the various roles of a spouse less adequately

Similarly, boys who score high on *quantitative* aptitude may thirty
years later

> Be more masculine in interests and temperament and unin-
> terested in aesthetic activities
> Be less well-integrated and self-confident
> Be judged by their peers to have less integrity
> Describe themselves in interviews as less emotionally stable
> Be more interpersonally immature, as shown in their more
> tense, distant, and conflictual relationships at work as
> judged by their colleagues, have fewer warm and intimate
> relationships, not have a sexually compatible marital re-
> lationship, not feel their own closest relationship to be
> very close or loving, not feel understood by others, be in-
> hibited about talking openly and frankly with others
> about their feelings, and be rated by their peers as not
> being sympathetic, gentle, or loyal persons

Remember that such statistical generalizations tell us only what
may be probable, not what is certain. The study contained some
exceptionally high-scoring men who were exemplars of human
excellence.

Though the internal pattern of results made sense according
to other studies (for example, high quantitative ability is typically
found in masculine persons who may not be as mature in their
interpersonal skills), I still questioned how true they were. So the
study was repeated with other men that I had been following,
though much less thoroughly; their results were similar.[20]

By now, I no longer questioned my findings about the
meager predictive ability of academic grades and tests and the close
and probably inseparable relationship between academic and character strengths. But I still doubted that the same patterns would be
found in more varied students from other colleges. In the meantime,

the results attracted national attention. I was inundated by confirming letters from faculty and heads of graduate and professional schools. Because droves of young people have been drawn to law, engineering, and medicine during the past decades, schools have relied heavily on academic grades and aptitude test scores to select whom to admit. What has the result been?

The chief justice of a state supreme court wrote me a troubling letter. The court's judges had become so unhappy with the quality of the lawyers appearing before them that they had crafted resolutions urging law schools to place less emphasis on the law aptitude test. They wanted them to select students for their "strength of will and character." "How do you measure such qualities?" he asked.

Inquiries came from deans of one selective research-oriented engineering school. They expressed concern that half of their exceptionally talented students would fall apart when they left the school's protected environment. "They know nothing about people. They don't even know that the opposite sex exists." "Typical dean talk," faculty might say. Two years later, some of the school's faculty expressed the same concern to me—confidentially.

Medical schools have selected some of our country's most intellectually capable and highly achieving Type A personalities for more than two decades. Thoughtful members of the profession now wonder whether academically talented people turn out to be good healers or ethical people.[21] Bright students accepted for early admission to one prestigious university's accelerated medical program are reputed to be "sociopathic zombies." CBS's "Sixty Minutes" reported that some bright young doctors are avoiding their commitments to work in poor urban or rural areas to "repay" taxpayers for supporting their medical school expenses.

Are tests of intellectual talent really of so little value? Definitely not! Hundreds of studies have confirmed that for the *population as a whole,* intellectual capability is a major contributor to success in various adult activities, such as occupational[22] and managerial level attained.[23] Furthermore, almost every person familiar with the work of Lewis Terman, the psychologist who followed gifted youngsters into their adult years, has accepted his claim that high intelligence contributes to some types of adult success.[24]

However, evidence now suggests that high abstract intelligence, say IQs of about 120 (the average of students going to selective colleges), may not be that contributory.[25] Studies of above-average but not as uniformly gifted Harvard men found that SAT scores (which are highly correlated with IQ) did not predict any measure of adult success; eleven of the highest-scoring but twelve of the lowest-scoring had been cited in *Who's Who in America* and *American Men of Science*.[26] The most intensive study of America's creative poets, physicists, architects, and others found that sheer abstract ability did not predict creativity for people with IQs higher than 120.[27] So intellectual level contributes to certain types of adult success; but within a bright group of adults, it may not contribute as much as character may.[28]

Are the hints that the mental health of very bright people may be more at risk true? Even Terman found that about 25 percent of his gifted people never fulfilled their talent because of motivational and personality limitations.[29] I thus re-searched the literature to discover numerous fragments that supported the hunch that high talent these days may be a mixed blessing. Growing up bright in the 1920s, when Terman's classic study began, may have been easier than it has been since the 1950s—a hypothesis that the changing personality of today's youth supports.

I report only a few fragments of what I discovered. A study of 1,454 Harvard students who had dropped out of college was reported to have found that "the more academic promise a student shows before entering college the greater the likelihood that he will drop out for psychiatric reasons. As a group, the psychiatric dropouts were clearly more intelligent than those who dropped out for non-psychiatric reasons."[30]

McClelland, who had studied Harvard alumni, also found what I had. Academic aptitude scores predicted no positive adult outcomes, including measures of occupational success. Instead, high academic aptitude scores tended to be negatively related to measures of well-being, including happiness and adjustment, as well as predictive of having fewer children.[31] We must be cautious, however, in accepting such a dramatically disturbing conclusion. Harvard alumni, like Haverford's, while highly talented, are not intellectually typical of the college-going population.

So let's turn to Ma Bell, who was, before she died, about as quintessentially American as anything could be. Her studies of college graduates from many different parts of the country showed that scholastic aptitude contributed only marginally to managerial success by the first five years after graduation, though more so after twenty years. But those who had higher scholastic aptitude scores upon graduation from college were reliably less happy and more psychologically maladjusted by their mid-adult years.[32]

Clearly, the popular view that academic success is *the* premier route to adult success and the widely accepted Terman view that high intellectual talent is a great blessing had to be qualified. But in what way was not yet clear. So I dug deeper into why academic success and high talent do not guarantee success—and why they might even create negative effects that may not show up until later and that could undermine adult success in *some* individuals.

The Limits of Academic Success and Talent

Why might some talented youth not turn out to succeed? Why might they be interpersonally immature? Success requires a variety of personality strengths that achievement and aptitude tests just don't measure. Scholastic aptitude tests measure too few high-level intellectual and other strengths to be used as good indicators of a person's success, even in college. About 85 percent of the reasons why college freshmen's grades differ may have nothing to do with SAT scores. SATs do *not* assess mind's varied strengths, such as imaginativeness, judgment, inductive skill, reflectiveness, and organizational and synthetic ability. Nor do they measure character strengths, such as curiosity, doggedness, and the maturity necessary to do well in one's work. Aware of this argument, the College Board is creating tests that measure more varied skills.

Some people high in scholastic aptitude may not succeed because they are immature interpersonally. Their early-emerging high talent may isolate them from their peers who don't speak the same language or have as focused interests. Peers may put down the "brain" of the class more frequently nowadays than formerly. My youngest daughter got A's in her algebra course the first six weeks.

Then one day she announced, "I've decided to no longer get A's. The girls at school are calling me a 'brain.'" She stubbornly stuck by her resolve to suppress her quantitative talent for years. To be labeled "gifted" risks social ostracism and put-downs such as "wimp" and "nerd."

To compensate for growing social isolation, other youngsters may cultivate their talents even more single-mindedly to bolster their self-esteem. When talent blossoms early, as it does for those gifted musically, quantitatively, or athletically, and is encouraged by parents and teachers, its pursuit just absorbs hundreds, if not thousands, of hours working alone.

High talent has not always been found to be associated with immaturity. The issue is much more complicated. When studied in the fifties, intellectually talented youth were more self-sufficient, independent, self-confident, and mature than the less talented.[33] However, with the exception of studies such as Terman's, initiated more than sixty years ago,[34] remarkably little information exists about the interpersonal relationships and personalities of bright children who grew up since World War II *and what they now are like as adults.* Chapter Two showed how adolescents' relationships and personalities have been changing since the sixties in ways that may make findings on children born prior to World War II even less applicable to those born since.

Enough other fragments of evidence, though, suggest that the idea that highly talented people may be at risk of not maturing interpersonally must be kept alive. I recall a British study that found that academically talented first-graders initiated relationships with others less frequently than less talented ones did. Gifted people tend to be isolated from other children when young.[35] As a sixteen-year-old contestant in the U.S. mathematics olympiad said, "I was pretty isolated ever since I could remember. I didn't like to play games the other kids played. They wanted to play catch and I wanted to stay inside and think about things."[36] Quantitatively gifted pubertal boys and girls are impatient, sarcastic, argumentative, opinionated, and socially aloof.[37] Would these traits attract their peers to want to be friends with them? The most academically involved college student grows least in all other sectors of his or her personality.[38] At Harvard, writing a senior honors thesis "tends to predict a decline in maturity of adaptation among men."[39] More generally, intellectual activity tends to inhibit emotional spontaneity and the earthy expression of impulses that can contribute to warmer relationships.[40]

The more clarifying question may be "What distinguishes those talented people who fulfill their intellectual promise later in life from those who never do?" Terman found the former to be emotionally stable, persistently motivated, purposeful, self-confident, and stronger personalities.[41] Among my most intellectually gifted men, those who were more maritally, parentally, and vocationally successful were also more mature and stronger people. Their peers viewed them as assertive, dominant, and decisive people who acted like leaders and enjoyed using power. Others identify the more successful talented person as interpersonally mature as well as ambitious.[42] My more and less successful talented men did not differ in these qualities.

Another more complicated reason may help explain why talented college-going males, in particular, may be more at risk interpersonally than the average male. In a typical masculine peer culture, highly *verbally* talented boys stand out like sore thumbs. The more *verbally* gifted men had not when young had the typical interests of other boys their age. They had felt different from and out of step with them and had not been very sensitive to what went on between them and others. Might being so "different" lead to feelings of self-doubt and the failure to develop the empathic skills necessary to fulfill intimate adult roles?

On the other hand, the more *quantitatively* gifted boys, while more typically masculine, may not have developed the interpersonal traits necessary to succeed in their adult roles either. They less openly shared their feelings in their intimate relationships. Their spouses, friends, and colleagues described them as less developed on many typically feminine, especially interpersonal, attributes. Compared to the less quantitatively gifted youth, the more gifted ones were reliably *not* seen by their peers as being as loyal, eager to soothe others' hurt feelings, gullible, gentle, sympathetic to others, sentimental, or tender.

As youth, the study's quantitatively gifted men had been persistently ambitious, rational, logical, controlled, consistent, self-sufficient people who had functioned well under stress. Might such youthful strengths have got in the way of developing the "softer" and more emotionally warm qualities necessary to succeed interpersonally in their adult roles? Might such strengths have made them more vulnerable to subsequent emotional instability and difficulty in creating cooperative relationships with others? Such has been found to be so for gifted scientists. When young, their hobbies and interests interfered with their peer relationships, they had fewer close male and female friends, and they were not aware of or sensitive to others' feelings. [43]

One of my most quantitatively gifted men poignantly illustrates the long-term effects of these traits. When asked to identify the six qualities that he had learned contribute to a happy marriage, he could identify only one, "spend time together"; to a fulfilling sexual life, "I haven't learned"; and to being a good parent, only one, "patience."

We should know more than we now do if such hunches are true. Johns Hopkins University's Study of Mathematically Precocious Youth aims to accelerate pubertal children's mathematical competence to help them become more creative earlier in life. Unfortunately, the researchers have not *thoroughly* explored their interpersonal and psychological maturing in adulthood. [44] I hope I am wrong, but my findings compel me to predict that numerous negative effects may emerge once they leave the protected and supportive university environment. The dropout rate for those admitted in 1972 to the accelerated program was 75 percent. Hopefully, the more mature youth remained in the program. They would have character resources to cope with whatever negative effects might result from such accelerated but focused development. The graduates who are now adults have become successful engineers and computer programmers but not yet unusually creative. Nothing has been reported about how well they have succeeded as marital partners, parents, friends, and citizens, or how virtuous, healthy, and happy they are.

Clearly, being blessed with high talents is not sufficient for their effective use in adulthood. To succeed in any of our many roles requires many diverse talents, interpersonal skills, values, and interests, as well as other traits. To focus on and reward only a few intellectual aptitudes and dismiss many other important ones sets up bright children for failure once they enter the adult world. Have the talented youth you know learned that to be maritally happy requires more than just spending time with one's partner, that to create a reciprocally fulfilling sexual relationship requires numerous interpersonal strengths, and that to be a good parent demands more than just patience—if either they or you really value these types of adult fulfillment?

Although the ways we assess student achievement and school effectiveness predict so little about adult success does *not* justify concluding that schools contribute little to human excellence. Our impoverished ideas about what academic excellence means blind us. Obsessive demands for quick, objective, two decimal-point measures of achievement also blind us to schools' other potential contributions to a student's healthy growth.

Cocurricular Participation as a
Predictor of Human Excellence

If measures of mastering liberal arts courses, such as grades and test scores, predict only weakly, if at all, how students will turn out as adults, is there any other school-related index that does any better? Yes: students' cocurricular involvement. American schools provide and encourage their students to participate in a wide variety of nonacademic activities. They provide not just sports but also student councils, school newspapers, clubs of every color on an artist's palette, including computer, chess, drama, and band. Americans are ambivalent about the value of such activities—except in Texas when it is proposed that football be cut back. When faced by limited funds, legislatures and school boards first reduce the athletic programs and other nonacademic "frills."

Several longitudinal studies agree that involvement in a school's cocurricular activities is the most valid school-related predictor of adult effectiveness.[45] One summary of research compared the contribution that grades, aptitude test scores, and cocurricular activities made to later success. It concluded that "the best predictor of creativity in mature life was a person's performance, during youth, in independent, self-sustained ventures. Those youngsters who had many hobbies, interests, and jobs, or were active in extracurricular activities, were more likely to be successful in later life."[46]

Following 3,767 students through college, the College Board not unexpectedly found that rank in high school and test scores were the best predictors of academic success. However, students who had put sustained effort into one or two extracurricular activities while in high school were more likely to succeed in campus leadership and independent accomplishment than students who had not.[47]

The extent of and success in cocurricular activities depend, of course, on many varied human talents, not the least of which are intellectual and motivational qualities such as persistence and hard work. High school students more actively involved in extracurricular activities, including athletics, are also the ones who get better grades and score higher on achievement tests.[48]

I have confirmed these findings with several thousand public high school students. Those who frequently participate in cocurricular activities get higher grades, feel better about school, have higher morale, spend less time earning money during the week, drink alcohol and use drugs less often, and act more ethically.[49]

Such findings do not apply only to the affluent who go to college. George Vaillant studied the development of 392 underprivileged inner-city boys from fourteen to forty-seven years of age. He compared the adult outcomes of those who as fourteen-year-olds had participated in clubs, sports, and other cocurricular activities with the outcomes of the nonparticipants. The former participants were mentally healthier, had closer and warmer adult relationships, enjoyed their first marriages and children more, had been employed more frequently, and had higher incomes. In fact, engagement in work and cocurricular activities when fourteen consistently contributed more to adult success than any other attribute, including intelligence and parental socioeconomic status.[50]

The high school cocurricular participation of the men and women whom I studied confirmed its contribution to adult success, though more for the men than for the women. The more involved high school male turned out to be consistently more productive and fulfilled at every period of his adult life. He was more mature and more successful in his primary adult roles. Perhaps because I included athletic and leadership activities in the cocurricular index, the more involved young men were, when middle-aged, rated as more masculine and more desirous of and effective in using their power and influence.

The more involved high school girls seemed to follow a similar though not as clearly marked path. Twenty to twenty-five years later, they also tended to fulfill their primary adult roles more successfully than the less involved girls. Apparently, cocurricular experience contributes to how successful a woman will be in her vocation. The more involved girls turned out to be more satisfied with and fulfilled in their adult lives, particularly with their work, which their colleagues saw as a "calling" and not just a job to them.

The evidence from diverse studies suggests that cocurricular activities contribute more than traditional academic measures to a variety of adult outcomes. Should not this trouble legislators and other critics who rue using scarce resources to support nonacademic activities? While saving dollars today, we may be undermining youth's competence and resourcefulness tomorrow and beggaring our country of its future leaders.

Teachers know why active involvement in soccer, student government, drama, and glee club predict adult success better than academic grades. They believe that cocurricular activities develop many of the strengths that contribute to an adult's success: cognitive skills such as planning, organizing, scheduling, and meeting deadlines; interpersonal skills such as cooperation, teamwork, and leadership; values such as "doing one's best," persistence, and responsibility; and self-attitudes such as self-confidence and self-esteem.

As the subsequent chapters will show, schooling also enables students to develop many other strengths not now measured by academic grades and test scores. Because we don't assess such effects, we underestimate how effective our schools may in fact be. By valuing only one-dimensional students, we rob them of an ideal or vision of the potentials that their schools may in fact or could provide them. By substituting a tunneled view of academic excellence for human excellence, we have betrayed the liberal education tradition that could provide the missing vision today's schools lack.

The Inseparability of Mind, Character, and Self

Academic excellence is ultimately rooted in and draws its strength from our character—our interpersonal skills and values—and the self-attitudes that make us educable. Academic excellence will never be achieved if we fail to integrate the maturation of mind with that of character and self.

Take the most straitjacketed definition possible of academic excellence: accurately answering thirty multiple-choice items, such as questions about the history of Idaho or Pennsylvania. Think of the rich personality attributes necessary to achieve such a feat: some *curiosity* about the state; *persistence* in reading the boring text; *accuracy* in taking notes; *thoroughness* in preparation; *judgment* about what is and is not important to learn; *scheduling* time to begin studying three nights before the test; *cooperatively* reviewing the notes with one's friends; *inhibiting* the desire to party the night before; keeping mentally *alert* the day of the test; *resilience* to keep going when not able to answer the first three questions; ability to *tolerate anxiety* when blanking out on the fourth; a *sense of humor* to put the test into perspective (just in case the criterion of academic excellence is answering twenty-seven items correctly); and *psychological skills* to explain away the failing grade to one's parents.

Or consider the rich strengths necessary to learn how to write well: a *belief* that one can and the *desire* to write; *sensitivity* to and *precision* in use of words; *access to vivid images* of one's less conscious mind; ability to *articulate* one's inner voices; *patience* while searching for some *imaginative* ideas about which to write; *empathy* to understand one's audience; *toleration of the frustration* involved while *persistently* rewriting and rewriting again; *flexibility* to abandon a sentence that doesn't "work" and to reorder another that might; *meticulousness* to catch every misspelled word and misplaced comma; *valuing excellence* enough to proofread the paper patiently for the fourth time; a *tough skin, self-confidence,* and enough *faith* in oneself to not be destroyed by the teacher's rash of red marks; and, among a host of other traits, the *maturity* to not view failure as personal rejection and the *strength and courage* to pick oneself up and write again.

Thoughtful teachers know in their bones that academic excellence and character are inseparable. Research supports their intuition. The U.S. Office of Education commissioned a study of 12,000 students from financially poor homes to identify those most likely to achieve and so pull themselves out of their dismal poverty.

Those who succeeded had valued high academic achievement, enjoyed working hard in school, had parents who expected them to achieve, and were religiously committed. American researchers have concluded that "the development of character and intellect must go hand in hand";[51] British researchers also agree.[52]

While some Americans have ignored the wisdom of valuing the maturation of mind, character, and self, the Japanese have not. However, their telescopic vision of the intellectual strengths for which to educate and samurai approach to character development have not escaped severe public criticism.

The Japanese "Secret" for Students' High Test Scores

The academic achievement of the Japanese stems from their personality. Japan's educational, familial, and vocational values consistently cohere to support students' development. The Japanese believe that their schools should be "comprehensive" and educate students' cognitive, social, and moral development. Schools should prepare them with the personality strengths necessary to participate in their vaunted workaholic society.[53]

While acknowledging that students differ in talent, the Japanese believe that all students can achieve if they work hard enough. To fail is likely to be viewed as a defect of character for which a youth, rather than the school, is responsible. Doing well academically tells others that one has developed some of the personality strengths necessary to succeed. Recall that I, too, found that academic grades and teachers' judgments of intellectual competence predicted personality strengths such as ambition, self-discipline, and reliability twenty-five years later.

Because Japan's test-dominated schools emphasize the mastery of factual information, learning how to memorize (but not to solve problems, create imaginatively, or judge realistically) is the singular route to academic success. More than other intellectual skills, successful memorization is enhanced by character strengths such as diligence, hard work, and commitment. Japanese families provide tutors and weekend schools for their hardworking children to maintain their pace in school. Homework builds the character that the Japanese value. Only 35 percent of Japanese but 76 percent of American high school seniors report that they spend fewer than five hours a week on their homework.[54]

The honorific status of a Japanese teacher witnesses not only Japan's Confucian commitment to education but also its belief in the intrinsic moral character of education. Socially ranked as equal to physicians, teachers are addressed by the honorable title of *sensei*. They assume responsibility for the moral and social growth of their students, and expect parents to defer to and support their academic as well as moral demands in and outside school. I visited a school that had refused to allow its students to meet a visiting choral group from an American school with which its students had been corresponding all year. Its teachers feared that the American adolescents would, in their words, "corrupt" their students.

Japanese teachers are also personally accountable for the moral lapses of their students *outside* school. An adolescent advisee of one teacher had been seen observing a local political rally. The teachers' colleagues punished her for her advisee's misbehavior by moving her desk away from their desks to a corner of the room and ignoring her. Because she could no longer be trusted, another teacher every night monitored her students' work and her next day's lesson plans. After suffering two years of her colleagues' ostracism, broken in heart and mind, she abandoned teaching. What must her transgressing advisee have felt about what she had done to her *sensei*?

Japanese schools assume responsibility for developing their students' personalities so they will be able to adjust to their economy's needs. They explicitly value self-discipline, diligence, meticulousness, conscientiousness, punctuality, obedience to authority, cooperativeness, adjusting to others' expectations, responsibility to one's group, harmonious peer relations, and public morality.

Such traits also make students educable for their schools' demands. In contrast to current American efforts to accelerate academic development in early childhood, Japanese elementary school teachers focus first on teaching their children character strengths, such as perseverance, self-reliance, and the ability to work cooperatively and get along harmoniously with others.[55]

Despite Japanese students' enviably high test scores, their schools have not escaped severe criticisms about the unhealthy effects of their teachers' efforts to shape their students' character. CBS reported that Japanese teachers routinely use physical punishment to strengthen character. They speak of their "whips of love," wooden rods with which to strike children on their backs. An elementary school compelled its children to run in the snow in their underclothes in order to "toughen" them up. As a punishment for smoking, a principal put two adolescents in a cage, where they died from suffocation.

A Japanese governmental commission assessing the nation's schools issued a devastating report in 1985 that described them as in a "state of desolation," characterized by "rigidity, uniformity, and closedness . . . a tendency to impose excessive controls on students . . . [and] frustration." As a result, schools have "made wastelands of children's minds." Students are not taught "to think independently"; they are not allowed to develop "distinctive personalities or the ability to govern themselves"; and they are not encouraged "to be creative."[56]

Another governmental commission, which included influential business leaders, has since recommended that colleges should no longer admit students solely on the basis of examinations that measure rote memorization but should also rely on students' school grades, extracurricular activities, and references.[57] Although recognizing the centrality of character to academic achievement, the Japanese apparently are struggling to create a consensual vision of human excellence that could enrich their understanding of academic excellence.

On the other hand, by not frankly accepting the *inseparability* of mind and character maturation, American educators remain paralyzed at first base. They wonder why their lethargic and bored students score so much more poorly than Japanese students. By purifying their liberal arts courses of their liberally educating goals, they have created schools that are characterological wastelands.

Liberal Arts Does Not Mean Liberal Education

To recapture American students' commitment to their own growth, schools must teach Spanish, history, and physics to empower students to teach themselves Arabic, induce an embracing idea from a plethora of fact, and frame a hypothesis that can be rigorously tested. Teachers know that liberal arts does not mean liberal education. But they fail to implement that distinction when talking about curricular issues and when teaching their courses. They know that students can take forty liberal arts courses but not deepen their love of learning or become self-educating persons in command of their talents.

Teachers should teach their liberal arts courses to produce the educating outcomes of maturation that contribute most to their students' adult success and well-being. Consider empathy, which is critical to success. An English teacher should explicitly explain to students how rewriting their themes three times to reach three different audiences teaches them empathy.

Or consider mathematics. It has been a core liberal arts course for more than two thousand years. Why should all American students pass some national standard for algebra? When I have asked teachers that question, none has ever given the politicians' answer: to score higher than every other country's students on math tests by the year 2000. Nor do any reply as the futurists do: to get along in the technological world of the future—the argument for requiring more math. They know that only a small number will need advanced math. When was the last time you needed to solve a trigonometric problem? Instead, teachers answer as liberal educators: to learn how to think logically and solve problems. Algebra, or math more generally, is a logic. More than most other liberal arts disciplines, it has the potential to help us think logically and solve problems.

Does math really help us learn these important skills? No. I know of no evidence whatsoever that taking two years of algebra necessarily improves logical thinking. I know no educators, including algebra teachers, who when invited to do so, defend the idea that mastering algebra helps any student to write logically organized papers or argue logically about the advantages of nuclear power. Learning to solve textbook math problems does not ipso facto enable a student to solve other problems more effectively. Math's liberally educating potential will never be realized until its teachers deliberately teach math in ways that help students to think logically and solve problems. They must also teach students to apply such skills to other areas of living. A liberal arts course not taught to produce liberally educating effects bores and turns off today's pragmatic stapler-students.

We lack an articulated vision of human excellence. We ignore the characterological roots of academic excellence. We replace liberally educating goals with disciplinary liberal arts ones. We become vulnerable to each new medicine man's pitch that he has the miraculous cure for all our educational ills. Lengthen the school day and year. But risk boring students even more. Require more math, science, and foreign language and cut back art, music, and vocational education courses. But risk pushing even more students out of school who don't learn well using only their left brains. One of the medicine man's more poisonous medicines has been the "back-to-basics" homemade brew.

We can't character-proof schools by isolating students' minds from their values, interpersonal relationships, and attitudes about themselves. We should have learned this from the failure of the "back-to-basics" movement—the seventies' parent of the eighties' test-defined academic excellence obsession. Its adherents sought to purify schools of their "frivolous" concern with students' self-concepts, feelings of self-worth, values, and social skills, to which they falsely attributed the nation's declining test scores. Is it not ironic that since dominating education's center stage in its various guises, test scores have not improved? In most other responsible professions, bankrupt slogans would have precipitated critical reexaminations of their assumptions and methods rather than the current reform proposals of "more of the same."[58]

Simplistic slogans such as "back to basics" and "academic excellence" can irreparably damage a student's healthy growth. Any too channeled understanding of how we grow healthily risks stretching us out of shape and distorting other aspects of our growth. Lags in growth of self-confidence, curiosity, and personal relationships relative to growth in mind eventually cause an inner strain that creates resistance to further growth and may lead to mind's death.

My daughter's teachers did not understand the destructive effects of their myopic view of what is "basic" to academic excellence. Her ninth-grade algebra and eleventh-grade history teachers destroyed her mathematical interest and historical curiosity. Cast in the mold of Japanese samurai, without supporting Confucian- and Meiji-like cultural traditions and parents committed to the "back-to-basics" ideology, they reprehensibly conformed their diverse students to the same pages and instructional procedures. Quantitatively talented, intuitively quick, and assertively articulate, my daughter soon made her boredom known to her algebra teacher. The department head insisted that a "basic" that she had to learn was how to conform to her teacher's methods and memorize verbatim the text's definitions of commutativity, even though she might be bored and getting A's. My daughter had been raised to be a questioning, initiating, self-reliant, thinking American—not an obedient, acquiescent, conforming, and memorizing Japanese student. We protested, but, sadly, not persuasively enough to prevent the permanent suppression of her mathematical interest.

Placed in an eleventh-grade history section for gifted students, my daughter failed a "more-of-the-same" final exam—a 500-item true-false test. She "knew" her history too well; she could see too many qualifications and shaded meanings. When asked to explain what knowing 500 historical facts had to do with academic excellence, her teacher insisted that it was "basic" that she know her historical "facts." This time we confronted the superintendent and high school administrators and demanded that they tell us what the school meant by "basic."

I asked, "In addition to disciplined knowledge, should not a 'basic' outcome be increased curiosity, deepened intellectual interests, joy in learning, and self-educating skills such as inducing new ideas, judging, and evaluating historical information?" Their response: "No. Those are not 'basic' goals of this school. Our purpose is to teach the facts to do well on national achievement tests."

If I had been more contentious, I would have taken the school board and administrators to court. Why? For destroying one of the most preciously basic of all human adaptive qualities—genuine curiosity—and suppressing the empowerment of a mind as a result of a puristic slogan of "back to basics." My charges? Professional ignorance of how children grow healthily and the attributes needed to succeed as an adult. Ideological blindness. Toleration of professionally incompetent teachers.

Too constricted a view of what is "academic excellence" destroys minds. It defeats efforts to improve our schools. It is too narrowly applied, too irrelevantly measured, and too neglectful of the rich character strengths necessary to do well not just in school but in the world outside school as well. Perceptive students know these truths. They have not made the slogan their own. So they don't slave like Japanese students to achieve their society's test-defined goal of academic excellence. Their schools are places of despair, not hope.

The Betrayal of Liberal Education's Vision of Human Excellence

When experienced teachers describe the most important gift that they received from their teachers when young, they cite richly humane ones such as "a new way of thinking"; "courage to face a difficult situation"; "the will to follow my dreams"; "belief that I was special"; "knowing that I was responsible for my own decisions and acts"; "an understanding of what compassion was all about"; and a "lifelong interest in philosophy." And like educators before them, they believe that a liberal education is society's most empowering organized route to human excellence. *None of these teachers would dispute the primacy of basic academic skills and knowledge of innumerable and varied specialized ones.* But they believe that schools should and can teach far more than "basic" skills and facts.

The spirit of the teachers' gifts can be traced back to those of fifth-century Greeks, made concrete in "the generous Homeric conception of *arete* as an all-round excellence and an all-round activity . . . [that] implies a respect for the wholeness or the oneness of life, and a consequent dislike of specialization."[59]

For centuries, philosophers have claimed that education should be person-centered and not just mind-centered. The *Iliad*, the *Odyssey*, and later the liberal arts, whether mathematics, rhetoric, Greek, or music, were taught as powerful means to arete, or all-around excellence. From Socrates' "Know thyself" to Alfred Whitehead's "complete development of ideal human beings"[60] and Jerome Bruner's "achieve a good life and make an effective contribution to . . . society,"[61] educators talk not just of intellectual but also of interpersonal, value, and self-attitudinal strengths.

Since *Sputnik*, however, we have imperceptibly substituted the goal of filling up minds for that of liberally educating students. Don't misunderstand me. Educating liberally *must* include disciplining minds, but not *just* filling up minds with five thousand facts so that they may be called culturally literate.[62] An empty mind has nothing with which to think. But to educate liberally demands much more than memorizing, even comparing and evaluating, five hundred facts about European history.

Fortunately, many voices have begun to call on schools and colleges to do "much more than just fill up minds."[63] Even William Bennett, a former secretary of education gadfly, has urged educating character. Others, including Presidents Carter and Ford, concerned about Americans' lack of civic responsibility, want schools to educate for commitment to "liberty, equality, and justice" and to teach students to "tell right from wrong."[64] The California Board of Education more pallidly insists that the state's textbooks must help students "see the connection between ideas and behavior, between the values and ideals that people hold and the ethical consequences of those beliefs."[65] The AIDS campaign provokes other calls to help students make more mature value choices about their sexual impulses. Educators of all stripes now acknowledge that schools should strengthen students' beliefs in their own competence if they are to do well academically. Arkansas legislators "are pushing a statewide effort to build self-esteem, but they can't agree on a proposal they all feel good about. . . . One bill would put instruction in morals and values alongside math and science on the public school curriculum."[66] Teachers of financially poor as well as of learning-disabled children now recognize that they must educate for social skills if those children are to survive in an increasingly service economy.[67] Such calls eloquently show how anemically limiting is the slogan of "academic excellence" and how inadequate are its measures—achievement test scores.

We can avoid producing one-dimensional students by creating what I call schools of hope dedicated to arete's classical vision of human excellence. The next chapter begins that task. More than most other adults, teachers and parents know contemporary students and how they need to grow. Let us first listen to their collective hopes for youth to clarify the goals of schools of hope. I then examine the strengths that research tells us that they need to live successful, healthy, and happy lives in the twenty-first century. Finally, I introduce in more abstract and technical language a model of human excellence, which I will redefine as maturity, to replace Benjamin Bloom's taxonomy of educational outcomes.

PART TWO

The Missing Vision

Chapter 6

A Vision
of Human Excellence

Where there is no vision, the people perish.
—Proverbs 29:18

Teachers and parents agree about the meaning of human excellence. Whether in Minneapolis, Hong Kong, or Cairo, they identify the same type of gifts that they wish their students or children might some day thank them for: self-confidence, joy of learning, sense of what is right, ability to teach themselves, curiosity, sensitivity to others, compassion. When describing the most mature, fulfilled, all-around effective adult they know—the ideal person they wish they or their children were like—they invariably identify similar strengths. Heading their list is sense of humor, followed by self-confidence; enthusiasm and high energy; interpersonal strengths such as empathy, caring, and sensitivity to and tolerance of others; motivational strengths such as curiosity and openness to challenges and change; ethical values such as integrity; and self-directing qualities such as commitment and perseverance.

Teachers also agree quite well about the five most important core strengths that students will need in their rapidly changing, technology-dominated, interdependent, less coherent communities of the future. Whether in Lansing, Jakarta, or London, they agree that adaptability should head the list. Communication and problem-solving skills come next, followed by interpersonal attitudes such as tolerance of different peoples and skills such as cooperatively working

125

with others, ethical values such as honesty, and a self-concept as a member of a global community.

The Japanese have asked themselves the same question, and they answer similarly. They, too, hope to teach their youth to cope more flexibly, learn to identify and settle problems, and develop a strong moral sense. But they also hope to rectify damaging inadequacies in their schools. They want their students to become more independent and creative as well as to enjoy studying more and so become better lifelong learners.[1]

Notice something missing from everyone's answers? Not one of the thousands of parents and teachers I have asked has ever wished to be thanked for having helped a student or child to get an A in chemistry, to speak French like a Parisian, to solve a quadratic equation, to accurately locate the countries of Africa on a map, or to memorize the 5,000 facts that Eric Hirsch believes every "educated" person should know.[2] Nor do they spontaneously identify specific intellectual skills, except communication and problem-solving ones, as the most salient strengths of their ideal person or the critical ones needed in the future.

What do these anecdotes and impressionistic surveys of teachers' and parents' hopes tell us about their implicit vision of what a human could become?

> Wherever we search and whatever questions we ask, we discover that adults share some similar values about human excellence.
>
> Attributes of character and self-attitudes are more frequently cited than those of mind, even by educators dedicated to mind's cultivation.
>
> The promise of parents' and teachers' hopes is that there may be a limited core number of strengths that contribute most to human excellence and successful adaptation.

Might there not be some universal objective "reality" to the idea of human excellence that research can confirm? Might we then be able to construct a defensible vision of it that has specific implications for how we could educate youth for the future's demands?

Beginning Steps Toward a Scientific
Definition of Human Excellence

To answer such questions, I rely on thirty-five years of studies of optimally functioning people in the United States and elsewhere, liberal education's effects on high school and college students, the course of healthy growth from adolescence to middle age, and the personalities of men and women who succeed in their principal roles and who are also virtuous, healthy, and happy. Since the results have been published elsewhere, I only briefly summarize those most relevant to schools to illustrate how varied are the strengths that students need to become fulfilled and successful adults.[3]

As you read about such strengths, keep in mind students' changing personality. Ask how well prepared they now are to live in the twenty-first century. Also ask which strengths academic grades and test scores measure and how accurately they communicate to students how well prepared they are to succeed as adults. And then ask why today's perceptive stapler-students are not more enthusiastically committed to schooling as it now goes on.

Can we really define human excellence? Yes. Its core meaning has persisted for centuries and will continue well into the future. Words such as *fulfillment, success, virtue, health,* and *happiness* surely must capture facets of its meaning.

The route to adult fulfillment is successful adaptation to our six primary roles as workers, citizens, marital partners, parents, lovers, and friends. Since youth cannot foretell their personal futures, they should develop the core strengths necessary to adapt successfully to *whatever* roles they eventually elect. The following list presents in rough declining order of importance the core strengths that students need to adapt to all six and to any five of their future adult roles.[4] That is, "patience" is not as cardinal a strength for fulfilling one's role as a citizen as it is for fulfilling the remaining five roles well, especially the familial ones. Note how well they mirror teachers' and parents' gifts and their ideal adult.

Needed for All Six Roles	*Needed for Five Roles*
Caring, compassion	Patience
Honesty, integrity	Shared interests, values, and
Sense of humor	responsibilities

Openness, capacity for self-
disclosure
Tolerance and acceptance of
others
Dedication, commitment
Understanding of others
Respect for others
Empathy for others
Adaptability, flexibility
Self-confidence

Intelligence
Knowledgeability
Affection
Sensitivity to others' needs
Trust in others
Willingness and ability to listen
to others
Responsibility, reliability
Consideration of and thought-
fulness about others
Ability to prioritize use of time
High energy level
Fairness and treatment of others
as equal
Good judgment

The list is imposing but provocatively troublesome. Its richness and diversity may overwhelm us. Yet the strengths are all necessary. Clearly, if we value human excellence as a goal for living—or for schooling—then we cannot ignore ethical *values* such as honesty, integrity, commitment, and fairness—nor *self-attributes* such as openness, confidence, or reliability, nor *cognitive strengths* of intelligence, good judgment, and knowledgeability. What surprised me most, however, was how firmly *interpersonal strengths* are at the core of our adaptability. Except for elementary school teachers, most ignore such strengths. Some even belittle those colleagues— the Mr. Chipses among us, as well as deans of students and counselors—who concern themselves with students' interpersonal maturation. While we may dispute the list's specific attributes and certainly their crude ordering, we cannot dismiss its message: interpersonal skills such as understanding, sensitivity, tolerance, and empathic listening skills are indispensable to adult success.

The list also tells us why exclusive attention only to academic development may put highly talented students at risk of failing as adults. It warns us that a single-minded emphasis on academic excellence obscures to students the centrality of their character to their future success.

The sheer number and variety of strengths necessary to adapt dismay most teachers. Much as they themselves value character and self-attitudinal strengths, high school and college faculties, especially, shrink from assuming responsibility for their development. They already feel overloaded by their schools' academic demands. More pointedly, few have any ideas about how they might teach for character maturation other than to use their lecterns as pulpits from which to sermonize and exhort.

When I hear educators speak of their goals, I hear them talk primarily about preparing students for their future vocational roles. I hear little about future citizenship and community leadership roles, even less about familial roles as marital partners or parents. Even when talking about preparing students for work or citizenship, educators emphasize almost exclusively their cognitive requisites. But succeeding in work and being a good citizen depend also on a wealth of other strengths. Note the strengths of character and self as well as of mind that our vocational and citizenship roles require.

Strengths Needed for Vocational Success

Students aspiring to enter the business or professional world need

> Mind's communication, analytical, and organizational skills, good judgment, and imaginative perspective as well as disciplined knowledge and specialized skills of their chosen occupation
>
> Character's interpersonal skills of understanding, care, and patience, as well as motivational attributes such as commitment to working hard and ethical values such as honesty and integrity
>
> Self-attitudinal strengths such as self-confidence and self-directing skills such as self-discipline, reliability, and decisiveness

To remind us that specific vocations require more of some and less of other strengths, I searched out those needed to be a white-collar manager and a blue-collar automobile worker in the future.

A 1990 graduate management admission report for American business schools calls for students who can frame and solve problems, particularly those that require adapting to rapid international changes. It also calls for students who respect, value, and work cooperatively with diverse peoples and who are skilled in anticipating their own effects on others. Intellectual curiosity, self-direction, and self-reflection round out the strengths that managers will need in the twenty-first century.[5]

Japanese managers of Toyota and Nissan automobile plants located in the United States want workers to have varied and high-level strengths quite similar to those I've already cited. Their workers must be flexible, with the ability to learn several jobs, shift easily between them, and ceaselessly reflect about how to improve their efficiency. They must be able to devote themselves to a team's goals, be sensitive to others, and control how their tone of voice affects others with whom they are cooperatively working. They also must be able to accept as well as know how to give constructive criticism. Finally, they should be able to set priorities, plan, be accurate and thorough, and be highly motivated and willing to work overtime.[6]

Strengths Needed to Be a Good Citizen

All societies use their schools to lead their children into their ways of thinking, believing, relating to others, and assuming communal responsibilities. What strengths do good citizens need who voluntarily work for and serve their communities? Again, note the varied strengths needed to be a sterling citizen:

> Mind's strengths, such as articulate and persuasive speaking and writing, problem-solving, and organizational skills, good judgment, and informed knowledge of issues
>
> Character's interpersonal strengths, such as tolerance of and caring concern for others who differ from oneself, leadership skills, and values such as energetically committing energy to persevere for a cause as well as a strong ethical character and ideals

> Self-attitudinal strengths, such as self-confidence and opti-
>   mism, as well as good self-organizational skills
> A sense of humor

Have you asked just how many of these varied strengths schools
educate for and measure? Is it not now clearer why academic grades
and tests don't predict complex adult outcomes, such as good citizenship, very well?[7] Or why too exclusive reliance on them as measures of future effectiveness endangers youth's confidence about
their future success?

Are you thinking at this moment that I have taken a micro-
scopic or at least too narrow view of human excellence? Focusing
on the strengths needed to adapt to our day-to-day roles ignores our
personhood, the quality of our nonrole lives, our more ineffable and
subjective selves. So let us step back from our daily activities to
discover the strengths of virtuous, healthy, and happy people—
surely other signs of human excellence.[8]

Personality of Virtuous, Healthy, and Happy People

From the days of the early Greeks until about the 1950s, many
educators believed that they should educate for virtue first, even if
academic excellence took third place after athletics in some schools.
Nowadays, academic excellence and athletic excellence uneasily
compete for first place in schools. Virtue has disappeared except for
a nod or two in some schools' mission statements. However, having
lived without virtue for several decades, some schools have begun
to resurrect it as a, though not *the*, primary goal for which to
educate.

Academic excellence itself presupposes universal ethical
values that every great religion has prized for centuries: honesty,
compassion, empathy, integrity, commitment, and courage. Who
wants students who cheat, fail to enter empathically into the inner
world of a book's characters, slant their own judgments to please
their teachers, perform their chemistry experiments perfunctorily
without commitment, and fear standing up and defending what
they discover? Teachers have been remarkably adept at hiding from
their students the intrinsically ethical nature of the pursuit of truth.

For the first time, we have the scientific evidence to support religions' claims that virtue—defined by ethical values such as honesty and compassion and maturity of ethical judgment—is indispensable to human excellence. More virtuous men and women are more successful in their adult roles and are healthier and happier than less virtuous ones. They also are more mature, especially interpersonally. Understanding others and being sensitive to their needs and feelings, they excel in forming cooperative relationships.

Of course, people's mental health and happiness are also relevant to their success and human excellence. Mentally healthy people are successful and happy; happy people are mentally healthy and successful. Like any important success, our well-being also depends upon strengths of character and self as well as of mind. Again for the first time, scientific evidence identifies the core strengths necessary for men and women to be mentally healthy and happy. Such people are well integrated, stable, and autonomous. Their command of themselves produces the self-confidence and optimism necessary to take risks to learn how to adapt more effectively. They are also androgynous. Healthy and happy men are judged by those who know them best to be sensitive to others' needs, cooperative, and warm; healthy and happy women are rated as strong and courageous individualists who can stand up for their beliefs.[9]

Personality Contributors to Human Excellence

What should the primary goal of education be? Chapter Five mentioned some views. "Arete," said the early Greeks. "Virtue," claimed others. The "valuable intellectual development is self-development," said philosopher Alfred Whitehead;[10] "healthy growth," insisted John Dewey.[11] "Make maturity the more it might become," urged Esther Raushenbush, former president of Sarah Lawrence College.[12] "Teach students to be human," writes Lloyd Averill, former president of the Kansas City Regional Council for Higher Education.[13] "Adaptability to the future," say contemporary futurists and many teachers. "Academic excellence," claim others. "High test scores, high school graduation, and literacy," among other, more practical goals, demand politicians.

How can we make some manageable order out of teachers'

and parents' kaleidoscopic lists of gifts and traits of their exemplars of excellence, the rich and diverse strengths necessary to adapt successfully, and educators' differing goals for schools? Research on adolescents and adults provides the key to creating a systematic, empirically based model of healthy growth and the ideal exemplar of human excellence.

A person's androgyny and psychological maturity are far more important contributors than academic measures to the widest variety of adult outcomes that describe human excellence.[14] Why? Because they enrich a person with the strengths for adapting. Rapidly changing technology and vocations, as well as familial relationships, require youth to become as adaptable as possible. Androgynous people share many of the traits typical of both males and females and thus are better equipped to adapt to their future's uncertain vocational and familial demands. For both men and women, typically masculine strengths, such as assertiveness and self-reliance, contribute to making a lot of money and being leaders. Typically feminine interpersonal strengths, such as caring and empathy, make possible strong and fulfilling familial, friendship, and ethical relationships.

More than adults' androgyny, however, their maturity contributes most to human excellence in all of its varied meanings. Mature men and women are happily married, are satisfied as parents and have mature children, are sexually fulfilled and good lovers, and have close friendships. They are well adapted to their vocations and are good citizens. They are also ethical, physically and mentally healthy, and happy adults.

That androgyny predicts many though not all of the same adult outcomes as does maturity does not mean that they are identical concepts. Androgynous people share some of the strengths of mature people; mature people share some of the strengths of androgynous ones. They are fraternal, not identical, twins, we might say. On the other hand, that psychological maturity predicts all the possible meanings of human excellence tells us that it and human excellence are essentially interchangeable. Mature people are exemplars of human excellence, who, in turn, are exemplars of maturity.

Another inescapable conclusion that I draw from these findings about maturity is that for the first time we now have scientifically based clues about where to discover the core strengths necessary to adapt: those, for example, that define the technical psychoanalytical concept of ego strength and educators' primary goal of adaptability. I now begin to speak of psychological maturity rather than of human excellence. As Dewey claimed, education should further healthy growth or maturing. The idea of maturing can more readily be anchored empirically and theoretically to others' ideas than human excellence can.

A Model of the Maturing Person

In 1956, Benjamin Bloom and his colleagues published their influential *Taxonomy of Educational Objectives, Handbook I: The Cognitive Domain.*[15] In 1964, they published their much less influential *Handbook II: Affective Domain.*[16] The authors proposed a rationale for identifying and ordering the course of cognitive and affective (their word for value) development. They argued that cognitive outcomes could be classified by their increasing complexity (or abstractness) or difficulty of acquisition. Value-related outcomes could be ordered by increasing internalization or what I later will call autonomitization.

Without reviewing their thoughtful and still cogent ideas about how both cognitive and value development occur, I will point out that their effort was necessarily flawed by limited research on and thus limited understanding of healthy growth at the time. They were unable to provide educators with a rationale that *integrated* both cognitive and value development. They proposed essentially two separate ordering dimensions for describing healthy growth: complexity and internalization. Furthermore, by focusing on value but not also on concurrent interpersonal development and self-development, the authors effectively told educators that the latter were unimportant or at least outside their responsibility.

The efforts of Bloom and his colleagues fostered two unintended and unforeseen effects. Psychology's inability to provide a unified multidimensional model of healthy growth reinforced teachers' inclinations—recognized by Bloom—to *not* understand affective goals as *intrinsically* related to cognitive outcomes and so to dismiss them. The second inadvertent effect resulted from labeling value development as "affective" development. Those inclined to think dichotomously might equate "affective" with "emotional" and then unthinkingly assume "cognitive" development to be opposed to or undermined by affective goals. After all, cognitive maturation, as Bloom also recognized, demands control, even suppression, of interfering emotions. The label "affective" should never be used to describe values, which are only one aspect of character. To say that teachers should be responsible for "affective" goals just creates needless resistance.

What we need now is a model of healthy growth that integrates the whole person. It should not ignore interpersonal and self-attitudinal growth. It should comprehend teachers' hopes as well as the historical goals of educators and research findings about education's actual effects. It should eschew labels such as "affective" that encourage dichotomous thinking. And, mirabile dictu, it should have practical implications for how we organize healthy schools, a liberating curriculum, and maturing classroom environments. In the following pages, I integrate such a model with others' ideas about development.

Maturing Is Systemic

A person-centered model of maturation must be *systemic*. Although humans are complexly organized and interdependent systems, we can talk about maturing only by abstracting out component structures and activities one at a time. The earlier chapters have prepared us to talk about the whole child's mind, character, including interpersonal skills and values, and self. Here I briefly summarize first the principles that describe growth and then the interrelated underlying dimensions that define the growth of mind, character, and self.

A healthy living system must have self-organizing and self-regulating capabilities to adapt to changing events. Biologists such as Ludwig von Bertalanffy,[17] cyberneticists such as William Ashby,[18] and psychoanalysts such as Heinz Hartmann believed similarly.[19] We, as vulnerable as we are to disruption by changing inner and external stresses, must be able to resist those stresses' effects and recover our essential stability when it is upset and disorganized.

One fundamental capability of a living system is its *equilibrating principle*. Excessive growth of mind, for example, relative to that of interpersonal skills can so distort and warp healthy functioning as to impede if not destroy further growth of its potentials.[20] We have the self-righting potential to recover our system's health.

Anecdotes are legion about gifted youngsters, such as musically or mathematically precocious children, who are pressured by ambitious parents and burn out early, never fulfill their promise, become mentally ill, suicidal, even homicidal. William Strubsall, a seventeen-year-old valedictorian, was the "smartest guy in the whole school," according to a classmate. He was a "handsome and popular teen-ager, who hoped to become a lawyer and attend the highly selective University of Chicago in the fall." Ten hours before graduation, he argued with his mother and crushed her skull with a baseball bat. William had apparently been pushed to the psychic abyss by a mother reported to have constantly "pressured him to do more."[21] Such a tragedy might have been prevented if someone had been aware of his equilibrating principle's psychic warnings.

A related systemic principle is that healthy growth of a *person* is necessary for the optimal development of mind. A gifted Haverford College senior, sensitive to his own interior warnings, reflectively said:

> The college's severe academic emphasis turned some of my friends into walking textbooks. But it made me decide when I was a freshman after I had come out first in my class that I wanted to have more time to myself and with other people than just with books. I've always been pleased with the intellectual horizons that the college opened up to me, but I adamantly insisted upon my freedom to walk in the woods, go bicycle riding, or do wood carving, which I do . . . but I've become very aware of the dangers of becoming overacademicized. I have learned how to keep the poetic, my mystic, self alive.

Ignoring the fact that humans need to grow wholly leads to foolish and wasteful educational prescriptions. Excessive cultural pressure on Japanese adolescents to pass their university entrance exams results in emotional collapse and hostile resistance to and flight from serious study during their university years—Japan's educational disaster area. Reformers who prescribe refresher courses for teachers don't understand what really contributes to their continued growth. A mentally and emotionally exhausted science teacher knew, however. He told me that the last thing he needed in July was a brush-up course in physics; he really needed to go white-water canoeing to regain his "sanity." Maybe he would be "ready" in August for renewed intellectual growth.

Maturing Is Developmentally Dimensional

From birth, healthy humans develop in five interdependent systemic ways that eventually provide them with the minds, character, and selves that mark them as mature and liberally educated adults. Although I focus on their manifestations in adolescents and adults, their roots reach back into infancy and childhood, as Jean Piaget has brilliantly documented. For example, five-year-olds show no visible evidence of the modes of thought that they will need when they are fourteen to understand and solve algebra problems. However, they begin to learn from building with different sized blocks the underlying or genotypic operations of combinativity and reversibility that algebra will later require them to use. Learning that they can combine blocks in various ways to produce the same tower prepares them to learn later at a more abstract symbolic level that they can remake $(a + b + c)$: they can reverse b and a to make the equation $(a + b + c) = (b + a + c)$.[22]

Symbolization. Jerome Bruner says that "the very essence of being human lies in the use of symbols."[23]

The capacity to represent in awareness our visible world and inner experience with symbols—images, words, numbers, art, music, mime, dance—provides immense adaptive power. We can imaginally combine, break up, and reverse ideas, such as $(b + a + c)$. Symbolization frees us to transcend the chains of time and space. We can imagine the future, as the writers of "Star Trek" have done. We are free of instinctual programs to react willy-nilly to our inner needs and external threats. Because we can inhibit our immediate reactions, we can imagine alternatives, think about their consequences, and choose among several ways of adapting. We become more adept at abstractly and honestly representing our inner and external worlds for adapting.

Other-Centeredness. According to John Dewey, "the individual is always a social individual. He has no existence by himself. He lives in, for, and by society."[24]

Healthy growth moves away from self- to other-centeredness, again vastly increasing our adaptive power. Other-centeredness frees us from viewing the world only from our pinpointed or self-centered view. When not imprisoned by our narcissism, we can stand outside ourselves to monitor how well we are communicating with another. Maturing people become more empathic and objectively realistic as they take multiple perspectives about themselves, others, and their world. The result is that they learn to care for others.

Integration. As Mark Van Doren puts it, "Man is in the same breath metaphysician, philosopher, scientist, and poet."[25]

Growth is toward increasing differentiation, complexity, connectedness, and integration. Internal coherence and external harmony greatly enhance adaptation, as religionists and educators since the early Greeks have told us. To not be torn by creating a way of life that integrates the inner scientist and poet, the feminine and masculine, the demonic and godlike is to act out of wholeness with integrity. To live and work with others with minimal strain and strife frees energies and talents for adaptive purposes. The maturing person becomes progressively more integrated and acts with integrity.

Stabilization. Earl J. McGrath tells us that growth is toward a "provisionally firm set of convictions, an examined philosophy of life . . . [that] structures the purposes and directs the activities of his existence . . . [that] give stability to his being."[26]

Any healthy living system must preserve its essential being while adjusting to new demands and stresses. Learning how to de-

velop adaptive habits enhances efficiency, frees awareness and
energy for new learning, and provides resiliency to recover from
temporary disorganization. The maturing person develops a more
stable identity, centered in predictable values and purposes, as well
as more enduring individual and community relationships and
commitments.

Autonomy. In the words of Alfred Whitehead, "the creative impulse
comes from within. . . . [T]he discovery is made by ourselves, the
discipline is self-discipline, and the fruition is the outcome of our
own initiative."[27]

As we become more stably grounded, our growth moves toward increased self-discipline, self-regulation, and self-education,
thereby bringing our potential strengths under our own control.
The knowledge and skills that we have learned become more mobile
and thus transferable for creating new adaptations. Autonomous
people command their drives and talents, discriminatingly respond
to environmental seductions and manipulations, and are able to
make of their lives what they consciously choose. Maturing people
become the agents of their own growth and so of their own identities and destinies, which they can fearlessly witness, if need be.

If such developments accurately map a person's healthy
growth and the course of adaptation, then they should clarify what
mature cognitive, character, and self-development means. Appendix
A portrays the complete model of maturity and its twenty attributes.
Study of it now will provide a more concrete overview of the
strengths that any person needs to adapt. It presents the language
and ideas that organize the rest of the book. Chapters Seven through
Nine define and illustrate each of the model's dimensional sectors,
relate them to philosophers' goals for education, and summarize the
research that shows that schooling can produce such effects.

Remember that I describe the growth of a healthy person.
Excessive development in any dimension or sector of the personality
distorts growth in the others. It ultimately brakes continued maturing and, if the calls of the equilibrating principle are not heeded,
results in stasis, unhappiness, ill health, and possibly death.

Consider unbalanced *dimensional* maturing. Relative to
growth on the other dimensions, excessive symbolization can lead

to paralyzing arguments and hairsplitting, as so frequently occurs in anguishing faculty meetings. Exaggerated other-centeredness produces an empty conformism and blocks the growth of a strong sense of self, as happens in the stereotypically feminine girl who is being raised to accommodate to and please others. Too tight integration can reduce spontaneity and openness to productive chaos, as occurs in the compulsively efficient and ordered administrator or pedant. Entrenched stabilization becomes rigidity, as seen in successful but complacent middle-aged teachers. Unbridled autonomy breeds self-centeredness, as is visible in the macho boy being raised to dominate and be self-contained and self-sufficient. Chapter Twelve uses this way of thinking to understand teachers' handicaps that impede or distort their personal and professional growth and so block the improvement of schools.

Maturing Is Genotypically Similar for All

The model of maturing is perfectly general. It describes how every person grows, regardless of his or her gender, social class, ethnic status, nationality, or cultural values.[28] For example, mature men and women differ similarly from immature ones. Mature northern Italians, Sicilians, eastern and western Turks, and Americans differ similarly from immature ones.[29] Visible or phenotypic differences such as gender and nationality do not *qualitatively* alter the underlying or genotypic meaning of healthy growth. They can affect, however, the hows, whens, and whats of maturing.

Some feminists and cultural relativists, for example, do not believe that a general model of healthy growth can be valid for both sexes and diverse cultures and regions. Their argument confuses apparent dissimilarities with less visible similarities. The lack until recently of a validated general model of maturing has limited their empirical efforts, which might otherwise have revealed more fundamental organizing principles of healthy growth. When men and women have the opportunity to become more mature, they grow in similar ways. Their level of maturity predicts the same patterns of adult outcomes.[30]

Until recently, cultural relativists have been the staunchest opponents of the idea that all humans can be described by the same developmental principles. They might contrast the Japanese with Americans. As dissimilar as their two cultures appear, however, they can also be understood in terms of their *different positions on the same underlying developmental dimensions.* Historically, the Japanese have valued other-centered group harmony much more than autonomous individualistic opposition. Now they seek to encourage greater autonomy, which they believe is necessary if they are to have a healthier and more creative society in the future. Historically and today, Americans have valued their individualistic autonomy more than communal other-centeredness—at least for their males. Historically, American females have been expected to become more other-centered than autonomous. Now they are expected to develop a stronger sense of themselves and become more autonomous.[31]

Comparative studies of people within cultures or of societies becoming more industrialized and educated confirm the model's generality. When studying rural Sicilians and northern industrialized Italians, I found that both described the Sicilian culture as much less mature on the model's dimensions than the more modern northern one.[32] Studies of peasants moving from less mature or more traditionalist societies, such as the Sicilian, to more modern urban ones show that they change in many of the ways that the model of maturing predicts.[33] Inkeles, a long-time student of modernization, argues, as I do, that "what defines man as modern in one country also defines him as modern in another. It argues for the actual psychic unity of mankind in a structural sense and the potential psychic unity of mankind in the factual sense. . . . [T]he nature of the human personality, its inner "rules" of organization, is evidently basically similar everywhere. . . . [T]his structural unity provides the essential basis for greater factual psychic unity of mankind."[34]

Maturing's dimensions identify Inkeles's "inner 'rules' of organization" and map how all humans grow healthily when freed or enabled to do so. Transcultural studies of mature and immature males in five cultural areas support Inkeles's and the model's assumption that the generic process of maturing is similar regardless of divergent cultural values.[35]

Maturing Can Occur Throughout the Life Span

Healthy growth can continue throughout much of a person's life. Because the model is developmental, it assumes that growth on each dimension is rooted in underlying trends visibly heralded earlier. Yes, we can fall prey to the resistances that slow, even stifle, continued growth as we age. But it is a myth that, as some administrators have told me, middle-aged and "old" faculty can't change for the better. Grandma Moses, who took up painting in her later years, Elizabeth Crosby, who earned her master's degree in political science from the University of Maine at the age of ninety-six,[36] and Armand Hammer, the former head of Occidental Petroleum Company, who continued to lead his company into new ventures in his nineties, show us that continued change is possible. While the ravages of aging and its handicaps may impede maturing, people of indomitable will and optimism have overcome even the most crippling of physical handicaps to live as fully as their handicaps permitted them.

Maturing Involves Successive Stabilized Adaptations

I use the awkward phrase "successive stabilized adaptations" instead of the popular "stage" concept because I wish to emphasize that maturing occurs primarily in response to how we adapt to either inner or outer challenges and also to avoid some of the implications of the "stage" concept.

Maturing and Adaptation. Throughout our lives, we must learn to adapt to different biological and social imperatives. To grow healthily, a child must learn to adjust to her teacher's demand to stop asking so many questions without suppressing her inquisitive and high-spirited nature. A pubertal boy must learn to adjust to his testosterone-driven itchiness in ways that don't annoy his teachers and peers without retreating into apathy or aggressively acting out at home. A college student must learn to adjust to the analytical and logical demands of his faculty without abandoning his imaginative poetic self.

Maturing and adapting reciprocally enhance each other. The

mature person has the strengths to adapt more effectively. Apparently, William Strubsall, the high school student who killed his mother, had the intellectual but not the character strengths. Conforming to his mother's and school's demands for academic excellence had not prepared him with the strengths to cope adaptively to his impulsive murderous wishes. By learning how to integrate adjustment and self-fulfillment, we become more mature. The Haverford senior who as a freshman had created some personal space to keep his "mystic self alive" while adjusting to the college's academic demands had matured in awareness of himself and autonomy of his values.

Obviously, there is a crude sequence to the kinds of tasks to which we must adapt. We learn how to be a student (childhood) before we fashion an integrated and stable sense of ourselves (adolescence) before we care for subsequent generations (adulthood). Successful adaptation to one task prepares us for the next and results in the accumulated acquisition of the strengths that define a mature person. Erik Erikson, for example, identifies eight sequential life-span tasks that he believes every person should master, including industry, identity, and intimacy.[37]

Maturing Through Stages. The idea of "stage" technically implies that maturing proceeds from one qualitatively different, invariant, universal, hierarchical, and age-defined structural change to another. However, not all theorists use the concept so strictly. Stage theories are of interest to educators who must match their curricular and teaching methods to fit their students' developmental readiness. Piaget identified qualitative changes in a child's and adolescent's thought that have aided educators when planning curriculum. William Perry extended Piaget's ideas into adulthood by describing how college students' minds evolve from dualistic to multiple and relativistic stages.[38] Similarly, Piaget, Lawrence Kohlberg, and others have described stages of moral development that have sparked educator interest.[39] Robert Selman's model of interpersonal maturation in children could be helpful to those who value the acquisition of role-taking ability and empathy.[40] Other stage models, such as Jane Loevinger's model of self-development, are not known as well by educators, possibly because their implications for schooling are not as clear as those of the others. [41]

As popular as such stage models are, I avoid using the "stage" concept as a basis for an educational vision for empirical reasons. Well-designed and careful studies of students' growth designed to produce and measure the changes predicted by stage models have produced quite meager results. [42] Two different conclusions are possible. We may conclude that education, even when carefully designed to produce such effects, does not really affect maturing very much. Or we may conclude that the assumptions and methods of stage theorists do not tap the richness of a liberal education's effects. I believe that the latter conclusion is more correct.

I avoid the "stage" idea also because its measures do not well predict either a person's maturity or that person's adult effectiveness—both traditional goals of education. For example, a popular measure of Kohlberg's moral development scale is unrelated to maturity; furthermore, other stage measures don't predict the adult outcomes that index human excellence. [43]

Finally, some experts now question the notion that children's minds develop in discrete, discontinous, stagelike steps. Also, most studying adults *over time* now agree that there are no age-delimited, invariant, and universal stages describing *adult* maturing. [44] No good evidence exists that everyone who reaches forty or forty-five, for example, must have a midlife crisis. [45] There may be such "stages"; no evidence exists at this time that they describe all people everywhere at specific age periods.

Is it not provocative that most stage theorists ground their models on underlying *developmental* assumptions about maturing? Piaget is quite explicit, though his views are ignored by popular interpreters of his work. Each successive cognitive stage is a further abstract and symbolic development of the five underlying operations or dimensions of logical thought, such as reversibility and combinativity. [46] Erikson's stages are basically dimensional. Each is rooted in infancy, develops over time, comes to the psychological forefront in its proper time to provoke a crisis, and continues to develop until death. [47] Kohlberg's stages of moral growth also elaborate, though less obviously, underlying dimensions, such as other-centeredness and integration. [48]

Figure 6.1 portrays how stage and dimensional views of maturing might be combined. It adds time or typical life-span periods and their developmental tasks, following Erikson, as a third vector to the model. Theorists may select and order tasks over time differently. But because the model of maturity empirically predicts a wider variety of adult outcomes than stage models now do, it identifies the strengths necessary to cope with each stage successfully. Chapter Eleven will argue that there is an optimal sequential order to how we adapt to whatever task or crisis we face that can help us match curricular development to the process of maturing.

Given the questionable power of stage theories to encompass personality development as well as education's potential effects, might it not be time to explore more thoughtfully whether a *dimensional* understanding of maturation provides a firmer foundation on which to build a vision of the goals of education?

Maturing and the Goals of a Liberal Education

Because we have not listened carefully to students, we have failed to understand and assess and thus have underestimated schools' potential maturing effects on which to build a firm foundation for a vision of human excellence. Teachers devote 95 percent of their time to rearranging their liberal arts courses rather than learning how to teach them to fulfill their liberal educative potentials. Researchers use tests to assess schooling's effects that are not specifically designed to measure teachers' gifts or guided by any comprehensive model of schools' potential maturing effects. A critique of 2,600 research studies on colleges (almost none have been done on high schools) over the past thirty years questionably shows that they have quite meager effects. Few studies assessed the gifts that teachers wished for their students or the actual growth that students report. Joy of learning, enhanced curiosity, self-educating desires and skills, courage, compassion, and honesty, among other effects, were not even indexed.[49]

Accordingly, the next three chapters, which illustrate what schooling *could* produce *if* we created more maturing school and classroom environments, rely more on students' reflections of their growth than researchers' test results.[50] They examine in detail the

Figure 6.1. Maturing over Time.

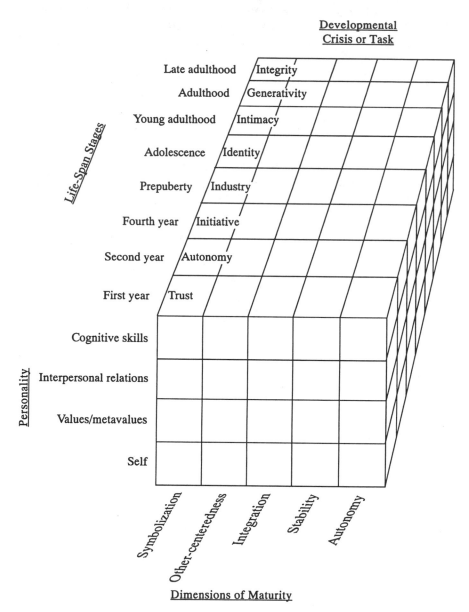

healthy growth of mind, character, and self that students can tell us about. They also draw on the wisdom of philosophers and the results of researchers of schools' measured effects.

The next chapter describes the maturing mind and how its strengths contribute to adaptation. Educators agree more about their goals for cognitive than for character development or self-development. We can get hold of, alter, even measure mind's products more easily than we can character's and self's. Because of the person's systemic unity, educating the mind also affects the maturation of character and self. So educating the mind has been societies' preferred route to forming the character and the self that are essential for adapting.

Chapter 7

The Maturing of Mind

The maturing mind is a wondrous miracle to behold. Its evolving powers are awesome: learning to understand and speak abstract words; wresting meaning out of written words; speaking and writing in an ordered, logical way; creating increasingly abstract ideas, such as n-dimensional spaces and black holes; bringing David out of a block of white marble; creating *King Lear* and *Tosca*; and in Cardinal Newman's words, securing "power over its own faculties." Our minds are our primary means of adapting and fulfilling ourselves.

What is the maturing mind like? Researchers and educators emphasize somewhat different ordering principles and attributes when describing its potentials. Psychologists such as Jean Piaget rely on logical operations,[1] Bloom and his colleagues on abstractness and complexity,[2] and Perry on multiplicity and relativism.[3] Influential educators have individually mentioned a great variety of powers: Charles Eliot, former president of Harvard, vivid imagination;[4] Edward Thorndike, pioneer educational psychologist, foreseeing consequences;[5] Robert Hutchins, former president of the University of Chicago, wisdom;[6] and John Henry Newman, foremost nineteenth-century Catholic educator, generalizing skills.[7] The College Board identifies thirty-five specific abilities necessary for work in college, including the abilities to separate one's personal opinions and assumptions from the facts and to use measurements in both traditional and metric units.[8] Agreement is not unanimous, however. Piaget, Bloom, and Perry, for example, do not mention imaginative, reflective, or inductive thought.

The five dimensional principles of maturing suggest one way to order mind's emerging principal powers. When categorizing a person's powers, we necessarily abstract ones that in real life do not function so purely. Also, the fewer ordering principles we use, the more arbitrary our categories may seem, particularly if our principles comprehend mind's most important adaptive powers. J. P. Guilford, a major researcher of the intellect, used different ordering principles to identify 120 intellectual abilities.[9] So the following list, which orders mind's principal adaptive strengths, may be incomplete, though it includes most of those that Bloom's pioneering taxonomy identified.[10]

Dimension	*Powers of a Mature Person's Mind*
Symbolization	Imagines possibilities
	Accurately and precisely represents, comprehends, and communicates internal and external experience
	Reflects about and induces from experience
Other-centeredness	Takes multiple perspectives
	Analyzes experience
	Judges realistically and objectively
Integration	Relates, synthesizes, and organizes knowledge
	Reasons logically and deductively
Stabilization	Has knowledge that is accurate, precisely differentiated, broad, complexly organized, readily accessible, resistant to stress interference, and, if temporarily disrupted or unavailable, readily recoverable
	Has skills that resist disorganization and if disrupted resiliently recover their efficiency

Autonomy   Judges appropriately, independently, and
                                critically
                            Has knowledge and skills that are mobile,
                                readily transferable, and available for
                                self-educating and creative purposes

In this chapter, I describe each cognitive power, its contribution to
adaptation, and a few of its philosophical adherents, and then cite
evidence of schooling's effects on its maturation. Referring to the
complete model of maturity in Appendix A while reading the chapter will aid in keeping the "whole" person and his or her systemic
complexity in view.

      Evidence is most scanty about middle and high schools' ef-
fects on their students. So I liberally quote students from several
independent schools and Bloomfield Hills' experimental Model
High School (MHS) as well as college students. Recall that the
MHS was designed to discover more effective ways to prepare students for their future. It created a competency-based and thematically organized curriculum. Chapter Ten describes its goals and
programs in more detail. The few studies that have followed students over time have relied mostly on self-descriptions about rather
than measures of education's specific cognitive effects. Since reflecting about one's own intellectual change is difficult, particularly for
youth whose reflective skill is just budding, researchers may underestimate schooling's varied cognitive effects.[11]

Highly Developed Symbolizing Skills

The skills of *consciously* articulating and manipulating our experience symbolically provide us great adaptive power. Philosophers
more than researchers of adolescent and adult development identify
such skills to describe maturing minds. Because such skills are so
basic to the maturation of mind's other powers, I examine in more
detail those that educators ignore in their preoccupation with teaching and measuring primarily reading and writing skills and those
of specific disciplines, such as mathematics.

Imagining Possibilities

By emphasizing *conscious* symbolization, I don't mean to devalue the contribution that less conscious modes of symbolizing make to maturing and adaptability. Night dreams and daydreams, reverie, intuition, and other forms of uncontrolled and unmonitored thinking that occur outside or at the edges of concentrated awareness can produce remarkably creative insights. They provide the imaginative ideas about how to adapt differently. They undergird reading comprehension, myths, poetry and other aesthetic and literary works, and, as Poincare told us, mathematical and scientific insight. Poincare describes how he had been wearyingly working on a problem without success and eventually yielded to dreamlike sleep, during which, he later wrote, "Ideas rose in crowds; I felt them collide until pairs interlocked, so to speak, making a stable combination. By the next morning I had established the existence of a class of Fuchsian functions. . . . I had only to write out the results which took but a few hours."[12]

Imagination secures its potential adaptive power by transforming images into disciplined forms of representation, particularly numbers and words. They are the principal ingredients of conscious thought and the carriers of accumulated knowledge. As Mark Van Doren, well-known interpreter of liberal education,[13] and Dewey[14] remind us, imagination then enables us to entertain many possibilities and anticipate consequences.

Evidence is sparse about how education affects imagination, possibly because few have studied it developmentally using similar measures. Imagination and its offshoots, originality and creativity, are not even indexed in the most comprehensive survey of studies of education's effects.[15] But why do about two-thirds of elementary school teachers but fewer than a third of high school teachers in excellent schools describe their typical student as imaginative? Or why do only a third of students and faculty judge their schools and faculties as imaginative? Or why do fewer than 20 percent view their schools as playful, an essential component of any imaginative activity?[16] The typical academic focus on mastering facts and developing analytical, logical, and critical modes of thought may crowd out if not squelch such growth from elementary school on. Harvard researchers believed that such suppression explained why seniors were no more creative than freshmen.[17] No wonder youth are so readily bored and depend on drugs to bring their deadened imaginative world back to life.

Representing, Comprehending, and Communicating Experience

Societies provide and value different modes of representing and communicating experience: hieroglyphics, words, numbers, mime, dance, graphs, music, art. Contemporary societies value most highly words and numbers, for, as Bruner reminds us, "the power of words is the power of thought."[18] A mature mind's accurate and precise verbal and numerical vocabularies powerfully contribute to successful adaptation, clarity of thought, and effective use of other cognitive skills. Television's and other audiovisual technologies' mode of representing reality may well be altering how highly we value words and numbers. Are they also limiting how well mind's adaptive potentials can be used?

Accurate and precise control of one's language, including its grammar and spelling, is also indispensable for effective communication, clarity of thought, and even survival, as the Eskimos well know—they need many more words for different types of snow than New Englanders do.[19] Enjoy these sad examples of the inaccurate and imprecise use of words.[20]

Ads

Used cars: Why go elsewhere to be cheated? Come here first!
Wanted: 50 girls for stripping machine operators in factory.
Vacation Special: Have your home exterminated.

Student Bloopers

We had a longer holiday than usual this year because the school was closed for altercations.
A triangle which has an angle of 135 degrees is called an obscene triangle.

Excuses

Teacher. Please excuse Mary for being absent. She was sick and I had her shot. Mary's Mom.
Please excuse Fred for being absent. He had a cold and could not breed well.

The past decade's cascade of national test results shows how dismally American schools are teaching students—and not just less privileged ones—to represent, comprehend, and communicate accurately and precisely. My more informal surveys show that only about 20 percent of teachers in our most favored high schools believe that today's students think clearly. As dismally, only 45 percent of teachers in such schools believe that their colleagues model clear thinking to their students.

Two of the many causes of sloppy and inelegant use of our language have been ignored. A language and how it is used reflect the experience and character of a people. We may not value accuracy, precision, and disciplined control as much as our grandparents did. Fewer than 15 percent of teachers describe their privileged students as self-disciplined and perfectionistic. Furthermore, many of today's teachers do not expect precise mastery of language or assume responsibility for its cultivation. I ruefully recall students' reactions to my constant correction of their imprecise use of words in class discussions and papers. After calling me "compulsive"—a particularly obnoxious type nowadays—they accusingly said, "Besides, you are not an English teacher. Other teachers don't turn back our papers to be rewritten because we don't spell or write carefully." When I urge teachers to become adjunct members of the English Department, most look glum, some even resentful. English faculty applaud; they know they fight a losing battle if not consistently supported by their colleagues.

Mastering reading, writing, spelling, and arithmetic is indispensable in contemporary information-service-technologically organized societies. So is mastering oral communicative skills, which are egregiously ignored by educators and reformers.[21] Our speech, more spontaneous than written words, directly mirrors the quality of our minds. Newman described early nineteenth-century people who lacked perfected oral skills as "madmen" who "once fairly started on any subject whatever . . . have no power of self-control; they passively endure the succession of impulses which are evolved out of the original exciting cause; they are passed on from one idea to another and go steadily forward, plodding along one line of thought in spite of the amplest concessions of the hearer, or wandering from it in endless digression in spite of his remonstrances."[22] Do our classrooms, committee meetings, and, yes, even faculty meetings have more mad people nowadays?

We learn to clearly articulate our ideas by articulating. A college freshman told me that when talking with his friends in bull sessions, "I was exposed to new ideas, and I was forced to respond to them, to defend my own positions as well as, perhaps, adjust to their positions, and this again had the overall intellectual effect of increasing my ability to express my thoughts."

A senior said that in trying to understand how the mind of his girlfriend worked, he learned that "some of our ideas are like anagrams. They are not really formed in your mind. But when you talk they all come out on the table and you can arrange them like anagrams and see what they mean. It's the ability to think out loud with someone in a very total and complete way, and when you say it a couple of times you begin to realize what the anagrams mean."

Since we learn to communicate orally from our relationships with others, it is not surprising that informal student activity rather than formal classroom activity spurs such growth.[23] Educators woefully ignore teaching students to "say it a couple of times . . . to realize what the anagrams mean." We educate for comprehending, writing, and passive listening but not for speaking, particularly in lecture-dominated and large classes. We delude ourselves to believe that students automatically learn even in smaller seminars how to communicate well from wandering, circuitous, and vague class discussions or question-and-answer sessions. Few educators self-consciously and systematically teach oral communication skills. Students, therefore, don't learn how to listen to and build on others' arguments, speak directly and economically, and logically organize and develop their own ideas or those of others. So they don't learn what they may really think.

Of the faculties I know, only that of Alverno College has

thoughtfully examined how oral and other communication competencies develop and also tenaciously evaluates how well it teaches them. Its researchers have independently shown that programs focused on oral and other communication modes can succeed.[24] Other researchers agree. College seniors write *and* speak more effectively than freshmen.[25] Such growth, of course, can occur prior to college. Effective communication, including speaking ability, is a priority competence for Bloomfield Hills' Model High School. When students described how they had changed during the year, improved communication skills ranked between four and six among maturing's twenty outcomes for three classes.[26]

Reflecting About and Inducing from Experience

As our minds mature, we increasingly can detach ourselves from the hubbub and confusion surrounding us to observe, describe, and monitor our minds. Reflection is fundamental to securing control over our minds. We have the unique ability to turn awareness back on itself, be aware that we are aware, and track consciously our own thought. Such ability is indispensable to communicating clearly and logically, regulating how we adapt moment by moment, hour by hour, and inducing from our immediate experience more general lessons about how to adapt to future situations.

My abilities to reflect and induce were recently tested when I substituted in a sick teacher's five social studies classes of ninth- and tenth-graders. Not knowing what they knew or their ability to think abstractly, I simultaneously monitored the words that I was about to speak, continuously observed their quizzical or blank looks, and occasionally interrupted myself to discover whether they knew a word that I had guessed they didn't know. I soon induced ideas about what ninth- and tenth-graders' minds were like in this teacher's classes and altered how I approached the remaining classes. That evening, I reflected about the day and induced what I had learned. I confirmed that forty-three-minute class periods encourage short attention spans and superficiality rather than thoughtful and sustained concentration. Can you now predict my reaction to those schools contemplating eight or nine thirty-four-minute periods per day to squeeze in more informational content?

Educators claim that reflective thought is a major goal and outcome of education. Alexander Meiklejohn, former president of Amherst, asserted that education should awaken "the impulses of inquiry, of experiment, of investigation, of reflection, the instinctive cravings of the mind."[27] Dewey also insisted that reflective behavior should be a primary goal, believing it to be "native to the mind," showing itself early in development, and blossoming into the scientific mode of inquiring, experimenting, and testing.[28] Hutchins called "intuitive knowledge," by which he meant inductive thinking, one of the basic intellectual virtues, as important as scientific, philosophical, and practical skills.[29] Knowing how to reflect and induce is essential to being a self-educating person.

Rudiments of reflective thought occur in childhood and more obviously by the pubertal years, as I have discovered when confronting eleven- to fourteen-year-olds about their relationships with each other. That fewer than 10 percent of high school teachers describe their typical students as reflective, however, may testify more to their didactic mode of teaching than to their students' potential to reflect. Though high school seniors are quite thoughtful about their relationships with others in interviews, they are still unable to describe in detail their own mental processes. As one perplexedly replied when asked, "How do I know? Sort of hard. I definitely know a lot more—a broadened horizon but that's about it."

A noticeable leap occurs in reflection and induction in the early college years, as noted by a freshman: "I think I've changed quite a bit here. I can truthfully say that Haverford has . . . made me look beyond the way things are, to look behind them. I was never aware of things behind. I lived, acted, did things. I had relations with people. I did not reflect beyond that to find out the causes, why I did them."

Though researchers report that students who go to college become more reflective than comparably intelligent peers who don't,[30] they may be more reflective about some aspects of their development than about others. A study of students at the University of New York, Buffalo, found that even juniors still had great difficulty reflecting about and describing themselves.[31] I have found that adolescents and adults more easily reflect about how their values or relationships have changed than about how their minds have.

This may be one reason so little good evidence is available about cognitive maturation during high school and college. Perry's study of the intellective changes of Harvard students is exceptional in revealing how reflective young adults can be about their maturing minds. However, he too found few who could describe in detail how their more relativistic mode of thinking came about.[32]

The ability to represent accurately and precisely our inner and outer experiences, the possession of a richly differentiated vocabulary, and the availability of imaginative, reflective, and inductive skills are simply "basic" to a mature mind. They are the essential foundations necessary on which to develop higher-order judgmental, relational, logical, and creative thought.

The mature mind is articulately discerning.

Other-Centered Cognitive Skills

Humans are inherently social. Other people enable us to survive early in life and to develop our potential more fully later in life. They provide us the language to represent our experience and the skills to use and communicate it meaningfully to others. Those, such as autistic or schizophrenic youth, who create their own language and grammar separate themselves from others and falter in adapting. The ability to know reality as others know it immeasurably extends our ability to adapt, particularly to our social world.

How do we learn what the reality is to which we must adapt? Piaget tells us that a child learns what a "thing," such as an orange, is by assimilating it to his different ways of knowing and existing categories of knowledge. By looking at, touching, holding, sucking, chewing, rolling, dropping, and throwing the orange, he learns that some round things are not like his ball. They taste better but don't bounce; they squash and squirt instead.

We learn similarly about social reality. The more diverse the ways in which we interact with others, the more likely we will know and understand them better. If we laugh, hike, play, sing, dance, hang out, and argue with others, not just talk or eat with them, we begin to know them and ourselves better. We may begin to understand more accurately how we are similar and dissimilar and why.

Taking Multiple Perspectives

Recognizing that others differ in how they view and interpret their world prepares maturing people to learn how to project themselves imaginally into the inner worlds of others and to view the outer world through their eyes.

The ability to understand accurately how another thinks and feels is critical not only to the development of later evolving cognitive skills but also to the maturation of our values, relationships, and self-concepts. Superb teachers know this. So do successful writers, advertisers, politicians, spouses, and parents. To write or persuade effectively, for example, requires understanding one's audience and the skill, in the words of the College Board, "to vary one's writing style, including vocabulary and sentence structure, for different readers and purposes."[33] To think relatively requires knowing that there are multiple ways of viewing and interpreting what is true. To work cooperatively with others requires understanding them well enough to anticipate how they may respond to criticism, sarcasm, or praise.

Educator after educator claims that education should teach a student the skill of empathically taking another's perspective on an issue. Newman says that a university should teach a student "how to accommodate himself to others, how to throw himself into their state of mind, how to bring before them his own, how to influence them, how to come to an understanding with them, how to bear with them."[34] William Cory, a master at Eton, told his students in 1861: "You go to a great school, not for knowledge as much as for arts and habits; for the habit of attention, for the art of expression, for the art of assuming at a moment's notice a new intellectual posture, for the art of entering quickly into another person's thoughts."[35]

Acquiring such a basic skill as "entering quickly into another person's thoughts," let alone empathically understanding that person's feelings, is most arduous. We trip over our own narcissism at every step. Our own perceptions of reality are extraordinarily coercive. What *we* believe must be true. Our own feelings are so immediately compelling that it takes persistent imaginative effort to transcend our embedded way of looking at and feeling about an issue to enter into another's. A college sophomore, feeling defeated trying to communicate with his girlfriend, plaintively said, "I am getting to know a little more about how a woman thinks. I guess it's going to take a long, long time before I ever know *what* a woman thinks."

Educators are right. A liberal education can draw students out of their subjective, self-centered, close-minded ways of looking at the world. While we cannot yet mark the approximate ages when such growth is *more* likely, my hunch is that it can occur in the high school years when appropriately educed. That high school debaters can argue opposing points of view tells us that. That social studies teachers tell me that their seniors can argue persuasively why Iranians were so hostile to the U.S. presence in the Persian Gulf also tells us that. That the College Board expects students to be able to vary their writing style, including vocabulary and sentence structure, to communicate to different audiences for different purposes and occasions also suggests that.

Focused interviews of high school students confirm that schooling can draw adolescents out of their egocentric way of thinking. A twelfth-grade boy in the MHS said that he had become "more objective now because I have been forced to look at many facets of particular problems." Other MHS students claimed similar effects. A ninth-grader said that his mind was "slowly becoming more open to new ideas and people"; an eleventh-grade girl mentioned that "students here have so many interesting viewpoints, I just have to listen in and contribute to them."

"Entering quickly into another person's thoughts" seems to take a quantum jump in a student's early college years. Numerous researchers identify "increasing openness to multiple aspects of the contemporary world" as a principal effect of higher education.[36] Alverno College's researchers have found similar growth in its women students,[37] as Perry has also found of Harvard men's cognitive development.[38] Students who think dualistically believe that there are right and wrong answers of which authorities are the arbiters. However, when confronted by diverse and conflicting views, students begin to recognize that there are alternative legitimate ways of viewing complex issues. They begin to think more relativistically.

Consistently reported signs of developing multiple perspectives are declines in black-and-white, authoritarian, and dogmatic modes of thought. Few other effects of education have been found so predictably, particularly in the first several years of college.[39]

Analyzing Experience

My analytical skill is being severely tested at this moment as I, a novice gardener, try to figure out why every morning three or four of my bean plants are cut off about two inches from the ground. Two weeks ago, I found that three rows of four- to five-inch-high plants had just disappeared. Stunned, then furious, then more calmly, I analyzed my "problem." Had the rabbit who has adopted me for the summer found a way in through the fence? No, the fence is impenetrable. Had I left the gate open? Possibly. But then I asked, "Could it have eaten three rows clean overnight?" Clearly not. What about deer? Could they jump from a standing position over my six-foot fence? Yes, my neighbor said. Next day my fence went up two more feet. But then I found three or four uneaten plants cut off every morning for the next several days. More deer? No. They weren't eating the leaves. Raccoons? No. They would have broken my flimsy fence. Porcupines? No. They eat only my spruce trees. Well, maybe deer after all. No. The plants were uneaten, and there were no hoofprints. Mystified, I despairingly watched my rows of beans systematically disappear, each time beginning at the end of a row and progressing methodically to the end. Stumped, I asked other neighbors. Hypothesis: something in the garden itself—a grub of some sort? Cutworms? How to test this idea? Put a barrier, such as a tin can, around each plant so the cutworms can't get to it. My epic will continue as I had to rely on more advanced "higher-order" skills to adapt to my disappearing garden.

The skill of accurately analyzing all of a problem's relevant possibilities and its solutions' consequences is essential to effective adaptation. After reviewing different views about education's goals, a team of Harvard researchers concluded that a "hallmark of the liberally educated person" is "disciplined flexibility in analytic thinking."[40] Assuming that analysis depends upon the skill of taking multiple perspectives, they assessed analytical skill by asking students to take and defend two opposing views toward a controversial issue.

Education does enhance analytical skill. The Harvard team confirmed others' findings[41] and what senior after senior told me also. "I think that I'm better able to analyze new questions than I was before. I always see things in perspective as a result."

Educating for analytical skill, as for every other skill, depends on the maturational level of students' imaginative, communicative, reflective, and other earlier developing skills. For example, Piaget found participating in arguments early in life to be a potent contributor to analytical development, as rabbis have known for centuries. Wandering the streets of Old Jerusalem, I heard a cacophony of boys' voices. I saw through an open door pairs of students intently arguing with each other while studying their open texts. Disciplined by their texts, they were learning through guided dispute how to articulate, anticipate the other's argument, search for meanings, and so analyze.

My patient grandfather taught me when I was fourteen years old what analysis means. He showed me how before moving a chess piece to think like a knight or bishop and then to view my intended move from the position of each of the opposing pieces. Only after I had told him how each saw the move would he let me go ahead to select my move. What a moment when, after years of being checkmated, I checkmated him. He proudly said, "You've begun to analyze." My disappearing beans tell me I've still got a way to go.

Judging Realistically and Objectively

As Dewey has told us, the development of an intellectual skill alters other attributes of mind and character. Learning how to take and analyze multiple perspectives, for example, increases open-mindedness, which for Dewey "includes an active desire to listen to more sides than one; to give heed to facts from whatever source they come; to give full attention to alternative possibilities."[42] Students know what Dewey means. "Slowly increasing openness to new ideas and people" is how one ninth-grade boy described MHS's effects. A tenth-grade girl simply wrote that "the faculty has taught me to be more open-minded when talking about world issues." One effect of becoming more open-minded is more realistic and objective judgment. When open to different viewpoints, even of those with whom we disagree m(st heartily, we see an issue "all the way around"; that is, more in terms of the issue itself than in terms of only our idiosyncratic stance or viewpoint.

Few educators have talked about judgment qua judgment as a goal or outcome. They refer to its processes using other terms, such as ability to discriminate, "observe keenly,"[43] compare, evaluate, and make "good sense."[44] Bloom's taxonomic effort identified judgment as "evaluation" as the highest form of cognitive attainment.[45]

What might realistic and objective judgment mean? We must often make judgments about problems when we have insufficient information, which we must either provide, infer, or assume; we then must evaluate its relevance, "fit," or importance according to some criterion of *appropriateness*, rather than of logical or deductive correctness or social convention.[46] Most real-life problems demand judgment because we never have complete information or consensual agreement about what an adequate solution is. Other modes of thinking, including reflection, logical deduction, analysis, and synthesis, may also be called for before we make our judgments.

Judgment has two frequently confused meanings. Realistic and objective judgment is basically an *other-centered* skill. Bloom's independent, critical, evaluative judgment is basically an *autonomous* skill, though it must involve realistic and objective judgment to be optimally adaptive. Just as a person may analyze well but make poor judgments, so a person may make realistic and objective judgments, show common sense, and demonstrate "good reality testing," as a clinician would put it, but not necessarily be good at independently and critically evaluating an issue. Lack of realistic judgment is a key diagnostic sign of schizophrenia; lack of independent critical judgment certainly isn't. As a later evolved form of thought, we do not expect even nonschizophrenics to think so maturely. The mature mind that can critically evaluate an issue must have first appraised it realistically and objectively before taking an independent stance toward it.[47]

Until the early seventies, researchers had few good measures of judgment.[48] They have now confirmed that judgment qualitatively evolves from what I label realistic or objective judgment to independent, critical judgment as students move from high school, through college, and into graduate school.[49]

The mature mind is realistically empathic.

Making Complex Integrations

Educators, students, and researchers studying education's effects agree that a mature mind makes connections—organizes experience into meaningful, consistent, and logical patterns. Recall Newman's description of chaotic minds: "contradicting themselves in successive sentences, without being conscious of it . . . after they have been driven from their opinions, [they] return to them the next moment without even an attempt to explain why."[50] A freshman woefully told me several weeks into his first semester, "My mind is like a thousand pieces going in a thousand different directions." A senior would never say that about his or her mind.[51]

What integrative skills contribute to and result in the mature person's more complexly ordered mind?

Relational, Synthetic, and Organizational Skills

A person may analyze superbly but synthesize dismally. A budding physicist freshman complained, "I know I've got all of the facts, but I can't find the keynote." I think I have noted all the relevant facts about my hapless bean plants, formed a reasonable hypothesis that makes sense of them, and taken steps to test it. But my synthesis may be wrong; I still may have missed some clues or put together incorrectly the ones I have.

Knowledge of facts is not enough. Every liberal educator agrees. To tell a student that he is educated because he knows a lot of facts, excels in Trivial Pursuit, and gets an achievement test score of 90 percent deludes him about the powers he will need as an adult. Meiklejohn would tell Amherst freshmen at their opening convocation to learn how "to take human activity as a whole . . . [and] understand human endeavors not in their isolation but in their relations to one another";[52] Henry Wriston, former president of Brown University, would tell them to develop the "discipline of reflective synthesis";[53] and Hutchins would tell University of Chicago freshmen to learn how "to connect man with man . . . connect the present with the past."[54]

As Piaget told us, the maturation of relational skills begins when an infant combines several habits, such as looking, grasping, and bringing his bottle to his mouth to suck, to make a more complex schema. These sensory-motor patterns are the roots out of which fifteen-year-olds will write increasingly more coherent, organized, abstract, and complex stories—eventually even books like this.

Schooling can produce more relational, synthetic, and organized minds. A ninth-grade MHS boy wrote, "I'm becoming better organized with work and time." Another confidently asserted, "I can relate many things without knowing much about them."

Researchers tell us that adolescents who go to college develop more flexible and complex minds than equally intelligent ones who don't.[55] Compared to freshmen, seniors form more complex concepts, integrate them better, and think more relativistically.[56] Their minds are richer, possessing more potential schemata, such as aesthetic interests, to which to relate their ideas.[57] If a new student at the University of New York, Buffalo, asked a sophomore how college had changed him, he would tell her, "Last year nothing tied in, this year everything is really tying in. . . . Logic is, sociology is, they're all fitting together in a groove, which makes me feel good that things are related."[58] A Haverford senior would talk about the maturing effect that a particular teacher had had upon him.

> He helped me develop an ability to go through the writings and thought of an individual and pull out just what is the meaning he is trying to express, what is the personal need that he is trying to satisfy for himself, how this all fits together with other philosophies either that he or others have held, or what it

says in general about the emotional or philosophical tradition in which he is writing.

Haverford's principal effect was, in fact, to encourage relational and synthetic thinking. Studies of its alumni ten to twelve years after their graduation showed that the integration of complex materials improves far into the adult years. The alumni became more able to "put things together" and "organize material for a purpose" as they learned how to integrate their theoretical knowledge with the practical problems of law, medicine, and business.[59]

Logical and Deductive Reasoning

The ability to deduce and order ideas logically is such a powerful adaptive skill that Piaget believed that logical operations are the core of intelligence. Formal operational or logicodeductive thought emerges in late adolescence and is, for Piaget, the principal contributor to adaptation. Others disagree.[60] They claim that postformal reasoning skills such as critical or evaluative judgment emerge later and contribute as much to adaptation. The dimensional view of maturing also questions the centrality of logicodeductive reasoning to adaptation.

What does research show about schooling's contribution to logicodeductive thought? A twelfth-grade MHS boy said that the school had "sharpened my thinking skills. Been using many different skills, such as deductive reasoning, logic, and intellectual broad mindedness." However, research shows that only about 50 percent of entering college students can think formally, in contrast to what Piaget had claimed. Furthermore, while college undoubtedly can spur logicodeductive thinking, particularly in the first two years, its development is not inevitable.[61] Why? Because we don't teach our courses in ways to educe logical reasoning. Mastering math and symbolic logic—the exemplars of deductive thinking—does not necessarily improve logical thinking. I agree with Lynn Steen, former president of the Mathematical Association of America, who believes that not until teachers self-consciously use math to teach logicodeductive reasoning, rather than *only* math, and then teach it for the skill's transfer and application to other, non-mathematical topics will mathematics' full liberally educating potentials be realized.[62]

Might not teaching a student how to outline a paper be a more efficient way to teach logical reasoning formally? Since the sixties, I have found that increasing numbers of students merely listed their ideas rather than ordering their relative importance. When teaching for logical thinking, I asked and helped students to outline their papers. I first guided them to order their ideas as follows:

I.   Principal idea
     A.   First subordinate idea
          1.   Paragraph
               a.-e. Sentences
          2.   Paragraph
               a.-g. Sentences
     B.   Second subordinate idea
II. Principal idea

I then asked them to defend why they put I. before II., A. ahead of B., A.1. before A.2., and, eventually, I.A.2.e. before I.A.2.f. rather than before I.A.2.c. When made aware of the logical structure of thought, and its absence in their own papers, some rapidly improved in writing logically coherent papers. One was so proud of his paper that he sent it to his former high school English teacher to show he "could do it." The word processor provides an ideal means for teaching today's stapler-students how to logically reorder their papers. To rewrite laboriously more than a paragraph or two in longhand nowadays trespasses too far on their ability to tolerate its frustration.

The mature mind is ordered and ordering.

Stabilization of Knowledge and Skills

Learning to solve problems produces knowledge and perfected skills that when readily available immeasurably improve adaptation. We stabilize knowledge by test and practice. My bean-preservation hypothesis proved to be stupendously wrong within five hours of its test. Four of my larger plants succumbed that afternoon, when cutworms were supposedly hiding deep in the earth. My analysis had been faulty and my proposed synthesis deadly. A belated call to the county agricultural agent told me that cutworms are attracted to moisture. The tin cans into which I had poured water in the early morning to resurrect my plants provided an ideal feeding ground for cutworms. Next year, I plan to be able to eat beans because I hope to recall the facts I have learned this year. More important, I hope that I have learned to think more clearly when I'm upset.

The beauty and power of the mind lie not in its specific knowledge but in how stabilized it is. Our minds have the remarkable ability to function efficiently under severe stress, such as deciding in four minutes whether to ignore, shoot at, or push the nuclear button upon seeing a radar blip of an approaching object—or instantaneously recalling at our command a fact that we have not thought of for forty years.

Dimensionally Mature Knowledge

Educators talk far more about what specific knowledge an educated person should have than about its generic adaptive qualities. Knowledge is essential, an empty mind can't learn how to reflect or synthesize. But what vocabulary and facts mark the mature mind? Americans have argued this question since the mid-eighteenth century, when Benjamin Franklin, America's exemplar of utilitarianism, rejected the European classical tradition. He insisted that Americans should learn useful knowledge and learn how to instruct themselves.[63] No other criterion than personal usefulness unites most educators. By "useful" facts, I mean facts necessary to survive and be a good citizen, such as knowledge about how to take care of one's body, eat properly, and fill out income tax forms. Surely, personally useful knowledge is a minimally necessary but scarcely inspiring or sufficient mark of the mature and liberally educated mind.

Different interest groups offer their own parochial criteria of what every educated person should know. Publishers rely on disciplinary experts and past texts; the National Assessment of Educational Progress also relies on widely cited textbook facts; the College Board's objectives are drawn from the judgments of educators, parents, and businesspeople about what students need to know for college;[64] St. John's College depends on history's "great books"; Brown University accepts a student's own interests; and Louisiana's legislators vote for religious beliefs such as creationism.

Agreement about what is useful or essential to know progressively fades when we climb the academic ladder. Geometry is considered useful by some but not by Dwight Allen, a former dean of education. Are two years of algebra necessary? Everyone says yes. But other than scientists and engineers, few other adults ever use its quadratic equations. College faculty vigorously disagree about what is essential to know. I recall a physicist arguing that every educated person should know the second law of thermodynamics. By his definition, an uneducated Shakespearean scholar replied, every person should know who Prospero was—which this particular physicist proceeded to identify in delightful detail. Hirsch's proposed core 5,000 facts that any culturally literate person should know aroused a sympathetic response, but I doubt many faculties incorporated such facts into their courses.[65]

Perhaps out of despair from listening to such faculty arguments, James Conant, former president of Harvard, urged that education "should . . . [refer] to a process rather than a program of study. . . . [T]he idea that it describes a consistent and generally accepted pattern of studies . . . is a myth. I defy anyone to discover in the stated aims and practices of our colleges and universities anything consistent enough to justify the term 'liberal education' as it is commonly employed."[66]

Actually, such disagreement need not paralyze our quest to describe the mature mind in developmentally dimensional terms. Formal qualities rather than knowledge of 5,000 or 105,000 culture-specific or time-bound items may more properly describe any *generic* understanding of the mature mind that applies universally, irrespective of one's specific culture.

Growth in symbolization suggests that knowledge becomes more accurate and precisely differentiated.

Increasing other-centeredness suggests that knowledge becomes richer and broader. Given our social nature, individual self-fulfillment requires knowledge of what humans are and could be. "[No] man realizes himself as an *individual* man except as he comes to understand through the breadth of his knowledge his identity with all men."[67] Most philosophers agree, as do those who believe in a common core for general education. To take multiple perspectives accurately in an ever more interdependent world, one must know not only one's own but at least some others' history, language, culture, and psychology.

Progressive integration means that knowledge becomes more complexly organized and patterned, which makes its stabilization easier.

Increased stabilization enhances knowledge's ready accessibility, its resistance to interference by stress, and if temporarily disrupted or blocked, its ability to be resiliently recoverable. That knowledge and skills are dependable is essential to efficient adaptation.

Growth in autonomy leads to increased mobility and transferability of knowledge so that it becomes freely available for use in any novel situation.

I have found little research that has explored whether education contributes to the maturing mind in these generic ways. College students are predictably more knowledgeable than equally intelligent adolescents who did not go on to college.[68] College seniors have more aesthetic knowledge than freshmen.[69] Reassuringly, surveys show that the richer knowledge of cultural facts that postsecondary education provides persists into the adult years.[70]

Resistance to Disorganization

With the exception of Newman, who says that an educated person's intellect is steady and not easily "startled,"[71] I have found no educator who writes explicitly about the efficient use of one's mind in stressful situations. Freud, however, had some wise insights about the core attribute of the mature mind. He claimed that its "thinking . . . concern[s] itself with the connecting paths between ideas, without being led astray by the *intensities* of those ideas."[72] A mature mind's analytical skill would not be undone by fury about losing bean plants, its judgment distorted by a family's political arguments, or its logical thinking derailed by the stress of an SAT.

Transcultural research has demonstrated that Newman and Freud are correct: mature men's analytical, judgmental, and logical conceptualization skills are indeed more stable than those of equally intelligent but immature men's when they must use them to connect threatening ideas. Furthermore, the research found that when the mature men's skills were "led astray by the intensities of the ideas" of the problems they were solving, they recovered more resiliently and efficiently than did the immature men.[73]

Education can stabilize such skills. An eleventh-grade MHS girl said of her mind, "It has matured; I don't get so frustrated as easily when I'm faced with a problem." Perry claims that learning how to think relativistically protects one's thought from such emotional frustration and disruption. One of his Harvard students, aware of this effect, said, "The more I work here, the more I feel . . . [like] a detached observer of various situations. . . . I mean, one who can . . . detach himself emotionally from the problems and look at the various sides . . . in an objective, empirical type of way. . . . I think it all boils down to trying to remove emotionalism from your decisions."[74]

Intriguingly, apparently unaware of the transcultural study of cognitive stability and resiliency, Harvard researchers independently identified such skills as central to becoming educated. Using similar methods, they found that seniors' problem-solving skills were more stable than freshmen's.[75]

A mature mind's knowledge and skills are accessible when called upon.

Autonomous Command of Mind's Skills

"To the Athenian at least, self-rule by discussion, self-discipline, personal responsibility, direct participation in the life of the polis at all points—these things were the breath of life."[76]

From the time of Socrates to that of contemporary educators, students, and researchers, uncommon agreement exists. A mature person commands his or her own powers. Education liberates the mind from the rule of prejudice, dogmatism, and passion[77] to be able to "weigh evidence dispassionately"[78] and critically. It also frees the person from the domination of convention and authority to be self-educating and creative.

Appropriate, Independent, and Critical Judgment

The maturing of mind leads to the creation of internal standards or criteria by which to judge. A Harvard student said of his growth, "You get perspective on the world. . . .You have more facts at your command on which you can make decisions . . . hence you are no longer forced to rely on hearsay. . . . You can actually consider the questions yourself. . . . [Y]ou can exercise your own judgment."[79]

To adapt well, independent and critical judgment must also be appropriate and must consider the perspective of others and the facts of an issue. As an educator, I tried always to examine for such judiciousness: "State your position and defend it by citing relevant evidence, taking into account contradictory or opposing evidence and views." When examining seniors for college honors, I asked, "What are your criteria for determining what is fact, the truth of an idea, the worth of a theoretical position? Why are they more adequate than other types of criteria?"

Research compellingly confirms that schooling can produce more autonomous minds.[80] Compared to adolescents who did not go to college, those who did became "less stereotyped and prejudiced in their judgments, more critical in their thinking, and more tolerant, flexible, and autonomous."[81] Others have also found these maturing changes.[82] Ernest Pascarella and Patrick Terenzini claim that college's effect on evaluative or critical judgment is selective: College "appears to enhance one's ability to weigh evidence, to determine the validity of data-based generalizations or conclusions, and to distinguish between strong and weak arguments. There is less support for the claims that college has a unique effect on one's ability to discriminate the truth or falsity of inferences, recognize assumptions, or determine whether stated conclusions follow from information provided."[83]

Mobility and Availability of Knowledge and Skills

The maturing mind's knowledge and skills become increasingly independent and detached from the original context in which they were stabilized. They become freely available, mobile, transferable. While *stabilization* refers to strengthening habits or skills, *autonomy* refers to their internalization and so their ready transferability to new situations. Consider the miracle of learning to read: the months of laboriously stabilizing the skill and then its rapid transferability to every kind of material anywhere at any time. Reading has become autonomitized, no longer tied to current readers and workbooks.

The most meaningful test of what we know is not its recall but its effective use in other situations than those in which it was learned. That physics teachers complain that students cannot use their calculus with physics problems warns us that the calculus has not been autonomitized. That students don't write as carefully for history as they do for English courses tells us that good writing has not become an integral part of their brains. My test of whether a biology major has learned the skills of science is to give her problems from social studies, not from biology, to approach like a "scientist." No wonder our measures of factual recall predict so little later in life; they don't measure the autonomy or real transferable power of the maturing mind.

Philosophers such as Newman, Whitehead, and Dewey believe that education's ultimate goal must be to secure command of our own minds. It should so enhance our control over knowledge and skills that we can freely apply them to novel and complex situations. Another of mind's miracles is its ability to use its knowledge and skills to operate on its own knowledge and skills to direct, monitor, and further its own continued growth and adaptation.

For this reason, many educators value most highly the self-directing, self-educating person. Early Americans felt similarly. Benjamin Franklin and Thomas Jefferson believed that a democratic government needed a continuously self-educating people. Ralph Waldo Emerson urged us to become a self-reliant people. Abraham Lincoln is America's archetypal model of the self-taught president. Some contemporary psychologists believe similarly. Robert Sternberg believes, as I do, that intelligence must refer to how mentally adept we are in managing ourselves and so enhancing our ability to adapt.[84]

Self-Educating Minds. What is a self-educating person's mind like? It is the maturing mind that I have been describing, which is capable of using its knowledge and skills to teach itself new knowledge and skills. It is able to articulate and set goals for what it wants to know; reflect on and monitor the efficiency of its own learning; induce ideas about how to improve its own efficiency; anticipate questions others may ask of what it has learned; analyze, relate, organize, and judge what is more or less important to learn; organize what it is learning in ways that facilitate its memorization; test the availability of what has been learned by using it; and discriminatingly accept and learn from criticism about how well it has taught itself. It has learned how to learn efficiently.

Few have studied the self-educating effects of schooling, as central as they are to becoming mature and liberally educated. Chapter Three reported that neither teachers nor students judge most students to be able to educate themselves. Moreover, students do not describe themselves as able to teach themselves. Schools have a long, long way to go before their students, even college-bound ones, will be autonomous learners in command of their own talents.

Teachers must first learn how to give their students meaningful responsibility for their own maturing. The Model High School sought to do that by developing more self-educating cognitive skills. A ninth-grade boy wrote, "I'm now using my mind as a tool to do what I want to do; using it to see viewpoints other than my own." A tenth-grade boy spontaneously said, "I developed my own study skills and approaches so I am now a competent writer and know many new sources for finding information." A ninth-grade girl wrote, "I don't feel I have more intellectual skills than others; I just have learned how to use mine to my advantage."

The best formal evidence that schooling can empower cognitive autonomy comes from studies of the effects of Alverno College's competency-based curriculum. The students could transfer the skills learned in their classrooms to solve simulated real-life complex problems as judged by community professionals.[85]

Creative Minds. Finally, a mind in control of itself greatly enhances its potential creativity. Creativity requires that knowledge and skills be mobile and transferable; that is, freely combinable and recombinable into original products. *Divergent thinking,* a strength of creative people, is but another name for disembedding familiar ideas and concepts from their conventional contexts and meanings and imaginatively reconstructing alternative ones.

More critically, and paradoxically so, the autonomously mature mind is most capable of allowing itself to temporarily abandon its control. It can permit socially forbidden impulses, wishes, and fantasies into awareness and enter deeply into the imaginative underworld of dreams, archetypal modes of thinking, myth, even the inner illogical world of the psychotic—the essential stuff of creative ideas. Most important, it can recover its control at its own command. The maturely autonomous mind does not need drugs to get access to the unconscious. Failure to understand mature people's control over their own regressive and disorganizing experiences has led some researchers to misinterpret their findings that seniors describe themselves as more impulsive and, in some studies, more "neurotic" than freshmen.[86] The more autonomous seniors have accepted and integrated more of their humanness into a more complex level of maturity *but under their control.*[87]

The maturing mind is freed to use its full powers.

The knowledge and skills of the maturing mind contribute mightily to successful adaptation, self-education, and creativity. But mind's strengths are not enough. Character strengths are also necessary if mind's strengths are to reach their full potential. We have seen liberal education's potential effects on the maturing mind. What can it contribute to the maturation of character—our interpersonal relationships and values?

Chapter 8

The Maturing of Character

We educate students, not just their minds. So the maturation of one attribute depends on and affects that of others. Teaching how to take multiple perspectives encourages tolerance and understanding. Educating exclusively for analytical and critical thinking can suppress empathy and sympathy. Nurturing cooperative learning skills and demanding persistence enable mind's maturation. Snuffing out curiosity and eroding self-confidence impede it.

Every philosopher of whom I am aware attributes some character traits to liberally educated people. Though influential ones such as Newman and Hutchins firmly assert that schools' only goal is to discover truth and not educate for character, each backtracks from that position. Newman says an educated person is a gentleman who, among other traits, has calm and steady command of himself;[1] Hutchins says he has a "social consciousness and a social conscience" with moral standards "based on reason and not on authority."[2] Other educators expressly claim that character maturation should be a primary goal. Sydney Hook, within the tradition of early American educators such as Franklin, Jefferson, and Horace Mann and later ones such as Dewey and Van Doren, is emphatic. Schools should strengthen loyalty to democratic ideals and the ability to "stand alone" in their defense.[3] Marie Syrkin wrote of developing social interest,[4] Boyd Bode of cooperation,[5] Earl McGrath of respecting others' rights and views,[6] and Francis Parker of contributing to a "sound community life."[7]

Not one of the hundreds of school and college catalogues that I have analyzed ignores character in its mission statement. Most faculties prize the development of interpersonal strengths such as empathy and values such as tolerance. Sehome High School of Bellingham, Washington, committed to creating "a school for the twenty-first century," identified among other indispensable strengths caring, cooperative skills, and liking for others and oneself.

Alverno College selected interpersonal maturity and value maturity as two of the eight most important competencies that students need for their future. No other faculty of which I am aware has as thoughtfully identified how to educate for competence in social interactions. It has carefully created curricular sequences for its students to master before graduating and then rigorously assessed their effects. So I return to Alverno's views throughout this chapter.

How can we identify the interpersonal skills and values that should be liberally educating goals? I know of no comprehensive efforts to identify mind and character attributes that use the *same* systemic ordering principles. Bloom's effort focused on cognitive and value development and ignored interpersonal and self-development; Piaget's, Kohlberg's, and Perry's efforts have been similarly limited. Chapter Six argued that the model of maturing provides the systemic principles that order the development of mind *and* character *and* self. What do its assumptions tell us about a maturing person's interpersonal skills and values?

Interpersonal Maturation

Interpersonal, as well as mind's, maturation prepares the way for the maturation of values and self. Relationships provide the crucible out of which develop not only conscience and ethics but also self-attitudes and identities. Mature people sensitively understand and empathically care about others, can work together cooperatively, and, while able to create enduring interdependent work and intimate relationships, can accept aloneness when such relationships are not available. Again, refer to Appendix A to keep in mind that it is a person, not just his or her character, that matures. The following list summarizes the maturing person's core interpersonal skills.

Dimensions	*Attributes of a Mature Person's Interpersonal Relationships*
Symbolization	Being sensitive to and perceptive about others and one's relationships with them
	Being psychologically minded and understanding others
Other-centeredness	Empathically feeling for, caring about, respecting, and enjoying people who differ from oneself
Integration	Being genuinely open and spontaneous in relationships
	Creating cooperative mutual work and intimate relationships
Stability	Being loyal and faithful to friends and organizations
	Having friendships and work relationships that persist and are not readily broken by argument and strain
Autonomy	Being independent and self-reliant and tolerating aloneness if necessary
	Selectively forming interdependent relationships

In this chapter, I briefly describe how strengths in each of these areas contribute to a person's adaptation and their relationship to the liberal education tradition and then summarize the evidence that schooling can nurture their maturation. Evidence is practically nonexistent for elementary and junior high schools, rather flimsy for high schools, and firmer for colleges. Few have compared students to nonstudents to separate out schooling's effects from the effects of just "growing up." Nor are good objective ways available to measure directly many of the interpersonal strengths that the model of maturity describes. However, searching interviews of students in diverse schools consistently identify similar interpersonal outcomes and those aspects of schools that contribute most to their development.

Symbolization of Interpersonal Relationships

The roots of interpersonal skills reach back into an infant's early cognitive and social experience. Infants apparently begin to become aware of their mothers' voices when still in their wombs. Babies actively attend and react to others, empathically feel others' tension, learn how to mold themselves to their parents' ways of holding and nursing them, develop strong and selective attachments, and "amuse" themselves when others are not present. Such potential and rudimentary interpersonal skills, while programmed neurologically, depend for their maturation on how others encourage their cognitive as well as social development.[8]

We ceaselessly interact with others as spouses, parents, friends, and workers. Mature interpersonal skills, as Chapter Six demonstrated, obviously contribute to how well we get along. Awareness of another's needs, foibles, and strengths as well as of our own skills in getting along with others provides the information necessary to fulfill our roles well. Perceptive people are able to accurately infer the motives of others, even those unknown to those others, to understand telltale signs of tension and defensiveness, and thus to respond appropriately.

Until recently, only a few educators identified interpersonal awareness, understanding, and psychological mindedness as prominent attributes of a liberally educated person. Newman, Meiklejohn, and Dewey believed that educated people should understand humans and their social relationships. Today, more educators acknowledge that schools should develop such skills.

Intriguingly, Alverno's faculty, without any knowledge of the model of maturity's sequential ordering of interpersonal development, ordered its curriculum similarly to further social interaction. Becoming interpersonally *aware* is the first step toward that goal: "Level 1 initiates the student by requiring her to *observe and assess* her own behavior in a task oriented group . . . to identify and evaluate her interpersonal behavior patterns . . . to perceive the effect on others of her verbal and non-verbal contributions . . . to articulate her own goal in the situation and that of the group."[9]

Do students mature in their understanding of others and their relationships as a result of schooling? Yes. Measures of Haverford men's increased interpersonal awareness from their freshman to senior year ranked it fourth in importance of maturing's twenty possibilities. Reflecting about the effect of living in a dormitory, one said, "When I was in high school . . . I never got to know my friends' insides. Here I'd see guys getting drunk, having trouble with their girls, problems with their parents. I learned an awful lot about human beings. I had just been completely isolated from them before." A senior perceptively described his growing awareness of others this way: "I don't think I was aware before of the different levels you can take people on, you must take people on: how serious you have to be with them; how much of yourself you divulge to them; how much you go out of your way to adjust to them like doing small things for them; how much you see them as means."

Other researchers report similar maturing. Fifty percent of the resident freshmen at the University of New York, Buffalo, felt that they had become more sensitive to and better judges of others,[10] changes also found in Harvard and Alverno students.[11] Increased understanding of others was also found in a study of students at seventy-four colleges and universities.[12]

Not surprisingly, increased interpersonal understanding typically occurs as a result more of informal peer relationships than of formal academic or curricular programs. The character of a school's students, male and female friends, and especially roommates can provoke increased sensitivity and understanding.[13] However, a curriculum and faculty teaching methods designed to enhance such maturing can also contribute to interpersonal awareness. Studies of Alverno College's program[14] and cooperative learning-teaching methods[15] demonstrate that enhanced interpersonal awareness can be taught.

Other-Centered Interpersonal Relationships

Chapter Six showed that empathy, care, and respect for others are essential for us to succeed in our various roles. They will be even more indispensable in the future. As technology continues to shrink our planet psychologically, we will increasingly meet, communicate with, and work with people different from ourselves. To communicate clearly and persuasively, we must not only be able, as

Newman said, to "throw" ourselves mentally into the minds of others. We must also enter empathically into their hearts to feel as they feel. One faculty, grounded in a religious tradition that valued service to others, made other-centered interpersonal maturation a priority educational goal. It required all students to serve at least two semesters abroad in a Third World country. When I met with the faculty, it was wrestling with how to develop the empathy—the ability to appropriately experience the emotionally subjective meanings of a Third World person's perspective—that its students would need for their year abroad.

Educators as diverse as Newman, Syrkin, McGrath, and Mann agree that a truly educated person respects, empathizes with, and sympathizes with others.[16] Bode wrote for other American educators concerned that schools develop the character necessary for a democratic society to endure. He urged schools to develop "the sympathy and cooperation that spring from understanding. . . . Our first obligation is to learn how to live together. This . . . is the democratic conception of a liberal education. It subordinates utilitarian interests to the great aim of making men human through the cultivation of a common life."[17] Van Doren extends other-centered interpersonal maturity to include empathizing with all humans. Liberally educated people are able to transcend their own special way of knowing to empathize with how a universal human knows and feels. Such a person "endeavors to rear within himself that third man who is present when two men speak, and who is happy when they understand each other."[18]

After Alverno students become more interpersonally aware, they begin to develop other-centered interaction skills. They must learn to "assume roles designed to help the group achieve its objectives. . . . [A]t Level 2 [they begin] *analyzing* social behavior systematically."[19] Evidence is not yet available to tell whether such an intellectual approach to developing interactional skills produces the empathy, sympathy, and respect that are at the heart of other-centered interpersonal maturity.

Considerable evidence now suggests that a liberal education enables students to take others' perspectives intellectually. I am aware of no evidence that it as effectively encourages empathic caring and respect.

However, methods designed to assess the model's twenty maturing effects found other-centered interpersonal growth to be among the two most frequently reported types of growth of three classes of MHS students. A tenth-grade boy spontaneously wrote, "I have become much more accepting of others' little quirks"; a tenth-grade girl reported, "I have learned to listen, close my mouth, and open my ears so I might learn something." Other-centered interpersonal growth was the fifth most salient type of growth of Haverford College students.[20] Other researchers report similar maturing.[21] A junior at the University of New York, Buffalo, described his other-centered maturing this way: "I think this year I'm listening more. I'm understanding what they're doing, and that some of these people really believe in what they are doing and I can value their ideas. . . . I can respect a person for his ideas. No matter how radical or how bad they are, I can still respect them if he really believes in his ideas."[22] Impressed by students' increased acceptance of and respect for others from his studies of their growth in thirteen small colleges, Arthur Chickering included interpersonal maturing as a principal outcome of a liberal education.[23]

That schooling can produce other-centered interpersonal growth is clear. But is education's promise realized very widely? No, at least not in contemporary students. Chapter Two reported that only a minority of faculty and students describe the typical student in their schools as empathic, accepting, caring, and sympathetic. Even fewer use such words to describe students in America's most academically competitive schools. Too narrow a view of academic excellence can suppress rather than encourage other-centered interpersonal maturation; it entrenches defensiveness and self-centeredness.

However, we can create schools that produce students who are both other-centered *and* academically excellent if we are committed to doing so. The MHS faculty was so committed. It successfully created a trusting and accepting interpersonal climate. When describing their peers at the end of their school year, 41 percent fewer MHS students judged their peers to be defensive and 37 percent fewer judged them to be self-centered than the students of their home schools so judged their peers. More MHS students also viewed their peers as interpersonally other-centered and academically excellent than their home peers so judged their typical student: 59 percent more accepting, 51 percent more empathic, 36 percent more open, and 31 percent more excellent. Clearly, academically excellent schools do not have to deepen self-centered defensiveness, if they create and implement a more humane view of their goals.

Integrated Interpersonal Relationships

Increased understanding, empathy, and respect prepare the way for the creation of cooperative team, work, and personal relationships. When each party is similarly understanding, empathic, and respectful, then mutual trust and openness can lead to a genuinely spontaneous "we-ness." More mature people are able to create such cooperative relationships unencumbered by persisting conflict, tension, and defensiveness. They therefore fulfill their roles more effectively.[24]

Until recently, only a few educators other than Meiklejohn, Bode, and Dewey believed integrative, particularly cooperative, relationships to be a proper goal of education.[25] Today, educators know that an increasingly interdependent world binds us ever closer to other peoples. Japan's emerging competitive preeminence stems in large part from its people's consensual way of organizing their relationships. So more and more assert that schools should encourage collaborative decision making, cooperative learning, and team building in the classroom—not just on the athletic field.[26]

Let's see what the Alverno faculty believes that the third step to social competence is. After students have become more interpersonally aware and other-centered, they should learn how to organize and relate what they have learned in the classroom and then integrate it into their individual and group relationships. The faculty teach students how to apply their intellectual integrative skills to their social interactions. A student "learns theoretical frameworks for both one-to-one and group situations. . . . In her increasingly complex analysis of group processes, she learns to discern proximate and long-term goals, and to make critical judgments [autonomy] regarding the effectiveness of both her own and others' specific choices of behavior . . . to relate to things, to information and to people in accomplishing the task . . . [and to] enabl[e] others to cooperate in perceiving and achieving their goals."[27]

Alverno students must master one level of social competence, as assessed by diverse measures, including community examiners, before qualifying for the next level. Independently conducted interviews of the college's students and alumnae confirm that students can learn such complex interaction skills.

Perhaps because individualistic, competitive learning, rather than collaborative learning, distinguishes American schools, evidence of their integrative interpersonal effects is scarce. The Model High School's accepting and collaborative learning environment did, in fact, encourage openness and integrative relationships. A tenth-grade boy said that MHS helped him to "decide to be completely honest with all my friends; now I have truer friends." A senior girl said she had "learned from peers; shared our gifts; and worked with each other as opposed to against each other."

Such interpersonal growth ranked third among the twenty principal ways in which Haverford men matured. However, that growth was confined almost exclusively to becoming more trusting, open, and spontaneously impulsive in their relationships. A freshman said of his roommate's effect on him, "He was the first person that I've been really able to be open and quite frank with. Because he's been really open himself, I found it much more easy to say things that I wouldn't to other people before this. . . . I think it's helped me to be open with other people as well. . . . It's helped me to be more self-confident. . . . I think self-confidence [stability] and self-assertiveness [autonomy] go along with this being open."

A senior said of his relationships with women, "We have a much more free and open relationship . . . just spontaneously . . . just being able to discuss things that really are on your mind rather than sort of elaborating on them before they come out. I mean before it was a conscious effort to disguise things as they might be, rather than talk about what is really on your mind."

Stable and Autonomous Interpersonal Relationships

What interpersonal skills does it take to adapt in a rapidly changing and mobile society that disrupts work relationships, unsettles personal relationships, impersonalizes schools, and dilutes communal ties? According to a twenty-five-year-old college-educated migrant worker, in between raking Maine blueberries and picking Vermont apples, one must "know how to be independent and accept aloneness but have a stable 'home' and a few permanent friends to return to." These days, a youth needs to be self-reliant when necessary, to resist the seductions and temptations that come from the need to conform and be approved by others, and to create selective interdependent relationships that endure. Loyalty and faithfulness to friends, lovers, families, and work-communal groups reassure others of our commitment. We become trusted; others can count on us. Not to split prematurely but to stay in a relationship and persist in working out its inevitable stresses and conflicts marks the mature person.

I combine stable and autonomous interpersonal maturation because educators have tended to ignore both as explicit goals of a liberal education. As one might expect of Dewey, he urged schools to educate students to free themselves of an authority's dictates. "For freedom is power to act and to execute independent of external tutelage. It signifies mastery capable of independent exercise, emancipated from the leading strings of others."[28]

The AIDS epidemic may force educators to pay closer attention to how they educate for interpersonal maturity. The Presidential Commission on AIDS urges that we educate students to develop "assertiveness to resist coercion by partners [autonomy] to engage in high-risk sex and develop . . . social skills to maintain stable relationships."[29]

If properly organized to sustain interpersonal maturation, schools can enhance the development of stable and autonomous relationships. When comparing their current with their ninth-grade friendships, three MHS senior girls used phrases such as "They are stronger now," "I'm more choosy about the relations I want, and therefore I give more to them," and "I'm no longer influenced by people who don't care for me."

The Alverno faculty explicitly recognizes that educating interaction skills requires their stabilization and autonomitization. Students achieve such maturation by practicing those skills in immediate academic and related situations and then by using them in increasingly different settings.

> At Level 4, the student is required to demonstrate *effective behavior* in a variety of settings, according to criteria she and her assessors have agreed upon. . . . Level 5 extends the student's operating range, by having her demonstrate her interaction skills during task oriented activities amid various cultures and subcultures. . . . Both Level 5 and Level 6 require consistency—the demonstration of competence over a period of time. [Stability] At Level 6 this commitment of sustained effort is directed toward organizational activity. This level demands that the student take responsibility and initiative, and employ her theoretical awareness and active skills in leadership. [Autonomy][30]

The Alverno researchers report that the undergraduates identified their interpersonal skills as the competencies most useful outside the classroom. They had learned to understand others better, overcome their shyness, and become more confident and thus more assertive in their relationships, over which they felt more control. The college's alumnae agreed.[31]

Residential universities contribute more than commuter universities to stable and autonomous relationships, particularly in the early college years.[32] Though upperclassmen report much deeper and lasting friendships than freshmen do,[33] more stable and autonomous friendships are not schools' salient effects. Compared to the twenty maturing changes that could occur in college, more stable and autonomous relationships ranked fourteenth and twentieth, respectively, as outcomes for Haverford men. They had yet to learn how to accept and integrate their suppressed emotionally dependent and affectional needs with their relationships. Not until some had had their own children did they become freer to develop more mature interdependent relationships.

Schools will not fulfill their potential for furthering interpersonal growth until they create learning environments that encourage it rather than thwarting it, as many do now. Large schools, impersonal and competitive learning climates, anonymous lecture courses, teachers swamped by 160 students a day, and single-room residential dormitories betray a flawed understanding of how critical interpersonal maturity is to the development of mind and character.

Value Maturation

The term *value* has numerous meanings, including interests, beliefs, attitudes, morals, ethics, preferences, and motives. I use *value* to refer to a dynamic dispositional tendency to seek out or avoid various goals. The following list indicates that a maturing person's values are accurately represented, socially centered, consistently organized, enduring, and free of determination by both impulsive wish and environmental control. Such maturation opens the way, prepares the characterological ground, so to speak, for valuing higher virtues or metavalues.

Dimensions	*Attributes of a Mature Person's Values*	*Metavalues*
Symbolization	Is aware of and articulates biases, assumptions, and values	Honesty Truth
Other-centeredness	Accepts and appreciates diverse views	Fairness
	Has humane values	Compassion
Integration	Sets priorities among values	Integrity
	Has values and behavior that are consistent with each other	

Stabilization	Has values that endure	Commitment
	Persists purpose-fully to achieve long-term goals	
Autonomy	Is motivated by considered principle rather than impulsive wish or envi-ronmental persuasion	Freedom
	Accepts responsi-bility for own values and maintains them in face of opposition	Courage

At first glance, such a dimensional view of value maturity seems to have no relationship to the hierarchical stage views of well-known researchers of moral development such as Piaget, Kohlberg, Perry, and James Rest.[14] But note, for example, the *underlying* dimensional assumptions of Kohlberg's three levels of moral matura-tion, each consisting of two stages, which are extended into adulthood by Perry.[35] Children at the egocentric level are initially *aware* only of their own interests but subsequently recognize *others'* interests, al-though they don't take them into account in their choices. Adoles-cents at the conventional level initially *integrate* others' feelings and interests into their own choices by following the Golden Rule and trying to live up to others' expectations. They subsequently extend their view of the individual other to include more abstractly society's rights and laws, which they take into account and seek to *integrate* into their own value choices. Adults at the postconventional or prin-cipled level are aware that their values, as well as those of others, are relative to their particular group. Initially, they believe that laws should be adhered to impartially and objectively because they consti-tute a social contract guaranteeing the rights and welfare of the largest number. Adults at the highest stage of moral development rationally choose their values and *make them their own* and commit themselves to universal *other-centered* principles of justice, such as equality and respect for others.[36]

Stage views of value maturation—indeed, of development generally—depend on underlying systemic dimensional development. Increasing awareness enables recognition of specific others' and then, more abstractly, society's values. Increasing other-centeredness encourages consideration and respect for another's views. Increasing integration enables people to harmonize their own and others' value choices. Increasing stability and autonomy prepare people to make their own enduring commitments to principles that transcend their own and their society's special interests.

Value maturation also depends on cognitive and interpersonal skills. Skills such as abstractly representing our choices, integrating our values into a coherent philosophy, empathically taking multiple perspectives, and mutually cooperating with others are essential for making mature value choices. Research shows, for example, that more empathic people make more mature value choices.[37] Kohlberg, as did Dewey, believed that the route to more mature values led by way of interpersonal growth. He proposed that if schools choose to educate for moral maturation, they must alter their teacher and student relationships and their decision-making processes and become genuinely democratic institutions.[38]

A dimensional understanding of value maturation assumes, as it does of cognitive and interpersonal development, that its roots are traceable back to our earliest experiences. Consider the roots of value autonomy. A person learns how to say no when six months old by spitting out the oatmeal his mother has just stuffed into his mouth, when sixteen months old by shaking his head back and forth, when two years old by being "stubborn," when six by refusing to go to school, when fourteen by threatening to run away from home, or when nineteen by consciously re-creating his values. He is learning how to make more autonomous value choices, first in relation to his family and then, gradually, in relation to others— his school, peers, and society.

How does value maturation affect our adaptation? Should

a liberal education seek to further such maturation? Does it in fact do so?

Symbolization of Values

Accurate awareness of our values and how they affect our decisions and actions greatly enhances our adaptability. Freud demonstrated how powerfully our less conscious wishes and motives can distort our view of ourselves and of others and propel us to act inappropriately. It is very human, even for the most mature, to see, hear, and interpret what we want to see, hear, and believe. Science's ethic of public verifiability provides a bulwark against scientists' tendency to discover their own biases in their observations, results, and interpretations. When students critiqued my courses, I recorded every comment, particularly negative ones—though reluctantly at times—knowing that I would otherwise "forget" the negative ones.

Liberal educators such as Bode, Thomas, and Van Doren agree that education should make students aware of their desires, beliefs, and prejudices and how they affect their moral and intellectual judgments.[39] Dewey and Hook, in particular, go further. They want schools to teach students how to reflect about the moral implications of social issues and become aware of the value assumptions of different proposed solutions.[40] Dewey recognized how our needs and wishes influence our choices and how those choices in turn alter our character. More than any other educator, he wanted students to become reflectively aware of why they choose as they do. Believing that the scientific mode of thinking frees intelligence from prejudice and bias, he urged that students learn how to apply it to the process of making more objective value choices.[41]

Little research has been done to assess how well schools and colleges teach students to reflect about and clarify their values. I recently listened to interviews with bright seniors from five independent schools about how their values had changed since ninth grade. Despite persistent questioning, few could identify significant changes. All that the most reflective person could say about how her values had changed was "I just question more. When I think of something now, I think of why. Take abortion. I think about how I got such ideas. I try to understand the reason I am what I am. I don't want to be different."

However, a reflective school ethos and programs designed to provoke awareness of one's values can further such maturing in high school students. An eleventh-grade MHS boy wrote, "Last year, I had no goals. Through the year I began to realize that without goals, I am really working for nothing." A senior MHS boy wrote, "Now I see things in perspective. I feel an inner desire to do well in school and to have a future that I can be proud of."

Interviews with college students reveal a noticeable maturation of their awareness about their values, more, I think, than what researchers have measured by tests.[42] Reported attitudinal change is greater in the freshman than in subsequent years. Their first experience of living away from home and challenging dormitory environments prod them to reflect about how to adapt to numerous troubling issues. How am I to get along with my obnoxious roommate, who gets drunk every weekend and smokes cigars? What am I to do with my freedom? By their sophomore year, only 9 percent of students at the University of New York, Buffalo, claimed that they were *not* aware of any change in their values since they had matriculated.[43] Education can signal to students to be aware of their values. This change was one of the three principal *enduring* effects of Haverford College that I found from interviews of its alumni fifteen years after graduation.[44]

Apparently, life experiences and relationships more frequently heighten awareness of students' values than their academic courses do. The confrontational sixties and seventies, for example, produced painfully acute maturing effects for many—at least in forcing increased awareness of their values. As one freshman told University of New York interviewers, "I'm beginning to question my values—all of them. Sometimes I'm not sure . . . about anything I value. . . . I started thinking about Vietnam for the first time . . . the thought that I might be dying over there for something like that started me thinking about things . . . from there on I started questioning everything."[45]

Other-Centered Values

Growth from egocentric to other-centered values is just crucial to adapting to our principal roles, even vocational ones, in a predominantly service economy and a shrinking, globally interdependent world. Chapter Six reported that other-centered values such as respect, compassion, acceptance, and tolerance are even more important than intellectual talents and knowledge for success as an adult.[46]

There is near unanimous agreement among educators that a liberal education should and does promote the maturing of other-centered values. While their specific words differ, they agree that education should produce good citizens[47] who value others' beliefs and rights[48] and are interested in, are sympathetic to, and value cooperatively serving others and their communities.[49] Nel Noddings, a Stanford educational philosopher, goes further to claim that the principal goal of schools should be nurturing the ethical ideal, by which she means maintaining and strengthening caring.[50]

There is also near unanimous agreement among researchers that education has the potential to and frequently does humanize values, more in some schools and colleges and at different periods than others. Students become less prejudiced, stereotyped, and ethnocentric, more accepting and tolerant, and, depending on the ethos of the school, possibly more interested in political and world affairs.[51] Students who go to college become less authoritarian and more open-minded than comparably bright high school students who don't.[52]

Bloomfield Hills' MHS was especially effective in encouraging its students to develop more other-centered values. A tenth-grade boy said that the school had "showed me you can still be powerful but yet loving and to have open arms toward people." An eleventh-grade girl said that the school's interpersonal code of "no put-downs" had taught her to "respect everyone for what and who they are." Finally, a twelfth-grade boy spoke for others when he said that the school had helped him to "come to an understanding of how different people come to be and therefore [I] gained a greater compassion for all people."

Maturation of other-centered values does not automatically occur as a result of education, however. Such growth occurs more in some institutions than in others. Chickering found that students in thirteen colleges, some religiously oriented, generally did *not* change in their concern for the welfare of others. So he did not include the humanization of values as a salient vector in his model of student development.[53]

Finally, more powerful forces than education can affect the maturation of other-centered values in young adulthood. For more than fifteen years, graduating high school students have valued earning money and security increasingly more and serving others less.[54] They have flooded business and other money-earning courses and professions to become instant yuppies. So it would not be surprising to discover that a liberal education did not have as powerful humanizing effects on students' values in the United States in the 1980s as it had in a different cultural era.

Integration of Values

Identifying and setting priorities and not following every whim and fad contribute mightily to effective adaptation. Failure to develop coherent priorities and consistently implement them bars meaningful sustained improvement in schools. When one school's teachers were asked to list every activity of the preceding week that they could have eliminated to give them more free time to work toward improving their school, only two of forty-five cited even one unessential activity. Apparently, everything that most of them had done was too important to give up. The consequence is that schools add ever more meritorious straws but never take any less worthy ones off the shoulders of anyone. No wonder backs break, morale sags, energy drains away, resistance to change becomes fixed, and nothing really changes.

To make value choices based on principles also greatly enhances consistent decision making. A friend met Nathan Pusey, former president of Harvard, walking one morning along the Charles River. At one point, he asked Pusey how he made the hundreds of decisions that he had to make every day. Pusey replied that he didn't have to anguish about every one because he had some basic principles that guided his choices.

Bloom and the other authors of the *Taxonomy of Educational Objectives* claim that integrating one's values into a consistent "philosophy of life . . . a code for governing all of one's conduct" is "the ultimate goal of education."[55] They quote Harvard's 1945 report on general education: "Education must look to the whole man. It has been wisely said that education aims at the good man, the good citizen, and the useful man. By a good man is meant one who possesses an inner integration, poise, and firmness, which in the long run comes from an adequate philosophy of life."[56] For the *Taxonomy* authors, attaining such value integration is attaining maturity, another way of labeling the "ultimate goal of education."

Researchers agree that a major effect of education can be the progressive integration of one's values, as seen in the numerous and diverse ways in which students change. In their critique of research completed over forty years on the impacts of college, Kenneth Feldman and Theodore Newcomb conclude that students become "less moralistic and more liberal and flexible . . . [and more] morally consistent and manifest a higher level of judgment in their moral thought."[57] Research since has confirmed that from junior high school through college, students respond to moral problems with increasingly principled judgments.[58] The amount of growth is modest, though, even in colleges, such as Alverno, that deliberately design programs to enhance value integration.[59] Chickering's studies suggest that integrity, the progressive integration of one's values and acts, is one of seven principal effects of education.[60]

Not unexpectedly, some schools encourage their students' integration of values more than others do. Philip Jacob critiqued 354 studies of the effects of college on the maturation of values that had been completed by the early 1950s and concluded that most colleges just confirm or stabilize the traditional values that students bring with them to college. Only a few, such as Bennington, Harvard, Haverford, and Reed, produced distinctive integrative effects on their students' values.[61]

A Harvard junior described how he tried to make sense of his own values and interests: "There are so many values you can't possibly line up all of them. . . . It means that you have to drop certain things and focus more on others. . . . You just let these things become peripheral."[62] A Haverford senior had sorted out his relationship to society this way: "I think that perhaps the whole idea of what you work for and what you gain from society is really not all your own, that you are only a part of a long continuing process and what you have accomplished is in part, as a result of your own endeavor, and also in part a result of the people who have gone before you, so that any claims that society may make on what you have done or have accomplished I think are valid claims."

Stabilization of Values

A lack of firm values and long-term goals to guide decisions and actions and failure to value thoroughness, persistence, and sticking to a valued course of action when the going gets tough undercut the effectiveness of almost any activity. American educators have long been bedeviled by "here today and gone tomorrow" fads, impetuous enthusiasms that promise "the answer," and quick monetary solutions to their problems. The resulting patina of change produces no long-lasting improvement. Recall the convulsive post-*Sputnik* effort to improve scientific, mathematical, and language skills. Thirty years later, we are similarly convulsed. Furious educational reform that is not guided by a coherent, integrated, humane view of healthy growth that is adhered to for the long haul will not create enduring character changes in teachers and students.

Only a few philosophers write explicitly about developing enduring values. However, many implicitly assume that guiding values will emerge as a result of the formation of an integrated philosophy of living. Hook advocated nurturing loyalty to the ideals of a democratic community;[63] Dewey valued persistently working for an ideal and maintaining an "unswerving moral rectitude"[64] while overcoming obstacles.[65] But educators rightly aware that change is a law of living are worried that stability can slip into rigidity. McGrath, for example, prefers to identify the development of *provisionally* firm convictions as a mark of the educated person.[66]

Researchers have shown that as students mature, learn how to adapt to school, become aware of and integrate strengths and interests, and make plans for the future, they develop a firmer sense of themselves, more often than not organized around enduring values.[67]

Students recognize that they are becoming more directed, purposeful, and stable, particularly in powerfully transforming schools that capture their interest. Four MHS students tell us the motivational potentials that schools can educe. A ninth-grade boy claimed that he had become "more motivated to learn, as opposed to just finishing and turning in work." A ninth-grade girl wrote that "I take time to go further and have a deeper understanding of what I learn." One eleventh-grade boy wrote, "My determination has increased tremendously; I actually apply myself to school and find the self-motivation to stick it through." Another echoed him: "I am following through with projects more than I have in the past." On the other hand, private high school seniors, having adjusted to years of *traditional* schooling, report that the only change they sensed in their values was that they were "strengthening."

College students become more purposeful, another of Chickering's seven principal types of growth.[68] Interests and values become more integrated, frequently around an emerging vocational identity that can persist throughout life. A Haverford student told me, "I just think the atmosphere of constant academic pursuit really got me in the swing. Got me working, got me interested in a lot of things and really sort of encouraged me; it encouraged me to really throw myself into the pursuit and really open myself up to different academic pursuits."

Education can produce stable values that persist far into adulthood. A critique of thirty-eight national surveys of college graduates conducted between 1949 and 1975 concluded that schooling had permanently altered their values and attitudes. They valued more highly civil rights and the freedom to hear controversial viewpoints, as well as ethical conduct.[69] Theodore Newcomb also found that Bennington's liberalizing effects on its students' values persisted for twenty-five years after graduation.[70]

I too found that Haverford alumni graduating in the forties and fifties had been enduringly influenced by the college's ethos. They had learned to enjoy working hard and persisting, regardless of the odds, to realize their goals. Subsequent studies of the college's alumni of the sixties revealed that its ethos continued to influence and stabilize their value maturation into adulthood. The alumni reported that Haverford had provided them with "an anchor to windward," "a bedrock of love and humanity." An agnostic alumnus said of its persisting impact on his values, "Haverford taught me to listen to others, to respect them for what they are, to be tolerant and, in the Christian sense, to love them. . . . I do not think I realized that I had learned this at the time, for each year I am more keenly aware of the value I place on the standards of personal fidelity and tolerance that I learned at the college."[71]

Autonomous Values

When our choices between values are freed from compulsive wishes, the dictates of others, and societal conventions, then decisions can be made in terms of the given realities of the situation itself. We face the world more as it is than what we wishfully project it to be or what others say it is. Adaptation becomes more deliberate, self-conscious, and rational. We then become fully responsible for our choices. We can more objectively and selectively respond to criticism. We can defend our choices with a greater purity of heart.

Educators highly prize autonomous value choices, which most interpret to mean choices so freed from the influence of personal fears and prejudices as to be reasonable and rational.[72] Dewey spoke for many when he wrote, "If a man's actions are not guided by thoughtful conclusions, then they are guided by inconsiderate impulse, unbalanced appetite, caprice, or the circumstances of the moment. To cultivate unhindered unreflective external activity is to foster enslavement, for it leaves the person at the mercy of appetite, sense, and circumstances."[73] Such writers mention less frequently that an educated person can form a philosophy of life or values that transcend parochial conventions or prejudices and can stand alone, if need be, in their defense.

The authors of the *Taxonomy of Educational Objectives* highly regarded the development of autonomous values as education's proper outcome. They used the degree to which youths internalized their values and made them their own the sole criterion for describing character maturation. They only implied, however, that internalizing values meant forming values independently of societal influence and control.[74]

A liberal education can encourage more intrinsic or self-owned values. Provoking its students to develop more autonomous values was the Model High School's fifth most salient maturing effect over a three-year period. By giving students meaningful responsibility for their own growth, MHS freed them from studying primarily for grades and enabled them to learn to work for more intrinsic reasons. "I'm now reading more books for pleasure and satisfying my curiosity than just for a specific grade," a ninth-grade boy wrote. An eleventh-grade girl claimed, "I'm learning more than I have in my entire life. I seem to learn better when working for myself; I'm more motivated and generally self-directed. Friends and family find me to be a happier person."

Pascarella and Terenzini's comprehensive critique of schools' effects confirmed that increased internalization or autonomitization of values continued through college. "Increases of about 20 to 30 percentage points are reported in the proportion of seniors [compared to themselves as freshmen] who find intrinsic value in a liberal education and exposure to new ideas."[75] College seniors make more responsible and autonomous value choices than freshmen.[76] However, a school's maturing effects are mediated less by their formal academic courses than by their ethos and opportunities, such as residential living arrangements, for provoking relationships.

From his review of the research, Jacob claims that most colleges only stabilize but do not radically alter students' values.[77] However, his failure to examine whether their values become more autonomitized may have led him to underestimate schooling's qualitative effect. A junior at the University of New York, Buffalo, explains why: "Well, I believe in God in a way now, because it's hard not to, but I mean, He's a different kind of God than the one my parents probably believe in. I never really was that far away. It's just, I revolted against it 'cause my parents believe in it. It was forced on me since childhood and now I'm just sort of going back of my own free will, I guess."[78]

That education can increase critical and objective thinking, independence, tolerance of ambiguity, and less dogmatic values provides other supporting evidence, though less direct, that it can further value autonomy.[79] Paradoxically, such maturing can free people from enslavement by their appetites, biases, and social convention. They can freely will to indulge their appetites, assert their biases, and playfully provoke convention—more maturely so for seniors than freshmen—so researchers report.[80]

Educating for Metavalues

Many educators are wary about educating for value maturation. Fearful of potentially wrathful parents, contentious students, eager lawyers, and proscriptive judges, some tell me they leave value maturation to the family and church. But as earlier chapters have pointed out, teachers cannot escape educating character, even in the most purely academic school. Mind and character are inextricably linked. The issue is not whether we should educate for value maturation. The fact is that we do, whether we want to or not. The issue is what specific values we should encourage.

A core set of values is intrinsic to a liberal education that most of us can accept. They are the metavalues that every great religion, most educational philosophers, and many teachers and parents agree describe the good, educated, and ideal person.[81] The model of maturing identifies them as follows:

Dimensional Growth	*Metavalues*
Symbolization	Honesty and truth
Other-centeredness	Fairness and compassion
Integration	Integrity
Stabilization	Commitment
Autonomy	Freedom and courage

Other educators emphasize similar metavalues. For Newman, liberally educated people search for truth and are known by their "supernatural charity" because they are free of "littleness and prejudice."[82] For the feminist Noddings, the foremost attribute of an educated person is caring, which she says means moving away from self to regard or desire another's well-being as primary.[83] For Dewey, educated people act with "unswerving moral rectitude" and integrity because they consistently live their ideals.[84] For Hook, they are loyally committed to democratic ideals.[85] And for Bertrand Russell, they are courageous because, freed of their fears, they can stand up for their beliefs against the crowd.[86]

Metavalues are not disembodied capricious abstractions. They are the universal values that maturing of our minds and characters makes possible. They are the naturalistic potential outcomes of maturing, as some theologians and social scientists now recognize. The theologian Paul Tillich says that metavalues develop out of what he calls the "essential structures of being."[87] Psychologists such as Erich Fromm claim that they are "found in man's nature itself."[88] Abraham Maslow insists that they are "instinctoid."[89] Donald Campbell proposes that they are universal for "they make complex social systems adapt better . . . because they have contributed in the past to the survival and reproduction of certain social systems in competition with others."[90] I agree.

To educate liberally requires schools whose climates and adults articulate and model such metavalues. To ignore or suppress any one value is to teach illiberally, to indoctrinate, and to distort healthy growth. Few faculties that I know have thoughtfully and deliberately identified such metavalues and clarified their characterological roots. Few have consistently demonstrated their centrality to becoming an educated as well as a successful and happy adult. I know of no school, for example, that has shown its students that applying the scientific method, one of the most powerful ways to know truth, depends on developing the humanistic character that results in the metavalues. The cultural gap between humanists and scientists is not one based on character, in other words. The scientific method requires the metavalues of honesty so as not to falsify observations, fairness and compassion in evaluating others' evidence and interpretations, integrity in the conduct of research, dogged commitment in the search for the truth, the inner freedom or self-control to keep bias and wish from distorting the search, and courage to defend what is discovered.[91]

The authors of the *Taxonomy of Educational Objectives* claim that the most mature character outcome of education should be the development of a consistent philosophy of life. It should be organized around ethical principles that regulate one's personal and civic life in ways consistent with democratic ideals. The metavalues are those principles. The *Taxonomy* authors believe that such values can be "so encompassing that they tend to characterize the individual almost completely";[92] that is, become the core of a person's self.

Let us now examine the attributes of the liberally educated self.

Chapter 9

The Maturing of Self

I have talked of the mature *person's* mind, relationships, and values. But as the biologist Edward Sinnott reminds us, every living thing is an organism that is, first of all, an *organized system of structures and activities.* "It is not a sprawling mass of semi-independent parts and processes but is held together under a coordinating control. This system is far more significant than the materials of which it is composed."[1]

I use self as the subjective counterpoint of the visible person.[2] *Self* refers to that superordinate "organized system of structures [the me's] and activities" (the I's) that results from the progressive integration of mind, interpersonal skills, and values. It is an ambiguous and thus confusing word because it is used reflexively. Self has the unique capacity to act and to act on itself. For most contemporary educators and many psychologists, *self* refers to "me," or a person's self-concept, particularly one's ideas about who one is and feelings of worth and confidence about what one believes one can do. For other educators and psychologists, self also includes "I," or ego— the executive self that commands, controls, evaluates, and actualizes itself. Teachers tend to talk primarily about self as an object—that is, about a student's self-concept—and ignore self's attributes as an actor. Philosophers and researchers studying schooling's effects also refer to self as actor.

The Maturing Self

What is the maturing self? It is both actor and object of itself. As an organized system, self matures similarly to the way in which its component mind and character do. As the following list tells us, a mature self accurately understands itself as well as understanding how others see it. It accepts its shared humanness and coherently unifies its various ideas of itself under the guidance of a dominant self or identity. Self-confident, it realistically affirms its own worth and believes in its ability to direct and control itself, which it in effect can do. Again, Appendix A will help in understanding self's development as part of our systemic nature.

Dimensions	Attributes of a Mature Person's Self
Symbolization	Accurately understands its own strengths and limitations
Other-centeredness	Accurately understands how others view it
	Accepts its own shared humanness
	Identifies itself with increasingly diverse others
Integration	Strives to unify and make more consistent its component private and public selves and actual and ideal selves
	Acts spontaneously as a result of resolving conflicts between and guilt about divided selves
Stabilization	Maintains its identity over time
	Positively values and is confident about itself
Autonomy	Discriminatingly accepts and rejects others' views of itself
	Affirms its own worth independently of others' evaluations
	Directs and controls growth of itself

Origins of Self's Maturation

The sources of the self—more accurately, of its component selves—are numerous. The genesis of the bodily self is assumed to occur during an infant's preverbal months, when it acts as if it "knows" what it can do and that it differs from others. When an eight-month-old grasps for a spoon on the table only when it is within reach, it must have some "awareness" of its bodily capabilities. When a baby sees itself shaking its hand back and forth in a mirror and then turns away to watch its hand shake, it has some sense of being a stable physical self.

When a child learns in her second year that she is a girl, she begins to play like one and so learns what her gender self is to become. Throughout these early years, she learns what others think of her and so forms her social self as a huggable or untouchable, good or bad, trusted or distrusted person.

By four or five, children form their work selves. Regardless of how teachers disguise how they are achieving, children know from observing others whether they are slow or fast workers. They also learn about their other selves from how they act and what they can do: class clown or screw-up, athlete or cheerleader, loner or gang member, leader or follower, dropout or valedictorian. Acquiring new roles, such as spouse, parent, or retiree, constantly challenges adults to refashion and reconsolidate their views of themselves throughout their lives.

How does a maturing self contribute to one's adaptation? What do philosophers believe a liberal education contributes to that maturation? What is the evidence that schools affect the development of the self?

The Symbolized Self

Our ideas about ourselves are primary determinants of what we do. So our self-concept can become a self-fulfilling prophecy. A six-year-old boy may get the idea that he can't read because he can't keep up with the girls who call him dummy. He may resist learning to read when he later becomes more ready. An adolescent girl who thinks that she is a pimply wallflower may withdraw from social activitites and not try to develop compensatory strengths such as an engaging sense of humor.

Accurate self-insight is a cardinal attribute of maturity because of its adaptive consequences. It enables us to realistically anticipate, plan, direct, and control our lives to enhance our effectiveness in our various roles. Knowing the potential and actual strengths and weaknesses of our various selves and how they affect each other can mean not just our survival and well-being but also our success and happiness. Repression of our body's signs that it is too stressed can kill us. Failure to understand how ingrained may be our need to please and keep others happy can undermine our work selves when we should assert ourselves. Examples of the effects of limited self-insight are endless.

So it is not surprising that Socrates, Thomas,[3] and Meiklejohn,[4] among others, identify self-understanding as a goal of a liberal education.

Researchers, relying more on interviews than objective tests of improvement in self-insight, agree that education can deepen and hone it.[5] Increased self-awareness was the third most frequently cited effect of MHS for two classes; it was also one of the more prominently mentioned effects that private school seniors spontaneously cited in interviews about how they had changed since ninth grade. Speaking of what caused his increased self-awareness, a senior boy said, "I know myself now more. Not really the school but my classmates did that to me. The change of friends. Basically I saw myself more. What I was. My feelings. My personality. I saw it more and what it did to other people. I can better perceive what my emotions are now. That came about from sophomore to junior year with the change in my friends. Also, just the fact of talk about going to college. Getting ready for it made me look at myself. That's life. I still find little things about myself that are really interesting."

Finding out interesting "little things" about oneself continues throughout life, particularly when one is making big changes in one's life, such as leaving home about the time when one is capable of being more reflective. It is an especially critical time to discover who one is and what one could be. Because colleges provide freedom from premature responsibilities and fixed roles, they offer students the opportunity to explore possibilities and potentialities and so become aware of strengths and limitations.

For Haverford students, increased self-understanding ranked second among the twenty possible maturing changes that they had experienced in their four years. The students identified the college's intellectual expectations, in particular, as having enlargened their understanding of themselves. One said, "It has taken me down a peg or two in my opinion of myself." Another, however, said that it had revealed to him his future identity: "Before coming to college I knew that I had perhaps above average intelligence. But I didn't value that very highly. Now, perhaps I have swung too far the other way. But being able to do well here has made me feel that it is essential to my life. The role of the mind and its use. I couldn't do without it. I feel that the mind is more important than anything else. Using my mind, I not only do what I want to do but what should be done as the most important thing."

Though a college's intellectual tradition, a particular faculty member, or an occasional course can provoke self-insight, students' relationships produce the greatest self-understanding. Roommates and close friends are potent provocateurs of increased self-insight.[6] About twice as many residential as commuter students at the University of New York, Buffalo, reported increased self-awareness by the end of their freshman year.[7]

The Other-Centered Self

Predicting accurately what others think of us powerfully predicts our maturity. It is an important adaptive skill.[8] We live in a social world of reciprocal relationships. Understanding what friends, co-workers, and bosses think of us tells us the limits and possibilities of our relationships with them. Knowing that friends believe that we are egocentric tightwads or easy touches or that co-workers think that we are manipulative goof-offs or excellent team workers or that bosses believe that we are gifted hustlers or glittering rising stars can immeasurably affect how we act.

Maturing people also learn from others that while they are unique, they are also like others. Adolescents, in particular, experience sexual temptations as well as fears of rejection and failure that they believe only they feel. Some believe that they are so unique, different, even perverse, that no one can possibly understand or like them. Inhibition, guilt, loneliness, withdrawal, or suicide can result. To learn that others feel similarly can affirm one's own humanness, deepen self-understanding, and enhance understanding of and getting along with others. The guarded defensiveness of contemporary adolescents and their lack of empathy and trust, which Chapter Two identified, can formidably bar self's other-centered maturation.

Acknowledging and accepting one's shared humanity prepare the way to expand one's self-concept to identify with and feel akin to increasingly diverse people. Extending the boundaries of one's self-concept opens the way to increased empathic communication and respectful relationships with others. These are important adaptive skills that youth will increasingly need in their interdependent global future.

Philosophers talk more about expanding one's "common ground" with others than they do about developing the skill of understanding how others view them. For Athenian Greeks, identification with the polis's communal life superseded asserting one's special self.[9] Others, following within the tradition of Aristotle, believed that individuals don't realize themselves except by expanding their identity to include others. Thomas, reviewing the history of and defending general education, insists that "no man realizes himself as an *individual* except as he comes to understand through the breadth of his knowledge his identity with all men."[10] More than most others, Van Doren emphasizes that education should "produce in . . . [a person] the utmost of his humanity, on the assumption that this is what he possesses in common with every other person. . . . And when we praise him we praise his humanity . . . we praise persons for the virtues in them which they share with other men. . . . An old way of saying this is that good men . . . tend to be alike."[11] Good men (in my words, mature persons) share the same metavalues, recognize each other, and share a common humanity as the core of their image of themselves. They accept and respect themselves as they accept and respect others, as Russell asserts.[12]

We now know that a liberal education can produce more

other-centered minds, relationships, and values. However, evidence is scarce that students develop other-centered concepts of themselves in the way philosophers believe. I found only a few glimmers of such other-centered self-concepts in interviews with high school students but more in college students.

A high school girl spontaneously said of her fledgling other-centered self that "I am trying to get a better opinion of myself. Am trying to see myself as others see me. Trying to get a perspective on that. Before I didn't know how others saw me." About a third of sophomores at the University of New York, Buffalo, thought of themselves as having become more kind, compassionate, and unselfish than they had been when freshmen;[13] an additional third of the juniors had developed a more other-centered concept of themselves.[14] Speaking of the effects of his roommate, a college senior told me, "Just that I think much more of myself as a person, accepted by others, less feeling that I'm different from everybody. I don't mind being different from everybody; in fact I'm sure I'm as good as everybody else; but it's nice to belong—to the human race."

Chapter Six mentioned educators' belief that developing that "common ground," that "identity" with all people, is imperative if students are to adapt to the demands of a globally interdependent future. I don't know whether the paucity of evidence that students develop more other-centered identities is due to inadequate methods of researchers, the individualistic values of the American culture, schools' abdication of general education and the dilution of their communal values, and/or the divisive polarization that sometimes occurs among racially and sexually diverse student bodies. But education's hope for an interdependent global village is that we can develop a shared humanity—the implicit promise of a judiciously formed multicultural curriculum.

The Integrated Self

As living organisms, we are born more as integrated neurological-biological systems than as organized psychological persons. Infants' reflexes, such as sucking and grasping, and biological capabilities, such as visual and aural alertness, provide the organized templates for subsequent maturation. Much of development involves learning how to coordinate first our bodies and then our psyches with each other and with others'.

I agree with psychologists such as Carl Rogers, Abraham Maslow, and Prescott Lecky[15] that we have a given, natural impetus to grow, explore, coordinate, integrate, and actualize ourselves.[16] Achieving one adaptation or internal equilibration releases energy for other self- or other-generated adaptations. Though progressive psychic integration may slow or be blocked, mature persons value continuous striving to make more consistent their private and public and actual and ideal selves.

Though forty-three when I studied her, Mary still was seeking to "find herself." An accomplished medical secretary, she had put her husband through medical school. She was then encouraged to do research, which was of such high quality that she was urged to get a master's degree, and eventually a doctorate, to be able to get grants. When I interviewed her, she had published seventy papers in her specialty and was nationally respected. For participating in my study, I offered her an in-depth analysis of the numerous test results that I had about her.

"Mary, something is wrong with these tests; they don't seem to be valid. They don't agree with each other. I can't make sense of you. Your temperament is not similar to those who are successful in your field; you don't value scholarly work; your personality is kind of dangling over here. Nothing comes together."

"The tests are correct. I feel scattered."

"But why? You are so competent and successful."

"I've always been in whatever I do. But I hate getting up in the morning to go to the lab."

"What would you like to do in the future? What do you dream of?"

Mary resignedly replied, "That's the trouble. I don't have a dream." She wrote me five years later about a prestigious international honor that she had received, but concluded, "I still don't know what I want to be but I'm still hoping. I hope my children learn much earlier to get themselves together better than I have."

To "get oneself together" is to reduce inhibition and inner conflict. In Dewey's felicitous word, we can act with "wholeheartedness." To paraphrase Sinnott, a sprawling mass of semi-independent *psychic* parts isn't going to go anywhere until it "gets itself together." Mary's talent had got her somewhere but not where she really wanted to be—if she had only known where that was.

The freshman who plaintively told me several weeks into his first semester, "I feel my mind is a thousand pieces going in a thousand different directions" was paralyzed for months. Easily diverted by his noisy roommates, unsettled by imposing faculty demands, wistfully yearning to see his high school girlfriend, unknowing about his future direction, he drifted like a rudderless sailboat on a stormy sea for much of the year.

Among educators, Dewey most eloquently develops the theme that schools should be so organized as to develop a "coherent and integrated self" in their students. He would say of the freshman's self, and of Mary's also, that the "attainment of a single purpose or the defining of one final ideal indicates the self has found its unity of expression. . . . [W]henever the ideal is really a projection or translation of self-expression, it must strive to assert itself. It must persist through obstacles, and endeavor to transform obstacles into means of its own realization. The degree of its persistency simply marks the extent to which it is in reality and simply in name a true ideal or conceived form of self-expression."[17] He asserts that a school can develop coherent and integrated selves only by carefully creating a sequentially organized and cumulative curricular experience that "has a sufficiently long time-span so that a series of endeavors and explorations are involved in it."[18] A vision of the ideal, organization, discipline, and persistence in the face of obstacles describe the school for which the "development of character . . . [should be] the ultimate end of all school work."[19]

What is Dewey telling us about the kind of school that today's "ideal-less" stapler-students need?

Researchers agree that typical college seniors would say that they are going in one or two but certainly not a thousand different directions. They infer the seniors' growing self-integration from a host of assessed changes, such as their increased acceptance of interests that are stereotypical of the opposite sex, previously repressed impulses, and evolving aesthetic interests.[20] More than freshmen, seniors feel free to experience and able to consciously control their emotional impulses without anxiety and guilt. They have begun to create a way of a life, an ideal, that unites their intellectual talents, interpersonal skills, and values.[21]

Teachers who model the integration of their academic and personal lives can decisively contribute to a student's own integration. A budding intellectual commented about his mentor, "I really think he's a brilliant teacher. On the other hand, I think of him as a very warm—that's a funny thing to say about him—he's very warm and in a very funny exciting way, a very human person. I've seen him play with his kids. This is the kind of example for me, sort of the way I want to be." Another told me, "He pointed out in his teaching and his life and his relations with students a particular idea in philosophy. It's not only intellectual but also aesthetic, connected very intimately with literature and the arts but also with human beings seen in relation to the intellectual process. This is what made my decision to go into teaching. I was already leaning in that direction; he pushed me over the brink."

The Stable Self

Erikson claims that the integration and stabilization of our various selves, including our talents, relationships, and values, is the primary task of late adolescence. However, I think it is still the primary task today of many in their late twenties and thirties. Many remain uncertain about either what their ideal self, calling, and commitments to others are or how they can unify their competing selves' claims to be workers, partners, and parents.

We learn whether our ideal self and life plan really fit us only by testing and retesting our provisional identity. When we discover that our actual self approaches our ideal, or that our ideal approaches our real self—that we can be a brilliant teacher and a warm human being to boot—we develop a stronger sense of ourselves. We feel more firmly grounded and so more dependable and predictable to ourselves. Our competence in fulfilling our ideal girds us with confidence and good feelings about what we can do with ourselves. Such self-trust enables us to risk making commitments that we believe we can fulfill. And if we fail and fall down, we know we can resiliently pick ourselves up to risk again. Evidence from the studies of mature persons convincingly shows that persons who have maturely stable self-concepts adapt more successfully than others to their various adult roles.[22]

Philosophers talk more explicitly about the integration and autonomy of the self than they do of its stabilization or consolidation. Might they have lived in simpler, more coherent and stable times, with fewer identity choices, which for many, in any case, were prescribed by their families and societies? Of the few who explicitly refer to the attributes of a stable self, Dewey again is the most articulate. For him, the sign that one has created a "final ideal," or identity, is the degree to which one persists in realizing or testing it.[23]

Researchers such as Chickering explicitly say that forming an integrated stable self is a major outcome of schooling.[24] Perry identifies a student's highest level of development as commitment, which rests on developing a strong sense of self, a "new inner strength," that in the word of a Harvard student, "puts a center and a focus into your life, into what you're doing. And it hasn't really anything to do with where you are or what particular society you're living in . . . , whether you're traveling around the world or whether you're sitting in your stall in [the library]."[25]

Another sign of students' more stable sense of self is their increased self-confidence. An eleventh-grade girl simply said that her MHS experience had made "me feel special, supported and celebrated; I feel confident about myself and my actions." These signs of an emerging stronger sense of self averaged seventh for three exiting MHS classes describing its impact on them. Pascarella and Terenzini report that "the percentage of seniors who have successfully examined and resolved their identity within occupational, ideological, or sexual areas is probably some 20 to 25 percentage points higher than among freshmen."[26]

The evidence that colleges nurture increased self-esteem is more conflicting. While seniors feel better about themselves than freshmen, particularly about their academic and social selves,[27] causes other than college, such as ability level, may account for most of such changes.[28]

The Autonomous Self

The maturing person develops a more autonomous self. An integrated and stable sense of self buffers one from indiscriminant criticism and put-downs. A mature woman can selectively accept or reject others' challenges to her ideas of who she is, for though knowing herself well, she remains open to understanding others' views. The consequence of being so centered is feeling in command of her potentials to adapt. She believes she is a free agent capable of directing her own life. She does not feel she is a pawn of her impulses, a prisoner controlled by others' opinions, or a victim hounded by bad luck.

Philosophers and educators use different phrases, but their meanings are similar. Most believe that education produces more autonomous selves. Newman says that it develops self-control and self-command.[29] Maria Montessori, pioneer educator among Italian slum children, believed that autonomous command of self was the ultimate "law of being."[30] Whitehead identified initiative and self-discipline[31] and Dewey self-conducted learning[32] as signs of liberally educated persons. Van Doren illustrates how interdependent self-maturing is when he describes the individual autonomy for which a democracy should educate: "As a ruler, he has first ordered his own soul [self-integration]. As the ruled, he likewise orders his soul. . . . For without autonomy, he cannot find the center in himself [stable self] from which in fact emanate the very generosity and lawfulness, the respect for others that is a form of respect for himself, necessary to the operation of society [other-centered self]."[33]

Researchers confirm educators' expectations that education can develop more autonomous selves. MHS powerfully enhanced its students' view of themselves as independent people in charge of and responsible for their own growth. Increased self-autonomy was MHS's second most important effect for its three exiting classes. A ninth-grade girl wrote that "I am being more myself everywhere. I take more ownership of my ideas and feelings." An eleventh-grade girl said, "I am an individual and my feelings and actions are mine; I know I am special."

Boys and girls who go to college reliably develop more autonomous self-concepts than those who do not. They become more inner-directed and think of themselves as more nonconforming and unique individualists.[34] Study after study of development in college agrees that students develop a greater sense of their own power to alter their own lives and environments,[35] become more independent and self-directed,[36] and become less adversely influenced by others' criticisms.[37]

A junior at the University of New York, Buffalo, explained how the merging of value and autonomy that schools can effect occurs. He reported that "I find that living on my own has accelerated my sense of responsibility for myself and that, in turn, has allowed me to mature faster. . . . Eventually you find that you're really determining your own life. Where if you do it, it gets done, and if not, it doesn't. So that gradually has changed my whole outlook on everything." Another said that the university helped him "to finally affirm myself, believe in myself, search for my own life style, without trying to copy somebody's else's, and that's the most valuable thing that has happened to me since I've been here."[38]

Perry's interviews of Harvard students as they matured from freshman to senior year reveal the meaning of growing autonomy. The first freshman he quotes in his book reveals the genesis of doubt that spurs increased autonomy: "When I went to my first lecture, what the man said was just like God's word, you know. I believed everything he said, because he was a professor, and he's a Harvard professor, and this was, this was a respected position. And-ah, ah, people said, 'Well, so what?' . . . And I began to-ah realize." Now contrast the tentative self-determination of the phrase "And I began to-ah, realize" with a senior's view of himself as an autonomous person: "just grabbing hold of myself and saying, 'This I want, that I don't want, this I am, that I'm not, and I'll be solid about it.' . . . I'd never believed I could do things, that I had any power, I mean power over myself, and over effecting any change that I thought was right."[39] Newman, Montessori, Whitehead, and Dewey would nod in agreement. They would say that he was becoming educated.

The Signs of a Liberally Educated Person

How can we identify the liberally educated self? We can ask people to describe themselves or measure directly or indirectly their maturity.[40] Transcultural research suggests that self's dimensional attributes more powerfully predict a person's maturity and adaptability than traditional personality measures.[41] Accurately predicting other people's views about ourselves, for example, is a particularly potent indicator of our maturity. Carl Rogers told me that he used this clue when interviewing prospective therapists to assess their potential to be empathic.

For outsiders to people's subjective selves, is there a core group of more visible behavioral signs that mark liberally educated persons? Yes. As their minds, characters, and selves mature, they become increasingly able to:

> Use their minds to acquire and demonstrate high-level competencies in several different areas, thus showing that they command their cognitive skills and can make them work for them
>
> Create enduring loving friendships with both males and females, thereby demonstrating freedom from self-preoccupation that enables them to be fully present to others
>
> Pursue interests and commitments with enthusiasm, thus suggesting an inner clarity or purity of heart that liberates energy for vital, positive affirmations
>
> Become good or virtuous persons, thus revealing their maturing humanity and growing shared identity with history's human procession
>
> Accept themselves, including their frailties, with playful and humorous objectivity, perhaps even humility, indicating that they have transcended pride to accept their own humanity

Chapter Five told us that academic grades and achievement tests are feeble measures of the potential powers of mind, character, and self. Students and teachers know this in their hearts. Society's obsessional preoccupation with test scores as *the* measure of students' worth and schools' effectiveness creates numerous balefully destructive effects. It robs students of a vision of what they need to become, demeans the nobility of teachers' calling to devote their lives to students' maturing, saps students' and teachers' motivation and commitment to human excellence, betrays the cumulative wisdom, now supported by research, of generations of educators about the proper goal of schools—and so destroys the very conditions necessary to create schools of hope and achieve human as well as academic excellence.

Now that I have sketched a vision of human excellence, I turn to the practical question of describing four diverse schools of hope. What do they tell us about the general principles necessary to bring the potential for human excellence into reality?

PART THREE

Fulfilling the Vision

Chapter 10

Four Schools of Hope

Research tells us that the school that generates hope has:

A distinctive vision of its liberally educating goals that is
widely shared by all members of the school and parents[1]

Adults that are as committed to the maturation of students'
character and selves as to their minds[2]

A leader whose primary role is to be the steward and artic-
ulator of the school's vision[3]

Teachers who empathically understand the interpersonal
world of their students *as their students perceive it*[4]

Adults and students who have alive relationships that are
growth-inducing for both (trusting, caring, adventurous,
and intellectually exciting)[5]

Teachers and students for whom teaching and learning are
a calling, rather than a job, and whose morale about their
work is high[6]

Teachers and students who emotionally own not only the
goals of the school but the means of implementing them
within the school *and* the classroom[7]

Adults and students who value risking together to discover
more effective ways to achieve their goals, who are willing
to hold themselves accountable for their success and failure, and who reflect about why their school and classroom
climates and methods have not been as effective as they
had hoped[8]

Schools of hope are similar to the Disneys, Hewlett-Packards, and international research organizations that achieve their goals. They have a clear vision and leaders who inspire everyone to ceaselessly seek to grow and perfect their organizations.[9] Note that the attributes of schools of hope cannot be bought off education's shelf, found in legislators' catalogues, or mandated by school boards. While not precisely measurable, they are assessable. They are a school's invisible ethos, ideals, values, commitments, dynamism, and quality of relationships and leadership.

Powerfully formative institutions, such as Catholic monasteries, have a coherent communion of value. They have a vision that is shared and emotionally owned by all, even by the monks who scrub the pots and kitchen floor. Their vision's invisible presence cannot be escaped. It affects every decision, whether about the curriculum, teaching methods, even architecture—every psychological nook and cranny, in other words. When a school's adults are emotionally committed to a vision of human excellence, the remaining attributes of a school of hope occur, one might say, almost "naturally."

Four Schools Valuing Human Excellence

No school with which I have worked is *the* ideal school of hope. You will not be surprised that when I reviewed the hundreds of schools that I have studied or know well, the four that responded most appropriately to their students' needs were small and distinctive. They were led by caring people called to a vision of excellence, which they self-consciously sought and achieved. I knew each from intensive studies and observations of their effects on their students. I will also use them in the next chapter to illustrate more *generic* principles about how to create maturing learning environments. I do *not* intend to suggest that the schools' specific programs and strengths should be copied. Each school must create its own identity or communion of values.

Proctor Academy, a boarding school founded in 1848 and located in Andover, New Hampshire, contributes to its fourteen- to eighteen-year-old students' self-empowerment by providing them with an activity-based experiential program. It is nationally known for its work with the roughly 25 percent of its students who have learning disabilities. The school tells us how we might better educate today's students who share the personality limitations that Chapter One identified as more noticeably seen in the learning disabled.

The Model High School, initiated in 1990 in Bloomfield Hills, Michigan, is the least formed of the four. It is an experimental high school applying Theodore Sizer's principles, such as meaningful student responsibility and accountability, by altering the students' learning environment along the lines that Chapters Two and Three recommended. It is an example of a public school that might leaven other schools' resistance to change.

Haverford College, founded by Quakers in 1833 and located in Haverford, Pennsylvania, provides for its eighteen- to twenty-one-year-old students (originally all males, but now coed) an education that integrates academic with character excellence. Maturity's metavalues are central to its identity. Long recognized by educators for its academic excellence, it illustrates a college also standing for ethical values and ideals that Chapter Two suggested today's students lack and need. [10]

Finally, the Monteux School for Conductors and Orchestra Musicians, founded in 1943 and located along Maine's downeast coast in Hancock, attracts twenty- to thirty-year-old advanced conductors and musicians for six summer weeks of intensive conducting experience. The school illustrates how a great teacher coaches students to achieve the self-confidence and self-command that Chapter Three identified as missing in many contemporary youth. Internationally known in the musical world, the school has been called by a music critic one of America's national treasures. It brings its students' command of themselves to higher levels of excellence.

Who are these schools? How do they speak to youth's needs to grow healthily? And what do they tell us about how to create schools of hope? I describe the schools and their effects as of the time when I formally studied them or, in the case of the Monteux school, when I informally knew it. I search to understand their underlying generic strengths that make them exemplars of schools of hope for today's youth.

Proctor Academy

David Fowler, Proctor's head, and the faculty asked me during its 1977–78 academic year to evaluate how effectively the school was achieving its twenty-three goals, such as increasing its students' social maturity and ability to put their classroom skills to practical use. The faculty was also concerned about how well it was educating its learning disabled students, who were not showing the academic growth that had been hoped for. To understand the school and its effects required designing, scoring, and interpreting numerous surveys, interviews, and observational procedures to assess its goals. No other school of which I am aware has so honestly and courageously explored itself so thoroughly. No question was turned away; no resource was withheld; no faculty member undermined our collaborative effort to understand itself, its effects on its students and alumni, and the causes of the school's immediate and enduring impacts.

Though struggling financially at the time, Proctor was rich in other resources. Located on 2,500 acres of White Mountain hills and woodland, its physical facilities and faculty homes, while not pretentious, were adequate. It had 220 high school students. Some had been badly hurt by absent or divorced parents; others had been bored by public school; about 25 percent had been wounded by learning disabilities that had turned them against schooling and themselves. Paradoxically, the students themselves were a resource. They viewed their caring and devoted faculty as their family and so felt emotionally identified with the school and its aims.

But Proctor's greatest resource was its head, who, steeped in Outward Bound's experiential philosophy, restlessly and adventurously led the forty-five full- and part-time faculty members in creating and exploiting activity-based experiences most appropriate to the needs of the students. New students were introduced to the school's philosophy by faculty-led outdoor camping experiences. The school's traditional classroom work was complemented by experiential activities that provided the avenues for its learning disabled students, in particular, to mature as rapidly as they did: a mountaineering seminar in the west to learn its geology, literature, and values; a school-based forestry and ecology course; a language practicum in southern French homes; and extensive sports, among other vigorous activities.

Recall that the signs of reduced willpower—such as distractibility, impatience, and impulsivity—that teachers frequently encounter nowadays are more exaggerated in students with attention and learning deficits. What does the Proctor experience tell us about how to educate today's nonhandicapped youth, who increasingly show the same traits as the learning disabled?

We must first understand how Proctor's students grew during their four years and then probe to discover why. Proctor's entering learning disabled students were reliably judged by the faculty (unaware of the study's purpose) to be less mature than their ninth-grade unimpaired peers on 90 percent of the signs of maturity. In a carefully controlled study, the learning disabled ninth-graders were reliably rated, for example, as less purposeful, determined, logical, and empathic and as falling shorter on fulfilling their potential than their nonimpaired peers. However, by their senior year, the faculty rated the learning disabled as less mature than their unimpaired peers on fewer than 10 percent of maturity's strengths, although they were still easily frustrated and upset, and their thinking was fuzzy. Other comparisons to the unimpaired showed that the learning disabled had matured most during their four years, especially in their educability.[11] The study of the alumni showed that most of the learning disabled students had gone on to college and subsequently graduated.

Which of its goals did Proctor achieve most successfully? It taught its students to:

> Become independent persons, able to stand on their own, think for themselves, and be self-reliant
>
> Think logically and critically and analyze problems
>
> Put skills they had learned in the classroom to practical use
>
> Become more open to learning from other students and adults
>
> Learn how to educate themselves and become independent learners

How did the school achieve these outcomes? The keys were its close, familylike faculty-student relationships and its activity-based experiential activities, which offered its students ways to discover strengths not usually educed in traditional didactic classrooms. The principal determinants of the largest number of maturing outcomes for the entire student body were, in roughly declining order of importance, quality of faculty and student relationships, athletic program, students' free time, the school's initial experiential orientation week, and the type of student attracted to the school. Other experiential courses, such as the semester abroad in France, profoundly affected the smaller numbers of their participants.

The assessment identified the specific maturing effects of the school's different attributes. For example, the quality of faculty-student relationships contributed, in roughly declining order of importance, to motivating students to become more responsible, self-confident, interpersonally mature, and adaptable. The athletic program contributed to the students' physical health, cooperative skills, abilities to accept responsibility and get along with others more maturely, openness to learning from others, independence, persistence, and adaptability. Some activities, such as a few academic departments, contributed little to achieving the school's goals.

One secret of Proctor's success was that it valued the maturation of character and self as highly as the maturation of mind. The learning disabled discovered that when competing with the nonimpaired students in their athletic and other school experiential programs, they had talents, such as interpersonal, leadership, and athletic skills, that everyone valued as much as they did academic ones. Their bolstered self-esteem, confidence, and interpersonal and other coping skills enabled them to get command of more of themselves. Though still deficient in academic writing skills, they eventually adapted successfully to their colleges' demands. Proctor had enabled them to develop stick-to-it-tiveness, self-reliance, and confidence to eventually cope with their colleges' academic and social demands.

Why is Proctor a school of hope? It shows us the type of ethos and schoolwide experiential and activity programs that could help today's students to develop the willpower to discipline and command their talents. By valuing both character and self-maturation,

Proctor enabled its students to eventually develop more mature minds.

The Model High School

The Bloomfield Hills school board and administration initiated the Model High School in 1988 to create alternative educational routes for its students. Three experienced teachers were charged to explore innovative approaches, such as Sizer's, for reorganizing schools, curricula, and teaching methods. They consulted with other schools, such as Alverno College, and members of Sizer's Coalition of Essential Schools, read extensively, planned, recruited, and persuaded students and parents to join their experiment. Partial funding by a three-year RJR Nabisco Foundation Next Century Schools Fund grant enabled MHS to assess its noncognitive goals.

MHS opened in the fall of 1990 in six rooms of a former elementary school that housed a preschool day-care program with eleven full- and part-time faculty members (6.6 full-time equivalents in 1993). All 77 students who applied were accepted (there were 105 in 1993). Students could opt to take some work concurrently at their two home-based high schools, which most did.

The school's distinguishing visible characteristics are faculty corporate and consensual governance, enrollment by choice, personalized learning plans for each student, student use of district and community resources, thematic curricular and core competency organization, guided but essentially self-directed small-group and individual learning projects, extensive up-to-date computer and other technological resources, nongraded portfolios, and student-initiated and -organized assessment of their independent work by groups of external evaluators.

Despite the actual chaos and apparently directionless freedom of its first months, the school successfully created a less visible ethos and a communion of values shared by teachers and students. They undergirded and directed the school's changing structural and curricular innovations. The school expects its teachers and students to care for, trust, and aid each other as well as to responsibly educate themselves. An outdoor challenging ropes course that demanded trust in and reliance on each other oriented everyone to the school's

values. Each participant agreed to a Full Value Contract requiring
them to be responsible for each other physically and emotionally,
accept others' decisions about their own limits, and not devalue
others.

Teachers guide and coach, not dominate and lecture. They
have sought to create integrative holistic curricular themes, relied
on experiential learning activities, and rigorously and honestly reflected about what they were learning from their innovations.

Assessment of MHS's accomplishments during its first three
years showed that, when compared to my public school norms,
everyone—students, teachers, and parents—believed the school to be
much more accepting, caring, empathic, ethical, adventurous,
changeable, enthusiastic, and self-educating—and definitely less
boring. Despite the severe frustration that creating a school from
scratch necessarily provokes, faculty and student morale was high.

I have quoted students at length about how MHS affected
them. More objective measures of their change confirmed their judgments. Student morale improved so significantly that many began
to think of themselves as students with a calling to learn. Students
also matured significantly, especially in their interpersonal other-
centeredness, autonomy, self-awareness, cognitive symbolization,
self-confidence, and self-motivation. Faculty and students agreed
that MHS had contributed most to students' increased understanding
of group dynamics, reflective and speaking ability, willingness to try
different tasks, time management, and curiosity, among other
strengths. How stabilized and autonomitized such growths have become can really be assessed only by how they adapt once they leave
MHS.[12]

MHS is a school of hope. It reveals education's potential to
meet some of youth's most critical needs for an other-centered,
responsibly self-educating, actively involving, and experientially
based education.

Haverford College

Others' research had found Quaker-initiated schools and colleges,
such as Bryn Mawr, Swarthmore, Earlham, and Guilford, to be
notably effective in furthering their students' academic maturation

and creative adult contributions.[13] In addition, Haverford College had also been identified as one of a handful of colleges that decisively influenced their students' values.[14] To find out why, I initiated in the early 1960s intensive longitudinal studies of how its students developed from freshman to senior year and its alumni grew from their twenties into their mid forties.[15]

At the time I studied five of Haverford's classes, the college had 550 male students and about 55 faculty members. Its president, Gilbert White, had exercised decisive leadership in the 1950s to vitalize the college's Quaker traditions. After his retirement, the college had become a more strongly faculty-run institution. Its Quaker values remained obvious in its ethos and programs during the undergraduate studies. The college's core values were maturity's metavalues of honesty, compassion and respect for others, integrity, commitment, and courage. They were embodied in student-generated and -enforced academic and social honor codes, student freedom in self-governance, faculty corporate consensual decision-making procedures, a powerful confrontational freshman English seminar that explored values through literature, and a weekly corporate meeting for meditation to which both faculty and students came (though fewer than 10 percent of the students were Quaker). Students occasionally and sometimes raucously used their collective meeting to reflect on and make moral decisions about community affairs, such as desegregating local barber shops and participating in freedom marches to Mississippi.

To both students and alumni, while uncompromisingly intellectual, the college's core ethos was indisputably moral, though not ideologically proscriptive or evangelical. The college's catalogue prominently featured President Isaac Sharpless's 1888 commencement admonition about integrity and value autonomy, which some students could quote from memory: "I suggest that you preach truth and do righteousness as you have been taught, whereinsoever that teaching may commend itself to your consciences and your judgments. For your consciences and your judgments we have not sought to bind; and see you to it that no other institution, no political party, no social circle, no religious organization, no pet ambitions put such chains on you as would tempt you to sacrifice one iota of the moral freedom of your consciences or the intellectual freedom of your judgments."

Haverford enduringly affected far more than its students' minds. It altered their character. When assessing how its alumni continued to grow during their adult years and the reasons for their growth, I was not prepared to discover that the college ranked eighth out of fifty possible determinants, such as type of occupation or spouse's personality, *in its contribution to their growth since graduation.*

How could a college continue to influence its alumni a decade and more after their graduation? The principal enduring and distinctive gifts that Haverford had given them explained the mystery. It had deepened the men's awareness of themselves as ethical persons and provided them with models of how to integrate its values and make them their own. While most of them were not Quakers, they attributed its lasting effects to the college's Quaker traditions. As alumnus after alumnus said, "Haverford College had a tremendous influence in forming my ethical opinions. It made me realize the importance of even having an ethical sense." One non-religious lawyer explained why the college's effects endured: "In some ways it is an oasis to me, just in terms of the spirit. It is sort of a counterweight to a completely secularized society. I really see that if I were cut off [from Haverford] I might really be a slick city lawyer, possibly with very little soul left." Or in the words of an English teacher, "Quaker ideals came through more strongly than I realized. Just their lingering impact. It is with me all of the time. I don't think the intellectual content stayed with me. That's mostly gone. But the values have remained."

The alumni had so internalized the college's values that it had remained a living inner presence long after they had physically left its classrooms and dormitories. It had created an ethos and programs similar to Kohlberg's democratic just community and fulfilled Noddings's goal of empowering students with an ethical ideal.[16]

President White advised the college in his last address before resigning to remain small and faithful to its intellectual and Quaker traditions. The studies of why the college so powerfully affected its students showed that he was right. Smallness made other-centered interpersonal maturation more likely. Rigorous intellectual demands supported by education's metavalues and Quaker beliefs created a coherent vision of what an ideal community of seekers could be. As a physician alumnus said, the college was a "bedrock of love and humanity. Haverford College was a hopeful kind of experience." It shows that schools can integrate academic excellence and character excellence to provide an ideal for which to strive.

The Monteux School for Conductors and Orchestra Musicians

Pierre Monteux, an internationally famous maestro, once said, "Conducting is not enough. I must create something. I am not a composer, so I will create fine young musicians." To understand the school's excellence, I interviewed its staff and students. Its lean budget, small staff, and barely adequate and unpretentious physical plant belie its superb achievement. Internationally known and respected, it annually draws one-third of its sixty-five to seventy musicians from Europe, Mexico, Canada, and the Far East for the most intensive, demanding educational experience of their lives.

The Monteux School is unique in the musical conducting world. Its twenty-five conducting students must also play in the orchestra to learn the importance of communicating their wishes precisely and clearly. They must master three times more musical scores in six weeks than they would in three or four conservatory years. Conducting weekly under the musical director's scrutiny, they must be prepared, sometimes with only a few days' notice, to conduct complex works that they may never have heard before. They test their mastery before most discriminating audiences in public concerts and then are rigorously critiqued by the maestro in exceptional detail.

The school is internationally known for its core values, which are adhered to by Monteux's student, Maestro Charles Bruck, and two staff members. Its commitment to musical purity and clarity, selfless devotion and fidelity to the composer's intent, and integrity are legendary. The maestro unremittingly expects and uncompromisingly demands excellence and doggedly persists until he gets it. Students are not expected just to beat time precisely and elegantly; they are expected to enter empathically into the musical score, search what it says to them, and then conduct with integrity and, I would say, soul. Fakers are scorchingly confronted; robotic conductors are firmly prodded to search themselves; sloppy habits, such as slouching posture and dangling hands, are rooted out. Conductors must know their scores in detail, conduct and play accurately, and be impossibly attentive 100 percent of the time to how each of the musicians is playing. The maestro relentlessly pursues them until they conduct or play superbly. I have never elsewhere observed (or winced so much at) such perfectionistic coaching.

Why do today's youth endure such a taskmaster and so much frustration and, for some, pain? Very simply. They experience the maturing effects of being held to a standard of excellence that most claim they had never experienced before and never knew they could achieve. They feel stripped of their defensive ploys, excuses, and ego to discover and become responsible for what they truly believe and value. They return to their schools and orchestras more empowered and responsible conductors and musicians.

The Monteux School is a lonely lighthouse beacon of excellence, standing tall among today's faddish currents and drifting institutions. Grounded on Maine's granitic old-fashioned virtues of honesty, integrity, hard work, and commitment, it is a school of hope to its students for the vision of what they could become—great conductors and musicians.

Schools of Hope and the Optimal Motivating Gap

You may be vigorously protesting at this point, saying, "Of course they can be hopeful schools. Their students have chosen to go there." Not entirely. Not true of Proctor's students. Some had been enrolled by desperate parents. A number of MHS's students were psychic dropouts forced to stay in school. Like many other college students, more than just a few Haverfordians matriculated because it was the thing to do, not because of a compelling desire to be so rigorously educated. And more than a few students new to Monteux were apprehensively ambivalent, some even resistant, about rising to its expectations for perfection. The real issue is how to create schools that generate intrinsic interest in learning, even in captive students.

"But their teachers taught so few students that they could spend more time with each." I agree. The two high schools could have taught more students if they had used their teaching resources, including advanced students, more efficiently. Large schools, however, also fail to use their resources wisely. They drain potential teaching resources. Haverford had one dean, one secretary, and one part-time counselor for its 550 students; it now has six deans, four secretaries, and four full- and part-time counselors for about 1,200 students. The real issue is our vision, the educational priorities to achieve it, and the discipline that it brings not to fritter away resources for less important ends.

"But what can we learn from such unique schools? What we need are examples of schools of hope that we can replicate." Recall the distinction I made when talking about the model of maturing. I claimed then that despite unique cultural, socioeconomic, or gender differences, people mature similarly when they are freed to do so. Underlying seemingly apparent singularities are universal principles of growth. Thomas Peters and Robert Waterman assumed similarly. They identified unique corporations such as McDonald's as exemplars of America's best-run companies in order to identify the common principles of excellent businesses that achieved their goals.[17] They were not advocating duplicating McDonald's; I am not proposing that we clone Haverford College. Instead, I want to discover the underlying principles that enable schools of hope to produce powerful maturing outcomes regardless of their visibly unique differences.

The four schools are exemplars of hope for more important reasons than their type of students, teaching resources, or special curricula or programs. For one thing, they understood how young people need to grow. Proctor and MHS understood youth's hunger for more than just directive, didactic, dependency-breeding, and noninvolving schooling. Haverford and Monteux understood youth's needs for ideals that challenge them to rise above themselves to discover what philosophers and the great religions have always known. Disciplining and so commanding not just minds but also characters in the service of a higher truth give life its meaning and purpose.

Schools of hope also understand the process of maturing. They intuitively understand the psychology of what I call maturity's gaps. Students vary greatly in their drive to mature. They differ in their nervous systems' excitability and need for stimulation, energy reserves, curiosity, comfort in exploring the novel, and expectations for their own maturing. Schools can dampen and quench or excite and strengthen the impetus to grow, explore, and enjoy learning for its own sake. Did you ask why 40 percent of teachers of reputedly fine high schools view their students as apathetic? Or why 56 percent of their students feel that school is boring? What answers can schools of hope offer us?

Students immediately experience gaps between their desire, study skills, talents, and interpersonal skills and those that their schools and peers expect. Schools that understand how maturing occurs know how to design gaps that motivate rather than discourage students.

Research tells us that students are most educable for a school's induced gaps during their first weeks. They arrive at the school's doorstep expecting to be changed. Uncertain, apprehensive, excited, they are vulnerable and ready to be stretched. Proctor took its ninth-graders during their first week on a strenuous outdoor exercise to fix its activity-based values. Haverford's upperclassmen introduced all entering freshmen to their honor system during their first days at the college. Freshmen learned that they were not to cheat and were to respect their peers.

The ways that students begin to work, the values they encounter, the kind of relationships they establish in their early weeks and months prefigure how they will mature throughout their next four years.[18] Schools should devote their closest scrutiny and best teaching resources to these early weeks. They are the moments to grasp a student's commitment to their vision. A midwestern college of despair didn't understand how maturing occurs. Isolated in a rural area, it was losing its brightest students in their freshman year. "Why?" it asked. Preferring to work with its departmental majors, the faculty had abandoned its academic ideal for its freshmen to its fraternities' "partying" for their pledges. The intensely competitive "rushing" of the freshmen their first month told them they should be social, playful, amusing, and heavy drinkers. The faculty had never been able to recover its lost gap's "playing field," so to speak.

If a school expects little and the students can easily adjust, then the gap is too small. They become apathetic and bored and may withdraw from the school's academic life to hang out, party, or listlessly wander through their four years. If the gap is too great, frustration, hostility, defensiveness, apathy, and withdrawal may result. Students respond differently to such gaps, depending on, among other factors, the type and importance of the gap, their ownership of it, their maturity, and the school's support for the gap's frustrations and hurts.

Types of Gap

Schools dedicated to human excellence expect growth not only of mind but also of relationships, values, self-attitudes, and self-command. Entering students vary in their willingness, ability, and ideals for achieving excellence in these areas. The gaps' sizes also depend on a school's goals for excellence. Chapters One through Three, discussing students' educability for maturing, claimed that the gaps between students' minds, characters, and selves and their schools' expectations are greater than faculty are adapting to. Proctor successfully sized the gap between its academic demands and its learning disabled students' views of themselves as educable. MHS self-consciously created an interpersonal ethos to moderate the gap between its students' former raw competitive relationships and its goal that they develop more caring and cooperative ones.

Importance of Gaps

When students value maturing in some areas of their personality, they can endure large gaps between a school's expectations and their readiness to respond. Haverford's expectations that students act ethically has created increasingly larger gaps in recent years as more students no longer value such growth. Monteux's maestro's exceptional expectations for technical excellence and integrity are accepted, though not without ambivalence, by his students. They know their fulfillment will contribute to their own professional advancement.

Authorship of Gaps

People who determine for themselves the size of their own gaps will mature more than those who have little say in their creation. Ambitious students with high expectations set large gaps for themselves. Students who have no ideal selves for which to work or who just "work to get by" can sometimes be reached by being responsible for setting their own goals. However, some resist responsibility's opportunity; they want to "be done unto," as the Kansas faculties said. MHS lost some students and a teacher who had not made the commitment to author their own expectations or accept responsibility for creating those of the school. Haverford's social honor code had more maturing effects than its academic code. The vagueness of its core value—respect for others—precipitated periodic community frustration when cases of alleged disrespect were brought to the students' honor council. Reflection, redefinition, and individually pledged reaffirmation and collective ownership then followed.

Maturity to Endure Gaps' Frustrations

The maturity of students to tolerate the frustration of large gaps while learning how to rise to demands for excellence and then persist until they close them critically limits the meaning of excellence. Chapter One told us that both teachers and students believe that today's stapler-youth cannot tolerate too much frustration and pain. They have not learned how to initiate and persist in their efforts to close gaps that could lead to excellence. In contrast to Proctor, which could select its students for their maturity, MHS accepted everyone who applied. Its expectation that its students educate themselves far outpaced some students' maturity. Unable to adapt to the school's seeming freedom and lack of daily controlling structures, some wallowed in emotional turmoil and guilt; though they complained that their teachers were not "teaching" them, only a handful left the program. The basic soundness and maturity of Monteux's students enabled most to remain educable and resilient to their very tough maestro's expectations. They knew how tough they themselves had to become to cope with the unique pressures that the competitive musical world would thrust upon them.

Supports for Enduring Gaps' Frustrations

Typically more inadvertently than self-consciously, schools provide their students varied supports to endure their gaps' frustrations. Haverford and Monteux were character "boot camps." Their rigorously demanding expectations for excellence were sustained by their recruits' shared frustration and pain. Haverford's demands for academic and character excellence were most visibly welded together in its freshman English writing seminars on values. Their challenge to students' academic self-concepts, motives for coming to college, and styles of relating created very large gaps. Confusion, disorganization, paralysis, and despair about meeting the college's expectations were severe. But they bonded the freshmen together. Knowing that others felt similarly, were not giving up, were beginning to cope, and might make it sustained motivation to try again and again. In contrast to marine drill instructors, their English faculty and small writing laboratory groups provided caring coaching and counseling. Proctor's, MHS's, and Monteux's students felt and reacted similarly to their schools' intensity.

If a school has succeeded in creating optimally sized gaps to motivate its students, what principles could guide how it proceeds to educate liberally? How does it create the learning environment to produce maturing's outcomes? Since the principles describe how any person grows healthily, I also use them in subsequent chapters to illustrate how to nurture a faculty's calling and then students' maturation in the classroom.

Chapter 11

Developing
Human Excellence:
Twenty Strategies

Schools expect growth. Its rate is high in elementary school but begins to slow as students encounter "more of the same" as they enter middle and high school, when school becomes noticeably more boring.[1] As students approach their later school years, they report that they are on a plateau. Ready to be tested and to use their powers in new situations, they anticipate that their senior year will be wasted; many itch to fly away with their new wings and explore other ways to grow, such as working at McDonald's, partying, and preparing to leave school and home. Ready for new adventures, they arrive at their new job or college in a state of high educability. Unfortunately, not understanding how educable students are at such transitional times, colleges provide only more of the same academic routines and modes of teaching. They early begin to lose many students, if not physically, then psychically. They fail to create the appropriate motivational gaps, especially in their curricula and mode of teaching.

How do people grow when they must adapt to new gaps, such as those provoked by such transitional periods as leaving middle school, entering college, or getting married? I first discerned an orderly pattern to the process of adapting to new expectations when studying how college students matured through four years. It resembled the process of solving problems and developing new habits that Dewey described in 1922 in *Human Nature and Conduct*.[2]

When Haverford's freshmen found that the college's expectations were much more strenuous than they had met earlier, their self-confidence wavered. Some despaired. Most naturally turned inward to *reflect* why. In the process, they eventually turned outward to seek others' opinions, advice, and new information and so grew more *other-centeredly*. Choosing a major in the latter part of their sophomore year precipitated an identity crisis for those who had not yet created an *integrative* path for themselves. Typically, their junior year was a quieter one, during which they explored, tested, and, if the path felt right, provisionally *stabilized* their vocational identities. Their senior year was marked, as it had been at a less mature level when high school seniors, by growing *autonomy*. They became more independent of the faculty and prepared for their next transition.[3]

Disruptions in this sequential pattern of maturing stalled and diverted subsequent growth, even undid less stabilized growth to provoke uncertainty, even disorganization. Rigidly following parental expectations about taking a premedical course, for example, and failing to reflect honestly about its "fit" with their personality eventually tripped up some. Being indecisive about selecting a major, unconsciously scraping by with D's in key premed courses, or not completing an independent senior project and so not graduating can be a sign of maturing having gone askew.

With this brief understanding of liberal education's ground plan, let's explore some principles that schools of hope use to further maturing.[4]

Empowering Reflection

Confrontation with a gap that causes frustration provokes us to reflect on and articulate our understanding. We begin to rely on mind's symbolizing skills that Chapter Seven described. Learning that our former A papers, while technically okay, are wooden and pedantic, or that our peers don't appreciate our witty sarcasm, or that we fall apart when given the opportunity to set our own deadlines prods us to reflect to figure out why and how to respond more appropriately. Schools of hope begin educating liberally, as Dewey reminded us, when they enhance students' awareness of their own thought processes, character, and selves. I have identified at least four educational principles that schools of hope—and, of course, many teachers also—have learned and use to nurture the ability to *symbolize*.

Since the principles organize the remaining chapters as well, I code them for ready recall. The first word abbreviates a *dimension* of maturing and the second the *principle*. To aid their recall, the principles are listed in Appendix B.

Symb Goals

A school of hope makes exquisitely clear its expectations of how its students should grow.

Most faculties cannot accurately describe their schoolwide goals when asked to recall them. Few students can either. This is not true of schools of hope.

MHS successfully used its Full Value Contract to establish its trusting and caring interpersonal climate. Like Alverno College, it sought to make explicit the competencies expected of its students in its public and later school meetings, though not with the clarity needed to help students focus their self-directed effort. The students used the language of the competencies but confessed, when pressed, that they really didn't know, for example, what aesthetic appreciation meant. So they did not know how to go about developing it. MHS devoted much of its second year to clarifying the outcomes it expected.

Haverford communicated its ethical goals more clearly. It placed Issac Sharpless's call to integrity on the back of its catalogue's front cover. Its admission interviewers talked about its values and honor codes. Student leaders oriented freshmen their first few days about the honor codes. All freshmen then signed a pledge to uphold the code's moral values. Letters to the student newspaper regularly seared the administration, faculty, and students for failing to live up to the college's Quaker ideals and ethical goals.

Failure to be clear about one's expectations and then to visibly and consistently implement them dooms attaining excellence.

Symb Confront

> A school of hope contrasts, confronts, and challenges
> to call out excellence from its adults and students.

Schools of hope understand the nuances of the power of motivating gaps, not just to initiate, as Chapter Ten described, but also to sustain growth's dynamic. Periodic assessment of how well one achieves one's goals reactivates and sensitizes awareness. Proctor's head knew that. He initiated the assessment to provoke his faculty to rethink how effective they were. They learned that some of their academic courses and departments made no identifiable contribution to the school's goals. They had not created large enough gaps between their didactic teaching style and their students' dependency on being so taught. The students did not feel the frustration they needed to spur learning of academic self-reliance.

Schools that fail to challenge, for example, their seniors' previous eleven years of irresponsibility, passive self-absorption, and unmotivated "do it unto me" attitudes make their last year a monumentally expensive educational wasteland.

Symb Model

> Schools of hope optimally use models of their goals to
> further student awareness.

Yesterday's one-room schoolhouses provided an ideal setting for less mature youth to have continual contact with more mature ones. They learned vicariously from them and visibly saw the power that they too could eventually have. MHS is essentially a one-room schoolhouse. Neither age-segregated classes nor its spatial arrangements separate students from learning from and about and working with each other.

Haverford's upperclassmen had unfettered responsibility for orienting the freshmen to the college's values. To have seniors explain and emphasize that Haverfordians did not cheat, even on take-home exams, copy other students' work, call other students names, or, more recently, use sexist and racist put-downs powerfully altered a freshman's awareness and ethical behavior.

Observing other Monteux conductors conducting each week and noting the demonstrable differences between the budding and blossoming ones' beats and interpretations of their scores alerted each about how to conduct precisely and economically. Growth in six weeks was palpably impressive, even to me, a naive musical observer.

Failure to provide clear models of a school's goals robs excellence of its potential compelling power to motivate one to achieve it.

Symb Reflect

Schools of hope teach their students how to reflect about the processes of their own growth.

Increased awareness of how one is maturing and why enhances the probability of securing control over one's own growth. Interviewing high school students has always depressed me; so few have insight—even the words with which to talk about themselves—into how they are maturing, why, and what they want from school. That so few can tell me how their schools and classes could be made more liberally educating no longer surprises me.

A college sophomore taught me how self-directing students could become when provided the opportunities to learn how to reflect about how they best learned and why. A physics professor accused me of undermining his course. After what he felt was an especially sparkling lecture—so my friend told me—a student approached him saying, "I've learned in Doug's class I don't learn best from lectures. Couldn't you occasionally ask us to teach each other in pairs or small groups or go to the board to work out a problem?"

MHS students wrote reflective journals about their growth and shared them, if they desired, with others. Furthermore, by being provided a rich variety of ways to learn, some MHS students decided they needed more structured, teacher-led guidance and so returned to their high schools. Others discovered that they learned best in the computer lab; others learned that they grew most in small groups.

Monteux's maestro socratically probed each conductor at the podium in front of the orchestra to delve inwardly and reflect about a score's message. "Why did you do this? Were you satisfied with that beat? What feeling did you want the English horn to communicate? How are you going to practice that measure?" With few exceptions, the students articulated in our conversations what being a conductor meant to them with extraordinary insight, even eloquence.

Schools fail when they do not empower their students to understand how they learn and so get more control of their own growth.

Nurturing Other-Centeredness

If turning inward to understand our confusion, indecision, and inadequacy is to be adaptive, we must eventually turn outward again to test our ideas against the reality to which we must adapt. What does MHS really mean by its competency of demonstrating citizenship? Does Haverford's social honor code expect me to respect, even talk to and practice for the wrestling meet with, a gay person? What did the maestro mean when he queried, "What did you feel conducting Berlioz's *Marche Hongroise*? Did you have any empathy for it?"

Schools of hope provide the opportunities and resources to grow through our relationships with others. In small schools, everyone can know everyone else. Students cannot easily lose themselves in anonymity and avoid learning how to adapt to others' expectations. They must respond. They must participate with others if the newspaper, glee club, and hockey team are to flourish.

Implementing four principles furthers other-centered maturation and its accompanying educating effects.

Other Trust

Schools of hope are trusting places that encourage non-defensive and open student and adult relationships.

From trust flow vulnerability and willingness to take risks, appear stupid, and not be shamed by failure. Who learns who fears to fail? Trust opens us to explore ourselves. We discover strengths when with others, especially if we know they care for us and will not judge, manipulate, exploit, and twist us to their advantage.

Each of the four schools was a trusting place. Proctor began to teach its students to trust others in its freshman orientation week. Their outdoor camping experience, rock climbing, and rappelling down a sheer rock face taught them to rely on each other.

MHS encouraged trust by using its Full Value Contract to establish the expectation that no one would judge, put down, or fail to listen to another. Its trusting ethos enabled students to share their most personal journal reflections with the entire community. In one group session that I attended, an eleventh-grade boy read about his changing relationships with another boy; a girl movingly described her reactions to the death of her closest friend seven years earlier. Their vulnerability told others how human they were—a classic other-centered liberally educating outcome.

Haverford students joined weekly in a collective meeting for meditation. They learned to listen without judgment to others' voices or censorship of their own nascent inner ones. Faculty and students who might rise to briefly share their insights trusted others to be accepting. Some of Haverford's most moving meetings occurred when the community spontaneously gathered to share its feelings and memories of those who had died. Four years of its discipline taught some to genuinely listen to and respect others as well as to so trust themselves to be accessible to their less conscious voices. I attributed the alumni's acknowledged creativity to their having learned how to release their minds from bondage to external distractions and internal defenses to pass to less conscious sources of inspiration and insight.

Monteux School taught students a different kind of trust—trust in the insight of a coach, an authority, perceived to care deeply for their growth under his gruff and authoritarian "old school" manner. Standing psychically naked at the podium, facing the maestro sitting at the head of the stage and gazed upon by sixty-five musicians, conductors had to trust his insight and suggestions. One female conductor, defensive, resistant, and reduced to tears, vowed that she would never return. In November while conducting back home, she suddenly realized that the maestro was right. She hemmed and hawed and after three letters to him was accepted back the following summer. Chastened but wiser, she said she now listened; she trusted his coaching.

Schools that have not created an ethos of trust will never nurture human excellence.

Other Care

Schools of hope expect everyone to care for and be responsible for the growth of others.

It is not just that each of us needs to feel that someone cares for us but that we have the opportunity and resources to care for others. Growth comes more from caring and being responsible for others than from being only cared for, as necessary as that is to feeling worthy and so being able to give to another. Teachers know this truth. They know that they learn more by teaching than by being taught. Parents know this too. Being a parent is a major maturing prod.[5]

Each school created an ethos that was not competitively cut-throat. Proctor was a tight family community; its students cared for the school. I counted on their caring when I challenged them to consider the moral aspects of their marijuana use, not just its effects on them but its effects on their school, which would suffer if it were busted. They rose to applaud—not me—and affirm that they should be caring and responsible persons for their school-family.

MHS taught its students how to listen to another in a group, a first rudimentary step to building trust and caring. It balanced the potential self-centeredness that valuing self-education could encourage by requiring students to learn how to contribute to sustained small-group projects.

Undergirding Haverford's ideal of service was its Quaker belief that each of us only partially understands the truth or the way to resolve problems and conflicts. Each needs the group's understandings to see more of the truth or the way to proceed. Only by helping others to grow to know more of the truth will a community—including oneself—know more of truth and so live more wholly. So the college's ideal of caring and responsible service set a tone, an expectation of how its members were to act. For example, the student honor council spent tens of hours, not infrequently during its final exam week, compassionately searching for the truth of a student's reported violation.

The musical world, especially of conductors, is intensely self-centering and competitive. Students typically do not share scores, tapes, instruments, or their interpretations and time with others. At Monteux, they do—even a prized early Pierre Monteux recording; a $60,000 violin; applause for a conductor who transcended what he had done in earlier rehearsals; or spontaneously remaining seated rather than standing to share applause to allow a beginning conductor who had conquered terror to receive the audience's appreciation for herself alone.

Failure to enable students to care and be responsible for others' maturing prevents them from discovering their own humanness—a central goal for liberal educators.

Other Skills

> Schools of hope educate for skills and attitudes necessary for corporate task learning.

Individualistically and competitively raised Americans, particularly males, are not taught the group-centered, cooperative, and consensual decision-making skills that contribute, for example, to Japanese managerial-organizational and competitive excellence. Increasing awareness that workers will move from one task group to another in the future provides an imperative to schools: teach faculty and students the skills necessary to work corporately with each other.

American schools have used competitive team sports to develop cooperative skills. Proctor's vigorous athletic programs, such as its ice hockey team, provided the playing field on which to excel in developing team-building skills. It aided its learning disabled students to excel in the eyes of their peers and themselves in a way valued as highly as achieving in the classroom.

Of the four schools, Monteux best illustrates teaching the attitudes and corporate skills necessary to achieve its primary mission. An orchestra is a superb metaphor of a playing field on which to learn such skills. The maestro self-consciously taught his individualistic students the other-centered attitudes (one might also say manners) necessary to create excellent, even occasionally flawless concerts. He expected each student to be in place when rehearsals began. He fined each who talked during rehearsals a dollar. He demanded that the bass fiddlers repeat several measures over and over until they played precisely together or that the horns repeat over and over until they entered on time. He taught conductors to publicly and graciously acknowledge exceptional solo playing.

Failure to teach for corporate task skills limits students' opportunity to grow through their work with others and so robs them of future success.

Other Roles

Schools of hope provide their members the opportunity to assume different persons' roles.

Recall that we learn to know reality or truth or ourselves when we assume different persons' vantage points or views. This was the rationale for mapping the collective perceptions of different groups about their schools or typical students. MIIS's teachers defined themselves as facilitators, not as didactic classroom lecturers, though not without misgiving and ambivalence when their hankering to lecture to cover the material more rapidly became irresistible. By creating more egalitarian, less authoritarian relationships with their students, they discovered that students saw them as real people who could be trusted to value their strengths and accept their weaknesses. Redefining their role freed them to experiment with other ways of teaching.

One reason Monteux's conductors grew so rapidly in only six weeks was that they had to be musicians in the orchestra that they were to conduct. They felt the confusion of being unable to follow unclear and wandering beats or recover where they were if they got lost. They also felt their buttocks' pains when a perfectionistic maestro pursued unprepared conductors far into the night while they had to sit patiently on uncushioned folding chairs. As musicians, they learned that as conductors they had to be prepared for rehearsals and to beat time clearly if the orchestra was to rise to their expectations.

Schools that fail have not heeded Dewey's admonition that we don't become educated by viewing truth only from our own self-centered perspective.

Encouraging Integrations

When faced by a gap, a problem to solve, not only do we reflect, try to understand, and search out others' knowledge about the problem and examine it from many points of view; we also try to resolve and make sense of discrepant facts and contradictory views. We frame hypotheses that unite or create ways of proceeding that provide realistic solutions. We begin to exclude some possibilities for our lives as leading organizing themes begin to emerge that prefigure our direction.

Schools of hope don't think of their students as Christmas trees on which to dangle haphazardly thirty or forty ornamental courses irrespective of their shapes and relationships to each other. I've identified to date four related principles that bring coherence to students' growth.

Integ Goal

Schools of hope provide coherent goals and learning environments.

Each of the four schools of hope has a keynote, a predominant theme or vision, that integrates, though not perfectly, its learning environment. The vision contributes to a coherence in approach and programs that mutually reinforce each other's effects.

Proctor's experiential educational philosophy seamed the school together, with some notable departmental exceptions. The availability of the computer may have encouraged its math department, for example, to create a hands-on laboratory for its algebra courses.

MHS had developed a competency-based curriculum. I could

not figure out what the competency of interacting effectively in group settings meant to the faculty, so I could not design ways to assess it. Prior to MHS's second year, the faculty defined its indices more precisely. It next had to learn to model, create, use, and monitor its project task groups so as to educe such behaviors while students worked on their projects' substantive issues. MHS needed to learn how to consistently integrate its teaching approaches with its goals.

Haverford had created customs and programs consistent with its core values. The college's coherence was centered in its weekly corporate meetings that reminded everyone of its core values. Intellectual- and value-focused bull sessions in the dorms served as the experiential laboratories for their required freshman English and philosophy-religion courses. The honor system articulated and its council enforced the integration of the college's values with the students' behavior. Students intuitively sensed the college's coherence and seamlessness, which they affirmed in the most memorable of their annual spring shows. Depicting the college as an intense Catholic monastery, an entire class, dressed in white monks' robes, carrying lighted candles, silently and reverently swaying in unison, moved down the darkened aisles as it broke out into a prayerful chant. When all had reached the stage, their equilibrating principle took command. The young men suddenly raucously frolicked in the nefarious ways that drunken monks are wont to do on saturnalia's one night.

Failure of a school to witness a coherently implemented vision dilutes purposefulness and meaning and so diffuses students' commitment and energy.

Integ Involve

Schools of hope ceaselessly create ways to actively involve their students in their own learning.

There is no more valid prescription for ensuring growth than to actively involve a student in learning. *Actively* does not mean sitting at the foot of a monk transcribing what he says, nor just reading a textbook, nor, when conducting, just beating time as if to a metronome. *Actively* means reflecting about, questioning, relating, searching for examples, and feeling what the monk, author, and composer are trying to say. Only by actively integrating one bit of knowledge with another—*Moby Dick's* Captain Ahab with our own obsessional ambitions or Copeland's Hoe-Down dance from *Rodeo* with our own bodily memories of square dancing—does education become meaningful. As Piaget told us, watching a scientist perform an experiment or a mathematician work a problem on the board is a feeble substitute for doing the experiment or working the problem ourselves. We most quickly master a language by using it, whether Russian, COBOL, or the dance.

MHS engaged its students. After sitting around for their first weeks, mystified about what they should be doing, they began to search for problems to research or to engage themselves with the technology center and its resources. Some became so involved that their parents complained they were getting home too late from school. One parent replied to a questionnaire, "She really looks forward to school. She's so busy now she has no time to look at TV any more."

The maestro set an intense pace. He required students to master sixty scores in six weeks—not just play them but play them accurately and with empathy. Conductors had not only to master their own instruments' parts to play other conductors' scores but also to know every instrument's part when conducting their own assigned score. One conductor took only three evenings off during the six weeks. They discovered resilient reserves they did not know they had.

Failure to actively involve students in their own growth makes learning a boring game to find ways to avoid.

Integ Exper

Schools of hope provide varied types of experiential learning about which to reflect.

Maturing must be tested in action in varied situations and then reflected upon if integrative growth is to occur. Active involvement is not enough; we must also integrate what we are actively learning with our minds, characters, and selves. When teaching a fellow student, debating another school's team, or playing in a concert, we act as people who must communicate with and be empathically aware of the other, make value choices, know ourselves, and be confident about our competence. And we reflect back on what we learned if we want to do better next time in other situations.

I have mentioned a few of Proctor's experiential programs. MHS also believed that such programs provided more effective ways to achieve its goals. As an evolving school searching for the best ways to achieve its competencies, it encouraged its students to find ways to apply and then reflect about their experiences. Adrienne, for example, independently researched women's changing roles. To prepare a demonstration about how competently she had achieved the school's goals, she not only read about the suffragettes but also wrote letters to women's groups and surveyed and then interviewed women working for equality. To publicly demonstrate her growth, she then prepared a monologue and a skit empathically portraying the frustrations and feelings of being an activist for women's rights.

Some Quaker educators assisting an impoverished Philadelphia community in improving its school convinced Haverford College to work with them. It provided academic credit for its students to live for a semester in the community in whose elementary school they taught. I gave an on-site concurrent seminar to provoke reflection and integrate theoretical and research issues with their practical experience. The seminar failed. The gap between the students' day-to-day intensely moving experiences with hungry, hurt, and occasionally defiant kids and the cool, rationally based seminar was too great to bridge. More important, the students matured dramatically as a result of their community-school involvement. They returned to the college questioning their career goals, rebelliously critical of traditional modes of learning, and more motivated to create their own ways of educating themselves.

Failure to provide students with the opportunity to learn simultaneously with their heads, hearts, and hands detaches knowledge from passion and power; students become one-dimensional, impotent to feel and act wholeheartedly.

Integ Context

> Schools of hope confront their students with complex
> and contextual problems that require the integration
> of different ideas and modes of thought, such as syn-
> thesis as well as analysis, intuition as well as logic,
> induction as well as deduction.

When I visited MHS, one entire classroom wall portrayed
intricately labeled boxes, circles, and connecting lines. The faculty
and students had collaboratively mapped the complex relationships
between the components of a humanities–social studies thematic
topic, such as the nature of power and influence. Students next
worked in small groups researching individual boxes and circles;
they then integrated their work with that of others by exploring
different approaches to the same theme. They sought to step back
to view the topic more holistically. The science-technology-mathe-
matics division has had more trouble developing integrated thematic
projects. "Covering" mathematics' logical sequentiality proved in-
compatible with integrating it with a specific thematic topic.

Schools that fail to provide some integrative thematic curricular projects do not prepare today's youth to adapt to their future's
complexity.

Building Strong Personal Foundations

A strong personal foundation does not mean just superb academic
mastery *or* a strong character *or* a resilient self. It means the stably
grounded, *not* imperviously rigid, *person* that the model of maturity describes. Wise teachers recognize this. They insist that character
and self-maturation, especially of self-confidence and self-command,
are essential foundations for academic success. However, such maturation must be won in turn by honest and genuine work, by mastering academic, extracurricular, or vocational tasks that demand
excellence—though at a level that one is potentially capable of
approaching.

As all coaches know, a single flawless tennis game does not
a successful tournament make. A new habit, skill, hypothesis, or

solution must be practiced and/or tested over and over again until
it has become so strong or reliable as to be predictable.

Schools of hope will recognize, just as great teachers will, the
following four principles for *stabilizing* a new integration as obvious. But when studying schools or visiting classrooms, I am reminded over and over how seldom they are self-consciously used to
create more effective maturing environments.

Stab Rehearse

Schools of hope encourage students to imaginally anticipate, plan, and rehearse.

Imagination is a powerful adaptive skill. It helps us to anticipate, plan, and prepare in great detail and to practice and stabilize our plans without producing the irreversible consequences
that occur when we must act in reality.

An experienced Monteux conductor knew this principle. Not
having an actual orchestra to practice with over and over again, he
retreated to an isolated spot by the shore and imaginally created his
own. Standing at his imagined podium with his score and each
player imagined in his or her place, he beat time to the music while
he sang it. Knowing that his orchestra was weak in the trombone
section but strong in the flutes, he anticipated every possible weakness and practiced how to bring out the flutes more prominently.
He rehearsed and rehearsed until he knew each instrument's entrance, was on top of the piece, and so could conduct with authority.

I am appalled by how schools impetuously rush to accept
and introduce new curricular or teaching fads or inaugurate fundraising campaigns. They fail to seek to imaginally understand the
conditions necessary for their success. Or imaginally map out the
steps to succeed. Or anticipate and correct possible glitches. Or
initiate small pilot forays to test their feasibility. While mental rehearsal increases the probability of success, only action's test can
"fix" the integration.

Failure to use imagination for rehearsing wastes institutional resources; failure to teach students *how* to use their imaginations for stabilizing new learnings creates flimsy foundations.

Stab External

      Schools of hope demand that students *constantly* externalize and then correct their learning.

      Ultimately, the measure of maturity is its demonstration in action, not just in words. Talking about what one knows is not enough. To achieve excellence, we must correct, demonstrate, correct, and demonstrate again. Students who are never required to rewrite their unproofread or poorly constructed papers until they achieve the level of excellence of which they are capable will never know the meaning of excellence. By failing to take the time to require demonstration *and* correction, we in fact teach failure and fix immaturity.

      Theodore Sizer, author of *Horace's Compromise,* proposed that teachers should be coaches, rather than continuing to be didactic information dispensers—a view that I too have long advocated.[6] Teachers ask me how to coach. Not facetiously, I recommend that they watch how winning athletic coaches coach; they know the importance of demonstration and correction.

      Despite its small size, Proctor fielded some excellent teams. Its coaches, consistently implementing this principle, taught their students the meaning of excellence. Its learning disabled students, not handicapped on the athletic field, learned from their coaches' disciplined expectations that they could learn to do something well that was valued by others. Proctor's outdoor program grounded their self-confidence and enabled them later to persist and eventually do well as alumni.

      Monteux's maestro coached similarly. While practicing Kabelevsky's *Colas Breugnon* Overture, the timpani and percussion musicians were out of time with each other. The maestro insisted that they play several measures over and over, each time interrupted by an emphatic and increasingly impatient no at the moment of their error. He progressively slowed their tempo until the cymbalist entered precisely at the right note. And then they were told to go practice together until they collectively commanded the piece. Repetition of a habit is one index of its strength or reliability.

      Failure to demand that students show what they know and

then correct it at some level of excellence teaches contentment with sloppiness and eventually snuffs out the meaning of excellence and the desire to excel.

Stab Conseq

> Schools of hope do not protect their students from the consequences of their decisions and acts.

The principle restates a fundamental law of learning: we learn as a result of experiencing the effects—such as rewards or punishments—of our acts.

A paralyzing bane of most schools is the failure to consistently enforce consequences when students fail to live up to their expectations. Students then learn that nothing may happen when expectations are not met, and expectations become meaningless. When not welded together by a shared communion of value or agreed upon values for excellence, faculty give confusing and contradictory messages. English teachers may lower their students' grades for spelling incorrectly; others may tell them that what is important is their creativity, not their spelling. Students who have some teachers who ignore their transgressions, others who don't, and still others who silently assent will more likely transgress.

MHS's students kept folders of their work to demonstrate their mastery of the competencies. When examining some, I discovered chaos; their portfolios were trash cans. Overwhelmed by the demands of creating a school from scratch, the faculty had not thoughtfully considered what an excellent portfolio was and then closely monitored its creation. Not experiencing any consequences of chaos, students did not learn how to use the portfolio's potentials for learning judgment, organization, the meaning of excellence, or compassion and empathy for their readers. The faculty has since agreed on its expectations for the portfolios. How carefully they educate for, monitor, and then *appropriately* reward students for excellence will decide whether the portfolio is a perfunctory time- and file-consuming fad or a useful way to encourage and assess student excellence. I emphasize *appropriately* because MHS attracts some individualistic and potentially rebellious students seeking

"freedom" from traditional forms of schooling. Too detailed imposed criteria, not emotionally owned by them, could undermine
the school's maturing effects on their autonomy.

Schools that fail to allow their students to experience the
consequences of their decisions and acts should refund parents'
taxes or tuition; they have not learned how to educate their students
appropriately.

Stab Affirm

Schools of hope appreciate and affirm students' *varied*
strengths.

When we seek to develop a strong sense of self shown by good
self-esteem and self-confidence, we are on surer ground if we appreciate and affirm *varied* strengths, rather than only one or two. A
sophomore taught me this. In trouble academically, he considered
dropping out. I cautioned patience and urged him to explore other
talents that he might have. That summer, he discovered a natural
talent for the guitar. Practicing around the clock, he judged he had
become the college's third-best player. He returned to tell me that
he now knew he could survive Haverford. He had taught himself
that if he worked hard enough, he could graduate. He did.

Academic excellence is difficult to achieve when it is isolated
from character. Healthy stabilization of mind's talents depends on
its integration with character and self. The more we can connect
students' minds with their characters and selves, the more likely will
their minds' knowledge and talents be strengthened and endure—
the assumption underlying experiential forms of learning. So the
more varied strengths we can affirm, the more likely they will support growth in other areas.

Schools of hope intuitively know this principle. By acknowledging that we grow wholly, they expect and reward holistic
growth. MHS and Haverford are my best exemplars. MHS expected
and rewarded not only *mind's* competencies, such as problem-
solving and communication skills, but also group interaction skills,
social responsibility, empathy, and fair-mindedness. When I studied
Haverford in the sixties, it expected its students not only to rigor-

ously pursue their minds' development but also to become ethical persons sensitive to the rights of others and their own teachers of truth. By placing a former president's call to this vision on the back of its catalogue's front cover, it told its students that it expected them to develop far more strengths than just academic ones. Students did prize their poets, mystics, and social activists as much as their athletes and intellectuals. [7]

Schools that fail to appreciate and affirm mind's *and* character's *and* self's adaptive strengths fail to educate liberally and so do not build firm foundations for future success and well-being.

Educating for Self-Command

The course of becoming educated begins with reflective efforts to discover ways to diminish gaps between expectations and our readiness to meet them. It next takes other-centering and integrative steps to create the best way, which it then tests and stabilizes. These steps, if adaptive, culminate in the autonomitization of the habit or skill. What does this rather arid abstract summary of education's ground plan tell us about the outcome? We have been permanently transformed. We have more command of our selves. We are more our own teachers in charge of our own growth.

Refer to Appendix A's description of the model of maturity. Growth proceeds from the upper left-hand quadrant—symbolizing and other-centered cognitive and interpersonal maturing—to the lower right-hand quadrant—increasing stabilization and autonomitization of our values and self. Cognitive development grounds interpersonal maturation, which in turn supports our values, which, as Bloom also suggested, become our self's core. Schools of hope use the principles I have described to guide and optimally spur liberal education's process from symbolization to autonomy in our minds, characters, and selves.

As Erikson would tell us, this plan, like all maps of healthy growth, is too neat and simple. It does not adequately highlight the *systemic* nature of maturing and could lead to unwise educational applications. Erikson's critical stricture is that infants grow from birth and students grow from their matriculation as persons, not as *a* cognitive skill becoming more symbolized or *a* value becoming

more other-centered. Infants, like middle schoolers or college freshmen, not only develop symbolizing cognitive skills but simultaneously also become a mite more autonomous; they learn how to reject
the nipple or spit out their spinach.

Acknowledging that we grow as persons does not mean that
we may not be more ready to mature in some sectors or dimensions
at some times in our lives than in others. Pubertal youth are most
ready for interpersonal maturing with others of the same sex; high
school freshmen or sophomores are most educable for reflection and
seniors for autonomy; college freshmen are ready to move to a more
mature level of reflection, particularly about their values, and college seniors are ready for autonomy. Schools that frame their curricula around these developmental vulnerabilities and teach to them
can have especially powerful educating effects.

We don't, however, have to wait until a student is a senior
to educate for self-command, the roots of which go far back into
infancy, as Chapter Nine illustrated. We can and should educate even
first- and second-graders to achieve the rudiments of liberal education's ultimate goal—self-command. Kathy, a first- and second-grade
teacher, taught me this valuable lesson, which Montessorians have
since confirmed. She taught her twenty-eight children, half of whom
were minority kids from the poorer section of the city, how to educate
themselves. When I visited her class at 8:30 one morning, she was in
the principal's office. Five of her children were already in class. Two
were working together building an Egyptian pyramid. One was practicing his numbers at the board. Two were reading. When she arrived
at 8:55, all twenty-eight had arrived and settled down to some task to
teach themselves. Not once during that time or the subsequent half-
hour planning period did I or she have to shush two giggling girls
or restrain a rambunctious boy or tell anyone what they should be
doing. Her kids knew their goals for that period and how to go about
achieving them. A wise teacher, Kathy intuitively knew the principles
of creating a classroom of hope. She had clear goals, paired the
second-graders as models with the first-graders, and implemented
most of the following four principles to help students learn how to
become self-educating people in command of themselves.

Aut Faith

> Schools of hope express a *realistic* faith in their stu-
> dents' capacity to be responsible.

Today's perceptive students can sense our faith in and hopes
for them and will live up to realistic expectations.

Assessing MHS's effects on its students reaffirmed again my
belief that when they are *appropriately* implemented, students will
rise to realistic expectations that they can be responsible for their
own education. Why did its students spontaneously describe developing more *autonomous self-concepts* as one of their two most
salient kinds of growth? Because MHS held its students to be meaningfully accountable for using their freedom responsibly. It therefore avoided the plight of the seventies free schools that crumbled
because they had not. Its teachers believed that students should publicly demonstrate their competence. So it required them to invite a
parent, a district employee, a peer, and an expert in the area of their
project to listen to, inquire about, and then evaluate their completed independent projects. During the school's first year, two
hundred panelists, including architects, Detroit's motor executives,
and the district's deputy superintendent, assessed its students.

The formal assessment of MHS's effectiveness produced clues
about the personality of the students for whom the motivational
gap between their former high school's expectations and MHS's was
forbiddingly too large to bridge. In contrast to students who grew
in autonomy, those who did not also did not grow as much on
maturity's other dimensions, were rated by the faculty as less mature, earned lower academic grades, were more dissatisfied with being a student at MHS, described their behavior as less ethical, and
were tested as being less empathic.[8] Strength enables strength; maturity enables autonomy.

Not to believe *realistically* that students can responsibly take
charge of their own education is to fail to tap the maturing power
that comes from being responsible.

Aut Early

> Schools of hope encourage students' assumption of responsibility for their own growth early and consistently.

Students are most educable during the early weeks and months of a school or class; how they begin to mature prefigures how growth will continue if consistently supported. If Kathy's students had had four years of traditional teaching first, they might not have responded as well by fifth grade to expectations that they be self-educating. Montessori teachers tell me that is what they have found.

Haverford illustrates the principle of expecting early and consistently that students will be responsible for their own growth. I have described how its upperclassmen introduced the freshmen to the college's values and honor codes in their first days. The college also early and consistently reminded them about its values in its collective meetings and values-oriented curricular courses.

Schools that fail to consistently expect students to be responsible for their own growth when they are most educable risk undermining their power to enable students to secure command of themselves.

Aut Test

> Schools of hope progressively reduce their expectations and structures to test students' budding autonomy to set and carry out their own hopes in increasingly varied situations.

Most schools fail to implement this principle consistently, just as most teachers fail to in their classrooms. Typically, seniors go through the same paces that freshmen do: imposed curricular requirements, scheduled classes, teacher-directed class activities and assigned work, reinforced dependency, and so on. Students are taught near the end of a course the same ways that they were at its beginning. With the exception of independent projects or student-initiated alternative learning opportunities, such as Proctor's French study abroad, seniors are channeled as freshmen are.

None of our four schools of hope wholeheartedly exemplified the principle of testing its students' autonomy in *progressively* diverse situations. Earlham College, in Richmond, Indiana, another Quaker school of hope, is my stellar example of how to encourage and test students' self-educating autonomy and growing self-command. Another daughter, intrigued by what she had learned about Richard the III when an eleventh-grader, pursued her interest in England, before entering Earlham. Disputing Shakespeare's portrayal of Richard, she elected to take an independent project course her sophomore year to research, create, and eventually present her interpretation in a three-act musical for the college. She wrote the play in verse and created its twenty-four musical scores, persuaded forty students to participate, selected a Richard willing to be taught to sing by a coach she found for him, directed and rehearsed the group, taught herself about lighting and staging, made the costumes as well as playbill scrolls, advertised the play, and charged one dollar for the two performances given two weeks before final exams to recoup her expenses.

Earlham's next challenge provoked her to test her self-educating autonomy more rigorously. Because it insisted she learn a language, she entered its nationally known program to teach English to public school students in Japan. She taught herself to speak, read, and write Japanese. She returned to Earlham to test her autonomy further by designing and offering a credited course on creativity to ten students as her senior project. She then returned to Japan to teach English in a private high school, live like a Japanese person, and teach herself to play and give concerts on the koto. Do you now understand what I mean by progressively reducing mandated structures to test students' autonomy and burgeoning self-command?

Failure to create developmentally appropriate motivational gaps in students' roles means that they do not become maturely autonomous and in command of themselves.

Aut Excel

> Schools of hope teach students to create their own
> standards of excellence and then affirm and reward
> themselves for approaching them.

Such schools must go beyond just rewarding students' correct
answers to stabilize their learning if they wish to encourage their
students' autonomy. Rewarding students with praise, gold stars,
good grades, or even money teaches them to depend on others for
signs that tell them what excellence is. Grades and honors become
the goals for which to work. Then we complain that students work
only for grades and have no genuine interest in learning.

Yes, rewarding learning is important, but teaching youth to
reward themselves for their own achievements is also necessary to
encourage their command of themselves. After all, the adult world
is a rather cold, unrewarding, and unappreciative place. Being mature enough to assess realistically the value of what we are doing
sustains motivation to pursue excellence in the face of indifference
or rejection. Creative people—authors, artists, inventors—who question the traditional and pioneer new pathways must be able to
affirm the worth of their efforts, sometimes for years, even for a
lifetime for the Van Goghs among us, until the rest of us recognize
their contribution.

Schools of hope create climates that encourage students to
create their own standards of excellence, hold themselves to them,
and reward themselves for their steps to their achievement. MHS's
struggles to create just such a climate have not been without pain.
It has eschewed daily quizzes and grades and sought other ways to
develop more intrinsic intellectual interests, strengthen desires to
excel, and encourage self-generated criteria of and rewards for excellence. But as most schools must, MHS must certify to the community its students' achievements and so is required to give
numerical course grades—hence the pain. Despite sharing in the
final grading process, two indolent graduating seniors angered by
their facilitators' judgments boycotted their graduation ceremony.

Monteux's maestro inculcated a standard of excellence that
students made their own. I complimented one student conductor for

what I and the enthusiastic audience believed to be a sterling performance. He responded by acknowledging that it was "okay." But then he severely criticized his own lack of authoritative presence, saying, "I know I still have a long way to go yet."

Schools that do not enable their students to become free of their external controls do not encourage maturing self-command.

We should never forget that a school is *not* its two miles of corridors, Olympic-sized swimming pool, up-to-date communication library, or budget. We should always remember that a school is a learning community of human beings. We don't really measure a school's worth by the number of its faculty's Ph.D.s, library books, or even students who graduate and go to college. An effective school is a school of hope that produces liberally educated students who have begun to secure command of their minds, characters, and selves. How well a school implements the twenty—undoubtedly there are more—principles that further maturing determines how educated its students will become.

Central to a school of hope are its adults. They create and model the school's vision; they implement the principles of maturing in their school and classrooms. Improving schools does not begin by mandating longer school days or more required math courses. It begins by establishing the climate and means that enable its faculty to continue maturing: developing their minds to educate, for example, interdisciplinarily and to creatively fulfill technology's promise; nurturing their interpersonal skills to work more collaboratively with each other and their students; reforming their values about what liberal education means; expanding their idea of what a teacher is to include—say, being more of a mentor, friend, guide, and counselor.

The U.S. Department of Education has identified the two principal impediments to school improvement as teachers' lack of desire to change and students' lack of commitment to their own growth.[9] Teachers are not *called* to teach or students to learn. No enduring improvement will occur until schools' adults view their work as a calling, not a job, and teach in ways to nurture their students' calling to learn. The next chapter suggests how to nurture teachers' calling by applying the twenty principles that contribute to maturing.

Chapter 12

Nurturing
the Growth of Teachers

We grievously misunderstand the meaning of vocation and what makes work fulfilling. Sociologists claim that Americans increasingly view their work more as an eight-hour job and less a lifelong vocation.[1] Today, more work primarily for extrinsic rewards, such as fat paychecks, power, and high status. Yesterday, so they claim, more viewed vocation as a calling, serving others or a cause; work implied craftmanship, even nobility—words that are passing out of our vocabulary. Young people look blankly at me when I ask what vocation means; few have heard of work as a calling. Chapter Two noted their pursuit of materialistic goals and the decline in their commitment to serve others or an ideal.

The demise of society's liberally educating vision for schools has devastated teachers' belief in themselves and their morale. Most still continue to be called to teaching for idealistic reasons—scarcely for its pay, power, or status. Their gifts that they hope their students will acquire—joy of learning, integrity, compassion—reveal that many remain idealists in their closeted hearts. They continue to believe in their profession's nobility, despite politicians' expectations that they be only technicians raising students' test scores, parents' views that they are only hirelings to get their children into the best colleges or jobs, and media's caricatures of them as dunces sitting on stools on *Newsweek* covers.

As a result of such demeaning expectations, teachers become conflicted about their identities as teachers. Erikson wisely observed that a healthy identity integrates a person's needs, talents, and values in a way of life that is *prized by society*.[2] Teachers do not feel respected for their vision of what they contribute to society's children. When surveyed about thirty attributes of a vocation that can make one feel satisfied, affirmed, and fulfilled, teachers express more discontent than other professionals with the rewards Americans use to measure success: pay, recognition, and status. They feel that they prostitute themselves to teach for goals that dismiss the ideals that called them into teaching.[3]

Unless one's identity is firmly and autonomously rooted, the consequences of society's devaluation are predictable: reduced morale, diluted calling, increased resistance to change, and guilt. We feel guilt when we fail to fulfill our potentials and deepest hopes. More than most other professionals, teachers are vulnerable to its ravages—not just because society blames them for their students' undistinguished test scores but because they believe, as Chapters One, Two, and Three showed, that few students are acquiring their gifts.

Teachers' morale is quite fragile, most so among public high school teachers, next among middle, and least among elementary school teachers. The morale of independent school teachers is higher than that of public school teachers at all levels and does not reliably differ from that of other professionals and managers.[4] Though the morale of college faculty has been higher than that of any of these other groups, it has declined as well, as has that of other professionals, such as lawyers.[5] But it is the erosion of teaching as a calling that most directly affects teachers' morale, schools' openness to change, and students' maturation. We can best understand the meaning of calling and how it can be revitalized by examining what we now know about vocational fulfillment.[6]

The Meaning of Vocational Fulfillment

Vocational fulfillment means high satisfaction with the varied attributes of one's work, such as type of occupation, collegial relationships, salary, opportunity to continue to grow throughout one's career, and competence.[7]

Vocational Fulfillment's Roots in Personality

Vocationally fulfilled adults have been happier since adolescence than unfulfilled ones. Because they are also more mature,[8] they have the coping skills to adapt (not just adjust) to their work to make it fulfilling for them.[9]

Regardless of occupation, sex, age, or nationality, the principal sources of vocational fulfillment are similar for all. They are not society's most valued job-related rewards. They are work's calling-related rewards. Therefore, we, not our supervisor or organization, are ultimately responsible for our own fulfillment and happiness.

The evidence for this is unusually consistent. For a lawyer or an accountant, a thirty-year-old male or a sixty-year-old female elementary or college teacher in the United States, Taiwan, or Israel, the same sources contribute *least* to morale. (Remarkably, the conclusion also holds for students as well, whether fifth-graders or college students.)[10] Surprisingly to many, satisfaction with salary, one's competence, work's demands on time and energy, and collegial relationships contribute least to one's overall morale. Of course, they do contribute, but not as much as other kinds of satisfaction. Raising salaries by $5,000 or reducing the number of courses taught will not increase morale unless satisfaction with work's other, more important attributes improves.[11]

To understand why satisfaction with one's salary and status, for example, doesn't contribute as much to morale as other factors, compare the satisfaction that they can provide with that provided by the five sources that contribute *most:* self-fulfillment, fulfillment of one's strongest needs, actualization of one's potential talents, opportunities to continue growing through most of one's professional life, and the type of work.

Teachers instantly recognize the difference between the least and most important contributors to fulfillment: work's extrinsic versus its intrinsic rewards, its objective versus its subjective meanings, and its union's demands versus individuals' personal needs. Work's extrinsic meanings—time, salary, and relationships—are not unimportant; it is just that satisfying them is not the most effective route to vocational fulfillment. They may be means to or conditions for fulfilling work's more important intrinsic meanings. But salary may or may not enhance the fulfillment of one's talents or growth through most of one's work life. Good relationships may further work's intrinsic meanings, such as continued growth, but in and of themselves, they do not contribute as much to overall morale.

Work that fosters continued growth and enables nascent talents to blossom provides the most direct path to fulfillment. It guarantees happiness and well-being. Regardless of its extrinsic rewards, work that summons and absorbs us gives us purpose, meaning, and fulfillment. Unfortunately, teachers are less satisfied than other professionals that their work provides them the opportunity to continue growing throughout their lives and so to fulfill their talents and needs.

Teachers in schools of hope have high morale. They are not governed primarily by extrinsic rewards. Proctor's poorly paid teachers were on duty twenty-four hours a day; MHS's teachers worked far into their dinner hours and planned during vacations; Haverford's pressured teachers, absorbed in their community's life, researched and wrote into their evenings and on their vacations; and Monteux's maestro met with individual students in the evening, critiqued their performance after a Sunday concert, and worked far into the early morning hours preparing the next day's scores. All those teachers were called by a vision that integrated their minds, characters, and selves. A romantic view of work, you might think. No. A practically idealistic one that is typical of mature people. Remember that vocationally fulfilled people are more mature than unfulfilled ones and that intrinsic rather than extrinsic satisfactions best predict their morale.

Signs That Work Is a Job, Not a Calling

Think of teachers—or colleagues at the law office, department store, or factory—that you know for whom work is a job, not a calling. If I visited your school or workplace, what visible signs should I look for to pick out those persons for whom work is just a job? For teachers, they are numerous. Not just one or two but their cumulative pattern indicates that teaching is a job, not a calling:

- The contract's conditions as the maximum: the teacher arrives at and leaves school at the specified time; resists additional faculty or in-service days or any additional responsibility unless paid; uses up every sick day though not really sick; is frequently absent; sits in the back of the auditorium during required school meetings to grade papers or read *Newsweek*.

- Ceaseless complaints: the teacher moans about salary, working conditions, students, other faculty, and, of course, the administration, board, and parents; does not keep up professionally— resists opportunities to go to conferences, visit other programs, read books such as this, alter lesson plans every several years, or teach a new course.

- Not being student-centered: the teacher is inaccessible to students outside of class; never varies teaching to meet students' different needs; doesn't care whether students say class is boring; never contacts parents if students are in difficulty; ignores or devalues their nonacademic talents; never watches their football games or musicals; puts them down; objects to teaching slower ones; rejects the role of "servant," in its best meaning, to students.

- Takes the easy way out: the teacher simply lectures; reads the text in class; lets the text define the course; assigns little homework and few papers that require time to evaluate; cursorily grades papers or lab reports; relies on multiple-choice tests.

- The classroom as a castle with the drawbridge up and the iron gate slammed shut: the teacher never invites others into the classroom; resists interdepartmental activities; is committed only to his or her own specialty; rules the kingdom by his or her own rules and ignores schoolwide expectations.

- Resistance to any idea that requires additional time, energy, or change: the teacher has a passive, negativistic attitude toward others, is actively critical of them, or overtly or subtly sabatoges their efforts to improve the school; principal commitment is to protect self, an out-of-school job, or personal interests.

Teachers know these signs in others and themselves. Students also know them. Ask them to identify the teachers for whom teaching and students for whom learning is a job. They know. The signs are death to individual happiness and well-being. They express attitudes and traits now known to produce unhappiness and ill health.[12] When work begins to become only a job that we seek to avoid, it is time to examine our lives, take ourselves in hand, and marshal the courage to either change ourselves or find work that is more fulfilling. When teaching becomes a job, not just teachers but, more important, students risk being hurt every day they enter school. How much enduring improvement will occur in schools whose committees work only on school time and insist that they be paid to meet after school or in the evenings?

When such signs become the collective faculty's self-image, then hope begins to die. If this book were about schools of despair, I could readily select exemplars—both public and independent. Their faculties think of themselves as losers. They are their own worst enemies. They are unable to agree about anything. Stuffy, traditional, and conventional, they predictably resist any change. Dispirited and irrevocably dissatisfied, they suspect and distrust their administrators, their boards, and each other. Not emotionally committed to excellence, they actively undermine anyone who works to improve the school. And on and on.

To create schools of hope, we must first enable ourselves to discover and fulfill our own maturing potentials. To do so, we must understand how we continue to grow, the handicaps and pathologies that erode our calling, and the kind of colleagues who nourish our calling. Merely providing a new technique and program and ignoring how personality must change if they are to "take" is ultimately futile. The technique will turn out to be but another passing fad to be resurrected with a new name twenty years later. Schools will not get better unless their adults are open to new ideas, encouraged to risk imaginatively and flexibly implement their own ideas, provided time to care for individual students, spurred to enthusiastically infect them with the desire to learn, and expected to make mistakes about which they laugh and from which they learn.

The Maturing of Teachers

An understanding of how adults continue to grow and fulfill themselves during their working years is only now emerging. Teachers' descriptions of their growth and studies of how adults mature into middle age suggest ways to further their growth and deepen their calling.[13] The suggested time periods for maturing are educated guesses. They certainly do not apply to everyone.

Motivating Gaps' Challenges

The gap between what teachers learned about teaching in college and what they discover during their first years of full-time teaching is huge for most. The gap can be such a chasm as to propel despairing teachers out of the classroom within their first few years of teaching.[14] Of fifty new teachers I worked with in one southern state, only five definitely planned to return the next year. The yawning gap plunges many into a high state of frustration and thus of educability.

Leaders of schools of hope know how to use such periods of enhanced educability to nurture maturing. They know that we are most educable during the first weeks and months of adapting to a new role. They understand that how we learn to adapt today may prefigure how we will adapt in the future. At this most critical moment in a teacher's maturing, schools typically respond in just about the most unhelpful way possible. Pressed by their own concerns, most leave their novice teachers to stew and struggle alone with their dispiriting baptisms—sometimes for the entire year. This conspiracy of silent isolation only confirms the novices' belief that they should be able to answer their questions by themselves and so aggravates their self-exploration and self-doubt.

Growing Awareness

Discovering that teaching is not what they had idealized, troubled beginning teachers immediately begin to reflect about why the kids are so apathetic. Why are they not prepared for class? What am I doing wrong? Am I not explaining things clearly? How do I control those disruptive boys? What do other teachers think when they hear how loud my class is? How can I get the students to like but also respect me? Will I ever get a night off? Is teaching really for me? Tens of similar questions flood into their awareness.[15]

Novices' maturity, particularly the maturity of their reflective skills, now becomes the decisive determinant of whether their heightened educability leads to further maturing. More mature teachers will deepen their awareness of themselves. Though shaken up, bruised, taken down more than a peg or two in self-esteem, forced to reorder their values, even question their calling, they can reflect in ways that spark and guide considered action. Teaching's first years are primarily self-revelatory ones. One teacher said, "I have learned I can intimidate unintentionally; I am trying to be less sarcastic, more sincere."

Less mature teachers can fall prey to either of two handicaps: reflective obtuseness or obsessional indecision.

Obtuseness means immature symbolization. Some may not have the skills to identify and articulate the reasons for their distress. Not understanding, for example, today's changing students and how they need to grow, and unskilled in reflecting about how to teach differently, such teachers can respond only as they were taught—to be slaves to their technique-based pedagogy, texts, and preformed teacher-proof curricula. Even if they dared to, they don't know how to break away from the tyranny of what become their permanent crutches.

Obsessional indecision can mean overdeveloped symbolization that is not well integrated with other coping skills. Teachers, more in departmentally oriented than elementary schools, are prone to develop this handicap even to the point of a pathology. Living in their minds, daily teaching students to live in theirs, entertaining every shade of gray, they learn how to obsess more than how to act decisively on the basis of incomplete knowledge. Such teachers, inclined to figure everything out to its last *t*, fear the uncertainty of taking risks. Like eloquent faculty meetings that want one more committee report before voting and so eternally postpone making a commitment, some teachers learn how to use their minds' symbolizing power to not act.

Other-Centered Growth

Teachers begin to leave their self-absorbed, even paralyzing despair behind when they learn that colleagues have gone through similar baptisms of doubt. They realize that they are not and never have been alone. More often than not, a caring colleague empathically says in the hall one day, "I had a hard time too when first teaching," or "Would you like me to visit your class?" or "Let's talk over lunch about what to do with these distractible kids."

More mature teachers are willing to and know how to turn to others, including their own students, to search out resources for perspective and assistance. In their first years, teachers say they become much more understanding of students. Other teachers become colleagues, not competitive adversaries. One said, "I'm more interested in other teachers' ideas and motives now."

Less mature teachers can react to teaching's frustrations in two ways: indulging their narcissism or becoming a camp follower or student groupie. Self-centered teachers can be tempted to use their classrooms' isolation and controls to force students to adjust to their style, needs, and dictates. The movie *The Prime of Miss Jean Brodie* beautifully illustrates how an experienced teacher, masked by a Ms. Chipsean love for her students, subtly destroyed their healthy growth by manipulating them to adjust to *her* demands and values. One angry tenured teacher said that it was the students' problem, not his, that they were bored with his class. He was not going to kowtow to them; they had to learn how to deal with boredom themselves.

Too other-centered teachers so compulsively conform to and please others that they don't develop a strong sense of themselves or enable their students to. They may be the enthusiastic camp followers of every passing fad or consultant. They may be groupies fawning over their students, gushing about them, and unconsciously seducing them to love them at the expense of holding them to expectations that might create frustration and hostility. In their first years, such teachers are especially susceptible to the temptation of seeking their students' love more than their respect.

Becoming More Integrated

Teachers are understandably absorbed by their own classrooms, students, and time-consuming preparations during their first years. They are centered in their own classrooms. Other teachers are there to help them, not to be helped by them. Not until they feel more in command of their own classrooms do they feel freer to grow beyond them to work less self-centeredly and more selflessly with others. This progressive integration typically becomes more prominent between the fifth and tenth professional years.

About this time, more mature teachers report that they begin to explore the relationships between their intellectual discipline and those of others, initiate collaborative work with others, and feel more a part of the faculty and more at home with themselves as teachers. Maturing teachers no longer feel at odds with their own humanness and their role as teachers; they can be themselves in the classroom and with their colleagues.

Less mature teachers may never experience this phase of professional growth because of two obstacles: scatteredness and tunneled focus. Teachers may fail to get themselves together because of impulsivity, inability to focus energy, limited intellectual resolving or synthetic powers, resistance to making commitments, or temperamental incompatibility with teaching's way of life. Scattered teachers just can't get themselves and their classrooms organized. As they are too responsive to every idea (some even creative) that pops into their heads, their classrooms can become a sparkling, even dramatic chaos. Students are zigged one way and zagged another; projects are enthusiastically started but seldom completed with excellence.

At integration's other pole are the compulsive teachers. They are so single-mindedly focused that they seem despairingly efficient to more casual colleagues. We recognize them by their superbly organized curricular units, religiously and meticulously completed by their planned dates; their beautifully ordered and neat classrooms; and their clear, logical, and cool descriptions of their goals on parents' night. Such paragons of academic virtue annoyingly produce students who score high on achievement tests. But at what price? The consequences of too tunneled a personality: susceptibility to breaking apart when unable to escape chaos or cope with negativistic students; inability to teach flexibly, work cooperatively or interdepartmentally, and play spontaneously; or apprehension about taking risks because they are too tightly organized to entertain other ways of being. So they are not open to exploring pathways to grow other than that on which they are already. They can be formidable obstacles to others' efforts to improve their school, which depend upon tolerance of ambiguity, risk taking, playfulness, even temporary chaos.

More Stably Grounded Maturing

Only by their early thirties, perhaps as much as ten years or more after beginning teaching, do most teachers feel centered and firmly grounded as teachers, certain about and committed to their calling. They feel their path's continuity and foresee it as their path for the future. Teaching fits them. Erikson is wrong about when young professionals fashion a stable identity; it is much later than the late teens or early twenties. A teacher of eleven years' experience reported that only recently had he affirmed his sense of teaching as his true vocation.

More mature teachers have been tested by many students and classes. They intuitively recognize and quickly respond appropriately to recurring types of students and crises. They are resilient, for they have been through "this" before. More self-confident, and, of course, predictably competent, they verge on joining the fraternity of their more experienced colleagues and becoming mentors to younger teachers, with whom they can still empathize.

Again, immature teachers are vulnerable to two handicaps: premature foreclosure of identity and too rigid an identity. Failure to understand how teachers mature has led unions and schools to inappropriately attempt to support teachers by advocating and granting tenure too early. Misunderstanding faculty maturing and granting tenure after only three to five years can become unassailable barriers to some faculty members' growth and school improvement. Immature teachers are vulnerable to foreclosing their identity prematurely, as Erikson warned against. Guaranteed security risks entrenching work's extrinsic meanings, prematurely fixing teaching as a job, and reducing motivational gaps that spur continued growth. More mature teachers will not be adversely affected, for they will continue to search, test themselves, and grow.

Tenure protects faculty from capricious administrators and guarantees that political pressure will not restrict their freedom to teach and pursue truth wherever it leads. But it has now become too great an impediment to significant improvement of schools. Other legal ways should be found to protect teachers from arbitrary disciplinary actions. Teachers who are called to serve their students and have high morale don't need tenure to spark and sustain their growth and work for improvement; teachers whose work is a job and have low morale need tenure to protect them from expectations for change. Independent school teachers who receive low salaries and no tenure have much higher morale at all levels than public school teachers who are paid noticeably more and are guaranteed tenure.

Even for faculty called to teach, too firm an identity can itself block further growth. Schools unwittingly abet this possibility by failing to provide the appropriate opportunities for teachers to continue to nurture their calling. When experienced teachers' satisfactions are compared to those of other professionals, such as poets, physicians, and managers, they are found to be less satisfied with their opportunities to achieve at their potential level of talent and to grow the rest of their lives—dramatically so for public high school teachers. Ironically, schools encourage faculty rigidity; they are *not* places in which many believe that they can continue to mature and find fulfillment even though their primary goal is to help their students learn how to grow throughout their lives.

Achieving Autonomous Command of Self

Teachers of fifteen years or more of experience agree with the model of maturing. They speak of having become more independent, self-directing, and able to stand up to authority. As one teacher wrote, "I shut my door and do what I think is best for my students." Beginning teachers never say that. Experienced teachers are more satisfied than novice ones with the amount of freedom and independence that teaching provides them. They have suffered each fad's cycles, lived through the turmoil and free school movement of the sixties, the back-to-basics of the seventies, and the legislated reforms of the eighties, and have seen little measurable improvement in their schools. Skeptical but wiser, they make their own judgments about what their goals should be and how to reach them. A twenty-year veteran said that "covering" his content no longer drove him; rather, he had learned how "to make it a vehicle for teaching other things." Another, with fifteen years' experience, said that she now felt responsible for her own learning and no longer needed a mentor.

Maturely autonomous teachers are not cynics or curmudgeons. They remain loyal to their schools and still feel called to serve their students; they remain hopeful and open to *considered* change. They are the faculty members whom others listen to; they are the ones who lead their colleagues to risk.

The handicaps that plague faculty in their middle and older years are the obverse of earlier other-centeredness. Overdeveloped autonomy shows itself in one of two ways. One is raising the drawbridge to one's castle and retreating in splendid self-sufficient isolation from the surrounding turmoil. The other creates more pathological effects. Most schools have one or two older, forceful, and charismatic paranoidal faculty members. They are inevitably very bright, eloquently articulate, psychologically shrewd, and suspicious of authority. They intuitively know how to achieve power by marshaling faculty and student dissatisfaction, which, rather than the welfare of the school or their students, is their consuming goal. Like magnets, they attract less maturely autonomous faculty members. They can create a festering oppositional group that fights and blocks every effort to change. Not astutely dealt with, such faculty members can forestall every effort to improve a school. They can devastate others' morale. As one teacher told me, "I've battled them and their hangers-on for years; I'm exhausted and about to give up working to improve our school." Woe to the school that has more than a few of these Joseph McCarthys and no leaders who can draw out their poison in ways that don't precipitate an out-and-out war between the rest of the faculty and its leaders. To one superintendent's query of what to do about them, I replied, "benignly neglect them. Tenure protects them. If you fight them, other marginal faculty will come to their support. Pour additional resources into those called to serve their students—not themselves."

Creating a School That Nurtures Teachers' Calling

Although relationships with colleagues do not *directly* contribute much to high morale, they and colleagues' personalities are certainly not unimportant. They contribute to creating a climate that can sustain one's calling. Both public and independent school teachers are more satisfied than other professionals and managers with their work relationships—a heretofore unknown fringe benefit of teaching on which schools need to capitalize.[16]

How do teachers perceive their colleagues? Though less than a majority view them as models of creativity or self-educating learners, they do judge them to be caring and decent people. At least 80 percent of teachers in independent schools, for whom I have more reliable information, believe that their colleagues are hard-working, dedicated, capable, caring, and conscientious. At least two-thirds also believe that they are academic, friendly, helpful, honest, and responsible.

While teachers feel positively about their peers, they agree less well that their typical peer is the ideal colleague who would most encourage and support their continued growth and calling. The following list presents the traits—in approximate declining order in frequency of citation—that teachers wish their *ideal* colleague had; it also lists the percentages who view their typical colleague as *actually* having such strengths.

Ideal Personality Trait	Percentage of Teachers Who View Their Colleagues as Having Such Traits
Intellectually exciting	33
Creative	49
Adventurous	29
Caring	86
Enthusiastic	58
Humorous	48
Imaginative	39
Cooperative	58
Trusting	35
Accepting	51

The majority of the independent school teachers believe that their colleagues have only four of their ideal strengths: caring, enthusiasm, cooperativeness, and acceptance. That about a third or fewer of teachers view their colleagues as trusting, adventurous, or intellectually exciting speaks volumes about where we must begin to create schools of hope that nurture teachers' calling. Some of our country's allegedly finest schools have not created a collective faculty self-concept that supports and strengthens each other's calling. How can we expect teachers to improve their schools if they do not believe they have the strengths that spark and sustain their growth?

To create a school of hope that nurtures its faculty's calling, we must first select teachers who are open to continued maturing and then create a school climate that expects and supports such maturing. Principals and faculties that have no say about who their colleagues will be cannot create or sustain over time the school's distinctive vision and the calling of its adults to serve its youth.

Selection of Mature Teachers

When asked how I would select faculty for a school dedicated to human excellence or arete, I answer, "First select for maturity; only then select for technical competence." Why? Mature but less competent persons have the strengths to develop the expertise they need. Because they command their own talents and are their own self-teachers, they can teach themselves the competence they need as well as continue to educate themselves most of their lives. They don't need the fig leaf of another summer course to increase their salary to motivate them to learn. Immature but technically competent teachers are risks; they may suffer immaturity's handicaps, be uneducable, and become nagging pains to their peers. I want models of mature self-educating teachers in my school to inspire my students to become likewise. I want models that approach arete, or human excellence.

"What specific strengths would you look for if head of Arete?" With the assistance of the faculty, I would search for those that the list above describes as the ideal colleague. I'd then look for the visible signs of maturity that Appendix A identifies. First, I want a teacher who has developed high competence in several areas, not necessarily only academic ones—say, being an Eagle Scout and captain of a winning team, or a superb chess player and choral singer, or an expert mechanic and an A math student—achievements that demand cognitive maturity and reveal a generalized desire for and commitment to an ideal of excellence.

Second, I want teachers who create caring and loving relationships with others and who believe that to teach is to serve students' maturing.

Third, I would choose teachers who have quite a lot of free energy. They should be contagiously enthusiastic about what they teach, able to juggle several commitments or projects simultaneously, excited about new interests and projects, and adventurously taking some risks.

Fourth, I would not select any teacher whose references *never* mentioned any of maturing's metavalues as salient attributes of character. I want teachers who overflow with goodness. Their honesty, compassion, fairness, integrity, commitment, depth of ethical concern, and courage should so visibly emerge in the way they relate to others and themselves that students cannot fail to know what *ethical* means.

And fifth, I want teachers on my faculty who accept and trust themselves and others enough to laugh at themselves. In our interview, I want them to unabashedly tell me—with a warm smile and a humane dash of humor—not just their gifts but the ones they wish they could give themselves. Every faculty needs some colleagues who have self-perspective and a sense of humor to help it to transcend its own handicaps.

Only then would I select for their technical competence.

And then I'd work darn hard to create *with the faculty* a school that kept alive and strengthened its calling to serve its students.

Nurturing Teachers' Growth and Calling

The highest priority of schools and school boards should be ensuring their leaders' and teachers' continued growth and calling to serve their students—essential qualities to further students' own growth and calling to learning. Ernest Boyer calls us to pay closer attention to school's "human dimension";[17] Phillip Schlechty urges us to nurture teachers' growth in ways consistent with the school's mission;[18] and Thomas Sergiovanni encourages leaders to enable their faculty's personal growth.[19]

To further teachers' growth, we should work with, rather than against, the direction of that growth. Teachers are most educable during their first months of teaching; the *best* resources should be dedicated to that period. A school's vision must become embodied early in their personalities. Teaching loads should be reduced so they can visit and work with teachers who model the school's goals. Mentors should be selected for their maturity, calling to teaching, and adventurousness, not for their disciplinary expertise. As their principal, I would ask beginning teachers to invite me several times during the semester to visit their best classes. I would ask them to share their hopes for their students, and I would then share mine.

If tenure must be retained, the faculty and leaders should consider it only when a teacher has demonstrated a self-educating person's mature autonomy and a number of an ideal colleague's strengths.

Experienced teachers should be encouraged to shake themselves up and take new risks. The fifteen-year-veteran fourth-grade teacher who needs a new challenge to avoid becoming stale should have the opportunity to work with the same kids in the fifth grade. Maturely autonomous teachers could be encouraged to assume leadership within the school *and* community.

How might the principles that further maturation be applied to strengthen or revitalize a faculty's calling? Rather than exhausting you with suggestions about how to apply each, I have selected critical attributes of a school of hope to illustrate how to apply some. But one warning! A program's purposes must be honestly stated, generated out of genuine care, implemented with integrity, sustained over time with commitment, and courageously risked. No hidden agendas. No manipulation. No deceits. No failures to follow through. Teachers have experienced too much of these.

Creating a Distinctive Vision and Expectation of Continued Growth

A school of hope has a distinctive vision of its liberally educating goals, of which the head is its steward. A change in a school's leadership is the most propitious time to form or reaffirm that vision. The leader's honeymoon period is the time when everyone is most educable. Uncertainty excites expectations that create gaps that can motivate change.

As Arete's new leader, my highest priority the first weeks would be to work with the teachers and other key staff to clarify and articulate our mutual hopes for our students and adults. Since Arete is a humanely sized school that enables more personal than bureaucratic relationships, I would devote an hour to leisurely exploring with each staff member four questions: What are the most important gifts you hope your students will thank you for ten years from now? When you reflect about what you achieved last year, of what are you most proud? What needs, talents, potentials do you wish you could fulfill or develop further that would make this year an even more fulfilling and productive one for you personally? And then, You know our limited budget and resources, but what do you need that could help you grow in these ways? To open a dialogue about the school's primary values, I'd then offer some of my hopes for Arete's students.

Only after I had *really* heard each person would I frame a working paper to articulate and clarify the faculty's gifts and hopes and their relationship to mine. Leaders cannot abrogate their most distinctive responsibility: stewardship of the school's vision. But the vision must resonate with that of most faculty if a genuinely shared communion of value is to guide Arete. I'd find some way, no matter how small, to let everyone know I had heard them. I would try to secure the resources each needed: a day to visit another school, a special request to the board for discretionary funds for travel or additional supplies, a copy of an article I had read, or a comment about what I'm trying to do for them but have not yet succeeded in accomplishing. To keep the school's primary values also in awareness, I'd ask what ways they had discovered to help Susan become more independent or Tim more caring.

Since my highest priority is to nurture teachers' growth and calling, my desk would not get in the way of my being with them in their classrooms, library, lounge, lunchroom, even bathrooms. And I would acknowledge growth or achievement whenever I sensed it.

In the following paragraphs, I illustrate how the principles that further maturing can be applied and describe in some detail the steps I would take in creating a school of hope. To minimize suspicion and avoid arousing feelings of manipulation and paternalism, I *must* be scrupulously honest, open about my motives, sincere, and genuinely caring about each colleague's well-being.

Encouraging Faculty Awareness. Maturing's first step is becoming aware of the vision's meaning. Because the ultimate sign of a mature or educated person is self-command, I encourage my colleagues (Symb confront) to form their own goals for the year (Symb goal). For them to tell how they plan to achieve them requires reflection (Symb reflect). By making my highest priority caring about the faculty's own fulfillment, I hope that they will rise to my implicit expectation that they as the leaders of their classes will find ways to nurture their students' calling to learn (Symb model). A school's climate of values reflects its interpersonal ethos; how leaders get along with their staffs influences how they in turn relate to their students or employees.

Fostering Other-Centeredness. Maturing also depends upon trusting relationships. Distrust between teachers and administrators is so endemic that it is a formidable barrier to generating and sustaining teachers' commitment to restructuring schools. For years, experienced teachers have weathered numerous changes in leadership and interminable efforts to change them. They cynically but correctly say that little ever really changes. Teachers most frequently wish that schools would anticipate the consequences of administrative and faculty plans, implement them consistently, and actually complete them.[20]

How do I create the trust that efforts to change will be worthwhile (Other trust)? By being willing to share my motives and personal hopes; making every effort early on to fulfill some part of my implicit promise to help them get the resources they need; persisting through the year to serve their growth; and modeling sustained interest in the hope that they too will assume more responsibility to encourage students to mature (Other care).

Promoting Integrative Growth. Teachers feel too great a gap between their schools' goals and their implementation. A mercurial head constantly violated his school's mission statement that valued respect for others. One day he burst into a new teacher's classroom to tell her in front of her shocked students that he was not reappointing her the next year. If I value caring as an outcome, then I had better consistently witness it in my relationships with others. If I expect teachers to be responsible and if I promise to find resources for them, then I must make a good-faith effort to do so. I must be willing to substitute for their class when they visit another school or loan my own book if the library can't purchase a copy (Integ goals; Symb model).

Beginning to Stabilize Maturing's Processes. Teachers have suffered enough one-shot efforts, quick fixes, here-today-gone-tomorrow fads, and erratic and unpredictable budgetary support. Priority outcomes must be clearly identified and resources conserved and dedicated to their *sustained* achievement. Better to husband one's resources for the most important priorities than squander them on demands to be and do all things for everyone.

People support each other in a school of hope. Exploring with them the specific steps that they will take begins to stabilize coping strengths (Stab rehearse). Best intentions wither away over the weeks unless reawakened. After reviewing each teacher's hopes and plans until I know them well (Stab external), I am primed to spontaneously inquire about their progress. Faculty tend to feel that they are not recognized by anyone. So acknowledgment as well as affirmation of their growth may encourage them to persist (Stab affirm). To the basketball coach in the gym after a game, "How did you ever get Eddie to focus his energies so well? He's a real cut-up in my class." To the drama teacher in the hall, "I never thought anyone could ever get forty-three eighth-graders to put on the *Mikado*." Just a few honestly felt words can spur us to persist and try again—and perhaps to more generously acknowledge and appreciate our students.

Nourishing Autonomy. A calling is a summons or impulsion to persist regardless of temporary disappointments and frustrations, limited resources, and inadequate extrinsic rewards: Billie disappoints us; the budget for supplies has been cut back 20 percent; salaries aren't keeping up with inflation; and no one seems to notice how hard I work.

How can I enable myself and my colleagues to hold on to and deepen the calling that brought us into teaching in spite of everything that erodes it away? I early want teachers to know my faith in their willingness to be responsible for their own continued growth (Aut faith; Aut early). So I invite faculty to become more involved in and responsible for their own growth. Providing individualized resources is one way to support their efforts (Integ involve). Next year I want to provide them the opportunity to reflect about their efforts and successes and request more resources. Faculty need to become their own self-diagnosticians freely in charge of prescribing for themselves (Symb reflect; Integ exper; Aut early). If they genuinely feel such self-command, maybe they'll have faith in their students' ability to assume more responsibility for their growth. Maybe they will risk giving students some measured freedom to learn how to use it wisely. Asking teachers to affirm their own strengths bolsters autonomy and can sustain them even in the face of *Newsweek* covers and societal charges that they are failing (Aut excel).

Schools of hope have leaders who, as stewards and articulators of their vision of human excellence, strengthen their colleagues' calling. Since trust is so critical to sustaining a calling, special steps sometimes need to be taken to sanction self-conscious efforts to strengthen it.

Creating a Climate of Trust

I had worked with a high school's improvement committee and then for a day with its faculty. After months of dedicated effort to fashion a long-range plan, the committee encountered budding sprigs of resistance: nit-picking, scheduling hassles, increasingly skeptical as well as cynical comments, and decreasing numbers of volunteers. So we surveyed the teachers', students', and parents' views of the school and students and the teachers' views of their colleagues. We found that fewer than 20 percent of any group believed the school or each other to be trusting.

Might the absence of an accepting, safe, and trusting climate have contributed to the faculty's growing resistance to commit itself emotionally to its own plans? Such resistance is not uncommon when a faculty must begin to fish or cut bait. It is much easier to plan and plan. A commitment is much more troubling to make. It demands that we take risks and that we really change our personalities. Before everything else, we need a dependably supportive and trusting interpersonal climate.

The survey's results were presented at a meeting of the school's faculty, which then broke into groups of five who did not know each other well. They explained to each other why they had not viewed their school, students, or each other as trusting. They were asked to be empathic and nonjudgmental. The challenge ignited prolonged and excited discussion. Forty-five minutes later, the faculty reunited, and each member selected one voiced idea that had been presented in his or her group's discussion and rephrased it in one sentence that described an *affirmative* step that might increase trust. After the first affirmative step had been presented, each teacher paused a minute or two before speaking to reflect about the preceding idea.

The faculty's ideas convincingly showed that criticizing each other really troubled many. Several felt that others so competitively and harshly put them down that they feared being hurt if they talked in meetings; they had gradually withdrawn their interest in improvement. I was not surprised. I had noted earlier how one teacher emotionally testifying to his hopes had been attacked with cynical and sarcastic remarks.

After the meeting, the principal collated the suggestions and asked each department to discuss them and agree about the steps to be taken to increase trust within the department and school. From that time, the tone of the faculty meetings radically changed. The chairperson of the improvement committee gave me an example: "Do you remember that man who wasted that teacher at our last workshop? He had been quiet all year, but at our last meeting he started to attack another teacher. The rest of us spontaneously, and

I have to admit quite aggressively, interrupted to tell him that we had agreed not to do that to each other any more."

What were the principles that contributed most to creating a more trusting climate? The survey of their own perceptions shook up the faculty but clarified how it collectively saw the school and itself (Symb confront). The opportunity to reflect about why so few felt that the school and faculty were trusting gave the faculty members greater insight about how to create a more favorable climate for growing (Symb reflect). The principal's follow-up request that each department and ultimately the entire faculty figure out how to create a more trusting interpersonal ethos among themselves was critical. It sustained reflection, brought hidden issues into the open, and resulted in the creation of a more open and vulnerable interpersonal environment (Stab conseq; Other trust).

Schools of hope have alive relationships that are growth-inducing. Mutual trust must be present if caring and risk taking are to occur. Strong enough to reflect about why they have not been effective, such schools can take appropriate corrective action.

Empathically Understanding the Role of a Student

A third way to provoke faculty growth is to offer teachers the opportunity to be a student for a day. For their personal in-service day, two or three teachers are given the names of randomly selected students unknown to them. They then shadow their students for the day, eat with them in their lunchroom, and go to the gym, even the student bathrooms. During the day's last period, the teachers reflect together about two questions: How do they feel as a student, and what changes could be made to make them feel better? Their anonymous report is added to their colleagues' to be later collated and analyzed for a reflective and action-commitment faculty day.

Experiencing what people in different roles undergo is a potentially powerful prod to new growth (Other roles). Participating teachers universally report two painful feelings: boredom and emotional exhaustion (Integ involve). Recall that only 12 percent of public high school teachers but 56 percent of students view school as boring. Teachers know that school, though not *their* classes, can be boring. But not until they have felt the pain of sitting for hours themselves in five dreadfully similar classes, rushing to be on time for the next class, needing a pass to go to the bathroom, where there is no toilet paper, shouting to be heard in the lunchroom, and sitting next to a sweating student who had no time to get a shower after gym do they really *know* the boredom and weariness that students report (Stab conseq).

Used to viewing education solely in terms of their own classes and their own courses, teachers glimpse for the first time the gap between a school's goals and their implementation (Integ goals) and the meaning of a year's 180 school days (Integ context). And not until required to reflect with others to understand why they felt as they did (Integ exper) and then brainstorm how they themselves might educate differently (Symb reflect) do some become more educable for rethinking their own goals and methods.

Schools of hope have adults who empathically understand what it means to be a student and can enter into their interpersonal world as they perceive it.

Sustaining Alteration of a Role to Stabilize Growth

Although shadowing a student or even being paired with another teacher for a day is a one-shot (and inexpensive) experience that can spark maturing for some, to stabilize growth requires more prolonged intensely involving experiences. Some schools contribute funds for more sustained growth-inducing experiences during summers: European history teachers may live in an Austrian village, science teachers work in an IBM or Silicon Valley lab, or a Japanese language teacher hike and bike in rural Japan.

Outward Bound's month-long Hurricane Island program taught me the transforming effects that a sustained experiential program can have. Each summer, twenty-four teachers arrived at Maine's Hurricane Island to be divided into two coed groups. Each group was given a thirty-foot open boat to learn how to sail and navigate along one of the world's most dangerous sailing coasts. Each boat had experienced Outward Bound leaders trained *not* to take over too quickly when the novice crew got into trouble. The sailors-to-be learned how to sail, navigate Maine's treacherous rocky coast, plot their daily runs, endure days of being fogbound, and live and get along with each other in an open boat with no bunks, tables, electricity, protection from penetrating fog, or toilets.

One summer, the two groups took half a day off the boats to participate in a reflective seminar about education. Their real treat, particularly for the women, was being able to use an outhouse. Be empathic and imagine how you might change as a result of such an intensely interpersonal (as well as potentially dangerous) expedition. The participants learned that growth does not occur if it is not constantly tested and corrected (Stab external). They learned to carefully think out their next day's course (Stab rehearse). One navigating team had inaccurately plotted its position, delaying its rendezvous with the other boat far into the scary moonless night; the Outward Bound leaders had not stepped in to protect the crew from its mistake (Stab conseq). Reflection about what and how they were learning (Symb reflect) from their experience (Integ exper) showed how pallid their former classrooms had been. To a person, they vowed that they would not return to their classrooms to teach as they had done, some for more than twenty years. Learning how to live cooperatively with each other to achieve a common goal—in this case, survival—under such stressful conditions had shown them the intrinsic inseparability of mind from character and self.

North Carolina provides a less scary week-long alternative experience for its teachers. The state's Center for the Advancement of Teaching (NCCAT) provides a free residential renewal experience for several groups of twenty experienced teachers each week in the Great Smoky Mountains. Its purpose is "to encourage professional strengths—the passion and the intellect that are their strongest allies in the daily business of teaching."[21] Intellectually stimulating seminars on far-ranging topics such as the global community combined with leisure time for reflective and spirited discussions (and tasty meals) not only refresh but call out potentials for renewed growth (Symb confront; Integ context). Teachers report a rekindled pride in their profession; they feel affirmed by the state for being a teacher to its children (Stab affirm).

Teachers in schools of hope willingly risk to create powerful involving learning environments and hold themselves accountable for their effects.

Learning How to Take Risks in a School

Not even a bare handful of teachers can experience the privilege of self-transformation by sailing along Maine's coast. But teachers can create their own privilege in their schools if they have the will and maturity. An elementary school faculty taught me that. The school claimed to teach its students to be self-educating learners. In a survey of its sixth- and seventh-graders and faculty, no one described the school or students as having any attributes of autonomous learners. Visiting the classes confirmed their impression; I saw no teaching that might achieve the school's publicized goal. So I assigned the faculty homework to complete before returning a month later: risk teaching in ways designed to achieve their goal (Symb confront). I assumed that they could teach themselves (Aut faith) and wanted to encourage them to step out of their traditional roles to try others (Aut early; Other role).

Two weeks later, the school canceled my visit. The faculty was not ready for me. Six months later, it was. In the meantime, it had divided itself into teams of three; each agreed to meet for a bag lunch once a week to share what they were learning and assist each other with their homework (Other trust; Other care; Other skills). They visited each other's classes and reflected together about what they saw (Symb reflect). So intrigued with what they were learning about how maturing proceeds, they created a monthly newspaper in which they described their exploratory efforts. Their failures were so helpful that they sent copies to their students' parents, inviting them to work with them to help their children become more self-reliant and self-educating (Integ involve). Reading about their adventures and what they were learning was most moving. They reaffirmed my faith that a faculty can raise itself by its collective bootstraps and, as one teacher told me, create an intellectually exciting school and have fun while doing it.

After engaging the faculty members in a reflective and humorous day about what they had learned from their homework (Symb reflect), I grounded their inductions on the model of maturing and its principles (Integ exper; Integ context). They have never needed me to return. They have become a responsible risk-taking and self-teaching faculty in command of its collective self.

Schools of hope have mature adults who trust, accept, and care for each other; their teachers can enthusiastically cooperate with each other to take imaginative risks to create an intellectually exciting school. They can laugh at their individual and collective mistakes. They can create the ideal faculty that nourishes each member's growth.

Students' Calling to Learn

Students who enjoy school and are called to learn are similar to teachers who have high morale and are called to teach. So I only briefly describe what I have learned about students' satisfaction with their vocational role as students.[22] The following chapters illustrate how maturity's principles can be applied in the school and classroom to nurture their calling to learn.

Students' morale remarkably parallels that of teachers. Elementary and middle school students are more satisfied with school than high school ones. Independent school students are more content than public school students with their schools. Public high school students are less satisfied with school than their teachers are.

Just as adults' morale is inextricably tied to their personalities, so students' morale is to theirs. Students who enjoy school predictably spend more hours on their homework and so secure better academic grades. Students who enjoy their vocation as students participate more frequently in cocurricular and community activities, spend fewer hours working for money during the week, drink alcohol and use drugs less frequently, and report behaving more ethically than students who do not enjoy it. MHS students who were most satisfied with being students described themselves as more responsible, more accepting and tolerant of peers who differed from them, such as the handicapped, minorities, and gays, and as more willing to be close friends with them. The MHS faculty viewed them as more flexible and interpersonally mature: trustful, gentle, understanding of others, and warm.[23]

From fifth grade on, the meaning of being a student as a calling or job is identical to the meaning of being a teacher. Teachers need to understand that what fulfills them also fulfills their students. The *least* powerful contributors to student morale are identical to theirs: satisfaction with their grades (comparable to salary), competence, quality of peer relationships, and school's demands on their energy and time. The *most* important contributors are also similar: satisfaction with their self-fulfillment as students, using their best potentials, opportunities to develop the skills and attitudes needed to grow the rest of their lives, and their role as students.

Work's meanings are deeply generic. Work expresses our personality and is a way for us to mature. Why not test how empathically you understand what being a student is like by identifying at least ten signs that students view their work as a job rather than a calling? If you need some hints, leaf back to the signs that suggest that a teacher's work is only a job.

How can we create schools and classrooms that nurture rather than snuff out a student's calling to learn? Recall that maturity is the most powerful contributor to fulfillment and morale, as well as achievement. The next three chapters apply the principles that further maturation to the school and classroom to educate mind, character, and self in ways that deepen students' calling to learn.

Chapter 13

Educating the Mind

The liberal arts curriculum expresses our values about what students should know and should be able to do with what they know. It ideally prepares them to adapt to their adult roles. However, its measures of students' achievement, such as academic grades and test scores, only marginally predict their adult success.

A school's maturing or liberally educating effects contribute far more to students' adult success. Earlier chapters have identified the strengths they ideally need for their future success and well-being. A school's liberal arts curriculum may or may not develop such strengths.

Guidelines for Creating
a Liberally Educating Curriculum

Current efforts to update and reorganize the curriculum focus more on its liberal arts' than on liberal education's outcomes. Reform will stumble if it treads the same path as previous curricular failures: the fifties' New Math, the convulsive post-*Sputnik* effort to spur foreign language and scientific competence, and the purifying "back-to-basics" reaction to the sixties' and seventies' curricular fragmentation. What paths should curricular reform take instead to succeed?

Assessing How Educable Students Are for the Curriculum

We must more thoughtfully identify how educable students are for our courses. As Chapters One, Two, and Three implied, reforms that ignore the personalities that students bring to school will fail. As Chapter Four also implied, ignoring the causes of the changes in students' educability will abort curricular improvement. Compensatory efforts such as creating smaller schools and altered teaching strategies are necessary to provide the optimal learning conditions for any innovative program to fulfill its promise, especially for minority youth.

A college that I call Typical illustrates why curricular innovations fail. Typical had created alternative programs, such as working at a National Institutes of Health laboratory for a summer, for which students could receive academic credit. These programs brought national recognition and foundation support. A visitor innocently asked what percentage of students had participated in the programs the preceding five years. Embarrassed to discover that fewer than 5 percent had and that the institution's integrity as an innovative college was at stake, the college sought advice.

The faculty had failed to identify the strengths that its programs assumed students needed to participate in them. When challenged to do so, it cited curiosity, initiative, autonomy, self-motivation, and self-educating skills. Surveys revealed that neither faculty nor students believed that the college had an ethos that supported and encouraged such traits or students who remotely possessed them or, most troubling, faculty whom students believed had them. The faculty had not altered its traditional teaching practices by replacing, for example, its lecturing with more involving methods that might develop the strengths its alternative curriculum required. Failing to understand how it could educate its students differently, the faculty shortly afterward abandoned its adventurous program.

Remembering That Students Are Persons, Not Just Minds

We must keep in the forefront of awareness that the maturation of mind, character, and self is inseparable. Trying to isolate mind from character and self eventually brakes its growth. Why, for example, do students begin to lose interest in math when they confront algebra—the most challenging discipline to teach today's "here-and-now" students? Math students have been called an endangered species in the United States and Great Britain, as a result, so mathematicians themselves claim, of "poor standards of teaching."[1] Math teachers as well as others, forget that they teach persons, not just mathematical logic. The gaps between students' minds and when and how algebra is taught are too great. Many eighth- and ninth-graders are not cognitively mature enough to really *comprehend* algebra's abstract operations—algebra was once a college subject. Also, students' "stapler" attitude, impatience, intolerance for frustration, and uneasiness with precise "right-or-wrong" answers make algebra threatening. It is also too remote from their lives to involve and sustain their interest. Finally, many girls lack confidence in their ability to work with impersonal and abstract algebraic concepts.[2]

The international math sweepstakes will not be won by requiring students to take more math courses unless their teachers heed the advice of their own forward-looking professional association. Math should be taught more liberally to develop generic adaptive skills such as problem solving, be made more relevant to students' practical interests, and rely more on participatory experiential activities and cooperative forms of learning.[3]

Giving Precedence to Liberal Education's, Not Liberal Arts', Outcomes

For a curriculum to be liberally educating, its outcomes must be primary. Each course should be *self-consciously taught to achieve some liberally educating outcomes*. The enhancement of students' desire to learn more about American history rather than perfect recall of 500 facts about it might be a course's principal goal.

The Michigan State Board of Education's current mandate to its schools begins to approach this guideline. It first identifies its primary liberally educating mission, such as encouraging caring, flexibility, and lifelong learning. It next details its liberal arts outcomes, such as foreign language and mathematical achievement. It then expects its schools to assess and report how well they achieve both its mission's and liberal arts' goals. The board's missing step is to clearly suggest that French and math should be so taught as to produce caring, flexible, lifelong learners.[4]

Using Liberal Education's Sequential Ground Plan to Guide Course Implementation

A curriculum succeeds only if teachers organize and implement it in ways that optimize its potential liberally educating effects. If we ignore the orderly sequence to becoming educated from freshman to senior year, we risk fixating students at its earlier phases, such as only mastering a course's language and facts. They may become restlessly bored, sense no meaningful growth, and feel unfulfilled and no more in command of themselves and their talents after a course than before. Learning remains a job; it is not encouraged to become a calling.[5]

Learning has much deeper meanings to students. It means maturing. Recall what MHS's students spontaneously wrote about how they had changed and what they had learned. They used the language of maturing, not that of their specific courses. Learning is much more complex than what we can learn from studying how sophomores memorize nonsense syllables. Teachers also know this powerful insight: they most want students to acquire their liberally educating gifts, not their courses' liberal arts content.

A Developmental Curriculum to Educate Mind

How can we organize the curriculum to be developmentally appropriate? How can we teach our courses so that students will acquire our gifts *as well as mastering their content?* It will be helpful to refer to the list of maturing principles in Appendix B while reading this and the next two chapters.

A Developmental Curriculum for Children: Montessori

Maria Montessori, an Italian anthropologist and physician, brilliantly designed a curriculum for early childhood that is one of the most developmentally appropriate ones for today's children of which I am aware. In 1907, she created the Casa dei Bambini (Children's House) in Rome to educate slum children, who had the same signs of weak willpower that retard mind's maturing, such as impulsivity and distractibility, that today's teachers increasingly see. From observing children's evolving interests, she formed ideas about growth remarkably congruent with the model of maturity, which is also induced from observing and testing older students' and adults' growth.[6]

Montessori asserted that education should develop children's personalities, not just their minds, to enhance their adaptability. Natural laws of being guide development and so should govern a curriculum's formation. Like Erikson, she believed that growth is systemic; it simultaneously involves intellectual, moral, affective, and volitional development. However, there are "special sensitivities" or critical periods for different types of growth. Educing mind's symbolizing powers, such as sensory-motor sensitivities, precise vocabularies, and the realistic imagination necessary for later abstract thinking, introduces the child's first school years. Educing character's other-centered strengths of respect and caring for younger children initiates moral development in the child's middle school years. A child begins to create from its first months its own self, first by absorbing much of its society's language, and next by working. Governing the maturing self is the child's inner teacher that seeks increased self-development, self-command, and autonomy.

Like Dewey, Montessori believed that interest sustains concentrated work and spurs mind's maturation. Work disciplines activity and is the child's principal route to the development of willpower and self-mastery. Concentrated work practiced over and over for hours at a time, of which children are capable, develops inhibition and patience. She claimed that work in a Montessori school also results in the maturation of interpersonal skills of respect and care for others.

Montessori's genius is seen in her curriculum, her materials, and their consistent implementation, which I only briefly highlight. The curriculum must follow, not lead, a child's interests. Children must have the liberty to reveal their interest and a responsively planned curricular environment that sparks and sustains working with that interest. Therefore, the curriculum is essentially individualized and provides for continuous progress. Montessori is best known for the varied materials she developed that enable a child's continued growth by enticing concentration, persistent effort, increased mental development, and self-correction.

Teachers should further children's self-discipline, control, initiative, and autonomy. Unobtrusively observant and responsive to their interests, teachers are the creators and stewards of a child's learning environment. Teachers use various ways to further self-control; for example, they teach four-year-olds to be silent, listen to others, replace materials in their proper places for other children to use, and carry bowls of soup without spilling from one lunch table to the next before sitting down to feed themselves. Teachers also ideally refrain from interfering with a child's concentration or diverting it to their own agendas.

Montessorians consistently implement the twenty principles that further healthy growth. I could identify most of them from Montessori's descriptions of her classrooms. Multi-aged classes of twenty-five to thirty-five children provide the varied social experiences and opportunities that enable peer modeling, caring, and teaching to occur (Other care; Other roles). The curriculum is not a "talking to," textbook and workbook one, but essentially a hands-on, experientially involving process that relies on manipulables and the natural social and work world for its materials (Integ exper; Stab external). With minimal interference from their teachers, students initiate and direct their own growth (Aut faith; Integ involve; Aut early). While teachers affirm student work (Stab affirm), Montessori's goals and related materials (Integ goals) are designed to encourage students to correct their own mistakes, create their own standards of excellence, and reward themselves (Stab conseq; Aut excel).

Reading Montessori's descriptions of her children's work and enthusiasm for learning suggests that her philosophy and pedagogy nurture learning as a calling. A dignitary visited her school on a holiday to find it closed. The children playing in the area, noticing his irritation, secured the school's keys, invited him in, and went to work. Not a teacher was around. Since the real test of genuine autonomy and calling is their demonstration in increasingly varied situations (Aut test), Montessorians should study more formally how their graduates adapt to more traditional schools and colleges and then to their adult roles. Do work, parental, and citizen roles become a calling, not just jobs, more readily for Montessorian than for traditionally educated children?

A Developmental Curriculum for
Pubertal Children: Carnegie Proposals

Reviews of research and extensive interviews with those knowledge-able about adolescents persuaded a Carnegie commission that middle and junior high schools do not provide appropriate learning environments and curricula for pubertal youth.[7] I agree. My understanding of students' changing character and the process of maturing during the pubertal years affirms and extends the commission's ideas.

Puberty is a time of heightened energy and distractibility but also of potential educability and thus maturing. Not only intellectual but also socioemotional behavior becomes more variable. Youth who have not stabilized and autonomitized their skills may be especially vulnerable to the stresses of this period. Their achievement as well as tested intelligence may vary considerably over time, making predictions of their future achievements hazardous.

The changing personality trends that earlier chapters have described can be exaggerated in twelve- to fourteen-year-olds. For example, teachers and students believe that they are more impatient, impulsive, distractibile, sarcastic, and defensive than children of other ages. The earlier sexualization of their relationships makes interpersonal other-centered growth now more urgent. Mind's maturation has become more vulnerable to being blocked or undone by interpersonal growth going off track.

Middle schools have failed the pubertal child; they retard maturing and even accentuate immaturing for too many vulnerable children. Chapter Three showed that they may dilute their students' calling to learning upon entrance to sixth or seventh grade. Their morale, particularly boys', precipitously declines during the pubertal years and then stumbles along at about the same level from eighth through twelfth grade. The pubertal years begin to generate increasing numbers of future dropouts.

In a nutshell, middle or junior high schools are too large; students' relationships are too mercurial and painful; the curriculum is too fragmented and departmentally organized as well as too abstract and remote from students' interest and experience.

The Carnegie Council on Adolescent Development agrees.[8] It first recommends that schools become much smaller. Given the centrality of interpersonal maturing at this age, in addition to its effects on the maturation of mind as well as of values and self, children need a much more personal, humane, caring learning environment than a school with more than three hundred youths can usually provide. Given the increased vulnerability and fragility of today's youth, they need a school in which every adult can know them and they can be known by most other students.

They also need a school whose interpersonal climate resembles that of MHS: empathic, accepting, and caring. They do not need the competitive, critical, self-centered, defensive, and interpersonally isolating climate of the typical middle school. They need a learning environment in which to learn what they were once like and so to care for younger children's growth, as well as what they will become like and so to be cared for by older students.

Today's pubertal youth do not need a miniature high school's curriculum. They need a more thematically than departmentally organized curriculum attuned to their interests. Teachers need to ask the Montessorian question about the themes with which to work: what are the evolving natural interests of this age group? They are their changing bodies and sexuality, authority, law, power, friendships and group relationships, conflict-resolving and negotiating skills, environmental issues, and the world over the immediate horizon waiting to be explored. A thematic curriculum makes possible a faculty *not* specialized in American history or biology. Middle schoolers should not encounter seven adult specialists each semester. They need continuity in their adult relationships, as with a team of three that includes a math-science, a humanities, and a social studies teacher.

They also need a more action- or experientially based curriculum that directs rather than suppresses one of a human being's most valuable assets—high energy level. They should not be sitting in chairs five periods a day being talked at, reading textbooks, or just doing problems. They should also be purposefully moving around, interacting and working with and teaching and learning from other students, and exploring their environmental, vocational, and service world.

And they need a competency-based curriculum that makes sense to them. Teachers should teach them how to interview their parents and other working adults about the strengths they will need to be a good marital partner, parent, citizen, engineer, factory worker, physician, or computer programmer when they grow up— and then begin to work *with* them to learn how to develop such competencies by the way the thematic units and other liberal arts courses are taught.

They need teachers who create classrooms that strengthen even further the meaning of learning as a calling. More than ever, they need schools of hope.

A Developmental Curriculum for High School Students: Model of Maturity

Piecemeal reforms of the high school curriculum that rely *only* on technology, teaching higher-order thinking skills, creating interdisciplinary courses, and using cooperative learning techniques are haphazard contemporary fads likely to fail. As adjustments to existing schedules and legislative and departmental assumptions, they ignore schools' systemic character and how students mature. They are not based on any rational or systemic model of adolescent healthy growth. They also fail to take into account students' underlying changing personalities.

Most teachers agree with three propositions about high schools. First, the senior year is not an exciting capstone year of high growth; it actually is a wasted year for many, especially once students know about their next year's future. Students begin to wean themselves from their schools, withdraw energy from their academic courses, and explore other ways to continue to grow. Second, the senior year contains more potential for growth than teachers have found how to spark. And third, high school, especially its last two years, is the tail that wags the curricular dog, the model or pacer of a district's values for everyone else: "It is grades and SAT scores that really count." Middle school teachers feel they must "prepare" students for high school; elementary teachers believe they must get their students ready for middle school. So altering the high school curriculum, especially that of the senior year, may be a more powerful lever to improve schools generally than heretofore believed.

What may an understanding of maturing suggest about organizing the high school? Within the larger cycle of schools' twelve to fourteen years, the senior year should test the maturity of its students, especially the autonomy or self-command for which kindergarten should begin to prepare them.

Within the high school's (and the college's) cycle itself, special care must be paid to the size and kind of motivational gap created for the incoming freshmen. Given their predisposition to be bored, they should not encounter just more of the same type of content or mode of teaching. The school's *best* resources should be used to create the optimal motivational gap, curricular program, and faculty care and support for them. Experiential adventurous bonding experiences, such as Proctor and MHS provided, should be thoughtfully used. They can establish the cooperative interpersonal climate necessary to encourage and support students' openness to learning.

The capacity to reflect more thoughtfully about one's character and self comes to the foreground of development at about this time. The curriculum, therefore, needs to educe it, beginning with the interpersonal and value issues that interest freshmen. Teachers and the curriculum should also be exquisitely clear about the competencies that students will need to demonstrate for graduation; teachers then must teach them throughout the curriculum.

For the next year or so, students should be mastering more of the language, the basic knowledge, of the key courses but in a way that stabilizes the competencies initiated earlier and encourages self-education. Alternative ways of understanding issues should be stressed, just as learning how to rewrite one's paper several times to address different audiences should be initiated. The second semester of the junior year should prepare students more directly for their senior year by providing them with a semester-long selected thematic unit mutually explored with a faculty member who is *not* an expert on the topic (Integ goal; Other roles).

I must now return to the nurturance of faculty's growth and calling. After teaching beginning Spanish or geometry ninety-nine times, just what incentive spurs increasing one's competence and excitement about the hundredth? Teachers called to teach *students,* not just Spanish or geometry, will always be excited; students' changing personalities provoke ceaseless spurs to understand and learn how to respond to their needs. So schools should also build into their curriculum the opportunity for teachers to keep educating themselves about their own interests and expanding their talents with their students without sacrificing one iota of their academic integrity (Symb goals). Of the gifts that teachers can give their students, the model of maturing suggests that enabling them to get command of their minds and characters is surely one of the most important. How can teachers best "teach" this gift? By modeling how they go about educating themselves while working cooperatively with students on a shared interest (Symb model; Other role).

Let's assume that a physics teacher has always been fascinated by China's Ming dynasty and its lasting effects on the Chinese character as expressed through its art (Integ context). She has always lamented that she never had the time to pursue that interest. Furthermore, let's assume that we have a school of hope that has *faith in and trusts its teachers and students to use freedom wisely* (Aut faith). So it provides each teacher the opportunity once a year to propose a course for juniors in an area of interest about which the teacher knows little—better yet, nothing. Since the teacher's gift is to model how a naive but educated person goes about teaching herself, she does *not* prepare for the course (Symb model). Rather, she works *with* students to clarify what they (including herself) need to know to understand China (Symb goals): its geography, history, language, and art, communism's effect on its aesthetic culture, even the effect of the policy of limiting families to one child on its Confucian values and historic family structure (Integ involv). Their pursuit of understanding should not be confined to the school's library or classroom. They should interview local experts and Chinese immigrants, visit museums, and perhaps even eat authentic Chinese food the way Chinese people do (Integ exper).

To hold themselves accountable, the class might develop a model curriculum for such a course to present to some external authorities in the field (Integ goal; Stab external). To model to the freshmen and sophomores the intellectual adventure and the skills they need to acquire by their junior year, the school could have a Day of Celebration. The teacher-student interest groups could prepare a brief description of their courses, collate them into the day's curriculum, invite freshmen and sophomores to choose three of those courses to attend during the day, and then present for ninety minutes or so their learnings (Symb model). Each teacher-student group would have to create ways to demonstrate their growth that would inform, interest, and excite other students (Aut excel). The ninth- and tenth-graders *and* their teachers should have the opportunity to question the substance as well as to probe the process of learning and its effects on the maturing of the participants, including the teacher (Symb reflect).

What might be the course's principal effects on students and faculty? Their course will have taught them how to go about collaboratively educating themselves. Students should reflect on what they have learned about how to educate themselves. They might even compare their ideas with the twenty principles that further growth in order to secure more conscious control over their own self-educating efforts (Symb reflect).

I once proposed a similar course to a governor's commission charged to suggest to the state's legislature ways to improve its schools. The commission's response? Union contracts and teacher certification requirements would not permit a physics teacher to "teach" Chinese history!

Those genuinely interested in improving their schools and colleges should radically alter their senior years to test how well they have furthered their students' maturity (Symb confront). Remember that it is youth's maturity, not advanced placement courses, grades, or SAT or Graduate Record Exam scores, that best predict how well they will adapt to whatever the future demands. How well students can take themselves in hand to further their self-development is the best test of their maturity.

How might schools of hope test their seniors' maturity? Alter their role to test their adaptability (Symb confront). How? Perhaps by providing them the opportunity once a day to assist their teachers with younger students in courses of their interest and so become models to them of the maturity that they too will shortly have (Other care; Other roles; Symb model; Aut test).

For the curriculum, the maturation process suggests that seniors should be freed from their tedious texts and lecture-dominated classrooms to test their growth in integration, stability, and autonomy (Aut test). How? Their junior year will have prepared them for a more adventurous year that demands that they stabilize and then demonstrate to the community their mastery of the *school's* mission goals (Aut excel). Concurrently with key courses, taught in ways to support their autonomy, students might participate in three successive faculty-student–led explorations that confront them with important value issues (Integ goals).

One of the three should be organized around a science-math theme, such as the greenhouse effect, that has implications for social science issues, such as its economic trade-offs, and humanities concerns, such as quality of life decisions (Integ context). The second could focus on a social science theme that has related scientific and humanistic concerns; say, the adequacy of U.S. governmental structures for adapting to global nuclear problems and their threat to U.S. sovereignty and individualism. The third could center on a humanities issue that has social science and scientific implications, such as artistic freedom and censorship as they have evolved in the social history of the United States and how changing technology may affect them.

Given that value concerns are beginning to emerge for seventeen- and eighteen-year-olds as the salient point of their maturing, each thematic course should ultimately expect its participants to wrestle with its value implications more maturely: to be able to identify and articulate the core value conflicts, empathically understand alternative stances, seek some integrative solution that is disciplined by factual information, hold it up to some criteria of worth, and then defend it in the face of criticism (Integ goals).

The organizing integrative themes would change each year. They should be generated by faculty *and* students, perhaps as themes growing out of the junior year experience (Symb reflect). Students should learn how to identify, define, and clarify their own goals (Symb goals); they should be trusted to do so responsibly (Aut faith). Each thematic course should have students whose interests and budding expertise represent one of the three components of each theme to broaden other students' perspectives (Other care; Other roles).

A school of hope welcomes being held accountable by its community. It seeks guidance about how well it has enabled its students to develop the maturity necessary to adapt to their future's demands. In late spring, the school might host a Day of Honor to which it invites its juniors and the community to learn how mature its seniors have become (Stab conseq). A day's curriculum could be prepared similar to that designed for the juniors' celebration. Each spring's faculty-student thematic group would plan to demonstrate how it has matured to three nonschool adults, knowledgeable about the course's themes and related issues, to serve as an assessment panel. Each group should inform the public and its panel about the school's and the group's specific academic goals, provide samples of its students' value-integrative papers, and prepare a demonstration of what it has learned (Stab conseq). As part of its two-hour demonstration, it might conduct an unrehearsed debate about one of the theme's value issues in which every member, including the teacher, has the opportunity to be randomly selected and assigned a position to defend (Aut test).

The assessors would be expected to query, probe, and seek additional evidence to assess *rigorously* how well the group has achieved the school's and its own goals. Integral to the assessment process, each group should be asked at the conclusion of its demonstration, first, to critique its own effectiveness (Symb reflect; Integ exper; Aut excel) and, second, to suggest how the school could achieve its goals more effectively. The assessors would then report their observations, affirm the group's strengths (Stab affirm), and suggest steps that the group could have taken to achieve even more excellently (Stab conseq). The collated critiques and suggestions would provide the district the information necessary to evaluate its own K–12 curricular program. Randomly selected demonstrations might be televised to show the community what its school has done for its children.

I hope you are not reflexively exclaiming, "How idealistically impractical. My school is too large; teachers will object to a cooperative relationship with students and subtly take over the course; time is being taken away from what is really important— completing the text; parents won't help; students aren't mature enough; we can't grade a student on his maturing; besides, there is the schedule; furthermore, . . ." I know these cautions. Remember, I write about schools of hope, for which such cautions are not intimidating irritations and excuses but valued prods to discover more effective ways to achieve human excellence.

A Developmental Curriculum
for College Students: Alverno College

Just as my own understanding of maturing arose independently from that of Maria Montessori, the Alverno College faculty's understanding of it developed separately from mine. Unaware of my research on maturing (as I was unaware of its first ten years' effort), the faculty induced from close observation of its students' development an understanding of education's course as remarkably similar to mine as mine was to Montessori's. That the three approaches, independently induced at different times from different types of students using different observational and experimental measures, are so similar strongly confirms the generality of the course of maturation. No other faculty has so insightfully and persistently sought to understand and assess its students' maturation as has Alverno's. Since the faculty's own reports are currently available,[9] I will not review its curriculum in detail. Instead, I summarize its curricular goals and developmental assumptions.

Alverno's faculty identified eight core competencies that its students needed to be effective adults, such as communication, problem solving, and the ability to make mature value choices. Students must master each compentency at four progressive levels of excellence before choosing a major. To complete their major, they must then achieve its two most relevant competencies at two additional levels of excellence. (Chapter Eight illustrated how the Alverno faculty applied its understanding of maturing to the teaching of social interaction skills.)

The levels generally describe the maturing process. The first requires becoming aware of or symbolizing, for example, one's own social interaction or aspects of the contemporary world. The next involves some attributes of other-centered growth, such as analyzing different modes of communication or discerning another's value assumptions. The next two levels are variants of integration and the last two variants of stability and autonomy. I underline the maturing dimension for emphasis. "Her development intensifies later, as she begins *integrating* her several competences into a *united* profile of her abilities and her approach to learning and *generalizing* abilities she has developed in one context into other realms of application. By her final semesters, she operates as a *self-directing* learner, planning appropriate learning experiences and helping to design techniques for assessing her performance."[10]

Alverno has not integrated its intuited understanding of students' maturation into an articulated theory of personality development that applies across the life span. So its insights remain bound to a narrow developmental range and thereby lose generalizing power. The college also cannot deal with systemic and other conceptual issues of development, such as flawed equilibration. However, as a working model of a developmentally based curriculum for young adults, it is currently unsurpassed.

Alverno's view of curricular development prefigures what I believe will and must be the leading edge of future curricular change. Not only mathematicians but also some historians now urge that liberal arts curricula be redefined to emphasize how they contribute to liberally educating competencies. Peter Stearns, chair of Carnegie Mellon's history department, argues that while students need to be aware of history's essential facts, however historians define them, they also need to take the next maturing steps of inducing, analyzing, and integrating comparative problem sets, by acquiring the "skills needed to develop coherent arguments based on primary evidence. They then would move on to consider conflicting interpretations of events and learn to identify arguments about social and historical causation. . . . History [should provide students] direct guidance in linking historical knowledge to the interpretation of present trends."[11]

I have long argued similarly. History and anthropology are the disciplines that best offer students the opportunity to learn the skill of induction, for example, if only their teachers would teach them in ways to educe it *more self-consciously and systematically.*

Let us agree that we can now roughly mark out some of mind's maturational sequences and so fashion a more appropriate developmental curriculum for meeting our liberally educating goals. We now face the practical question of how to create classrooms to achieve those goals. With the assistance of my students and a growing awareness of the principles that contribute to maturation, I worked for years to learn how to educate for maturity. I essentially became the "coach" that Sizer has since advocated that teachers become and that many teachers, such as Monteux's maestro, have always been.[12]

Not unimportant, refocusing the curriculum to make it more developmentally based can be teachers' route to revitalizing their work as a calling. By integrating my older role as a teacher with my emerging role as a coach, I challenged myself to continue growing for the latter part of my active teaching years. Classrooms are the most available and potentially the most growth-inducing environments that teachers have in which to renew their calling to teaching.

A Class to Educe Mind's Maturation

I always asked returning students what they had learned from their work with me. Dismayed by how many couldn't even recall the books they had read or a course's leading ideas, I questioned for years how to create a more effective learning environment. I had long felt that we really know something only when we can use it to adapt. To use what we know means to have skills to apply it. Potentially transferable skills that are practiced persist longer than information that is only occasionally, if ever, used. So with the assistance of my students, I began an eight-year search to learn how to use my liberal arts courses to teach important skills most useful to them in their future.

A junior-senior class on developmental issues throughout the life span provided a vehicle for learning how to teach oral communication, inductive, and critical judgment skills. Futurists had identified these skills as essential; the U.S. Labor Department's Commission on Achieving Necessary Skills has since recommended that all students learn, for example, listening and speaking skills.[13] Studies have also shown that as much as one-third of one's work time may require the use of oral communication skills in pairs or groups.[14] Within ten years, my students would occupy major positions of responsibility directing or working with others, chairing committee meetings, teaching, speaking in public, continually educating themselves, and making judgments about issues on which they might not be experts. They needed to learn how to communicate in groups, learn from their experience, and continuously evaluate cascading amounts of information about which they would know little.

I describe the last time that I taught the course but include examples from previous classes to illustrate how students taught me to teach. Eighteen juniors and seniors, most of whom I did not know, piled into our living room for the first session of a three-hour evening seminar. I had formerly introduced the course in many ways, such as showing a movie about the birth of a child or gathering in the nursery school where the students would work three hours a week to play with the blocks or in the doll corner (Integ involve; Integ exper). This evening we playfully introduced ourselves and our earliest memory. Each succeeding student repeated the names and memories of all the preceding students before citing his or her own. So we went until my turn. To the students' hilarious amusement, I stumbled and was the first to fail to recall a student's name. Was my time looming over the horizon?

After refreshments, I talked of the course's goals (Symb goals). When I mentioned the skill goals, I discussed why we had played the way we had (Symb confront; Symb reflect): because play, really work for a child, can be an important way to grow (Integ involve); because playfulness engages us as persons, not just as cool intellectuals, and when purposeful helps stabilize learning (Integ involve; Integ exper); because playing together encourages non-defensiveness and trust, so necessary to encourage students to risk conversing about ideas (Other trust). I had begun to help the students to develop oral communication skills by creating a playful camaraderie; even the shyest student could comfortably tell us her name and earliest memory.

Teaching Oral Communication Skills

I asked the class to reflect about the course in which they had grown most, next to identify why it had had such maturing effects, and finally how we could create as maturing a class for ourselves (Symb reflect; Symb confront). I remained quiet. In no more than fifteen minutes, the students agreed about eleven steps to or tests of classroom excellence (Aut excel). Later that week, I rephrased them in the form of queries, presented them for the group's revision and approval, made copies for each of us, and asked how we could use them to keep us pointed toward excellence. Some of their queries were:

> Are we adequately prepared for and have we reflected about our homework before class?
> Do we listen actively, seeking to understand what others contribute?
> Are we open to suggestions that we may occasionally need to divide into small groups to provide more opportunity to actively discuss the material?

The students suggested that each be assigned a query, monitor the class's activity, and every several weeks report to us how we were measuring up to it (Symb reflect; Stab external; Aut excel). Since a test of their maturing oral communication skills was to organize and conduct the class for forty-five minutes beginning the seventh week, the queries served as one way to assess their maturation (Symb goals; Stab conseq).

The course, a fast-paced, at first tightly but progressively less structured one (Aut test), included each week specific activities designed to practice and test the students' oral skills (Integ involve). Initially, they were limited to short time periods, involving other students as supports, but they soon demanded more complex skills. They included a several-minute team presentation of examples of Piaget's cognitive stages, progressively longer pair and small-group discussions to practice communicating technical concepts, three-person team presentations of a joint research survey of a topic, a solo several-minute report, and solo reflective assessments about how the class was meeting its criteria of excellence. Students demonstrated their communication skills by leading the class in any way they wished in a forty-five minute discussion of a major paper that the other students had critiqued in preparation for the demonstration. The class then reflected on how well the presenters had accomplished their purposes.

Teaching Inductive Skills

Induction is one of the most important self-educating skills that students will need in their future. But I have never been satisfied with how well I have taught students to form hypotheses or draw ideas from a collection of facts, really learning from one's experience, and apply them to other situations.

To clarify the meaning of induction, the students early read about the course of therapy of young Kenneth (Symb goals). Their task was to draw out or induce principles about how development proceeds (a most difficult challenge for those used to textbook condensations) and share them orally with each other (Symb reflect; Integ involve; Integ context). I then modeled how to induce some principles (Symb model).

Because some students mature most when responsibly involved in experiential activities, I had since the early seventies provided hands-on activities for every course I taught (Integ exper). Working for three hours in a nursery school during the first six weeks and then in a setting with the elderly, such as a nursing home, during the latter part of the course provided the opportunity to learn how to induce—and to be responsible (Aut faith; Aut early). After being alerted about how and what to observe (Stab rehearse), the students practiced finding examples from their fieldwork that illustrated ideas from their reading (Integ exper). During the following weeks, they wrote short papers describing their inductions about healthy growth as they had observed it in their fieldwork settings.

When we explored the meaning of healthy growth during the college years, the students interviewed their peers; of growth during the adult years, their parents at spring vacation; and of maturing during the later years, the elderly in their fieldwork settings. Because their interviews focused on tasks or issues of the age group, they acquired their own examples and knowledge with which to independently evaluate the merits of their reading (Integ context; Aut excel). The ultimate test of their inductive skill was their major paper, in which they demonstrated and used their knowledge to evaluate the research literature about an adult developmental issue (Integ context).

Although the fieldwork contributed significantly to their maturing, I learned that teaching induction ideally required my modeling. I should be present when occasions arose that illuminated growth's processes—a practical impossibility for me, though essential to being a superb coach, as athletic, dance, and musical directors know (Symb model).

Teaching How to Judge Appropriately, Independently, and Critically

The ability to make critical judgments is mind's principal autonomous skill. We are rapidly moving into a future that will give us instantaneous access to mind-boggling amounts of information about which we may know very little but which we must sift through and evaluate.

I had always asked students to judge and critically evaluate the articles they read. But I had never figured out how to monitor and systematically improve their judgment until a student suggested the key piece to my puzzle. To provide the information that students needed to conduct the class as their test of their oral communicative growth, each prepared a thirty- to forty-page paper on a topic on which they were to be the class's expert (Other role). The topics varied from evaluating the effects of the changing role of women on their own and men's healthy growth to religion's contribution to healthy growth in adults. At the end of the sixth week, the next week's leaders distributed copies of their papers to us to read prior to the coming class.

When the first teacher for the evening initiated her forty-five minute class, she discovered immediately that only a few had read her paper. Rather than letting her bail out the class by reading the paper to the miscreants who had undermined their colleagues, I immediately interrupted to ask what we should do now (Symb confront). One student suggested that every student write a critique of each paper before class. Since they all might have to suffer similar dilatory tactics when they were responsible for the class (Stab conseq), they hastily agreed. Knowing how critical competitive intellectuals can be toward their peers, I alerted them to this academic handicap. A judicious and helpful critique should also honestly affirm a paper's strengths (Other care; Stab affirm). Another student then asked what a critique was; I prepared some samples the next day for the class (Symb model).

Suddenly *the* idea for which I had been searching struck me. I asked them to prepare three copies of their typed critiques: one for the paper's author, one for me, and one for themselves. I promised to critique their critiques by the next class and expected improvement in their subsequent ones (Stab external).

Just as what we write can reveal the maturity of our minds, so our critiques of a book or article can reveal how actively we have read and evaluated a topic about which we may know little except what we have just read. I typed a detailed critique of each student's critique. After acknowledging their critiques' specific strengths (Stab affirm), I reviewed them for comments about the paper's mechanics. Had they noted that the author's style was sparse but delightfully humorous, paragraph three on page one might better have been placed at the paper's beginning, paragraph four on page eight needed to be reworked for clarity, the paper needed to be proofread more carefully from page twelve on?

And then I turned to the critique's principal task of evaluating a paper's substance. Had they noticed that the author had clearly defined "healthy growth" but then proceeded to ignore his own definition in his evaluation, had astutely drawn on his fieldwork for principles and examples but not well documented his opinions by citing research studies, and when he had done so, had cited reviews uncritically rather than examining primary sources, which he had incompletely and in some cases inaccurately notated in his references? Or might not the paper's author have brought to bear some information on the topic that had been discussed in the course or as a sociology major included anything from his own field about women's changing roles (Integ context)?

When I received a student's next critique, I reread my previous critique and then dialogued again with her about her reactions to the new paper. I congratulated her for paying closer attention to the author's style and identifying paragraphs to be revised (Stab affirm). But I also pursued why she had only cursorily evaluated the paper's content (Symb confront) and ignored some of my suggestions.

A few students quickly grew under this close tutelage. So by the last weeks I urged them to take weak passages or sections from the next authors' papers and help them by playfully rewriting or amplifying them to show how they could be more insightful, critical, or clear (Other care). Those who showed less growth continued to master the critique exercise (Stab conseq).

The coaching produced dramatic results. Students always complained about how much work they had to do, how detailed my critiques of their own critiques and their major papers were, and recommended that future students write fewer critiques and that I relax a little. However, to a person, they always recommended that I continue to critique future students' papers, though I should affirm more of their strengths. They and I could visibly see their growth by comparing their early with their later critiques. They said they had learned how to approach an unfamiliar topic, clarify its key terms and issues, assess it for its logical organization, articulateness, and evidence, and bring to bear their own knowledge and perspective to evaluate its worth (Aut excel).

I also grew a little more each year. I continued to strengthen my willpower to critique papers on time, learn more about how students mature, and develop a smidgen more humility. I learned to check my impulsive and impatient urge to interrupt a student's teaching to correct, steer, illustrate, and amplify her session's discussion. I doubt that I spoke more than an hour or two during the entire last seven weeks. I learned how well students can rise to genuine faith in their capacity for responsibility when prepared to assume it (Aut faith). I learned that students could become autonomous learners much earlier than I had thought. And, somewhat wistfully, I learned that they might not need me.

I know that the students would not have scored high on any national test of their factual knowledge about human development.

I believe, however, that they would be able to search out and learn whatever facts they might ever want to know in the future. Many would also have scored near the top for their age on any measure of oral communication, induction, and critical judgment and command of their own talents.

Although I have concentrated on mind's maturation, did you induce that growth of character and self continued apace as well? The next chapter focuses on what I have learned about how character matures and its primary determinants.

Chapter 14

Educating Character

Schools of hope believe that they should and *can* affect their students' character. Chapters Eight and Ten argued that schools whose students achieve well, graduate in large numbers, and don't get into a lot of trouble affect character by educing interpersonal and value maturation. What is it about schooling that calls out character's maturation?[1]

When asked that question by the leaders of the Association of Christian Colleges, I responded, "Not just a daily chapel service, sermon, and prayer; they may only confirm the values that already exist. Not just traditional courses on ethics and religion; they may increase mind's awareness but probably not interpersonal or value maturation." When asked by secular school heads, I respond, "Not most curricular changes made to enhance character maturation unless taught with the principles that further maturing. Not just inspiring assembly talks. Not just required one-semester service projects in the community, human relations and conflict-resolving courses, or even special programs such as Quest."

Research findings are not as discouraging as my replies suggest. The above activities may contribute to character maturation *if* they interpersonally involve students and are integral to and consistent with a coherent ethos that values their effects. The principal critique of why colleges can affect character concludes that "[t]he dominant source of . . . college effects consistently appears to be the frequency and nature of the contacts undergraduates have with the

312

major agents of socialization: their peers and faculty members.
. . . [T]he evidence . . . indicates that the structural, organizational,
and programmatic effects of college are largely indirect ones, being
mediated through the influence they exert on the nature and frequency of students' interpersonal interactions, as well as institutional and subgroup environments."[2]

Chapter Four described how negatively large schools affect
character by undermining the responsible and personal relationships
now known to further character maturation. A 1988 study of 4,843
students in 379 colleges and universities concluded that "attending
a large . . . institution had a significant negative influence on the
development of humanitarian/civic involvement values largely because it tended to inhibit student social leadership involvement."[3]

Characteristics of Schools of Hope

Much as humane sizing of institutions is necessary, it is not sufficient to encourage character maturation. It is a school's climate of
values, not just its specific programs, that alters character.[4] A
school's ethos may do so in healthy and unhealthy ways. The model
of maturing identifies the attributes of a healthy school and its ethos
that support specific programs and practices to educate for interpersonal and value maturation.[5] Healthy schools reflectively and accurately understand themselves, empathically respond to their members' needs, coherently organize and implement their values,
resiliently adapt to change, and create autonomously distinctive
identities.

Reflective Understanding of Themselves

Just as healthy people accurately understand themselves, so do
healthy schools. Typical College, which could not figure out why
so few students opted for its adventurous curricular options, is not
exceptional in its inability to reflect on and understand itself. I
could cite many similar examples. Consider Purity, a resource-rich
independent school. Its student enrollment had steeply declined in
only four years for reasons that the school misunderstood.

Responding to an earlier study that had suggested the high

school needed a new head, Purity hired the chair of a college science department, who not understanding today's students, implemented many of the changes proposed by reformers—also not understanding today's students. With his core academic faculty's support, he increased the number of required math and science courses, raised foreign language standards, pushed aside electives such as art and music, curbed the athletic program, and instituted an academic grade requirement for participation in cocurricular activities. Purity's declining enrollment was blamed on changing demographics.

A restudy of Purity four years later suggested a radically different hypothesis for its enrollment problem. Its rapid imposition of a purified academic ethos alienated its more casual, fun-loving constituency. While faculty morale had improved, its high school students' morale had plummeted; its middle school students' had also, though not as severely. In contrast to the faculty, the students believed that the school's ethos and their peers' character had dramatically changed—for the worse. Though Purity's core values— academic, competitive, demanding—persisted, the supportive context of values that had made a competitive academic school tolerable, even enjoyable, had been torn away. In only four years, it had become, from the students' perspective, a less enjoyable place to be. Thirty-one percent more students judged it to be moody, 26 percent more argumentative, uptight, and stubborn, 25 percent more unfair, 22 percent more distractible, and 21 percent more worrying and boring, which 60 percent now claimed it to be. As telling, 41 percent fewer students described the school as athletic, 37 percent fewer as open, 31 percent fewer as artistic, and more than a fifth as less realistic, self-confident, considerate, honest, and, significantly, hardworking.

The attributes that the largest increases in students *wished* for the school were athletic, artistic, expressive, open, self-confident, realistic, sincere, optimistic, trusting, playful, and sympathetic.

Unless some institutional earthquake occurs, a school's core values remain remarkably stable over time. A school's personality, like an individual's, can be stretched and altered at its edges. However, it retains its distinctive identity, even, paradoxically, if it has none at all. Apparently, Purity had been severely wrenched by the efforts to "improve" it even more academically. Its students saw the school as more emotionally tumultuous, not responsive to their needs; the school, not perceived by the majority of its students to be fair, open, and considerate, had become boring and less exciting and was not working as hard *for them*. It had become a school for the faculty.

The psychic bottom-line question is what had happened to the students. A massive change had occured in how healthily they viewed each other, which suggested why student morale had gone so far downhill and probably why enrollment had precipitously declined. A startling 68 percent increase in the number of students who saw their peers as worrying sets the stage: 63 percent more viewed them as moody, 58 percent more as uptight, 57 percent more as defensive and demanding, and 54 percent more as critical of each other and difficult to get along with. Not surprisingly, fewer students described each other positively. Only 18 percent of the students, for example, viewed their peers as honest, a striking 38 percent decline in just four years. Thirty-one percent fewer believed that their peers were friendly, 30 percent fewer enthusiastic and fair, 26 percent fewer relaxed and happy, and 24 percent fewer genuine, giving, and good-natured.

The curricular and other changes had transformed reasonably healthy peer relationships into irritating, defensive, and critical ones. No wonder the most greatly increased *wishes* that the students had for their peers were that they were more warm, trusting, sincere, sympathetic, honest, understanding, and considerate.

How can faculties that do not reflect accurately about themselves and their students ever become schools of hope? Flawed self-understanding creates resistance to or undermines efforts to improve oneself. Speculate what the effects might be of each of the following examples of inadequate reflection: faculties possessing inaccurate collective self-images, administrators unaware of faculty views of them, schools unaware of their real effects, and reformers misunderstanding the conditions that must be present if reforms are to take hold. Never forget Margaret Mead's insight: A clear understanding of a problem prefigures its lines of solution. If a remedy isn't curing a problem, might not the diagnosis and so the remedy be wrong?

Empathically Responding to Constituents' Needs

Accurately understanding how others view an issue or problem can lead to greater empathy for how they feel and therefore the ability to respond more effectively. Schools of hope have adults who understand and empathize with their students. Not understanding mind's and character's inseparable dependence on each other, Purity could not fully respond appropriately. The faculty subsequently sought to create a more humane ethos by removing its more irritating student dress and behavior codes. Do you really believe that Purity's mildly palliative remedies for its interpersonal illness would suffice? I don't.

Purity's empathic obtuseness is neither unique nor even rare. Why do we stumble so badly when responding to conflicting racial, ethnic, and gender issues? Unwitting prisoners of our own compelling perceptions, we believe that others view our school as we do. We believe that our views and solutions are *the* right ones. Like the elementary school faculty that preferred to talk about rather than empirically find out why its children no longer played in its sand pile, we don't try to find out others' views. Lack of institutional empathy and sensitivity can create an ethos that trips up and undercuts even a school's most heartfelt effort to provide maturing environments for its members.[6]

A school of hope would respond more empathically than Purity to its students' troubling concerns. MHS did. Understanding its students' interpersonal needs and their effects on their minds' and characters' growth, its faculty successfully altered its students' relationships. Seventy percent and more of MHS's students and parents agreed with the unanimous faculty belief that the school was accepting, caring, and empathic. Similar percentages of its students agreed with the faculty that the typical MHS student was caring, cheerful, friendly, and considerate. In contrast to most student groups with which I have worked, MHS students were so satisfied with their relationships that they did not even wish that they were more caring, sensitive, or understanding. No wonder three classes spontaneously reported that they matured most in their other-centered relationships.

You may be unconvinced that a school must empathically

understand and respond to its members' needs for it to be academically effective. Purity's principal was skeptical that mind's and character's maturation reciprocally depended on each other. He rejected the idea that Purity's altered character affected the school's primary academic mission. A school's interpersonal ethos was an irrelevant "frill," in other words, to be neither understood nor concerned about.

Studies of the relationship between an institution's character and its alumni's creative productivity suggest otherwise. Kenneth Hardy, studying the social origins of American scientists and scholars, found that the Quaker schools had educated proportionately more productive adults than other, intellectually comparable schools. He concluded that "these schools are so superior in productivity, not only among the denominational schools but also among all of the schools in the entire sample, that it seems probable that a specific Quaker influence is at work."[7] What might that "specific Quaker influence" be? Table 14.1 compares the collective perceptions of teachers (only a few of whom were Quakers) new to their schools with those of teachers in America's foremost independent and comparable public schools.[8] The table lists in declining order the attributes about which teachers in the Quaker schools disagreed most with teachers in the other two types of schools.

If I had continued the table, the Quaker schools would have been seen to be more caring, trusting, and warmer by margins of 25 to 45 percent for the independent and public schools, respectively. Table 14.1 tells us three things. First, the Quaker schools have highly distinctive climates; they share among themselves a widespread communion of value that we now know is essential to being a school of hope. Second, *if Hardy's inference is correct*, then valuing character's as well as mind's maturation may contribute to a student's future productivity by making it easier for students to be vulnerable and open to learning. When asked why so many viewed their schools as talkative, the teachers said that they had a greater say in the consensual decision-making process that Quakers use to conduct their business. And third, the Quaker schools were perceived as more open, accepting, and empathic than the other schools, which suggests that they might indeed be more responsive to their members' needs.

Table 14.1. Perceptions of Teachers in Quaker, Independent, and Public Schools of Their Schools' Ethos.

Attribute of school	Teachers' perceptions (%)			Difference between Quaker and independent (%)	Difference between Quaker and public (%)
	Quaker	Independent	Public		
Talkativeness	70	27	20	+43	+50
Openness	80	38	32	+42	+48
Expressiveness	70	33	27	+37	+43
Giving	80	44	34	+36	+46
Acceptance	89	56	44	+33	+45
Feeling for others	84	51	35	+33	+49
Imagination	71	38	33	+33	+38
Fun	77	45	29	+32	+48
Deep ethical sense	70	38	25	+32	+45

Schools of hope create empathic and humane climates that value what is most deeply human—their members' humanness, not just their minds.

Coherently Organizing and Implementing Their Values

In describing schools of hope, Chapter Ten referred to the character-forming power of a Catholic monastery. So coherently organized by its central values, it consistently implements them in every aspect of its community's life. Nooks and crannies to which to escape are scarce. A school that wishes to alter its students' character might also learn from its local McDonald's franchise. Note its youthful cooks' and servers' behavior. Learn how it taught Russian youth to fulfill its corporate cultural values. Not only is the company crystal clear about its core values of quality, service, cleanliness, and value (qualities reputedly not found in Russian stores), but it also rigorously monitors whether they are being consistently implemented in its more than 7,000 outlets.

My favorite example of the lack of integration between a school's goals and their implementation is a high school known for academic excellence. Its mission committee successfully secured unanimous faculty support for its priority outcomes, beginning with students becoming more autonomous learners. Two years later, its evaluation team's report began with this devastating comment, as closely as I can recall it: "We commend you for your mission statement and the process you used to create it. We visited every single class and did not note one example of teaching that we felt might enable your students to become autonomous learners." Typical of most faculty I know, it publicly approved virtue but privately taught the way teachers have taught for centuries, even before the invention of the printing press.

Of course, no school is so coherently organized as to implement its values with perfect consistency. A school of hope, responsive to its constituents' needs, is an exploring, changing place. But when schools are not unified by a coherent core vision and led by people who think *systemically*, they can become just collections of curricular bits and pieces that have no lasting effect on their students' character. Even some of Chapter Ten's schools of hope had not avoided the dangers of incoherence and inconsistency. Some of Proctor's departments were not sympathetic to the school's experiential emphasis.

Resiliently Adapting to Change

Schools that have articulated other-centered and integrated core values can adapt to their students' changing personalities to create healthy maturing environments for everyone. But like individuals, schools can become so rigid that they can't change to meet their students' evolving needs and so eventually die psychically. Or schools that lack any core values fail to marshal their corporate efforts to affect their students' character. Lacking unifying values to guide priorities, they wander hither and thither among the latest fads seeking the magical herb or remedy, frittering away their scarce resources.

A metropolitan high school with large numbers of minority youth paradoxically illustrates stability's two extremes in its purposeless rigidity. Though one of the sickest schools I know, it is qualitatively similar to a number of public high schools in its purposelessness. For years, Purposeless High School had been directed by a former naval commander, who ordered his teachers each new year *never* to smile at their students. His primary value was to maintain discipline and order. When the school was surveyed at the request of a concerned counselor, a younger, more caring principal had just come on board. The following list tells us how the faculty perceived the school:

Faculty View	Percentage Agreeing
Defensive	57
Conservative	57
Accepting	50
Authoritarian	50
Caring	50
Conventional	50

Faculty Wishes	Percentage Agreeing
Academic	68
Intellectually exciting	61
Consistent	54
Ambitious	39
Creative	39
Excellent	39

When at least two-thirds of a school's different groups share in common twelve or more values about their school, it has a defined ethos of values that can affect character. The faculty at Purposeless High School did not agree that the school had *any* liberally educating values; too few believed that it possessed any strengths whatsoever for it to be anything more than a school of despair. Fewer than 15 percent of the faculty thought that the school was adventurous, ethical, excellent, imaginative, initiating, self-educating, or trusting, among a host of other empowering strengths.

The faculty also did not believe that Purposeless was changeable. Its core self-concept was rigidity: defensive, conservative, authoritarian, and conventional. That half the faculty believed that the school was accepting and caring may have reflected budding results of the new principal's efforts or simply the faculty's views of themselves.

Purposeless was not a terminal patient, however. The faculty had not given up. Its severe frustration, seen in its widespread agreement about what it wished, was also a sign of hope. Far better to be frustrated, even angry about what you would like to be than contented, even drowsy about being nothing. The new principal learned that his faculty wished the school were more academically excellent and exciting; he also learned from the survey that although 68 percent of the students believed that the school was boring, about half of them wished it were more academic and intellectually exciting. So while the school was very sick, its prognosis would be favorable if the new principal could convert the faculty's paralyzing frustration into concerted efforts to teach differently. Unfortunately, the omens were not promising. After listening to the survey's results, the superintendent adamantly insisted that the solution to the school's problems was to create a computer center.

To produce character maturation, healthy schools not only must have a stable identity and be resilient; they must also stand for distinctive values, which they implement and defend.

Creating a Distinctive Identity

Studies of organizations that effectively achieve their goals, whether business, international research, or educational, paint a consistent portrait. They have clear, stable, and *distinctive* identities—they are not like Purposeless. Their leaders articulate and sustain the organization's core values. They are not afraid to hold themselves accountable for their results. Their strength provides them the autonomy to question their own efficacy, to pioneer, though remaining faithful to their mission, and to resist distracting societal drummers in order to be their own.

Haverford College is well known among educators and the Monteux School among musicians for their distinctiveness and vigorous autonomy. Given its pacifistic Quaker values, Haverford refused to seek and accept grants from the U.S. Defense Department. The entire college collectively went to Washington to lobby against the country's Vietnam involvement. Some of its students led the effort to send medical supplies to Vietnam. Misunderstanding the college's consensual decision-making procedures, an accreditation team felt that its individualism and internal arguments bordered on anarchy.

Such independent, even rebellious stances drew their inspiration and support from the college's distinctive values. Students perceived the college as having a special personality. At least two-thirds agreed that the college was intellectual, competitive, demanding, capable, self-conscious, introspective, idealistic, individualistic, honest, cooperative, and dedicated and that it had strong interests, especially ethical ones. Comparative data from a variety of schools show this ethos to be most atypical, even among religious schools. Values such as introspection, idealism, honesty, strong ethical commitments, and especially individualism are rarely mentioned in descriptions of schools.

How might such a distinctively individualistic ethos have affected students' character? Three pieces of evidence suggest that it prepared them to be potentially creative and productive alumni. The first is Hardy's study of the origins of creative scholars and scientists.[9] Haverford's ethos defines the attributes of the Quaker influence to which he attributed the college's success.

The second piece of evidence comes from the many studies of highly creative persons. Creative persons are not only autonomous, individualistic, self-consciously introspective, and intense, but also androgynous.[10]

The third piece comes from follow-up studies of Haverford students of the sixties. Ethical persons share stereotypically feminine interpersonal strengths, such as sensitivity to others. Haverford's social honor code, identified as a major cause of maturing, valued such strengths. Might not the college have encouraged the androgynous growth of its males, which, given its Quaker values, in turn contributed to their later autonomy and creativity?[11]

Monteux's young musicians and conductors also perceive their school as distinctively different. They come from many countries because of the school's standards of excellence. It has resolutely and single-mindedly upheld such excellence in the face of changes in musical taste and what some believe has been a national erosion of musical standards. Its alumni report that the school taught them how "sloppily" they had played before. The school's distinctive autonomy permanently altered many of its students' values of musical excellence.

Now that we know the key attributes of a healthy and hopeful school that can affect character, we can ask the practical question "What steps can a school take to nurture character maturation?"

The preeminent rule is *never* to ignore the invisible spirit, quality of relationships, and communion of values that define a school's ethos. Those who forlornly look to the typical American solution may despair. Character cannot be bought. No millions of dollars to the Harvard Business School to create courses on ethics will do. No magical curricular solutions, quick technological fixes, or specific teaching techniques will do. If they did, churches or enterprising consultants would have discovered them years ago. Furthermore, in the absence of a healthy ethos that values character, none of the steps that I will suggest can create enduring changes. Mind's maturation can best be encouraged by the curricular efforts described in Chapter Thirteen when those efforts are *supported by a congruent and healthy ethos*. Conversely, character's maturation is best nurtured by a school's ethos that is *supported by an appropriate curriculum*. The distinction is not a fatuous cop-out. It tells us where to begin, why, and how. It protects us from squandering resources on another medicine man's bag of interpersonal and value nostrums.

Creating School and Classroom Climates to Educate for Character Maturation

To educate for character, we must begin by creating the healthy relationships out of which value maturation develops. I illustrate how the principles that further maturing can be used to create a healthy institutional ethos. Those in large schools may vigorously protest or reflexively cringe at what they may believe are impractical or threatening ideas—one of many reasons why such schools should be abandoned and replaced by more adaptable smaller ones.

Becoming More Aware of Interpersonal Relationships and Values

Schools should be much clearer than they are about how they expect students and faculty to interact with each other (Symb goals). Haverford's freshmen learn in their first introduction to the college that their peers expect them to be sensitive to and respect their rights and opinions (Symb confront). MHS's Full Value Contract guided how its students should get along with each other. Colleges are now struggling to create similar expectations as women, blacks, Latinos, gays, and other groups insist they not be harassed. Such efforts can contribute to interpersonal sensitivity and value maturation *if judiciously framed with community ownership of the expectations.*

Though schools expect faculties to behave professionally, only recently have some begun to clarify how they should relate to each other as males and females. Recent laws and judicial rulings about sexual harassment will hold schools financially liable for their teachers' behavior. American males' macho styles have become increasingly inappropriate as women expect and demand equal respect; so males will be increasingly pressured to alter their character. Just as teenage girls now assert their right to join Little League teams, so some will soon initiate legal suits against male teachers who egregiously offend them by what they believe is sexist behavior. More than ever, schools should clarify appropriate faculty-student behaviors in and outside the classroom (Symb model).

The teaching profession could significantly contribute to students' character maturation if it created an enforceable code of ethical conduct for itself comparable to that of psychologists. The code could be made available for students to discuss as well (Symb goals; Symb model). Sensitive to the contribution that interpersonal and ethical expectations make to achievement, a teacher in an independent high school sought advice from her students about their expectations of her, which she promised to try to fulfill. The students expected her to be fair, patient, not belittle them, give extra help, and try to end class on time so that they could leave at the bell. She expected them to try their best, be honest, not to belittle others, cooperate, and observe the dress code.

Schools should also provide institutionalized ways for their faculties and students to become aware of their unconscious ways of relating and to reflect about their effects on their values (Symb reflect). In some schools, surveys of faculty's and students' perceptions of each other and their school have provoked considered reflection and altered faculty and student relationships (Symb confront; Symb reflect). Recall the school whose teachers, students, and parents had not viewed it as trusting and how, as a result of such awareness, its teachers created the ethic that they would suppress their sarcasm.

Schools of hope will find creative ways to use such surveys or ethical codes to periodically prod their adults and students to reflect about their relationships (Symb confront) and to create more interpersonally mature climates. Chapter Two mentioned the district whose middle school students were driving other students out of their schools by their persecutory put-downs. It surveyed its students' views of their peers in preparation for a two-day visit during which I worked for an hour with each schools' 300 to 400 sixth-, seventh-, and eighth-graders. Confronting them with the results, I asked them to identify the sarcastic comments they had heard the day before (Symb confront). I then asked why they and their peers (as well as their teachers) used such put-downs and to tell their teachers how sarcasm affected their classroom behavior (Symb reflect). A series of exercises helped some to develop healthier ways to deal with such comments rather than escalating their retaliatory put-downs (Integ involve). For their next hour's classwork, I asked them to reflect about how to create more safe and supportive classrooms for themselves (Symb reflect; Aut excel).

Because modeling desired strengths develops character much more effectively than didactically teaching or sermonizing students, a few courageous schools have sought to learn what their faculties model and what they don't. When they do, they inevitably are shocked, some humbled, to discover how few students perceive their teachers as models of interpersonal maturity and strong moral character. Consider the following list, which reports how students of one state's finest academic high school viewed their teachers:

Interpersonal Traits	Percentage of Students Agreeing
Caring	46
Accepting	42
Understanding	40
Feeling for others	34
Trusting	34
Open	29

Ethical Values	Percentage of Students Agreeing
Fair (just)	45
Honest	45
Strong convictions	24
Deep moral sense	22
Idealistic	18
Integrity	18

The faculty viewed itself similarly; the majority identified only caring and honesty as describing their colleagues. These results are not exceptional for competitively academic schools. However, they don't tell us that teachers are not interpersonally mature or highly ethical; they tell us that teachers have not created relationships in which they can be genuinely themselves. Only 16 percent of this school's students believed their teachers to be genuine human beings. Too small an academic circle within which to relate does not provide the opportunity to experience another's interpersonal and ethical maturity. Only coaches are known as fuller human beings.

The junior and senior curriculum proposed in Chapter Thirteen provides a larger educational compass. Working cooperatively with faculty to create their own course enables students to observe how interpersonally and ethically mature their teachers really are (Symb model).

The availability of means for an academic community to reflect about its critical values and conflicts could strengthen its ability to cope as well as enhance its awareness of its values. Despite its small size and family climate, Proctor had no community means to search for and discuss ways to resolve conflicts. Not until I talked of the assessment's results to the entire school did it as a community confront for the first time the moral issues involved in students' drug use. Kohlberg also relied on schoolwide "town meetings" to encourage more democratic relationships and reflection about values. [12] Haverford's collective weekly meeting among faculty and students for meditation provided an ideal opportunity for them to reflect together about ethical issues. However, its potentials for furthering student maturing were never fully understood and so were not interpreted to its increasingly resistant and restless students.

Needless to say, educating students to become more aware of their relationships and values requires that they learn the vocabulary of their inner and interpersonal worlds. They need the skills of differentiating and articulating their feelings and those of others as well as reflection and induction. Concurrent courses should be taught to make such skills generalized habits of mind to apply to character's issues (Aut test).

If a school has created an ethos of trust and openness (Other trust), taught the skills of induction and reflection (Symb reflect), and provided opportunities to become aware of interpersonal and

value issues, then the ground has been prepared for the seeds of
personal honesty to sprout.

Developing More Other-Centered
Interpersonal Relationships and Values

Maturing requires more than just becoming aware of one's relationships and values. Courses about ethics or different stages of moral
reasoning will not result in more mature value choices and acts
unless integrated with emotions and behavior (Integ exper).[13]
Awareness must be accompanied by learning how to empathically
feel how others feel. Other-centered values such as compassion and
fairness will not otherwise become truly incarnated and so sources
of action. If students cannot be moved to tears and anger seeing a
hurt child bruised by an abusing parent, or to take a crying child
into their arms to console, or to feel indignant viewing a black man
being kicked and beaten by several police officers, or to suffer the
shame and terror of a young woman being raped by seventeen fraternity brothers and then feel the angry despair of the college's
president about his faculty, who says it is none of its business—then
for what purpose is it to teach them ethics and Kohlberg's stages of
moral reasoning?

    Other-centered character maturation depends on learning
empathy, which is most directly called forth in relationships with
diverse people in varied situations. Of course, empathy can be
educed by dramatic works of art and literature when reflectively and
imaginatively taught to involve students personally and experientially (Integ involve; Integ exper). However, unless the school's climate of relationships prizes and reinforces emotional sensitivity to
others' feelings and opinions, then the effects of its courses are not
likely to be stabilized and so endure.

    The next step is to provide students the opportunity to be
responsible for the care and growth of others (Other care), whether
for other students in a course or, more ideally, for the school and
different age groups (Other roles). I remained to talk at the end of
a day with an eighth-grader in a wealthy school that expected its
students to be responsible for its upkeep. In trooped three seventh-
graders to sweep the floor, clean the blackboards, empty the waste

baskets, and straighten the desks (Other care; Aut faith). They even monitored how well they had done (Aut excel). Why could not inner-city schools spark and organize neighborhood cleanup drives that continued periodically throughout the year? Rather than complaining about their schools' physical conditions and janitorial negligence, students might learn how to be good citizens within their own classes and schools. In one urban school, the faculty actually monitored whether the bathrooms had been cleaned and toilet paper and paper towels were available.

Following the Carnegie recommendation that schools expect students to fulfill a community service project for graduation to teach "citizenship" will not produce enduring character maturation. Instead, the commission should have recommended that all students from kindergarten through middle school be responsible for serving their schools in some capacity every day to learn the habit and skills of serving others. They could feed the gerbils and plants, help put toys away, assist in the offices, correct younger children's papers, read to and tutor younger children, and adopt a little brother or sister for the year (Other care; Aut faith; Symb model).[14] If students had demonstrated that they could care and serve responsibly, then high school could introduce them to serving their local community, not for forty hours one semester, but for several hours a week for the school year every year (Aut faith; Aut test).

Colleges could offer students the opportunity to serve in and thus learn in different types of neighborhoods and countries (Aut test), as Haverford did for its students teaching in an urban school and Earlham did for my daughter teaching in a Japanese one. If a school is serious about educating for character maturation, *sustained* experiences that demand maturing are indispensable (Integ involve; Integ exper; Integ context) for its stabilization to occur (Stab extern; Stab conseq). Schools should not play games with character education; they should prepare students to develop their own altruistic ideals *from kindergarten on.*[15]

Might not learning and practicing the skills of empathy and caring provide the fulfillment that religions have taught us comes from giving to others? Might not learning how to care and give in school better prepare students to care as adults for their communi-

ties and to seek equity for everyone than our schools now prepare
them? Schools of hope teach their students to be compassionate and
seek justice for those who differ from themselves. They educate their
students to be responsible citizens caring for their planet's future
survival and their global neighbors' well-being.

Systematically Integrating Interpersonal and Value Maturation with Academic Maturation

To create a maturing environment that produces integrative character effects first requires clarity about the character desired (Symb
goal). Given such clarity, there must then be a continuing alive
understanding of the school's *systemic* nature and how its practices
and structures should consistently reinforce its vision (Integ context).

Steps taken to enhance the maturation of character must be
in harmony with the school's mission, ethos, and curricular and
teaching practices to produce optimal maturing effects (Integ goal).
Implied in suggestions to create means for communal reflection or
develop a code of ethics for teachers is the necessity to integrate their
implementation with a school's other practices, particularly its academic ones. Most proposals to alter relationships and further value
maturation fail because they are not integrated with consistent
changes in a school's primary activity—teaching the curriculum.

Consider the proposal to create means for community reflection and decision making about a school's activities and effects.
Kohlberg's proposal that faculty and students regularly meet to reflect about a school's moral issues suggests only an initial step.[16] If
a school's academic life is immune to such reflection, then it does
not consistently support character's integration (Aut test).

Haverford's reflectiveness supported my efforts to create with
my students the class's learning ethos that I did. It also taught some
students to reflect about their other courses. I always asked at the
end of a semester just one question: What changes should I make
in the course to better achieve its goals next year (Symb reflect)? To
keep myself honest, I recorded each suggestion, reflected about it,
altered my next year's course when appropriate, and then the first
day of next year's course reviewed the ideas, explained why I had
rejected some, and outlined how I planned to implement others

(Symb reflect). Students felt that I listened to and respected their opinions, trusted my innovations, sanctioned my taking the risks that I did, and felt more ownership of the course. Five weeks into a course on life-span development, a student said during our break, "Doug, I have a suggestion for next year's course." She viewed the course as an experience in growing up and had reflected about how it could help her to mature more (Integ exper; Symb reflect).

Because character growth is enhanced when it is integrated with the school's academic mission, I have never been enamored by hands-on activities as a means to character maturation if they are *not* part and parcel of concurrent academic courses (Integ exper; Integ context). Just turning students loose to serve in their communities may have other-centered maturing effects; but if their experience is not integrated with their knowledge and other values, its effects may be insubstantial and fleeting. For example, students in the life-span course recommended one year that they reflect about and induce ideas from their fieldwork and then relate them to the course's reading and discussions. They were correct to insist on such integration.

How else can we create schools of hope that educate for integrity?

Stabilizing Character and Encouraging Its Autonomy

Three tests of a permanent change in character are its predictability, resilience to possible disruption by stress, and occurrence in situations quite different from that in which the change was educed. Not until these tests are met can we confirm that the trait or value is no longer just being called out by the situation in which it was learned but has become an integral part of our character. The ultimate test of character stability is its autonomy.

Proponents of character education frequently forget that character is seldom changed by one-shot experiences. Even rare sudden conversions probably result from transformations that have been silently going on for months at the edges of consciousness. A Martin Luther King day may recall to students the values for which the civil rights movement fought and so temporarily reaffirm them (Stab affirm). Unless such values are exercised and monitored day in and day out and tested at home and in the neighborhood, the celebratory day contributes little to stabilizing such values (Aut test). Students don't learn to be responsible citizens by visiting polling booths every two years. Interest in voting and faithfully doing it can become more stable habits if students vote regularly on *meaningful* personally relevant classroom and school issues (Integ involve; Stab conseq).

How can a school aid its youth to test their interpersonal maturity and develop firmer and more autonomous values? Madeira, a girls' boarding school located outside Washington, D.C., uses its favored resources, setting, and location to teach its students how to create their own goals and become more autonomous. Each Wednesday, the students participate in some experiential day-long activity (Integ involve; Integ exper). Ninth-grade girls, for example, learn how to survive in their physical world (Symb confront). While visiting the school, I was taken aback to observe a crew of yellow-helmeted girls in work clothes pass by. They were learning how to cross a steep gorge on ropes (Aut early).

The sophomores are apprenticed for a year to social service agencies, where they are expected to act as caring professionals; they can even be fired if they miss appointments or act irresponsibly (Aut faith; Other care; Other skills; Stab conseq). Their work is evaluated by professionals (Symb reflect).

During my visit, I talked at breakfast with a worried junior who worked on "the Hill" at the office of her member of Congress. The previous week, she had inadvertently erased his mailing list on the computer and didn't know what to expect now (Stab conseq). Another told me how she had argued with Tip O'Neil, former leader of the House of Representatives, and now felt great about herself. Their experiential learning was integrated with a concurrent social studies course on government (Integ goals).

The seniors were expected to develop, without assistance, their own goals and plans and responsibly carry them out in their chosen year-long community program (Symb goals; Symb reflect; Aut test; Aut excel).

When hearing of such a program, some teachers bemoan how much time the program would take away from their courses. Others say that students in such programs won't do well on their

SATs or get into college because they will have missed some advanced courses. Madeira's counselor said that her most difficult task was to convince girls with mediocre grade records to raise their sights about the quality of college to which to apply. They had developed the character that selective colleges really want in their students. They not only had tested themselves in various interpersonal situations but also had learned to value being independent persons more able to survive whatever they might face.

You may argue that favored wealthy independent schools can create such programs but that large public schools can't possibly create programs to encourage students to develop more autonomously held values. Some can, if they trust their students to be responsible (Aut faith). Bored by school, my eleventh-grade son and ten of his like-minded friends petitioned a sympathetic superintendent to be released from all requirements. They wished to discover whether they could together teach themselves. Their faculty agreed, though it insisted they attend their regular mathematics and language courses.

Unfortunately, the gap between these students' hopes and the interpersonal and value maturity they would have needed to achieve them was not just a gap—it proved to be a despairing abyss. Argument, frustration, and chaos reigned. I eavesdropped when they met in our living room to plan their curriculum and how they were to go about teaching themselves (Symb goals; Symb reflect; Other roles). As the MHS students also discovered, they had not been prepared to even listen to and work cooperatively with each other. Nor had they been prepared to form their goals for their own growth. Dismayed that they couldn't agree about what they wanted to learn, they asked a parent to teach them conflict-resolution skills—just as MHS had to do (Other skills).

At one point, they asked me to teach them psychology. I misguidedly suggested that they look at some texts to discover what they might want to know. Some immediately turned off and didn't read their own assigned chapters. Their former texts had been one spur to their rebellion.

They continued to struggle for weeks trying to decide what their goals should be (Symb reflect). Eventually, they decided to go their own ways, though continuing to meet to educate each other about what they were learning.

"A disaster," you might be saying. Of too little faith, I too had begun to say that—to myself. However, some autonomous phoenixes rose out of the ashes of seeming defeat. Several persuaded the school board to create an alternative school the next year, which they helped to organize (Aut excel). Others found their direction, created their own goals, and settled down to work toward them. Some returned to their regular classes for their senior year. All graduated and, in spite of glaring gaps in their academic records, attended and graduated from highly selective colleges.

When later asked what they had learned from their experience, none expressed regret. All agreed that it had been their most formative high school experience. They unanimously said that they had learned how to create their own goals (Symb goals; Aut excel) and to pursue them. The real test of their growth is, of course, how they lived their subsequent lives. My son has been his own self-teacher since, most recently teaching himself how to sail a twenty-six-foot sailboat alone around the world. I have told you about my Earlham daughter who had joined the group the following year.

Few schools trust their students to be responsible and create their own goals and ideals—or prepare them to use freedom wisely. Fewer than a third of both teachers and students in independent and public schools and colleges use words such as *autonomous, independent, individualistic, strong convictions, deep ethical sense,* and *idealistic* to describe their schools, faculties, or students or even their wishes for them.

When assessing a school's ethos, I inquire whether the voices of feminists, black activists, Latinos, and gays are heard and respected in the school. Are the voices of faculty who disagree with currently fashionable political values heard and thoughtfully considered? How open is the school to hearing controversial speakers and the curriculum to including unfashionable ideas and readings? If it is rejected out of hand, ignored, ridiculed, or attacked, then how can any specific program or curricular effort to encourage healthy interpersonal and value autonomy possibly succeed?

Has the school that you know well created an ethos that prizes

faculty and student commitment and courage—the liberally educating outcomes of encouraging character stability and autonomy?

Liberal educators claim that the ultimate sign of our maturing is that we become agents of our own growth. Our maturing
minds and characters gradually come under our own command, as
the Madeira, MHS, and self-teaching students had begun to experience. The next chapter returns to the classroom to illustrate how
maturing's principles can be applied to educate students to be more
self-educating to better prepare them to adapt to a most uncertain
future.

Chapter 15

Educating the Self

Maturing proceeds toward increasing self-confidence and self-esteem as well as command of our mind and character; we begin to achieve our hopes by our own efforts.[1] What can teachers do in their classrooms to further such maturing without any sacrifice of the academic integrity of their courses? In this chapter, I first describe how one teacher worked with underprivileged high school Latino and other minority youth and then how I worked with privileged college students.

"Do You Have Ganas?"

Jaime Escalante, the inspiring teacher of the movie *Stand and Deliver,* has taught us that math does not have to be the most forbidding liberal arts course to teach to today's here-and-now adolescents. The movie, reputedly 95 percent accurate, pictures how Escalante taught math to bright but nonachieving Latino and other minority adolescents from a Los Angeles barrio. Their school, Garfield High, was on the edge of losing its accreditation because of its low test scores. Escalante overcame crushing forces working against him to exhort, cajole, push, and drive his students to achieve excellence: his chairperson's belief that his students did not have the talent and sturdy self-esteem to learn the calculus; the school's gang-ridden, unruly, and episodically violent ethos; unsupportive parents; and apathetic and hostile students.

Beginning the first day teaching them fractions and negative numbers, next geometry and trigonometry, and then calculus, he created such a classroom of hope that all eighteen of his students passed the College Board's advanced placement test in calculus. The next year, thirty-one passed it. By 1987, a cumulative total of 354 and, by 1991, 576 students had passed it since he had begun teaching. Students have gone to college who had never believed they were capable of doing so. His success "reinvigorated the school. Its seniors rank among the best in all subjects in the huge Los Angeles school system. Tough administrators have broken the back of gang influence among students, and there is little graffiti."[2]

How did Escalante create his classroom of hope that so radically altered his students' views of and hopes for themselves? His answer that other teachers could achieve what he did if they just cared more about teaching than they did about the system is neither helpful nor sufficient. Let's search more deeply to discover how to create a classroom of hope that nourishes self-confidence and self-esteem. Escalante's example suggests that classrooms of hope should have teachers who:

Care for and love their students and dedicate their lives to serving them
Empathically understand today's youth
Fervently believe their students can fulfill high expectations
Create a trusting, caring, and cohesive classroom ethos[3]
Consistently implement maturing's principles

And they should have students with ganas—the desire to learn and willingness to work hard to do so. While not discounting his achievement, a colleague told me that Escalante could select Garfield's most talented students for his classes; he also had the privilege of rejecting those who did not meet his expectations. Such privileges and his subsequent fame did not endear him to his colleagues. Due to union criticism and lack of collegial and parental support, he resigned from Garfield in 1991.

From the opening moment of Escalante's class, we learn about strengths that teachers need to reach today's youth. With firmness, playfulness, and humor, he told them of his expectations and commitment to teach them. They sensed his calling to care for and serve them; they knew he was *their* advocate. He convinced a father to allow his daughter to remain in school and the department to permit him to teach calculus. He then worked with his students without pay during the hot summer to prepare them for their calculus test. He entered into their troubles, such as publicly comforting in his arms a girl whose life was crumbling around her. His students knew that his mild heart attack resulted from his compulsion to serve them. As his wife told him when he was most despondent, the kids reciprocated his love for them.

The students knew that he not only cared for them but also empathically knew the lives they lived and the bleak future that they might be condemned to. So they accepted his direct, blunt, and humorous sarcasm as a sign of affection, not of hostility and rejection. He called them stupid. He made fun of Angel's hairnet but gave him extra copies of the text so his gang wouldn't see him carrying it in the corridors or taking it home at night. He dramatized the consequences of his students' current lives and decisions: "I'm afraid you are going to screw up the rest of your lives." He scared Pablo, who had been thinking of dropping out to make a lot of money as a mechanic, by racing his car, slamming on the brakes, and saying, "All that you see is the turn ahead but not the road beyond."

The students knew his faith in their ability to achieve. Holding college up as a realistic option for them, he prodded them, "Do you have ganas?" He did not compromise his expectations. He demanded that his students give up their vacations and immediate pleasures to work for longer-term goals, which he kept insisting they could reach. Why did they persist? Because he had faith in and cared for them.

As happens in other boot camps, the students became a strongly knit support group, sustaining each other's motivation through their grueling and intensely paced summer's preparation for the calculus test. When one student needed something to drink in the hot classroom, several others offered their own oranges to suck. I noticed no student putting others down, even when Pablo vulnerably and despairingly said that he was the most stupid person in the group. Angel humorously came to the defense of a fragile girl about to be grilled by a representative of the test agency who thought that they had cheated on their calculus test.

Escalante consistently applied the principles that contribute to maturing. He most effectively used several. He was very clear about the class behavior that he expected, which he consistently and impartially implemented (Symb goals; Stab conseq). Students were to do their homework, bring their books and pencils to class, not speak out of turn in class, and not be late. When Angel arrived late, he refused to listen to his legitimate excuse. He told him to go to his counselor and switch into woodworking and make shoeshine boxes. Claiming that there would be no "free ride" in his class, he rigorously held the students to his expectations. But more important, he clearly expected them to pull themselves up by their bootstraps and improve their lot. He expected ganas! He expected them to be winners, not losers (Aut excel).

He also made effective use of the principles of ceaselessly challenging, confronting, and affirming their worth (Symb confront; Stab affirm). He continually tested their ganas, whether by requiring them to sign a contract agreeing to assume responsibility for their behavior, or to come an hour earlier to school, or to work on Saturdays to review their calculus (Aut faith). When their ganas flagged, he cheered them on. "You are the best. You are the true dreamers. You'll prove you are the champs. Math is easy. Boy Scout stuff. You can do it. You have math in your blood. The Mayas, your ancestors, were the first to use the idea of zero."

Most appropriate to his students' cognitive developmental level and the psychology of today's youth, Escalante made math concrete, dramatic, fun, and pervasively experiential (Integ involve; Integ exper). The movie pictures him dressed as a chef on the second day of class calling on each student to tell how much of an apple each had that he had cut into fractions. He spoke their language— even that of the streets. When the students wanted to talk about sex, he phrased math problems in terms of numbers of lovers or gigolos to make abstract ideas meaningful. Using games such as tick-tack-toe, class chants, and visits to a company's computer division to demonstrate why algebra was useful, he playfully made math comprehensible and fun to learn.

Escalante's class of hope was far more than a class about

calculus. Like a school of hope, his class taught character. He altered the students' relationships and values. He taught them who they were and what they could be. Angel eventually found the courage to walk away from his domineering gang leader and abandon his antisocial behavior. Pablo persisted to pass the advanced placement course. The students became aware of their strengths, learned to put aside immediate pleasures for longer-term goals, became more self-confident, earned the respect of their teachers and themselves, raised their aspirations, and went on to college to become professionals. Escalante taught math in such a way as to produce liberal education's effects. That is the essential secret of his course's success—not that so many hundreds of his students mastered the calculus. He inspired confidence and hope in formerly defeated and defiant kids.

How well Escalante enabled his students to secure as mature command of themselves as they might have is more problematic. The movie illustrated teaching that could reinforce dependence on him: its rather quixotic title, *Stand and Deliver,* his humorously benign but authoritarian control, his students' deferential though respectful acknowledgment that he was "boss," the paucity of scenes showing students teaching each other, the failure of the class to work for a student who assumed the teaching role when Escalante had his heart attack, and his students' need for him to help them review for their placement exam.

What was Escalante's real secret? Might it not have been empowering students' self-confidence and esteem not by faddish techniques and theories but by faith in and love for his kids *and* high expectations of the competence on which genuine self-confidence must ultimately be grounded?

Teaching to the Teacher Within

Montessorians—and Kathy, the first-second grade teacher whose students worked independently on their own while she and I conferred—tell us that we each have an inner teacher. Even four- and five-year-olds can become their own teachers for a limited period when provided an appropriately structured learning environment. Not until Escalante's students had been freed of their texts, his step-by-step teaching, and his invigorating and motivational exhortations would they discover how maturely autonomous they had become.

To create his classroom of hope, Escalante had to overcome far more imposing handicaps and meet more forbidding challenges than I. My thirty-two sophomores and juniors came from favored homes and high schools, had tested and proved their academic talents, and were motivated to take one of the college's more demanding courses. I taught a course about personality, which was surely of more intrinsic interest to my students than fractions and negative numbers were to Escalante's. I also taught in a small college whose ethos valued academic growth and implicitly supported my educational views. I did not have to fight the system as Escalante had to.

Follow me into the most important moments of a class—its first days and weeks. Since forty- or fifty-minute class periods breed distraction and apathy more than concentrated effort and sustained involvement, I offered the course in two ninety-minute periods after lunch. I reserved a subsequent optional ninety-minute period for experiential enrichment. As the students entered the class their first day, I separated them into groups of five and sent them to different parts of the room and corridor. Each received a sheet outlining the goals for the day (Symb goals) and how to achieve them and another listing 125 technical terms that they were to master over the next few weeks (Aut excel).

The first day's three goals introduced the students to the course's interpersonal ethic. The first goal was to get to know the name of every person in their group and then of the entire class within two weeks—a small but crucial step to create an open and caring classroom environment (Other trust).

The second goal was to learn how to ask a stupid question. Today's students need to trust that they will not be slaughtered by the teacher or others if they expose their ignorance (Other trust). A shy future valedictorian had never said a word in the large class for several weeks. One day, she hesitantly raised her hand to say, "I have a stupid question to ask." While it was not stupid, she needed the sanction to expose what she felt was her ignorance (Other trust).

And the third goal was to begin to learn the skills of helping other students learn (Other care; Other skills; Other roles; Aut faith). Since students learn best when actively involved, I provided as many different ways as possible to engage them throughout the ninety minutes (Integ involve). Teaching another is the quickest way to test what one knows (Other roles; Stab rehearse; Stab external), so guided pair and small-group discussions dominated the early weeks while the students mastered the course's basic vocabulary.[4] Since I don't "curve" grades and so pit students against each other for scarce A's, students learned that cooperating is more productive—and more enjoyable—than competing.

I did not require prerequisites and quickly plunged the students into difficult Freudian ideas. The gap between their understanding of the clinical problems and the technical vocabulary that Freud created to understand them confronted me with a formidable teaching dilemma. I had to provide a great deal of support and close that gap immediately (Symb confront). So the students were each instructed to give their names and then to go down the second list of technical concepts word by word to find the first one that they didn't know that would make them look most stupid and to ask others to define and give examples of it (Aut early). Needless to say, even students who had had a traditional introductory psychology course immediately learned that they could not precisely define most of the terms or give accurate examples of them (Symb reflect). In the meantime, I moved from one group to the next to be available as a resource.

I had early learned that I needed assistance. So I had invited two former students to be my colleagues, for which they received partial course credit. Responsible for several groups, each was available to clarify a term in question and inductively draw from the group's experience numerous other examples (Symb model). The new students were awed by how much my colleagues had learned in just a fourteen-week course. We met once a week and discussed the course's pace and confusions and the students' morale and needs. We tracked each student to discover who needed individual tutorial or other assistance, which one of us would provide (Other care; Symb model). My colleagues offered optional group reviews of the technical terms to which four or five students came several times a week (Aut early). They also assumed responsibility for conducting one class, evaluated class and small group participation, and advised me about who should be my colleagues the following year.

After I had visited every group, we returned to class, and I asked why I had begun the course this way (Symb confront; Symb reflect). The students groaned when I confirmed that I planned to actively involve them throughout the course (Integ involve) and not lecture at them. However, to establish my credibility as a traditional teacher, I promised to give them one special, insightful, well-organized and sparkling ninety-minute lecture six weeks later. When I did, they blanked out and agreed that they preferred not to have another one.

In critiquing an earlier version of the course, a student who learned best from lectures had suggested that I prepare recorded background lectures and place them in the library so students could listen to them if they needed more didactic instruction. That summer, I prepared thirteen recorded lectures. The course outline indicated when it would be most appropriate to listen to them (Aut faith). I recommended that the students listen to and discuss them with one another (Integ involve), especially the questions I had included to prod them to think more relationally (Integ context). Initially, I gave out detailed outlines of the lectures to show that they were organized—an idea about lectures that I have found many of today's TV-bred youth to be unfamiliar with (Symb model). Gradually, I reduced their detail to wean students from depending on me for organizing their notes (Aut test). The students enjoyed this method, but over the years, more and more complained that the lectures were too long. About thirty-five minutes would be best, they said. I did not yield.

After these prefatory comments, I described the course's three goals (Symb goals) and explained how I would achieve them (Integ goals). First was to consistently teach in ways that would enable the students to teach themselves whatever they wished to know about the course's topics for the rest of their lives. Second was to teach them three generalizable skills: thinking clearly, inducing, and thinking relationally and critically. And third was to create a learning environment that would further their maturing. The examinations would measure their mastery of the three skills using the course's content.

I next shared with the class the preceding class's critique of the course and suggestions about how to reach my goals more effectively. I previewed how I planned to enable them to become more self-educating, develop each of the three skills, and create a maturing learning environment (Symb goals). Since Chapter Thirteen described how I used my liberal arts content to teach skills, I now present only a few of the ideas that students gave me for teaching them how to be more self-educating.

Because reflecting on how one learns brings greater self-control, I presented during the third week the twenty principles that further maturation (Symb reflect). After discussing each principle, the students induced examples of them from the past three weeks' classes. And, as I told you, one student began to take charge of his own learning when he subsequently asked his physics professor to use more varied teaching methods that would help him learn the material better.

So began a fast-paced in-depth study of the course's key theorists. I had early learned that students trained to depend on summarizing textbooks did not know how to read original works questioningly and critically. So I taught them to read actively to prepare them for the next class's discussions. I prepared detailed guides stating the goals for the next class and included questions that probed important issues presented in their readings that their randomly formed groups might discuss (Symb model; Integ involve; Stab external). As the students learned to think more critically about their reading, I loosened the prearranged structure of the small-group sessions to rely increasingly on their own judgment about the issues to identify, wrestle with, and clarify in class (Aut test).

Students learned the first week that though I would give brief lectures, I would not review their homework. I or other students would answer questions brought to class. Like Escalante, I assumed that they had read the material and had enough command of it to participate responsibly in their group and class discussions (Aut faith; Aut early). One group of five silent males fidgeted mutely when I visited it. Their task had been to make a close sentence-by-sentence analysis of an obscure passage of a most penetrating but impenetrable section of Freud's classic *Interpretation of Dreams* (Integ context). I noted no underlined passages in their open books, so assumed—correctly, as it turned out—that none had read the section. I sat silently among them while they embarrassedly hemmed and hawed, squirmed, and avoided my glances, not even knowledgeable enough to ask a question. After ten minutes of the very itchy silence, I left, saying that they knew where they could find me if they needed me (Stab conseq). By the next class, some, though not all of them, came to class prepared to work.

Despite these traditional instructional procedures, some students still had not mastered well the course's initial vocabulary. During the mid seventies, a student suggested that I program the course's vocabulary on a computer. So I created three self-examining tests of fifteen questions each to teach students how to induce the terms from contextual material (Integ context) as well as to use them precisely— one way in which I taught them how to think more clearly. I designed stories for each set that illustrated the various technical terms. Students had three chances to induce the correct answer and enter it into the computer. If they were correct, the computer responded ecstatically in true Escalante style (Stab affirm). If they were incorrect, the computer commiserated with them and then encouraged them to continue. At their first incorrect answer, they could request the computer to give them a brief lecture from which they could induce the correct term. They had to answer a question correctly before the computer permitted them to proceed to the next; if they failed their three chances, a most apologetic computer bid them goodbye and returned them to the first question to begin all over again—a most painful consequence to occur by the thirteenth question (Stab external; Stab conseq).

One night, the supervisor of the computer center called to tell me that there had been an emergency. A frustrated stapler- rather than paste-trained student had tried to smash the monitor. How had other students coped more adaptively with the task's potential frustration? Groups of students clustered around the computers with their notes and dictionaries arguing about the answers (Other skills; Integ involve). When one student claimed that the answer to the thirteenth question was "schizophrenia," I overheard another say, "Let's check it first." And before they entered the answer, another, who had noted me hovering in the background, said, "Be sure to check the spelling. This is a dumb computer."

As with the voluntary taped lectures and computer exercise, students learned when they needed to seek varied resources, take the initiative, work cooperatively with each other, and thoroughly check their answers and spelling. They had begun to develop the attitude, skills, and idea of themselves as self-educating persons. Students enjoyed the computer exercise and, in spite of its severe frustration, recommended making it an integral part of the course.

I knew, however, from students' discussions that some had only a verbal command of the material. They had not internalized its meanings and integrated them with their personal experience and character. So I offered a weekly optional experiential session focused on a theorist's principal method or concepts. To understand Freud's method of free association and defenses such as repression and intellectualization, pairs of us took in turn the roles of patient and analyst (Other roles). As a patient, each uttered whatever came to mind without censoring it. As an analyst, we noted each time the flow of words was interrupted. After experiencing each role for twenty minutes, we reflected about and induced the different defenses that Freud had identified (Integ exper).

The tightly organized course became progressively less structured through the semester to test students' growing autonomy (Aut test). I became less and less the students' authority. Groups assumed responsibility for teaching a particular theorist in panel discussions to the rest of the class (Other roles; Integ involve). Eventually, each student taught a group of four others one of the great religions' view of personality development, for which the class was held responsible (Stab conseq). Students also created some of their own questions for their final exams (Aut excel).

One year, when I was responsible for the concurrent introductory psychology course of about 100 freshmen, the students formed themselves into three-person groups to provide the freshmen an enriched experience about personality for a week (Aut faith; Other care; Other roles). Each created its own curriculum of readings that had not been assigned in their course (Aut test), collected copies of the readings, organized its several course meetings, and collated all the interest groups' offerings into a master curricular list from which each freshman selected a course. Each team had complete responsibility for its course as well as the evaluation of its students (Aut test; Aut excel). The freshmen also evaluated their teams' efforts (Stab conseq). The result? Great intellectual excitement, very (too?) heavy reading assignments, courses that went on for many more hours than required, freshmen awed by how much their teachers knew (Sym model), and personality students also awed about how much they had learned (Stab affirm; Aut excel). When students are trusted with meaningful responsibility appropriate to their maturity, they will be maturely responsible.

The final examination was apprehensively known to be tough. It explicitly tested for mastery of the course's skills, which meant that students had to know the course's content in detail to be able to think about it. They spontaneously formed themselves into small study groups. One group's members told me that they had worked for eight hours formulating questions to answer (Other care; Other roles; Stab rehears; Aut test). "Doug will ask a question using induction. What are some questions measuring it?" They then collectively answered the questions and graded their answers, thus learning how to hold themselves to their own defined criteria of excellence (Aut excel).

What did the course do to the students? Did it achieve its goals? By providing richly varied ways to learn and test their growth, it helped some to discover strengths they had not known they had. Its cooperative rather than competitive ethos provided a trusting class that spoke to both the women's and men's needs. Since it was appropriate to women's interpersonal strengths, they gradually emerged to lead the small-group discussions and to assert themselves more argumentatively in the larger class. The men, no longer dominating the small-group and class discussions, formed more collaborative working relationships. When I returned the final exams to the mail room, one male nearby asked not what most students usually did, "How did I do?" but instead, "How did my group do?" Had he developed a mite of caring from his sustained cooperative work with others?

Though this was not my principal goal, the students learned an impressive amount. Alumni who entered graduate programs claimed that they knew as much as second-year students or psychiatric residents. To assess the course's effects, the students anonymously rated on a seven-point scale how much they had learned compared to every other college course they had taken. Their rating was next to the top, 6.1; 23 percent of the students claimed that they had never learned as much in any other course; no one claimed to have learned less than in their typical courses.

The majority of students believed that they had grown in the ways that I had hoped. Eighty-one percent anonymously rated their greatest areas of growth to have been learning how to think more relationally, which I had independently confirmed from their exams designed to measure it, and becoming more aware of themselves, not an unexpected result of a course on personality. Seventy-seven percent believed that they had matured in reflecting about and understanding their own minds and in developing more autonomous cognitive skills. They had made the course's ideas and vocabulary their own. Some, so the English Department complained, too flagrantly used their new technical language to interpret their novels. They had not yet, however, so made it their own as to be able to translate it into ordinary down-to-earth words.

The course next affected the students' interpersonal maturing. Seventy-three percent believed that they had learned to work more cooperatively with each other; 69 percent claimed that they had become more sensitively aware of others and their relationships with them. Fifty-eight percent reported that they had become more caring and actually valued caring for other students more. Some reported that they had never had another course in which they knew so many other students so well and made as many close friends with whom they could talk about intellectual ideas. From about the seventh week on, small groups met for lunch to talk about their reading before class, much to the annoyance of nearby students. The last time I taught the course, a perpetually scowling woman who we felt had fought the course the entire semester surprised us. She invited the class to a potluck dinner at her place after the final exam; all but two came.

The effects produced by the course were similar to how students typically matured from freshman to senior year. However, it more effectively taught its students to become more aware of their own minds, which had become more reliably accessible and under their own control.

Had the students secured more command of *themselves?*

While numerous small signs said that they had, and 27 percent of the students agreed, they, like Escalante's students, would not know until they had tested their maturity in other situations (Aut test). But I felt that most had encountered—some for the first time—their own inner teacher.

If this and the previous chapters have identified some truths about students, adults, and their schools, then the way to create schools of hope dedicated to human excellence should be prefigured, as Margaret Mead would say. What prefigured steps should we take to create schools in which students learn how to be their own teachers?

Chapter 16

Creating
Schools of Hope:
Seven Essential Steps

To create schools of hope, we must:

> Secure leaders who are practical idealists emotionally committed to liberal education as an *alive* and attainable ideal
>
> Make liberal education's goal of human excellence *the* primary operative priority
>
> Understand and persist in surmounting ideological barriers to its fulfillment
>
> Abandon large schools and create humane and caring school climates
>
> Create a shared belief within the school and its neighboring community in the school's specific goals and ways to achieve excellence
>
> Create a *developmentally coherent* curriculum and programs that consistently implement the school's priority values
>
> Continuously reflect within the school and with the community about how well and why the school's goals are or are not being achieved and then judiciously experiment to achieve them more effectively

Educational reform is stalled because it has ignored what students really need: a coherent, compelling ideal of the strengths they need for adapting to their future. Boyer, William Glasser, Sizer, and others agree.[1] Teachers know that. They tell us that by the gifts that they wish they could give their students: the joy of learning, a sense of what is right, and self-confidence. Students also know that. They tell us that by their apathy and their lack of sustained commitment to a calling as teachers of themselves.

The book has pursued the ideal outcomes that educators have claimed schools should produce. *Fulfilling Lives* and other studies demonstrate that such outcomes do, in fact, contribute to an adult's success, virtue, and well-being. For the first time, scientific evidence confirms philosophers' views that a liberal education can powerfully contribute to a student's adult fulfillment and success. The model of maturing comprehends most of philosophers' and schools' actual outcomes. Its principles suggest how schools can further faculty's and students' growth, how the curriculum might be organized developmentally, and how the liberal arts can be taught to produce liberally educating effects without sacrificing their academic integrity.

Our understanding of today's youth and schools prefigure at least seven necessary steps to fulfill education's promise for its students' future.

Developing Educational Leaders as Practical Idealists

Schools of hope require leaders, including influential faculty, who are committed to the vision of human excellence—to the maturation not just of mind but also of character and self. The traits of excellent school heads, college presidents, and business leaders are similar. In their book *In Search of Excellence*, Peters and Waterman tell us that the excellent leader is "the value shaper, the exemplar, the maker of meanings . . . primarily an expert in the promotion and protection of values . . . calling forth and exemplifying the urge for transcendence that unites us all."[2] Such leaders are neither autocratic nor democratic. Autocratic leaders suppress individuals' ownership of their goals, initiative, and growth; overly democratic ones do not provide the consistently firm guidance necessary to efficiently achieve a school's goals.[3] Wisely experienced in promoting institutional change, Phillip Schlechty insists that leaders must be far more than superb administrators: they should articulate an organization's values; they should be the voice of its hopes; they should weld their colleagues together in service to the ideal that is the source of their calling and inspiration.[4]

An excellent leader knows how to reaffirm, enliven, and strengthen teachers' calling and thus a passionate commitment to their ideals. Chapter Six identified the gifts that teachers hope their students will make their own. They are liberal education's vision of the ideal. However, their vision has been so demeaned and dismissed by society and its media that many teachers now question their vocational choice and the validity of their calling. Too many, so my studies suggest, have accepted society's view of their work as a job, no longer as one of the noblest of all callings.

Schools of hope need leaders who themselves understand, draw upon, and have the courage to defend America's own quintessential tradition that justifies human excellence as schools' proper ideal. They will not rob themselves, for example, of John Dewey's wise insights about schooling's ideals. No other philosopher, American or otherwise, so accurately and insightfully wrote about healthy growth. Thirty-five years of research about how youth and adults mature has confirmed over and over the wisdom of his views. When mapping philosophers' goals into the model of maturing, I discovered no other that identified as many of maturing's outcomes. When empirically identifying the principles that further maturing, no other had so cogently applied so many to schools.

Making Liberal Education's Outcomes
the Operative Priorities

What should be a school of hope's priority goal and proper yardstick for measuring its accomplishments? Not students' test scores but their demonstration of becoming liberally educated in the ways that Chapters Seven through Nine described. Acquiring teachers' gifts is the route to increasing mastery of a liberal arts discipline. Not until students experience the self-command and power that their courses could produce will they begin to commit themselves to making learning their calling.

How do we get students to make this commitment? Clarify the strengths they need for their future success and well-being. Constantly demonstrate how their courses empower them with the strengths. Hold them accountable for acquiring them. I repeat my prescription for the last time. *Not until we explicitly teach liberal arts courses to produce liberally educating effects and assess and value such effects will today's pragmatic students become genuinely involved agents of their own growth.* Only then will mastering a course tap into intrinsic motivation, rather than the extrinsic motivation that it now does. As the MHS students told us, only then will they become self-motivated teachers who enjoy learning. I challenge you again. Ask students about the most important growths they have experienced as a result of schooling. They will describe the effects that liberal education produces, not the effects that liberal arts courses now test and grade for.

The implication is not that we dismiss tests of achievement. *They are one necessary index of excellence. But they are not sufficient indices of students' growth.* Students grow in many more far-reaching and significant ways—ones that will contribute more to their future success and well-being—than their test scores measure and predict.

Accrediting and legislative groups are beginning to recognize this truth. Some now hold schools accountable for more than narrowly defined achievement test scores. The North Central Association of Colleges and Schools requires its participating schools to select three cognitive and two character-self-related goals. They must then learn how to assess each and so hold themselves accountable for achieving them.[5] Focusing on liberally educative outcomes can contribute significantly to improving schools. Schoolwide measures, rather than only course grades or achievement tests, place the responsibility for growth where it should be—on the school, not just on a few departments and classrooms.

Understanding and Surmounting
Ideological Barriers to Improvement

Americans have mixed feelings about their schools educating for the growth of character and self. Religious fundamentalists charge "secular humanism," as, for example, failing to ground values on beliefs in God. The American Civil Liberties Union (ACLU) charges invasions of privacy, as, for example, using magic circles in elementary schools. Both charges are naive; they misunderstand how growth proceeds.

Fulfilling Lives tells the fundamentalists that it is not their religious beliefs, any other ideology, or daily prayers or catechisms that contribute to their children's future success, well-being, and happiness—if they value these outcomes for them. No, what is more crucial is the integration into the way their children live their lives of religion's values, such as honesty, compassion, integrity, commitment, and courage—the values intrinsic to becoming liberally educated as well as successful, healthy, and happy.

Fulfilling Lives also tells the ACLU that mind, character, and self are inseparable. Efforts to build Chinese walls between them cause children to fail as students and eventually as adults. What are children to talk and write about? Only trees? Rocks? Butterflies? Never about what is most important to them, such as their feelings, beliefs, experiences, and dreams? Education *must* intrude into the privacy of students' minds, engage their values, "civilize" how they listen, argue, and feel, help them communicate and cooperate with others, alter their views of their strengths and weaknesses, and encourage their hopes while discouraging their despairs. If it doesn't, we produce only academic impotence and personal futility.

The seeming dissolution of Americans' consensus about their basic values acutely concerns educators. The issue of character education as it has been simplistically phrased is divisive. While 43 percent of adults believe that schools should offer a value- or ethics-based curriculum, 36 percent say that values or ethics should be left to parents and churches. The remainder take no strong stand for either.[6] If instead of this too vague question, adults had been asked whether schools should encourage honesty and compassion, would not most agree?

If we understood why we have become ambivalent about liberally educating students, perhaps we could begin to remove some ideological barriers to improvement. Since the sixties, societal values have changed in at least four ways that affect schools. They explain why we are so unsure, resist doing much about our ambivalence, and flee to objective test scores that safely measure noncontroversial academic facts. Since I have described some of the four earlier, I only briefly review them now.

Replacing Proscriptive Authority
with the Right to Self-Fulfillment

Chapters Two and Four claimed that during the watershed-rebellious sixties and seventies, we permanently altered our relationships with traditional authorities. They lost their ordained power. Role and position no longer automatically commanded respect and obedience. We no longer trusted anyone to tell us what our values should be.

The death of traditional authorities spawned self-fulfillment as the raison d'être of being and the arbiter of our choices. But in the absence of restraint and maturity, self-fulfillment deteriorates into self-seeking pursuit of greed and pleasure. The effects of the deteriorated vision of self-fulfillment on teachers' commitment to character education have been woeful. Faculty self-interest, resistance to expecting ethical behavior of others, and fear of moralistic vigilantes and prowling lawyers raise formidable barriers to educating character.

Usurpation by Special Faculty Needs and Interests of Communal Ones. Schools have become collections of self-seeking and turf-protecting departments. Increased faculty self-interest undermines a school's vision. Teachers cast off self-restraint and go their own way. Departments compete for scarce resources. Schools lose perspective, make decisions reactively, and seek to provide every possible resource or curricular option that faculty and students demand. They become financially strained and educationally bankrupt.

"Don't Lay Your Personal Hang-Ups on Me." Distrusting authority and not sharing a vision of the educated person result in students' resistance to and faculty's reluctance to assert the centrality of character maturation. Schools have lost their moral authority to prescribe not only academic but social-ethical standards of excellence. Faculty and students silently conspire to dilute expectations of human excellence. Today's teachers are wary about assuming responsibility for the moral and interpersonal maturation of their students. That is the "business" of the clergy, parents, counselors, assistant principals, and deans in charge of discipline. Even a gang rape of a drunken freshman woman by seventeen fraternity brothers was not, so one faculty claimed, its business.

Teachers rightly suspect those who facilely advocate educating character. I do. Such advocacy too easily slips into parochial indoctrination, too readily imposes moralistic proscriptions, and too frequently confuses education with therapy. Why? Because teachers are not clear about what the education of character means. They do not know how to defend themselves against charges that "character" refers to values that are relative, arbitrary, "middle-class biases" that should *not* be expected of or imposed on anyone else.

Educators' Fear of Moralistic Vigilantes. When we believe that we are the sole arbiters of our own choices about what is best for us, we become vulnerable to being hoisted by our own guilt. We cringe from telling others how they should live their lives, particularly when our school has no consensually shared vision of its goals. We then can become overly sensitive to the cries and demands of even the tiniest minorities who believe that their rights are being stepped upon. School boards let the noisy few limit the freedom of the many to know. So they ban *Huckleberry Finn* and *Catcher in the Rye*. Texts don't get written that might provoke thought about the pros and cons of nuclear power, abortion, evolution, premarital relations, teenage pregnancy, and the answers that different religions propose to such issues. We remain silent about just those topics that youth struggle with and should learn how to make more mature judgments about. Schools are stuck with utterly bland, nonprovocative, insultingly boring texts that squelch students' curiosity and tell them that learning is irrelevant. So they drop out—if not physically, then psychologically. We then sanctimoniously complain that youth are interested only in rock music, sports, drugs, sex, parties, and cars.

Whereas some moralistic vigilantes believe that schools can corrupt and irreversibly alter students' character, others doubt that they have such power; they insist that schools should not indulge in ineffective frills but they should stick to their academic knitting.

Ambivalence About the Power of Education to Alter Character

Americans question that schools can powerfully alter and should improve a student's mind *and* character and self. Teachers and parents waver between saying, "Character is set by the age of five and can't really be changed much" and "Who controls education controls a nation's destiny."

Schools Cannot Alter Character. Some teachers believe that they don't need to be concerned about character; interpersonal skills and values have already been irreversibly set, as if in concrete, by parents. Chapters Eight and Nine, which described schools' effects on the maturation of character and self, and Chapter Ten, which illustrated schools of hope, prove them wrong.

From a different perspective, those who claim education should not be concerned with character because it wastes resources may be right. B. F. Skinner, psychology's well-known behaviorist, once said that people tolerated education because it was so ineffectual. He did not mean, nor do I, that schooling could not affect character. He meant, as I do also, that educators didn't know and apply the best principles of learning to change behavior.

The issue is not that we cannot liberally educate a youth; the issue is that most teachers have not devoted the same concentrated effort to figuring out how to do that as they have to mastering and reviewing the content of their next day's class.

Education Can Be Too Powerful. Though parents spend thousands and society billions of dollars on education, believing that it can alter character, they, like the vigilantes, rightly fear how that power will be used. Don't we really want schools and colleges to be safe, predictable, and benign? To not change students' values or relationships but just give them a degree? It is human nature to not want to be changed too much. How many of us would go to church if the chances were 95 percent that we really would be "saved" and transformed?—not just sign a pledge card; I mean really change our way of life: take a vow of poverty, chastity, and obedience; tithe 25 percent? Give up our job to follow the way of the cross or retreat into Plato's cave? Go to Calcutta to work with Mother Teresa? Forgive our parents?

When asked why so few of its students applied to colleges in the Northeast, a South Carolina counselor said, "The parents around here are afraid of what those colleges will do to their children, particularly their girls."

A black sophomore told me that he was dropping out because he felt that he was changing in ways that he liked, but he feared that if he stayed, he would become a stranger to his mother and friends. He tearfully said that his girl back home had left him. "She said she couldn't understand me any more."

The president of an evangelical Christian college said that his board insisted that its mission should be to confirm and deepen, not challenge and disrupt, its students' faith. The religion department's head musingly said in our workshop, "I wonder if our students show so little curiosity about anything because we don't encourage them to question what is most important to them." I had reached the same conclusion from an independent assessment of the college's ethos.

Beliefs Can Character-Proof Education

When we isolate mind from character, thus ultimately enfeebling mind, we then believe that education should and can be "value-free." Teachers should be responsible only for their courses. Counselors and a panoply of deans should take care of students who are confused about their values, mired in their relationships, and mixed up about who they are. And never the twain shall meet!

Chapter Five mentioned the futility of fooling ourselves that education can and should be character-free. No choice of a goal and its means can be purified, objectified, and freed of someone's values and biases. American schools blatantly tell their students that abstract verbal competence is more prestigious than mechanical or artistic or social proficiency. Better to be an ambulance-chasing lawyer than a decent skilled machinist. Choice of what to require students to learn, topics to introduce, books to assign, classroom climate to encourage, ways to test growth, and standards to require for an A all inextricably involve someone's values, biases, prejudices, opinions, and needs. Tell me, just what is "basic" for a twelfth-grader or a college sophomore to learn that does not depend on someone's prior value judgment? Chemistry? Read the scientist Bronowski. He identified a rich variety of values intrinsic to scientific inquiry, including freedom to inquire and dissent, honesty, integrity, perseverance, independence, and tolerance.[7]

Nothing that we do in class is character-free. Chapter Five described the numerous character strengths required to take a history test and to write well. Even our modes of teaching affect character. Consider even the most sanitary lecture's potential effects. It more likely encourages today's students to sink another millimeter into a dangerous dependency on some authority to entertain them than teaching them how to educate themselves. What a price to pay for believing that we have character-proofed our classrooms.

Willy-nilly, teaching even pure and "safe" subjects may alter character. A student may become a little more careful working on the computer, more persistent when dissecting an earthworm, or more objective, even tolerant, when analyzing the effect of a social policy on minority groups. Evolutionary theory may change one's views about the Bible's authority. Reading the Bible may deepen one's spiritual life. An American history text that fails to mention women's or Hispanics' achievements may reinforce males' chauvinistic values and females' and Hispanics' inferiority feelings. No matter how carefully censored by a local vigilante group, any novel may wake a youth to a provocative insight about himself or others. Art can encourage a youth to discipline his impulses. Drama may help a youth become more empathic. Football practice teaches competitiveness and teamwork. Compulsory showers can provoke fear of loss of control and shame over their rising penises for pubescent boys, and embarrassment about their budding breasts for girls.

If we cannot character-proof education, then let's become aware of what education's actual effects are and could be, reintegrate mind with other attributes of character, clarify our goals, and so more self-consciously learn how to reach them more efficiently.

Reductionistic Disciplinary Bias

Another ideological barrier to creating schools of hope is more subtle and silent. Its benefits are widespread. Its embodiment in the curriculum and teachers' identities is deep. Only a bruising shift in our perspective could possibly lead to its integration into a more embracing goal of personality maturation. It may well be *the* insuperable barrier to creating a more enabling vision of human excellence.

We have entrenched a reductionistic theory of how humans grow in our curriculum, teaching methods, and professorial mentality and identity. Beginning in first grade, American teachers prefer to parcel a student out to experts in art, music, reading, science, to counselors, and to other specialists. We have created a cadre of teachers certified to teach only a limited range of increasingly specialized subjects. Schools and colleges are now organized into narrow departmental enclaves that separate, isolate, and so tear apart their connectedness to each other.

Accumulating knowledge has inexorably advanced toward specialization and away from communalization. The chair of the biological sciences division of a research university told me that its faculty was divided into many autonomous departments. To my naive surprise, he then said that they had as much difficulty talking with each other as I knew mine did. Paradoxically, more powerful unifying forces now undermine traditional science department definitions of their boundaries. Simultaneously, however, such changes create even more imposing problems for humanists and social scientists. Science's technical language and knowledge barriers have become incomprehensible and so impenetrable.

As beneficent as the effects of such centrifugal forces have been for technology and medicine, their effects on commitment to human excellence have been most destructive. Departmental goals now undermine most colleges' liberally educating ones. Shared general education courses disappear; faculty resist accepting responsibility for teaching outside their disciplines; they abandon collective efforts to assess how liberally educated their students have become to rely on departmental grades and evaluations; collegewide programs succumb to departmental needs when finances become scarce. Without a commonly shared vision and the self-restraint that it calls out, faculty and their departments go their own ways.

A midwestern college asked me to evaluate a long multiple-choice test that its departments had collectively created to assess how educated its seniors had become. I shuddered when I read its anarchical view. The faculty proposed to certify a student as educated only if he or she could be twenty departmental experts! I (and most of the faculty) would never be certified for a degree; we would have done better with Trivial Pursuit.

Because we have not had a defensible and operational vision of liberal education that could be implemented, one person's vision is another's ideology is another's slogan. "Educating for character" rapidly deteriorates into just another polarizing ideology or ineffectual slogan; the choice of the values for which to educate then becomes arbitrary.

Might not empirically grounding education on a developmental model of maturing open a way to surmount the formidable barriers to improving schools? The model in Chapter Six identifies universal liberal educating values that all religions share. Its supporting research demonstrates that other-centered rather than self-centered definitions of self-fulfillment contribute to success and happiness and that schools can affect maturing. It also tells us that separating mind from character impoverishes mind. Chapter Eleven's principles for furthering maturing and later chapters' recommendations for implementing them in our classrooms illustrate that teaching liberal arts courses to produce maturity's outcomes can enhance the mastery of their content with integrity.

Creating the Most Favorable Learning Environment

If a school's leader, faculty, and supportive community are genuinely committed to creating a school dedicated to human excellence, then they must create the most favorable learning environment for achieving their vision: a small school with a humane and caring ethos.

Abandoning Large Schools

In 1971, *Humanizing Schools* predicted that until large urban "school-prisons," as I called them then, were replaced by numerous small, humane neighborhood schools, their students would be "crippled." The research about school size and work with large inner-city and suburban schools summarized in Chapter Four have so strengthened that judgment that I despair that any radical reform other than *first* downsizing schools will succeed.[8] So do parents, educators, researchers, and foundations. When asked what kind of school they wished for their children, parents identified small "school size . . . and proximity to the student's home" as important.[9] Teachers in small schools are more optimistic than those in large ones that improvement could succeed. Researchers such as Goodlad agree.[10] The Carnegie Commission recommends that urban schools be broken up into units of no more than 450 students.[11] Observers of New York City's honored District 4 Afro-American schools believe that their small sizes—fewer than 300—create the personalized learning environment that contributes to their increased achievement, a belief also shared by consultants to Philadelphia's small "schools within schools" downsizing effort.[12]

Vulnerable youth need small, emotionally safe, personal, humane, and caring schools that their parents know, trust, and don't fear visiting. They need teachers who work with them for several years and forge a close relationship with their parents. They need older students to tutor and be friends with them. They need as urgently the non-age-graded experiential and flexible classrooms and curriculum that I have suggested. They need more integrated school, home, and neighborhood environments. Removing schools from local neighborhoods has robbed their residents of visible potential sources of caring, community resources, and hope around which they could coalesce to create healthier communities.

Chapter Four identified the ideal-sized school necessary to prepare today's youth for their future. Schools larger than several hundred for elementary and about four hundred for upper-school students do not provide ideal interpersonal learning environments. Chapter Six told us that successful and healthy adults need interpersonal and ethical strengths. Chapter Two alerted us that today's typical students are not developing them. Chapter Four summarized the evidence that large, bureaucratically controlling schools make mature and ethical relationships inordinately difficult. Such schools are not believed to be caring, cooperative, sensitive to the needs of their students, or ethical.

Furthermore, large schools impede sustained efforts to improve them for several crucial reasons, some of which strong leaders might possibly overcome—at least temporarily. They are less likely than smaller schools to be perceived by their faculty and students as having a distinctive identity, as my studies dismally show over and over; no widespread communion of value unites their faculty or students, who tend to go their own ways. Faculty agree only on the narrowest of goals, usually minimal academic ones. When faculty are not united by a commonly shared view of their goals, consensus and emotional commitment to change become frustratingly difficult to secure.

Sustained commitment to improving schools depends on teachers viewing their work as a calling, not a job. Large schools provide unfavorable conditions for nurturing teaching as a calling. I infer from my data that the reliably *lower* morale and sense of calling among public than among independent school teachers is attributable in part to their larger schools' bureaucratic impersonality and inflexibility. Prove me wrong. Try to carry out Chapter Twelve's ideas about nurturing a faculty's calling in a large school.

Large schools are education's dinosaurs. They must die if students can have the schools of hope they need. Radical and logistically complex, yes. But absolutely necessary. Decades too late for millions of youngsters.

At its root, what has damaged and killed so many children's spirit has not been lack of money but lack of a compelling vision, imagination, commitment, and will to create healthier school environments for all children. We have not asked the right questions about the steps necessary to nourish that spirit. For example, why have we not asked why we persist in building large schools when the evidence is so compelling that they just don't work for vulnerable kids?

At least four reasons come to mind. Boyer suggested one: we and our leaders do not sense the urgency or have the will and commitment to create small schools of hope, especially in our inner cities, where they are most needed. They might initially require more taxes. [13]

The second reason is that racially integrating schools has taken and continues to take precedence over creating hopeful schools. We have uncritically thought that integration could more easily take place in large comprehensive schools that could meet needs of very diverse students. In 1971, I questioned that it would produce the effects proposed if it occurred within large schools. Tracked resegregation could more easily occur in them than in small schools.

Two decades of research since show, though ambiguously to some researchers, that integration has produced slight to moderate academic gains (a "slight" gain being no more than one to two months' gain in reading scores and even less gain in math scores).[14] Critical questions should now be asked. Have the quite modest gains been worth the personal and communal costs, especially to minorities? What have large depersonalized schools done to vulnerable children? What have been the costs of white flight, loss of neighborhood schools, and community fragmentation? To what extent has the mixture of these personal and communal costs contributed to student and parent alienation from their schools and to drugs, crime, and hopelessness? We cannot assess these costs, because researchers have not comprehensively studied schools' effects on character. Nor have they disentangled schools' size from their racial composition as causes of character's and self's as well as mind's maturing. Integration's effects are much more complex than have yet been explored.

Because we dare not wait for the years necessary to answer such questions, we should become open to asking whether minority-controlled small neighborhood schools might provide more effective learning environments than large remote, establishment-controlled integrated schools. Heretical perhaps. But studies of eighty-two minority-controlled small private schools suggests "possibly."[15] I have no firm evidence on which to base an answer to this question.

Or should we not ask how we can create integrated *small* schools of hope? Small magnet schools might be one way. Or as some state courts now ask of their legislators, "How can equal or *compensatory* resources be made available to deprived communities to create more hopeful schools for all children?" The answers we give depend on clarifying and ordering our priorities, creating more imaginative solutions, and then summoning the will to implement them.[16]

The third reason we continue to build large schools is the belief that they offer a better education than smaller ones. We naively believe that a "better" school has every fashionable academic resource to meet every need of every student. Such shopping-mall schools that indulge every whim and fancy should provoke the question of "better for achieving what?"[17] Research conducted more than two decades ago showed no relationship between what schools buy, such as number of library books or number of faculty with advanced degrees, and any objective measure of mind's achievement.[18] We've already learned that large schools are death to character.

Chapter Four rejected the fourth and most frequently cited reason for building large schools: they are cheaper. No full accounting of their costs, including their psychological ones, has been done to determine whether they are cheaper than several smaller schools for their estimated lifetimes.

The policy issues should be clear. We should no longer perpetuate a failed decision, no longer build large schools. One out of eight of today's schools needs to be replaced because of old age, structural flaws, or inadequacies, such as lack of air conditioning, that prevent their more extended use.[19] Federal funding should be made available to any district, especially poor ones, to recreate more humanely sized schools. Schools should no longer be mindlessly consolidated if there is the remotest possibility that creating and sustaining a school of hope would be impossible.

You may be thinking that small schools can be as cold, despotic, and destructive as large ones. You are right. I know a few. But small size more readily permits creating a school of hope; it is not sufficient to guarantee it.

You may also be thinking, "Be practical. We can't afford to abandon our existing large schools." But what is more practical than to make a long-term investment in creating healthy learning environments for all children? Given, however, that we are stuck with large schools, what can we do?

Creating Humane and Caring Learning Climates

Effective leadership and educational rearrangements may moderate some unhealthy effects of large schools. The quality of a school's leadership is crucial. Interpersonally astute, determined, charismatic, practical idealists might by the force of their personality create the climate of a hopeful school. Their charge: integrate the ideal of human excellence with the curriculum, fix it in the core faculty's character and practices, and embody it in the school's culture. If they don't accomplish these steps, then the suppressed unhealthy potentials of large schools will eventually demand their voice after they leave.

Large schools' effects might be moderated by creating a core group of respected Escalante-like faculty. They then become the de facto carriers and respected models of education's values. Their classrooms can become havens from the ills of large size. They can provide the care and inspiration to inoculate students against the otherwise unhealthy viruses of a large school. Mature students can adapt to large schools and even make their benefits, such as their richer resources, work for them. But less mature ones, especially, need a supportive "home" and an Escalante cheering them on.

Large schools could be divided into "neighborhood houses" or minischools to which students ride the same bus and in which they stay for their school years. Ideally, such "houses" should have their own teams, student newspapers and governments, eating and recreational areas. Shared cocurricular activities, cafeteria, library, and bus rides with other houses' students dilute a house's distinctive culture. Only if a house could be physically isolated and had genuine autonomy, as some Philadelphia leaders now propose, might sharing some common facilities, such as media centers and athletic fields, not erode its distinctive ethos.

I have never seen a successful example of the house plan that has persisted. *If* its ethos and autonomy could be guarded, then a house plan might be a realistic though not a fully desirable structural way to create a school that promotes human excellence.[20]

Large schools' impersonalizing effects might be countered by downsizing them psychologically. We could build in greater continuity in faculty-student and student-student relationships for several years: elementary school teachers could teach the same students for four years; small teams of middle school teachers could work several years with the same students; the high school curricular changes proposed in Chapter Thirteen could create more cooperative sustained student relationships with fewer teachers; counselors could be responsible for the same students for their entire school stay.[21] We could free the school from the tyranny of the seven-period day and anarchic curricular schedule to encourage more intensive faculty and student relationships.[22] We could free faculty's imagination and charge them to create ways to work with fewer students in more depth. We could free teachers from their didactic information-dispensing role and enable students to be their own information gatherers by creative use of technology. Though such changes may be too expensive, awkward, and even ultimately impractical for large schools that must maintain order among several thousand students, they point the ideal toward which to strive.

We could create more caring and favorable learning environments by providing nearby small alternative schools for students to elect to attend for varying periods of time. MHS has confirmed what my children's efforts to create a more favorable school environment for themselves taught me. Schools must provide alternative ways for students to discover what they want for themselves and learn how to go about achieving their goals. Small auxiliary experimental centers—even in neighboring houses or vacant stores—still linked to their home-based school's resources could offer varied routes to growing up that students need to explore. Minnesota's move to create teacher-initiated small schools chartered by local school boards is promising. Freed from proscriptive rules and regulations, such smaller schools can be more responsive to students' needs. Every student should have the opportunity to attend a Model High-like school that offers a really different way to become educated than is practically possible in large schools.[23]

Creating smaller, more caring schools can produce another most eminently practical effect: principals and teachers can work more effectively with each other and with their neighboring communities and parents to educate their children.

Creating a Shared Belief in Goals

Chapter Ten claimed that the institutions that created powerful maturing environments were like Catholic monasteries: they stood for a shared vision that was implemented consistently throughout every activity of the institution. While not walled-in monasteries, Proctor Academy, the Model High School, Haverford College, and the Monteux School were similar. Each had a vision of human excellence that was emotionally owned by most of their faculties and supported by their constituents and was consistently implemented.

Creating a Communion of Belief Within a School

To achieve their goals, schools of hope need the flexibility to forge faculty commitment to their primary values. Their leaders and faculties need the freedom to admit like-minded faculty to their fraternity of believers if their schools are to retain their distinctive character.

Not one of the large public middle and high schools that I have studied had a distinctive vision that was widely shared by its teachers and students. Public elementary schools do. Most independent schools do also. Colleges vary too much to say whether they do or don't. Why such differences? Elementary school faculties are welded together by a vision of the "whole" child and understanding of how he or she grows. Public secondary schools' lack of a distinctive communion of value may be due to several factors: administrators rather than educational leaders; large size; belief that they must be all things to everyone; central office control over the assignment of teachers; inflexible teacher certification, seniority, and tenure requirements and rules. The pioneering Rochester, New York, board and union contract recognized that such policies weakened their schools; it provided a modicum of freedom to its principals to select their own teachers.[24]

The opportunity to create a like-minded teaching cadre is not enough, though, to sustain a distinctive vision over time. Continuing efforts to strengthen the faculty's calling to human excellence are essential.

Creating Shared School and Community Goals

The more similar a community's, school's, and parents' expectations and ways of raising children are, the more likely each will affect their maturation. Chapter Four described the dethronement of authority, rise of self-fulfillment, and secularization of religion that have produced conflicting and incoherent expectations. National and state leaders propose goals that ignore teachers' gifts and conflict with students' values. Teachers do not feel that parents are on their side. Other than a passport to a good job, parents are confused about what they want for their children. Though both teachers and parents value a more humane vision of the personality that their children need to be successful, happy, and healthy adults, each thinks that the other doesn't share that vision—which is not true.

Many voices call for communities and especially parents to be more involved in their schools. Parental participation is even more imperative for schools of hope dedicated to human, not just academic, excellence. If such meritorious calls are not to become another empty and ineffectual remedy, we must find answers to two questions. What currently bars meaningful and effective involvement of parents in their schools? What practical parental involvement can most help schools to assist their children to mature?

Barriers to Effective Community and Parental Involvement. The barriers to direct and constructive community and parental contributions to schools are numerous; some are practically unscalable. Only a few parents will sustain their involvement for the time needed to produce lasting effects. Family instability—single-parent and two-career families, for example—limit parents' available time and energy, as community volunteer agencies now report. But other barriers, especially school-related ones, must be torn down if meaningful community and parental involvement is to occur.

Schools' large size is a formidable barrier to sustained and meaningful parental contributions. Remote from local neighborhoods, large schools are emotionally inaccessible and forbidding. Parents don't know how to cope with schools' mazes, in which they feel like strangers and know no other parents; they never meet their children's teachers or principals outside school to know them as human beings. Parents in inner cities fear going to unknown areas at night. Vulnerable parents with unhappy memories of their own school years may feel that their children's large, impersonal schools don't really want them there—unfortunately true for some I know.

To attract and sustain parental involvement, a school's leaders and teachers must alter their attitudes about their relationship to their communities and parents. They must *genuinely* value such support, *actively* initiate reaching out to ask individual parents and the community for their aid, *wholeheartedly* believe that their community's and parents' resources are essential to the healthy growth of their students, and *visibly* move a portion of their students' education beyond their walls into the community.

The smaller schools of hope must ceaselessly articulate and garner community and parental ideas about and commitment to its goals. Less bureaucratically encumbered, their leaders and faculty can know their parents and community more directly; they should be freer to communicate and work with larger percentages of their parents to clarify their schools' vision.

Most Effective Type of Community and Parental Involvement. Only a few parents can serve on policy-forming committees or will contribute the time and energy for such sustained involvement. However, *all* parents can give the most important gift a school needs from them. They can consistently clarify to their children that they support the schools' goal of human excellence. They can expect their children to be good school citizens, fulfill their academic responsibilities, serve others, and participate in cocurricular and community activities.[25] Students whose parents encourage their ethical behavior like school more, do better academically, and participate more frequently in its co-curricular activities than students whose parents don't encourage such ideals. I have found that parents whose children turned out to be successful adults had encouraged them to do well, been accessible when their children needed help with their homework, talked with their children about intellectual and cultural ideas, and modeled maturity's strengths.

Schools of hope that are humanely sized and have a vision of human excellence, educational leaders who can articulate it, teachers, community, and parents committed to it, can create a curriculum and programs that will more likely "take" and produce lasting personality changes.

Creating and Implementing
a Developmentally Coherent Curriculum

Mathematicians, scientists, historians, and others are reordering their liberal arts curricula. Such efforts will fail, as similar ones in the past have failed, unless they are explicitly integrated with a coherent vision of human excellence. Schools dedicated to such a vision may find that the developmental model of maturing proposed in Chapter Six and elaborated in Chapters Seven through Nine offers the systematic guidance they now lack. It comprehends philosophical ideas and research-based findings about education's potential outcomes. Individual schools will prioritize the model's outcomes differently and create their own pathways to achieve them. Chapters Thirteen through Fifteen illustrated some pathways that I drew from the model for educating mind, character, and self. If such ideas have merit, then the issue becomes how to implement them.

Rolland Barth's *Improving Schools from Within*, Schlechty's *Schools for the Twenty-First Century*, and Sizer's *Horace's School* identify some of the issues and prescribe steps to take that I too have learned are the way to go.[26] Barth claims that schools must become more collaborative, trusting communities of learning in which everyone—students, faculty, and principals—respects their differences, reflectively seeks to create high standards without creating high anxiety, and laughs and, I would add, plays together.

Schlechty focuses on, among other attributes, leaders who are committed to nurturing a school's human resources and who capture the commitment of others to a clearly stated vision.

And Sizer, whose suggestions are more specifically programmatic, recommends that schools divide themselves into small houses with their own distinctive cultures, simplify their curricula and order them more thematically; abandon the time-honored six-period forty-five-minute schedule; reduce the number of students taught by a teacher, who can then attend to individual students' needs more as a coach than as a dispenser of information; provide students more responsibility for their own education and the welfare of the school; and require students to exhibit their work publicly, among other changes. He claims that such radical alterations are financially possible within schools' budgets.

It is much easier to create a school and its curriculum afresh, as MHS did, than to reshape an existing school and its curriculum, as most schools must. Sizer believes that given schools' systemic nature, they cannot be improved incrementally bit by bit but must be rebuilt from the ground up, so to speak. Consulting with and assessing schools influenced by his principles suggests that this is a high-risk Yeltsian strategy. While theoretically desirable, it may be unrealistic, especially for large schools.

Since school or instructional change means altering teachers' personalities and arousing parental fears, careful attention must be paid to the size of the gap between the ideal and the educability of a school's constituents. Joseph Carroll, principal of Masconomet High School in Massachusetts, ignited a fire storm in his community when he suggested replacing the traditional 45-minute period with two 100-minutes ones—a most modest step compared to those that Sizer proposes.[27] Bloomfield Hills sidestepped such resistance by creating the MHS, though it too angered traditional teachers, who resented that a few of their better students opted to educate themselves differently.

Alternative, lower-risk strategies to introduce curricular change may be more practicable.[28] First, understand how faculty and students view their school and students. Map their morale as well as their judgments about and wishes for each other. Assess the degree of their pain, hopes, and emotional commitment to education's outcomes. Identify the optimal "levers" or conditions necessary to initiate change, such as generating trust, altering decision making, or nurturing work as a calling.

Second, prioritize hopes and focus schoolwide efforts to fulfill *the* priority for the year to which the largest number of faculty are emotionally committed. Seek student ownership of the priority as well.

Third, expect and reward faculty and students' risking and exploring ways to teach and learn differently to fulfill their collective priority goal.

Fourth, begin to alter the traditional teacher-student relationship by encouraging their collaborative effort to create alternative classroom activities that might fulfill each other's wishes. Students should be encouraged to share responsibility with their teachers to learn how to become their own teachers.

These four steps are not enough, however. Faculty and students must reflect continuously about the whats, whys, and hows of their schools' and classrooms' effects if both are to secure command of their own talents to improve their school.

Reflecting and Experimenting to Achieve Goals

Fifth, collaboratively reflect periodically as a class and as a faculty about what all are learning about how to create as maturing a class and school environment as possible. They should systematically apply Chapter Eleven's twenty educational principles to their classrooms and school.

Sixth, examine what is being learned about how to achieve the priority goal and how the school's ethos, schedule, and other attributes may work against achieving the year's priority goal.

Seventh, initiate other changes to achieve their priority goal.

Eighth, commit themselves at the end of the school year to learning how to achieve their next-highest-priority goal.

Schools of hope also seek out other, more formal systematic ways to reflect about their goals and hold themselves accountable for achieving them. They develop the research capability to economically monitor their own ongoing improvement efforts. Schools need to learn how to understand themselves as systems, not just measure how much information their courses teach. They also need to learn how to develop measures of their ethos and morale as well as their priority goals and how to use their own research to improve themselves. I know of no schools that have sought to study themselves as thoroughly, comprehensively, and holistically as have Alverno College, Proctor Academy, and the MHS. Proctor initiated numerous changes as a result of understanding its effects. MHS has created measures of its ethos, morale, and competencies that provide base-level data for assessing the effects of its future innovations.

Schools of hope also search out and rely on the reflective

judgments of their communities to evaluate how well they are educating their children. Chapter Thirteen described one way a community could assist in evaluating its high school seniors' maturation. MHS relies on panels of community representatives to assess its students' projects. Chapter Fourteen illustrated how Madeira's seniors had to plan, initiate, and assume responsibility for demonstrating their maturity by serving or working in neighboring communities that evaluated their readiness to enter the adult world.

Such collaborative bootstrap efforts among faculty, students, and community could empower both faculty and students with the attitudes and skills to be their own change agents: strengthen their ownership of their classes and school; deepen their calling as teachers and students; enhance their confidence that they can create a school of hope; and bring them into greater command of themselves.

To create schools of hope is not impossible. All it takes is a vision of human excellence, imagination, commitment, the will to persist—and a supportive community as well as responsive state and national governments. What other educational choice do we have given the uncertain future for which we and our children must prepare ourselves?

Model of Maturing Attributes That Contribute to Adapting Effectively

Developmental dimensions of maturing

The person	Symbolization	Other-centeredness	Integration	Stabilization	Autonomy	Effects of successful adaptation
			Mind			
Cognitive skills	Is imaginative Has precise control of words and numbers Comprehends oral and written words Speaks and writes articulately Is reflective Is inductive	Takes multiple perspectives Analyzes well Has realistic and objective judgment	Has relational, synthetic, and organizational skills Has developed hypothetical-deductive and logical reasoning skills	Has knowledge that is accurate, precise, broad, organized, readily accessible, and resistant to interference Has skills that resist disruption or can recover resiliently	Has judgment that is independent, critical, and appropriate Has knowledge and skills that are mobile, readily transferable, and available for self-educating and creative purposes	Increased mastery, competency, and sense of power
			Character			
Interpersonal skills	Is sensitive to and perceptive of others and of relationships Is psychologically minded and understanding of others	Empathically feels for, cares about, respects, and enjoys people who differ from self	Is not defensive but genuinely open and spontaneous in relationships Is able to create cooperative mutual work and intimate relations	Is loyal and faithful to friends and organizations Has enduring friendships and work relations not readily broken by argument and strain	Can be independent and self-reliant and can tolerate aloneness if necessary Selectively forms interdependent relationships	Increased ability to create intimate and loving relationships

			Self			
Values	Is aware of and articulates biases, values, and assumptions	Accepts and appreciates diverse viewpoints / Has humane values	Sets priorities among values / Has values and actions consistent with each other	Has values that endure / Persists purposefully to achieve long-term goals	Is motivated by considered principle rather than by impulsive wish or environmental pressure / Has courage / Has freedom	Released energy for new interests, enthusiasms, and adaptive efforts to meet new problems
Metavalues	Is honest / Is truthful	Is fair / Is compassionate	Has integrity	Has commitment		
Self	Has accurate self-insight and understanding	Accurately understands how others view self / Identifies self with increasingly diverse others	Strives to unify component selves: private, public, ideal, and actual / Acts spontaneously with self not conflicted or divided	Has sense of self that is strong and stable; firm identity / Positively values and is confident of self	Discriminatingly accepts and rejects others' views of self / Can affirm own worth independently of others' valuations / Believes in ability to control growth of self	Heightened capacity for self-transcendence and sense of humor

Educational Principles
That Contribute to Maturing

Empowering Reflection (Symbolization)

Symb goals: Make expectations about how one should grow exquisitely clear

Symb confront: Contrast, confront, and challenge to call out excellence

Symb model: Use models of goals to further awareness

Symb reflect: Teach how to reflect about the processes of one's own growth

Nurturing Other-Centeredness

Other trust: Create trust that encourages nondefensive and open relationships

Other care: Expect care and responsibility for growth of others

Other skills: Educate for skills necessary for corporate task learning

Other roles: Provide the opportunity to assume different people's roles

Encouraging Integrations

Integ goal: Provide coherent goals and learning environments

Integ involve:	Ceaselessly create ways to involve students actively in their own learning
Integ exper:	Provide reflected upon and varied types of experiential learning
Integ context:	Confront with complex and contextual problems that require the integration of different ideas and modes of thought, such as synthesis as well as analysis, intuition as well as logic, induction as well as deduction

Building Strong Personal Foundations (Stabilization)

Stab rehearse:	Encourage anticipation, planning, and rehearsal
Stab external:	Demand *constant* externalization and then correction of learning
Stab conseq:	Do not protect from the consequences of decisions and acts
Stab affirm:	Appreciate and affirm *varied* strengths

Educating for Self-Command (Autonomy)

Aut faith:	Express *realistic* faith in capacity to be responsible
Aut early:	Encourage assumption of responsibility for own growth early and consistently
Aut test:	Progressively reduce expectations and structures to test budding autonomy to set and carry out own hopes in increasingly varied situations
Aut excel:	Teach to create own standards of excellence, affirm them, and reward selves for approaching them

Notes

1. Healy, 1990.
2. Byrne, 1989b; Moses, 1991a; Rothman, 1990c.
3. Viadero, 1986, p. 5; Gold, 1987; Rothman, 1991b.
4. Results from mapping students' and teachers' perceptions of the schools come from twelve suburban public high schools with national and state recognition for their excellence. Data from additional schools do not significantly change the reported percentages.
5. Heath (1981a) describes the Word Check List procedure and illustrates how it can be used for institutional assessment.
6. The Word Check List (WCL) provides information about an institution's distinctive ethos; areas of potential miscommunication between its varied constituencies; degree of frustration with the school, students, or teachers; collective faculty and student self-concept; degree of emotional commitment to the school's goals; and other attributes of schools.
7. Independent school normative results are highly stable; they no longer change when other school results are included. Norms for views of students were secured from 1,789 teachers and 2,253 students in National Association of Independent Schools high schools. Data from only a few Catholic parochial schools are included.

8. Hechinger (1992) summarizes evidence on the relationship between students' health and their education; see also Lawton (1991c); Tugend (1986); Viadero (1987a); Wynne (1979). Heath (1976a) evaluates how healthy the changing character of youth is.

9. Commission of National Association of State Boards of Education, 1990.

10. Lawton, 1991d.

11. Tavis & Offir, 1977; Hechinger, 1992.

12. Hechinger, 1992.

13. Kozel & Adams, 1986; Landers, 1989.

14. Jennings, 1988a, p. 23.

15. Freiberg, 1991a.

16. Cohen, 1991b; Rothman, 1990e.

17. Mischel, Shoda, & Rodriguez, 1989.

18. Rothman, 1990c.

19. Sizer, 1984.

20. Travers, 1991.

21. Dodge, 1991; Janko, 1987; Rothman, 1990d. Fifty-six percent of top-achieving high school students spend seven hours a week or less on homework.

22. See Sternberg (1988, chap. 12), who describes how weak willpower and undeveloped academic coping competencies limit mind's effective use.

23. Rothman, 1990e, p. 11.

24. Hedlin & Wolfe, 1979.

25. Carnegie Foundation, 1986.

26. Lawton, 1991b.

27. Marston, 1989, p. 8.

28. Rothman, 1990a.

29. Rothman, 1990a.

30. National Assessment on Educational Progress, 1987.

31. Astin, 1975.

32. The Student Role Satisfaction Scale (SRS) is modeled on the Vocational Adaptation Scale (Heath, 1991, chap. 16) for adults. A comparable measure exists for fifth- to seventh-graders.

33. Heath, 1991. Chap. 16 examines identity's changing meanings.

Chapter Two

1. Niebuhr, 1992.
2. Shogren, 1993. The American Association of University Women (1991) reports that more than 90 percent of such students had been harassed themselves. Girls' self-esteem was especially harmed.
3. Snider, 1987.
4. Winkler, 1990.
5. Handy, 1988.
6. Heath, 1991. Androgynous males are more happily married than stereotypically masculine ones, have happier partners, are better lovers and more competent fathers, and make better friends.
7. In a study of 35,000 students by Flax (1992), 26 percent of twelve-year-olds report that they are unsure of their sexual orientation; the percentage declines rapidly to 5 percent in eighteen-year-olds.
8. Heath, 1978, 1991. Fathers become more mature than nonfathers over time, especially in becoming more other-centered.
9. Ricklefs, 1983.
10. Bercovitch, 1975, pp. 14–15.
11. Heath, 1969.
12. Walshe, 1990.
13. Thompson, 1981.
14. Levine, 1980.
15. Association of Governing Boards of Universities and Colleges, 1982.
16. Astin, 1991. Seventy-three percent of 1990 entering freshmen wanted to be well-off financially, their most frequently cited goal. Forty-three percent wished to have a meaningful philosophy of life and influence social values.
17. Simpson, 1986.
18. Association of Governing Boards of Universities and Colleges, 1982.

19. Sevener, 1983.
20. Association of Governing Boards of Universities and Colleges, 1982.
21. Yankelovich & Immerwahr, 1983.
22. Gallup & Castelli, 1987.
23. Kilpatrick, 1986, p. 10.
24. Fallon, 1986; Schmidt (1990b) describes a Girl Scout–sponsored national poll reporting that 65 percent of high school students would cheat on an important exam. Poor children are more pressured to commit antisocial and self-harmful acts.
25. Heath, 1991, chap. 19.
26. Heath (1991) found that more virtuous men and women are more likely to succeed in their adult roles and are healthier and happier than less virtuous ones. Virtue is not associated with amount of income.
27. Heath, 1991, chap. 19.
28. Heath, 1976b, 1979.
29. Veroff, Douvan, and Kulka, 1981.
30. Bellah et al., 1991.
31. Heath, 1991, pp. 132–135.

Chapter Three

1. Heath, 1991, chap. 1.
2. American Association of University Women, 1991.
3. Segal, 1987.
4. Rothman, 1991a; Viadero, 1985.
5. American Association of University Women, 1991; Freiberg, 1991a; Moses, 1991b.
6. Winkler, 1990.
7. Rothman, 1990a.
8. The Copernican, Darwinian, and Freudian revolutions altered our ideas of our importance, origin, and rationality, but they did not affect as immediately and profoundly how men and women live their lives.
9. Parelius, 1975.
10. Astin, 1991.
11. Widnall, 1988.

12. Adelson, 1980; Freiberg, 1991b; Gilligan, Lyons, & Hanmer, 1990.
13. Heath, unpublished results from studies of fifth- through twelfth-graders' satisfaction with thirty attributes of their school and their role as students.
14. Heath, unpublished results; Crispell, 1991.
15. American Association of University Women, 1991.
16. Stanley, 1988.
17. Adler, 1989; Feingold, 1988; Linn & Hyde, 1989.
18. Heath, 1991, chap. 27. University of California, Berkeley, longitudinal intergenerational studies (IGS) also found that adolescent girls' personalities did not predict their adult behavior, possibly because of girls being raised to please others at the expense of developing their own identities and talent (Bayer, Whissell-Buechy, & Honzik, 1981; Brooks, 1981).
19. Heath, 1991, chap. 29.
20. Grannon, Kulick, & Schenck (1981) studied the effects on maturation of single and coed schools with warm and cold climates. "Warm" and "cold" climates were measured by the percentage of students describing their schools in stereotypically feminine interpersonal terms such as *understanding, caring,* and *warmth.*
21. Perry, 1970, p. 158.
22. Fiedler, 1989, p. 9M.
23. Handy, 1988.
24. Heath, 1991.
25. Heath, 1991.
26. Heath, 1991.
27. Travers, 1991. A poll of 72,000 teenagers found that 68 percent want "self-help courses that teach independence and coping skills" (p. 5).

Chapter Four

1. Heath, 1977b.
2. Heath, 1968.
3. Heath, 1991, chap. 20, notes 20–22.
4. Heath, 1991, chap. 27.

5. Rothman (1992) reports a study's finding that 62 percent of fourth-graders, 64 percent of eighth-graders, and 40 percent of twelfth-graders watch TV more than three hours a day.

6. Since no longitudinal follow-up studies have comprehensively examined the potential maturing and immaturing effects of television programs, even of "Sesame Street" (Walsh, 1988, 1989), no firm conclusions can be made yet about its delayed effects on healthy growth. Healy (1990) summarizes and critiques TV's possible effects in detail.

7. Fisher, 1989.

8. Lawton (1991b) reports an observational study of middle schools that documents their unresponsiveness. A National Research Council study of college mathematics teachers says that "teaching methods have changed little in 3 centuries" (Holden, 1991, p. 382).

9. Byrne (1989b, p. 729) reports a National Research Council committee's claim that lecturing is the "most prevalent method of math instruction . . . [and] has been proved the least effective." Not student laziness but "teaching that is out of date and mired in pointless pencil-and-paper competition, rote memorization, and multiple-choice tests" explains poor achievement.

10. Heath, 1991.

11. University of Michigan Institute for Social Research, 1986; Weisman, 1990.

12. Falbo's summary of research on one-child families (1984) illustrates the complex issues involved in determining how birth order and sibling status affect later personality development. No comprehensive model of healthy growth has guided such research to enable it to identify long-term delayed effects.

13. Rothman, 1990e, p. 11.

14. Freiberg, 1991b.

15. Moses (1992) reports Jaeger's analysis of reasons for international math score differences.

16. Doyle Dane Bernbach, Inc., 1985.

17. Heath, 1991, chaps. 24–25.

18. Barker & Gump, 1964; D. D. Heath, 1971. For a summary of research, see D. H. Heath (1971, 1972); Garbarino (1980).

19. Goodlad, 1984.
20. Wehrwein, 1986.
21. Boyer, 1987.
22. Campbell, 1981.
23. Pavuk, 1987; "Across the Nation," 1992.
24. Giffin & Felsenthal, 1983, p. 133.
25. Hoge's critique (1974) of the available research illustrates the factors that complicate generalizing about changes in religious values.
26. Public Broadcast System, 1992.
27. McKinney, 1977.
28. Barrett & Wermiel, 1991, p. A7.
29. Heath, 1991.
30. "Teenagers Who Work," 1986.
31. Elliott, 1992.
32. I have consistently confirmed these findings for college preparatory public high school students. Freiberg (1991c) confirms the detrimental effects on high school students as researched by Steinberg & Dornbusch (1991).
33. Greenberger & Steinberg, 1986; "Teen Jobs . . . ," 1992.
34. Greenberger & Steinberg, 1986.
35. Heath, unpublished results.
36. Heath, 1991.
37. American Association of University Women, 1991.
38. Lawton, 1991b.
39. Rothman, 1990a, p. 1.

Chapter Five

1. Pascarella & Terenzini, 1991.
2. Heath (1991) describes the study's purposes, participants, methods, and findings, on which much of this chapter is based.
3. Lewis & Nelson, 1983.
4. Cohen, 1984; Pascarella & Terenzini, 1991; Samson, Graue, Weinstein, & Walberg, 1984.
5. Willingham, 1974.
6. Kelly, 1957.

7. Rhoads, Gallemore, Giantureo, & Osterhout, 1974.
8. Pascarelli & Terenzini, 1991. Arnold & Denny (1992) report that valedictorian graduates of 1982 had only average vocational success ten years later.
9. Craeger & Harmon, 1966.
10. Cohen, 1984.
11. Hudson, 1976.
12. Goertzel & Goertzel, 1962; Goertzel, Goertzel, & Goertzel, 1978.
13. Taylor & Ellison, 1967.
14. Pascarella & Terenzini, 1991, p. 518.
15. Heath, 1977a, pp. 625–626.
16. Winter, McClelland, & Stewart, 1981.
17. McClelland, 1973.
18. McClelland, 1973, p. 3.
19. Heath, 1977a, 1991.
20. Olney & Peters, 1979.
21. McCue, 1985.
22. Clausen, 1981.
23. Bray, Campbell, & Grant, 1974; Bray & Howard, 1978.
24. Terman, 1954.
25. Block, 1971.
26. Vaillant, 1974.
27. Barron, 1963.
28. Wallach, 1972.
29. Terman, 1954.
30. Reinhold, 1970, p. 38.
31. D. C. McClelland, letter to author, October 8, 1975.
32. Bray, Campbell, & Grant, 1974; Bray & Howard, 1978.
33. Warren & Heist, 1960.
34. Terman, 1954.
35. McCurdy, 1960.
36. N. Elkies, quoted in Kleiman, 1981, p. B4.
37. Haier & Denham, 1976. Using data from the Berkeley IGS studies, Eichorn, Hunt, & Honzik (1981) found that high-IQ adolescents were judged to be calm, dependable, overcontrolled in their sexual relationships, and socially aloof from their peers.
38. Astin, 1977.

39. Winter, McClelland, & Stewart, 1981, p. 132.
40. Doob, 1960.
41. Oden, 1968; Terman, 1954.
42. Benbow & Stanley, 1983; Gough, 1955; Kegel-Flom, 1974.
43. Heath, 1991; Roe, 1953.
44. Benbow & Stanley, 1983.
45. Jennings & Nathan, 1977; Willingham, Young, & Morris, 1985; Office of Educational Research and Improvement, 1986; Vaillant & Vaillant, 1981.
46. Jennings & Nathan, 1977, p. 569.
47. Willingham, Young, & Morris, 1985.
48. Office of Educational Research and Improvement, 1986.
49. I have consistently confirmed this pattern of results for several high schools, including MHS.
50. Vaillant & Vaillant, 1981.
51. Mirga, 1986, p. 10.
52. Rutter et al., 1979.
53. Ranbom, 1985.
54. Ranbom, 1985, pt. 1; "Column One," 1991; Leestma, August, George, & Peak, 1987.
55. Stevenson, Azuma, & Hakuta, 1986; Tobin, Wu, & Davidson, 1989.
56. Marshall, 1986, p. 268; Walsh, 1987.
57. Regur, 1991.
58. Howe, 1984.
59. Kitto, 1951, p. 16.
60. Whitehead, 1929b, p. 60.
61. Bruner, 1966, p. 167.
62. Hirsch, 1987.
63. Massey, 1993; Schmidt, 1990a.
64. Rodman, 1987.
65. Rothman, 1987, p. 6.
66. "Self-Esteem Bill Causes Blues," 1991, p. 5B.
67. Viadero, 1987b.

Chapter Six

1. Marshall, 1986.
2. Hirsch, 1987.

3. Heath, 1991.

4. Heath (1991, chap. 1) reports how the core strengths, as well as their adult correlates, such as virtue, androgyny, and maturity, were identified.

5. Evangelauf, 1990.

6. Hampton, *Business Week*, 1988. Rosenfeld (1988), director of the Southern Technology Council, identifies similar strengths needed by factory workers in the future: flexibility to perform various tasks, ability to learn, willingness to accept responsibility, initiative, ability to contribute innovative ideas, and so on.

7. Lewis & Nelson, 1983.

8. Heath, 1991.

9. Heath, 1991.

10. Whitehead, 1929a, p. 13.

11. Dewey, 1964i.

12. Raushenbush, 1965.

13. Averill, 1983.

14. Heath, 1991.

15. Bloom et al., 1956.

16. Krathwohl, Bloom, & Masia, 1964.

17. von Bertalanffy, 1952.

18. Ashby, 1956.

19. Hartmann, 1960.

20. Cannon's homeostatic principle (1939) is a physiological analogue of the psychic equilibrating principle. Cognitive researchers within the Thorndikian tradition, such as Gardner (1983), reject a *systemic* view of personality organization in favor of a view of mind composed of separate or independent domains.

21. "Valedictorian Kills Mother on Graduation Morning," 1988, p. 12.

22. Piaget, 1950.

23. Bruner, 1966, p. 89.

24. Dewey, 1964c, p. 109.

25. Van Doren, 1943, p. 57.

26. McGrath, 1959, p. 6.

27. Whitehead, 1929c, pp. 50–51.

28. Heath, 1977b, 1980, 1983, 1991.

29. Heath, 1977b.

30. Heath, 1991.

31. Heath (1991, chap. 4, note 3) critiques the claims of researchers such as Gilligan who confuse phenotypic differences with underlying genotypic similarities.

32. Heath (1977b, chap. 8) illustrates how Sicilian and Turkish male differences in autonomy must be interpreted in reference to maturity's other dimensions if judgments about healthiness are not to be misled by phenotypic differences.

33. See Heath (1977b, pp. 41–43) for an analysis of the effects of modernization on personality changes and their similarity to maturing's effects.

34. Inkeles, 1969, p. 212.

35. Heath, 1977b.

36. "96-Year-Old to Receive Degree," 1988.

37. Erikson, 1950.

38. Piaget, 1950; Perry, 1970; Gardner, 1983.

39. Piaget, 1932; Kohlberg, 1970.

40. Selman, 1980.

41. Loevinger, 1966.

42. Mentkowski & Loacker, 1985; Whitely, 1982.

43. Miller & Moser, 1977; Rest, 1979. Heath (1991, pp. 377–378) reports that Loevinger's measure of ego development predicts no adult outcome.

44. Neugarten & Neugarten, 1987. Gardner (1983) relies on post-Piagetian research to reject a stage view of cognitive development.

45. Levinson, 1978.

46. Piaget, 1950.

47. Erikson, 1950.

48. Kohlberg, 1970.

49. Pascarella & Terenzini, 1991.

50. Feldman & Newcomb, 1969; Pascarella & Terenzini, 1991.

Chapter Seven

1. Piaget, 1950.

2. Bloom et al., 1956.

3. Perry, 1970.

4. Eliot, quoted in Thomas, 1962.

5. Thorndike, 1912.

6. Hutchins, 1943.

7. Newman, 1891.

8. College Entrance Examination Board, 1983.

9. Guilford, 1956. See Gardner (1983) for a thoughtful critique of Guilford and an alternative view about mind's organization. Gardner identifies seven basic independent intelligences to encompass mind's potentials, including musical, spatial, and bodily-kinesthetic domains. His model of maturing includes the cognitive domains of linguistics and logico-mathematical cognition and the interpersonal and intrapersonal domains as the critical contributors to character and self-adaptation.

10. Bloom et al., 1956.

11. Feldman & Newcomb, 1969; Pascarella & Terenzini, 1991.

12. Poincare, 1913, p. 387.

13. Van Doren, 1943.

14. Dewey, 1964g, 1964h.

15. Pascarella & Terenzini, 1991.

16. See notes 4, 5, and 6 in Chapter One.

17. Winter, McClelland, & Stewart, 1981.

18. Bruner, 1966, p. 105.

19. Whorf, 1958.

20. Lederer, 1987.

21. Willis, 1991.

22. Newman, 1891, p. 139.

23. Chickering, 1969; Feldman & Newcomb, 1969; Heath, 1968; Pascarella & Terenzini, 1991.

24. Mentkowski, Moeser, & Strait, 1983.

25. Pascarella & Terenzini, 1991.

26. See Chapter Ten for a fuller description of the MHS.

27. Meiklejohn, 1920, p. 36.

28. Dewey, 1964g, p. 253.

29. Hutchins, 1936, p. 62.

30. Pascarella & Terenzini, 1991; Trent & Medsker, 1968.

31. Rott, 1972.

32. Perry, 1970.
33. College Entrance Examination Board, 1983, p. 12.
34. Newman, 1891, p. 178.
35. Madan, 1938.
36. Feldman & Newcomb, 1969, p. 326; Pascarella & Terenzini, 1991; Trent & Medsker, 1968.
37. Mentkowski, Moeser, & Strait, 1983.
38. Perry, 1970, pp. 102-103.
39. Pascarella & Terenzini, 1991.
40. Winter, McClelland, & Stewart, 1981, p. 32.
41. Feldman & Newcomb, 1969; Mentkowski & Doherty, 1984.
42. Dewey, 1964h, pp. 224-225.
43. Eliot, quoted in Thomas, 1962.
44. Newman, 1891.
45. Bloom et al., 1956.
46. Heath (1965, pp. 188-189) analyzes how judgment differs from synthetic thought and logical deduction on the basis of Bartlett's analysis of thinking as completing gaps (Bartlett, 1958).
47. More recently, Kitchener & King (1990) have similarly differentiated judgment.
48. Heath (1965) describes measures designed to assess judgment, synthesis, and logical conceptualization.
49. Kitchener & King, 1990.
50. Newman, 1891, p. xvii.
51. Chickering, 1969.
52. Meiklejohn, 1920, p. 38.
53. Quoted in Thomas, 1962, p. 89.
54. Hutchins, 1936, p. 71.
55. Trent & Medsker, 1968.
56. King, 1973; Perry, 1970; Pascarella & Terenzini, 1991; Winter, McClelland, & Stewart, 1981.
57. Feldman & Newcomb, 1969; Pascarella & Terenzini, 1991.
58. Wolfe & Claar, 1971, p. 109.
59. Heath, 1976b.
60. Kitchener & King, 1990; Pascarella & Terenzini, 1991; Perry, 1970.
61. Pascarella & Terenzini, 1991, pp. 116-117.
62. Steen, 1988.

63. Cremin, 1970, 1980.
64. College Entrance Examination Board, 1983.
65. Hirsch, 1987.
66. Conant, 1963, p. 92.
67. Thomas, 1962, p. 301.
68. Trent & Medsker, 1968.
69. Feldman & Newcomb, 1969; King, 1973.
70. Hyman, Wright, & Reed, 1975.
71. Newman, 1891.
72. Freud, 1956, p. 602.
73. Heath, 1965, 1977b.
74. Perry, 1970, p. 126.
75. Winter, McClelland, & Stewart, 1981.
76. Kitto, 1951, p. 128.
77. Dewey, 1964h; McGrath, 1959; Newman, 1891; Van Doren, 1943.
78. Gardner, 1956, p. 6.
79. Perry, 1970, p. 150.
80. Chickering, 1969.
81. Trent & Medsker, 1968, pp. 129–130.
82. Feldman & Newcomb, 1969; Heath, 1968; Pascarella & Terenzini, 1991; Perry, 1970; Winter, McClelland, & Stewart, 1981.
83. Pascarella & Terenzini, 1991, p. 156.
84. Sternberg (1988) rejects the Guilford (1956) and Gardner (1956) view of mind as composed of discrete independent talents. He views intelligence in adaptational terms and identifies (chap. 12) the factors that limit the effective use of intelligence—most of which I describe in Chapter One as increasingly occurring in today's youth.
85. Mentkowski & Doherty, 1984.
86. Feldman & Newcomb, 1969.
87. Sanford, 1962.

Chapter Eight

1. Newman, 1891.
2. Hutchins, 1943, pp. 30, 63.
3. Hook, 1946.

4. Syrkin, 1944.
5. Bode, 1927.
6. McGrath, 1959.
7. Cited in Curti, 1963.
8. Selman, 1980.
9. Alverno College Faculty, 1976, p. 28.
10. Wolfe, n.d.
11. King, 1973; Much & Mentkowski, 1982.
12. Pace, 1990.
13. Heath, 1968; Pace, 1990; Pascarella & Terenzini, 1991; Wolfe, n.d.
14. Much & Mentkowski, 1982.
15. Johnson & Johnson, 1989.
16. Newman, 1891; Syrkin, 1944; McGrath, 1959; Thomas Mann, cited in Curti, 1959.
17. Bode, 1927, p. 321.
18. Van Doren, 1943, p. 68.
19. Alverno College Faculty, 1976, p. 28.
20. Heath, 1968.
21. King, 1973; Much & Mentkowski, 1982.
22. Rott, 1972, p. 83.
23. Chickering, 1969.
24. Heath, 1991.
25. Meiklejohn, 1920; Bode, 1927; Dewey, 1964c, 1964d.
26. Harp, 1992. The U.S. Department of Labor's commission on achieving the necessary skills for future vocations urges schools to stress "problem-solving, teamwork that extends beyond school grounds; teacher and student interaction in projects, grading, and planning; and teachers cast as team leaders and guides rather than lecturers armed with all the answers" (p. 1).
27. Alverno College Faculty, 1976, pp. 28-29.
28. Dewey, 1964g, p. 256.
29. Landers, 1988, p. 25.
30. Alverno College Faculty, 1976, pp. 28-29.
31. Mentkowski, 1988.
32. Rott, 1972.
33. Heath, 1968; King, 1973.

34. Rest, 1979.
35. Perry, 1970.
36. Kohlberg, 1970.
37. Greif & Hogan, 1973; Mosher & Sprinthall, 1971; Selman, 1980.
38. Kohlberg, Wasserman, & Richardson, 1975.
39. Bode, 1927; Thomas, 1962; Van Doren, 1943.
40. Dewey, 1964e; Hook, 1946.
41. Dewey, 1964c.
42. Heath, 1968.
43. Wolfe & Claar, 1971.
44. Heath, 1976b.
45. Wolfe & Claar, 1971, pp. 11–12.
46. Heath, 1991, chap. 1.
47. Newman, 1891.
48. McGrath, 1959.
49. Dewey, 1964c; William deWitt Hyde, president of Bowdoin College, quoted in Thomas, 1962; Russell, 1931.
50. Noddings, 1984.
51. Feldman & Newcomb, 1969; King, 1973; Pascarella & Terenzini, 1991; Whiteley, 1982.
52. Trent & Medsker, 1968.
53. Chickering, 1969.
54. Astin, 1991.
55. Krathwohl, Bloom, & Masia, 1964, p. 172.
56. Krathwohl, Bloom, & Masia, 1964, p. 74.
57. Feldman & Newcomb, 1969, pp. 23–24.
58. Pascarella & Terenzini, 1991; Rest, 1979.
59. Mentkowski, Moeser, & Strait, 1983; Whiteley, 1982.
60. Chickering, 1969.
61. Jacob, 1957.
62. Perry, 1970, p. 156.
63. Hook, 1946.
64. Dewey, 1964a, p. 197.
65. Dewey, 1964b.
66. McGrath, 1959.
67. Feldman & Newcomb, 1969; Heath, 1976b; King, 1973; Perry, 1970.

68. Chickering, 1969.
69. Hyman & Wright, 1979.
70. Newcomb, Koenig, Flacks, & Warwick, 1967.
71. Heath, 1968, p. 169; 1976b, p. 179.
72. Gardner, 1961; Thomas, 1962; Hutchins, 1943.
73. Dewey, 1964g, pp. 258–259.
74. Krathwohl, Bloom, & Masia, 1964.
75. Pascarella & Terenzini, 1991, p. 325.
76. Heath, 1968; Lehmann & Dressel, 1962; Pascarella & Terenzini, 1991; Perry, 1970.
77. Jacob, 1957.
78. Rott, 1972, p. 87.
79. Feldman & Newcomb, 1969; Pascarella & Terenzini, 1991; Trent & Medsker, 1968; Webster, Freedman, & Heist, 1962.
80. Feldman & Newcomb, 1969; Sanford, 1962.
81. Heath, 1977b.
82. Newman, 1891.
83. Noddings, 1984.
84. Dewey, 1964a, 1964b.
85. Hook, 1946.
86. Russell, 1931.
87. Tillich, 1959.
88. Fromm, 1947, p. 7.
89. Maslow, 1967.
90. Campbell, 1976, p. 382.
91. Bronowski, 1956.
92. Krathwohl, Bloom, & Masia, 1964, p. 185.

Chapter Nine

1. Sinnott, 1959, p. 15.
2. Heath, 1965, 1977b.
3. Thomas, 1962.
4. Meiklejohn, 1920.
5. King, 1973; Feldman & Newcomb, 1969; Wolfe, n.d.
6. Heath, 1968.
7. Wolfe, n.d.

8.   Heath (1977b) confirmed this finding for college students in five different cultural areas.
9.   Kitto, 1951.
10. Thomas, 1962, p. 301.
11. Van Doren, 1943, pp. 22–23, 33.
12. Russell, 1931.
13. Wolfe & Claar, 1971.
14. Rott, 1972.
15. Rogers, 1959; Maslow, 1967; Lecky, 1945.
16. Heath, 1991, chap. 31.
17. Dewey, 1964b, pp. 282–283.
18. Dewey, 1964f, p. 178.
19. Dewey, 1964c, p. 132.
20. Feldman & Newcomb, 1969; Pascarella & Terenzini, 1991.
21. Heath, 1968; King, 1973; Mentkowski, 1988.
22. Heath, 1991.
23. Dewey, 1964b.
24. Chickering, 1969.
25. Perry, 1970, p. 162.
26. Pascarella & Terenzini, 1991, p. 202.
27. Heath, 1968; Whiteley, 1982.
28. Pascarella & Terenzini, 1991.
29. Newman, 1891.
30. Montessori, 1973.
31. Whitehead, 1929a.
32. Dewey, 1964f.
33. Van Doren, 1942, p. 39.
34. Trent & Medsker, 1968.
35. King, 1973.
36. Chickering, 1969.
37. Heath, 1968.
38. Rott, 1972, pp. 113, 114.
39. Perry, 1970, pp. 61, 158.
40. The appendix in Heath (1991) describes measures of self's dimensional maturity.
41. Heath, 1977b.

Chapter Ten

1. An organization is said to have a distinctive climate when at least two-thirds of its various constituencies agree about at least 10 percent of the Word Check List's 150 words when describing the organization.
2. Rutter et al., 1979. Commitment is measured by the WCL procedures described in Chapter Two.
3. Abelson, 1983; Peters & Waterman, 1982; Blume, 1980; Silcock, 1983.
4. Chapters One, Two, and Three illustrate how teachers' empathic understanding can be assessed. Pipho (1988) describes how Iowa's Heartland Humanities Program helps teachers develop the human relationship skills needed to better understand today's students.
5. Data about such relationships can be secured from faculty's and students' perceptions of each other and from teachers' identification of faculty attributes most contributory to their continued maturing by modifying the WCL instructions. Chapter Twelve describes the growth-inducing traits that teachers feel a nurturing faculty should have.
6. Heath (1991, chap. 16) describes and illustrates how morale and calling can be measured.
7. See note 2.
8. Researchers on school effectiveness have not studied most attributes of schools of hope, which are drawn from unpublished research on the Word Check List (WCL) and morale measures reported in Chapters One, Two, and Three. Heath (1981a) describes how the WCL can be used to diagnose institutional health.
9. Peters & Waterman, 1982; Abelson, 1983.
10. Hardy, 1974; Jacob, 1957.
11. Proctor's faculty rated how well each knew every student. The two most knowledgeable about each ninth- and twelfth-grade student then rated each student on the Self-Image Questionnaire, a thirty-item personality scale measuring attributes of maturity (Heath, 1977b, 1991). The faculty did not know the

study's purpose. Faculty ratings of ninth- and twelfth-grade learning disabled and nonlearning disabled students were then compared.

12. The MHS assessment relied on faculty, student, and parental ratings, specially designed measures of MHS's character and goals, focused written essays about change, morale scales, WCLs, self- and teacher ratings of personality and maturity, and other tests. See Boughner (1992) for an "insider's" view and assessment of MHS's first year's effects.

13. Hardy, 1974.

14. Jacob, 1957.

15. Heath (1968) reports methods for assessing the college's effects and their results; Heath (1976b) also reports the results of the persisting effects of the college on its alumni revealed by a study on a different sample.

16. Power, Higgins, & Kohlberg's analysis (1989) of their just community high schools convincingly demonstrates that a school's moral culture will not affect student maturing unless teachers and students create more democratic relationships congruent with the school's values. See also Noddings (1984).

17. Peters & Waterman, 1982.

18. Heath, 1968; Pascarella & Terenzini, 1991.

Chapter Eleven

1. Lawton, 1991b.

2. Dewey, 1922.

3. Heath, 1968, pp. 225–236.

4. Hunter (1981, 1983), also drawing on psychological research on learning, has contributed a more detailed, perceptive, and prescriptive set of principles for classroom use. In contrast, this chapter's twenty principles are designed to be appropriate for furthering the growth of any person and to serve as a guide for improving institutional learning environments.

5. Heath, 1978.

6. Sizer, 1984; Heath, 1971.

7. Heath (1968, 1979) explores the psychological dynamics of the Quaker meeting for meditation and how its effects contributed

to the college's coherent ethos that produced enduring value changes in its alumni. The dynamics of the meeting are remarkably similar to the ethos and town-meeting mode of Kohlberg's just community schools.

8. Objective measures of each trait and outcome made it possible to discover the kind of student who might not be ready for MHS's program. For example, empathy was measured by the degree of agreement between a student's predicted ratings of how knowledgeable faculty would rate him or her on the Self-Image Questionnaire's thirty trait scales and those teachers' actual ratings. See Heath (1968, 1977b, 1991) for the measure's extensive validation as one index of maturity.

9. Rothman, 1990a.

Chapter Twelve

1. Bellah et al., 1985.
2. Erikson, 1950.
3. Heath (1981b, 1991) describes the Vocational Adaptation Scale (VAS), which measures satisfaction with thirty critical attributes of one's vocation. Its total score correlates with happiness and maturity for both men and women as well as with numerous measures of success for males and judged personality traits. Reliable norms are now available for teachers.
4. Of the suburban public high schools for which I have teachers' morale scores, no faculty is as satisfied with its vocation as are faculties of the typical independent school. The Carnegie Commission's study of 13,500 teachers found that morale had declined substantially (Olson, 1988b).
5. Morale of other professionals, such as lawyers, is also reported to be declining (Steptoe, 1987; Munneke & Bridge-Riley, 1981).
6. Heath, 1991, chap. 16.
7. See note 3.
8. Heath (1991, chap. 16) reports that regardless of type of vocation, satisfied males are judged by knowledgeable others to be more mature than dissatisfied males and more typically masculine: self-sufficient, independent, willing to take risks, and ambitious, among other traits.

9. Heath (1991, pp. 209–210) reports that satisfaction in typical nurturing professions, such as teaching, requires typically feminine interpersonal strengths. High morale is associated with such strengths for both female and male teachers.

10. The Student Role Satisfaction scale (SRS) parallels the VAS, described in note 3; a similar scale, phrased in language appropriate to fifth- through seventh-graders, is now available. Stable norms are now available for students in independent schools but not yet for those in public schools.

11. These conclusions are based on item analyses that correlated rated faculty satisfaction for each of the VAS's thirty items with the total VAS score. With remarkably few exceptions for hundreds of all types of schools, the least and most predictive items of overall morale have been similar. Clausen (1981) found similar discriminating attributes.

12. Heath, 1991, chap. 16.

13. Teachers' quotations come from workshops in which groups of teachers with varying lengths of teaching experience wrote about and then discussed how teaching had changed them.

14. Bradley, 1991.

15. Ryan (1970) reports six teachers' similar views of their first year's effects.

16. Heath, unpublished data from VAS studies. See note 3.

17. Boyer, 1988.

18. Schlechty (1991) agrees that a leader's priority should be to nurture teacher growth in ways congruent with the school's mission.

19. Sergiovanni, 1990, 1992. The February 1992 issue of *Educational Leadership* discusses many of these issues.

20. In declining order of agreement, K–12 independent school teachers wish that their schools were more consistent, adventurous, intellectually exciting, and creative; that they anticipated consequences; and that they were more efficient, imaginative, and flexible. Less reliable norms are available for public school teachers, who seem to have similar wishes.

21. McPherson, Rinnander, & Rud, 1987, p. 45.

22. See note 10.

23. As note 9 in Chapter Eleven describes, it was possible to iden-

tify statistically the judged personality strengths of MHS's students who achieved different school competencies and outcomes.

Chapter Thirteen

1. Anderson, 1991.
2. Freiberg, 1991a.
3. Byrne, 1989a.
4. Michigan State Board of Education, 1991.
5. Heath (1971, chap. 11) describes a course's maturing sequence in detail. Repetition of maturing's "natural" sequence at more advanced levels of maturing is analagous to Bruner's idea of recurring curricular cycles or spirals (1960).
6. Montessori, 1912, 1949.
7. Rothman, 1989.
8. Carnegie Council on Adolescent Development, 1989; Lawton, 1991b.
9. Alverno College Faculty, 1976, 1979.
10. Alverno College Faculty, 1976, p. 33.
11. Stearns, 1991, p. A32.
12. Sizer, 1984. Healy (1990, chap. 14) describes coaching techniques to deal with students' changing minds. Rosenshine and Meister (1992) have independently identified, illustrated, and applied many of maturing's twenty principles to teaching cognitive skills. Willis (1992) summarizes studies of how to teach thinking skills.
13. Karr, 1991, p. B3.
14. Willis, 1991, p. 6.

Chapter Fourteen

1. Lickona (1991) comprehensively summarizes school and classroom techniques for educating character.
2. Pascarella & Terenzini, 1991, p. 264; Pascarella, 1985.
3. Pascarella, Ethington, & Smart, 1988, p. 431.
4. Averill, 1983. Kohlberg's democratic just community in three small alternative public schools is perceptively analyzed and critiqued in Power, Higgins, & Kohlberg (1989).

5. Heath (1981a) illustrates how the Word Check List can be used to describe an institution's character and diagnose its problems.

6. See Heath (1981a) for other examples.

7. Hardy, 1974, p. 502.

8. Teachers from some twenty K-12 Quaker schools completed the WCL about their schools six weeks into their first teaching semester. Reliability checks over a ten-year period confirm the stability of the Quaker schools' ethos. Their students are similar to comparable NAIS independent and public schools.

9. Hardy, 1974.

10. Barron, 1963; Holden, 1987; MacKinnon, 1962; Stein, 1974; Torrance, 1983.

11. See note 7 in Chapter Eleven; Heath, 1991.

12. Kohlberg, Wasserman, & Richardson, 1975; Power, Higgins, & Kohlberg, 1989.

13. Whiteley, 1982.

14. Schmidt (1990a) reports the growing acceptance by schools of the concept that they must educate for values such as respect, responsibility, compassion, and tolerance. Jennings (1988b) summarizes school programs requiring community service as a means to educate for such values.

15. Boyer (1983) suggests that schools include a Carnegie unit on community service. Students need preparatory service-related attitudes and skills, so such a recommendation can be both formative as well as a test of their character maturation.

16. Power, Higgins, & Kohlberg, 1989.

Chapter Fifteen

1. Bloom, 1977.

2. "Depart and Deliver," 1991, p. A6; see also Mathews (1989).

3. Prawat (1992) identifies similar guidelines for creating "learning communities."

4. Glasser's quality schools also rely on learning teams as well as other methods that I describe (Glasser, 1990).

Chapter Sixteen

1. Boyer, 1991; Glasser, 1990; Sizer, 1992.

2. Peters & Waterman, 1982, pp. 82, 83, 85.

3. Rutter et al., 1979.

4. Schlechty, 1991.

5. North Central Association of Colleges and Schools, 1991.

6. Graham, 1988.

7. Bronowski, 1956.

8. Heath (1971, pp. 127–129) reviews the evidence that small high schools, those with several hundred students, can still offer a "comprehensive" curriculum. Lawton (1991a) reports that a Georgia legislative task force claims that "the national trend is going away from large schools" (p. 23).

9. Olson, 1990, p. 12.

10. Goodlad, 1984.

11. Boyer (1983, p. 231) proposes that large high schools break themselves up into houses of "several hundred each." Sizer (1992) agrees, urging existing schools to form separate units of about two hundred students each.

12. Snider, 1989b; Bradley, 1992, 1993.

13. Boyer, 1991.

14. Coughlin, 1991; Mirga, 1983; Snider, 1989a.

15. Walsh, 1991.

16. Olson, 1988a.

17. Powell, Farrar, & Cohen, 1985.

18. Coleman, 1966; Jencks et al., 1972.

19. Schmidt, 1991.

20. Snider (1989c) reviews conditions necessary for house plans to succeed and assesses New York City's efforts to integrate them into its large high schools.

21. Cohen (1989) reports increasing use of multi-age elementary classrooms that teachers teach for several years. West Germany's Cologne model, adopted by more than twenty U.S. schools, creates small personal learning environments in which autonomous teams of teachers educate the same students from the fifth through the tenth grade (Viadero, 1989).

22. Rothman, 1990b.

23. Olson, 1992; Bradley, 1992.

24. Bradley, 1989.

25. Cohen (1991a) describes Carnegie's recommendations for par-

ental and community conditions necessary to enhance children's educability.

26. Barth, 1990; Schlechty, 1991; Sizer, 1992.
27. Carroll, 1990; Rothman, 1990b.
28. Sparks (1992) suggests other more, tactical steps necessary for improvement efforts to succeed.

References

Abelson, P. H. New biotechnology companies. *Science*, 1983, February 11, *219*, 9.

Across the nation. *Education Week*, 1992, March 11, 2.

Adelson, J. *Handbook of Adolescent Psychology*. New York: Wiley, 1980.

Adler, T. Sex-based differences declining, study shows. *APA Monitor*, 1989, March, 6.

Alverno College Faculty. *Liberal Learning at Alverno College*. Milwaukee, WI: Alverno Productions, 1976.

Alverno College Faculty. *Assessment at Alverno College*. Milwaukee, WI: Alverno Productions, 1979.

American Association of University Women. *Shortchanging Girls, Shortchanging America*. Washington, DC: American Association of University Women, 1991.

Anderson, A. British mathematicians count their numbers. *Science*, 1991, August 16, *253*, 733.

Arnold, K. & Denny, T. Study reported top scholars have average careers. *Bangor Daily News*, 1992, May 26, 3.

Ashby, W. R. *An Introduction to Cybernetics*. New York: Wiley, 1956.

Association of Governing Boards of Universities and Colleges. *News Notes*, 1982, *13*, #2, 1.

Astin, A. W. *Preventing Students from Dropping Out.* San Francisco: Jossey-Bass, 1975.

Astin, A. W. *Four Critical Years: Effects of College on Beliefs, Attitudes, and Knowledge.* San Francisco: Jossey-Bass, 1977.

Astin, A. W. *The American Freshman: National Norms for Fall, 1990.* Cooperative Institutional Research Program. Los Angeles: Graduate School of Education, University of California, 1991.

Averill, L. J. *Learning to Be Human: A Vision for the Liberal Arts.* Port Washington, NJ: Associated Faculty Press, 1983.

Barker, R. G. & Gump, P. V. *Big School, Small School: High School Size and Student Behavior.* Palo Alto, CA: Stanford University Press, 1964.

Barrett, P. M. & Wermiel, S. Judge Thomas, billed as conservative, may prove unpredictable. *Wall Street Journal,* 1991, July 19, A7.

Barron, F. *Creativity and Psychological Health.* New York: Van Nostrand Reinhold, 1963.

Barth, R. S. *Improving Schools from Within: Teachers, Parents, and Principals Can Make a Difference.* San Francisco: Jossey-Bass, 1990.

Bartlett, F. C. *Thinking: An Experimental and Social Study.* New York: Basic Books, 1958.

Bayer, L. M., Whissell-Buechy, E., & Honzik, M. P. Health in the middle years. In D. H. Eichorn, J. A. Clausen, N. Haan, M. P. Honzik, & P. H. Mussen (Eds.). *Present and Past in Middle Life.* New York: Academic Press, 1981, chap. 3.

Bellah, R. N., Madsen, R., Sullivan, W. M., Swidler, A., & Tipton, S. M. *Habits of the Heart: Individualism and Commitment in American Life.* Berkeley: University of California Press, 1985.

Bellah, R. N., Madsen, R., Sullivan, W. M., Swidler, A., & Tipton, S. M. *The Good Society.* New York: Knopf, 1991.

Benbow, C. P. & Stanley, J. C. (Eds.). *Academic Precocity: Aspects of Its Development, Revised, Expanded, and Updated.* Proceedings of the tenth annual Hyman Blumberg Symposium on Research in Early Childhood Education. Baltimore, MD: Johns Hopkins University Press, 1983.

Bercovitch, S. *The Puritan Origins of the American Self.* New Haven, CT: Yale University Press, 1975.

Block, J. *Lives Through Time.* Berkeley, CA: Bancroft, 1971.

Bloom, B. S. Affective outcomes of school learning. *Phi Delta Kappan*, 1977, November, 193–198.

Bloom, B. S., Englehart, M. D., Furst, E. J., Hill, W. H., & Krathwohl, D. R. *A Taxonomy of Educational Objectives. Handbook I: The Cognitive Domain*. New York: Longmans, Green, 1956.

Blume, S. S. A managerial view of research. *Science*, 1980, January 4, *207*, 48–49.

Bode, B. H. *Modern Educational Theories*. New York: Macmillan, 1927.

Boughner, C. Bloomfield Hills Model High. *Journal of the Michigan Association of Secondary School Principals*, 1992, *33*, #3, 7–18.

Boyer, E. L. *High School: A Report on Secondary Education in America*. New York: HarperCollins, 1983.

Boyer, E. L. *College: The Undergraduate Experience in America*. New York: HarperCollins, 1987.

Boyer, E. L. *The Conditions of Teaching: A State-by-State Analysis*. Princeton, NJ: Princeton University Press, 1988.

Boyer, E. L. Elementary and secondary education. In D. W. Hornbeck & L. M. Salamon (Eds.). *Human Capital and America's Future*. Baltimore, MD: Johns Hopkins University Press, 1991, chap. 6.

Bradley, A. After two tough years in Rochester, school reformers look to the future. *Education Week*, 1989, October 18, 1.

Bradley, A. First year blunts teachers' idealism, survey finds. *Education Week*, 1991, October 9, 10.

Bradley, A. N.Y.C. to create small, theme-oriented high schools. *Education Week*, 1992, April 1, 5.

Bradley, A. Gains seen in Philadelphia schools with "charters." *Education Week*, 1993, March 24, 10.

Bray, D. W., Campbell, R. J., & Grant, D. L. *Formative Years in Business. A Long-Term AT&T Study of Managerial Lives*. New York: Wiley, 1974.

Bray, D. W. & Howard, A. Career success and life satisfactions of middle-aged managers. In L. A. Bond & J. C. Rosen (Eds.). *Coping and Competence During Adulthood*. Hanover, NH: University Press of New England, 1980.

Bronowski, J. *Science and Human Values.* New York: Julian Messner, 1956.

Brooks, J. B. Social maturity in middle age and its developmental antecedents. In D. H. Eichorn, J. A. Clausen, N. Haan, M. P. Honzik, & P. H. Mussen (Eds.). *Present and Past in Middle Life.* San Diego, CA: Academic Press, 1981, chap. 10.

Bruner, J. S. *The Process of Education.* Cambridge, MA: Harvard University Press, 1960.

Bruner, J. S. *Toward a Theory of Instruction.* Cambridge, MA: Harvard University Press, 1966.

Byrne, G. Overhaul urged for math teaching. *Science,* 1989a, February 3, *243,* 597.

Byrne, G. U.S. students flunk math, science. *Science,* 1989b, February 10, *243,* 729.

Campbell, A. *The Sense of Well-Being in America: Recent Patterns and Trends.* New York: McGraw-Hill, 1981.

Campbell, D. T. Reprise. *American Psychologist,* 1976, *31,* 381–384.

Cannon, W. B. *The Wisdom of the Body.* (1932) New York: W. W. Norton, 1939.

Carnegie Council on Adolescent Development. *Turning Points: Preparing American Youth for the 21st Century.* New York: Carnegie Council on Adolescent Development, 1989.

Carnegie Foundation. Frustrated students. *Wall Street Journal,* 1986, February 7, 23.

Carroll, J. M. *The Copernican Plan.* Andover, MA: Regional Laboratory for Educational Improvement of the Northeast and Islands, 1990.

Chickering, A. W. *Education and Identity.* San Francisco: Jossey-Bass, 1969.

Clausen, J. A. Men's occupational careers in the middle years. In D. H. Eichorn, J. A. Clausen, N. Haan, M. P. Honzik, & P. H. Mussen (Eds.). *Present and Past in Middle Life.* San Diego, CA: Academic Press, 1981, chap. 13.

Cohen, D. L. First stirrings of a new trend: Multi-age classrooms gain favor. *Education Week,* 1989, December 6, 1.

Cohen, D. L. Carnegie proposes seven-point action plan to ensure children's readiness for school. *Education Week,* 1991a, December 11, 1.

Cohen, D. L. Task force offers broad vision of school readiness. *Education Week*, 1991b, December 11, 10.

Cohen, P. D. College grades and adult achievement: A research synthesis. *Research in Higher Education*, 1984, *20*, 281–293.

Coleman, J. S. *Equality of Educational Opportunity*. Washington, DC: U.S. Office of Education, 1966.

College Entrance Examination Board. *Academic Preparation for College: What Students Need to Know and Be Able to Do*. New York: Office of Academic Affairs, College Entrance Examination Board, 1983. (Excerpted in *Education Week*, 1983, May 18, 12–13.)

Column one. *Education Week*, 1991, October 9, 6.

Commission of National Association of State Boards of Education. Report. *Bangor Daily News*, 1990, June 6, 24.

Conant, J. B. *The Education of American Teachers*. New York: McGraw-Hill, 1963.

Coughlin, E. K. Amid challenges to classic remedies for race discrimination, researchers argue merits of mandatory school desegregation. *Chronicle of Higher Education*, 1991, October 9, A9.

Craeger, J. A. & Harmon, L. R. On-the-job validation of selection variables. Technical Report no. 26. Washington, DC: Office of Scientific Personnel, National Academy of Sciences–National Research Council, 1966.

Cremin, L. A. *American Education: The Colonial Experience. 1607–1783*. New York: HarperCollins, 1970.

Cremin, L. A. *American Education: The National Experience. 1783–1876*. New York: HarperCollins, 1980.

Crispell, D. People patterns. *Wall Street Journal*, 1991, July 1, B1.

Curti, M. *The Social Ideas of American Educators*. (1959) Paterson, NJ: Littlefield, Adams, 1963.

Depart and deliver. *Wall Street Journal*, 1991, August 30, A6.

Dewey, J. *Human Nature and Conduct*. Troy, MO: Holt, Rinehart & Winston, 1922.

Dewey, J. What psychology can do for the teacher. (1895) In R. D. Archambault (Ed.). *John Dewey on Education*. New York: Random House, 1964a.

Dewey, J. Interest in relation to training of the will. (1896) In

R. D. Archambault (Ed.). *John Dewey on Education*. New York: Random House, 1964b.

Dewey, J. Ethical principles underlying education. (1897) In R. D. Archambault (Ed.). *John Dewey on Education*. New York: Random House, 1964c.

Dewey, J. The school and society. (1899) In R. D. Archambault (Ed.). *John Dewey on Education*. New York: Random House, 1964d.

Dewey, J. Logical conditions of a scientific treatment of morality. (1903) In R. D. Archambault (Ed.). *John Dewey on Education*. New York: Random House, 1964e.

Dewey, J. Progressive education and the science of education. (1928) In R. D. Archambault (Ed.). *John Dewey on Education*. New York: Random House, 1964f.

Dewey, J. The process and product of reflective activity. (1933) In R. D. Archambault (Ed.). *John Dewey on Education*. New York: Random House, 1964g.

Dewey, J. Why reflective thinking must be an educational aim. (1933) In R. D. Archambault (Ed.). *John Dewey on Education*. New York: Random House, 1964h.

Dewey, J. The need for a philosophy of education. (1934) In R. D. Archambault (Ed.). *John Dewey on Education*. New York: Random House, 1964i.

Dodge, S. Little study reported by top high-schoolers. *Chronicle of Higher Education*, 1991, October 23, A36.

Doob, L. W. *Becoming More Civilized: A Psychological Exploration*. New Haven, CT: Yale University Press, 1960.

Doyle Dane Bernbach, Inc. Youthful worries. *Wall Street Journal*, 1985, December 4, 33.

Eichorn, D. H., Hunt, J. V., & Honzik, M. P. Experience, personality, and IQ: Adolescence to middle age. In D. H. Eichorn, J. A. Clausen, N. Haan, M. P. Honzik, & P. H. Mussen (Eds.). *Present and Past in Middle Life*. San Diego, CA: Academic Press, 1981, chap. 4.

Elliott, D. Teen jobs often lead to trouble, study finds. *Miami Herald*, 1992, January 10, 9a.

Erikson, E. *Childhood and Society*. New York: W. W. Norton, 1950.

Evangelauf, J. Business schools are urged to rethink the curriculum of MBA programs. *Chronicle of Higher Education,* 1990, May 23, A30.

Falbo, T. *The Single-Child Family.* New York: Guilford Press, 1984.

Fallon, M. "Success at any price": Cheating common, California survey finds. *Education Week,* 1986, April 30, 6.

Feingold, A. Cognitive gender differences are disappearing. *American Psychologist,* 1988, February, 95–103.

Feldman, K. A. & Newcomb, T. M. *The Impact of College on Students.* San Francisco: Jossey-Bass, 1969.

Fiedler, T. Youthful apathy: Who cares? *Miami Herald,* 1989, December 10, 9M.

Fisher, K. Pushing preschoolers doesn't help, may hurt. *APA Monitor,* 1989, August, 9.

Flax, E. Significant number of teenagers unsure of sexual orientation, new study finds. *Education Week,* 1992, April 15, 4.

Freiberg, P. Self-esteem gender gap widens in adolescence. *APA Monitor,* 1991a, April, 29.

Freiberg, P. Study: Disorders found in 20 percent of children. *APA Monitor,* 1991b, February, 36.

Freiberg, P. Teens' long work hours detrimental, study says. *APA Monitor,* 1991c, June, 19.

Freud, S. *The Interpretation of Dreams.* (1900) New York: Basic Books, 1956.

Fromm, E. *Man for Himself.* Troy, MO: Holt, Rinehart & Winston, 1947.

Gallup, G., Jr., & Castelli, J. Pope's popularity down in '86. *Miami Herald,* 1987, January 30, 4B.

Garbarino, J. Some thoughts on school size and its effects on adolescent development. *Journal of Youth and Adolescence,* 1980, February, *9,* 19–31.

Gardner, H. *Frames of Mind.* New York: Basic Books, 1983.

Gardner, J. W. *Fifty-first Annual Report 1955–56.* New York: Carnegie Corporation of New York, 1956.

Gardner, J. W. *Excellence: Can We Be Equal and Excellent Too?* New York: HarperCollins, 1961.

Giffin, M. E. & Felsenthal, C. *A Cry for Help.* Garden City, NY: Doubleday, 1983.

Gilligan, C., Lyons, N. P., & Hanmer, T. (Eds.). *Making Connections.* Cambridge, MA: Harvard University Press, 1990.

Glasser, W. *The Quality School: Managing Students Without Coercion.* New York: HarperCollins, 1990.

Goertzel, M. G., Goertzel, V., & Goertzel, T. G. *Three Hundred Eminent Personalities: A Psychosocial Analysis of the Famous.* San Francisco: Jossey-Bass, 1978.

Goertzel, V. & Goertzel, M. G. *Cradles of Eminence.* Boston: Little, Brown, 1962.

Gold, D. L. Study disputes link between reforms, rise in test scores. *Education Week,* 1987, September 9, 1.

Goodlad, J. I. *A Place Called School: Prospects for the Future.* New York: McGraw-Hill, 1984.

Gough, H. G. Factors related to differential achievement among gifted persons. Paper presented to American Psychological Association on the gifted child, San Francisco, 1955, September 1.

Graham, E. "Values" lessons return to the classroom. *Wall Street Journal,* 1988, September 26, 29.

Grannon, P., Kulick, W., & Schenck, L. Effect of single and coed schools on maturing. Unpublished senior thesis, Haverford College, 1981.

Greenberger, E. & Steinberg, L. *When Teenagers Work: The Psychological and Social Costs of Adolescent Employment.* New York: Basic Books, 1986.

Greif, E. B. & Hogan, R. The theory and measurement of empathy. *Journal of Counseling Psychology,* 1973, *20,* 280-284.

Guilford, J. P. The structure of intellect. *Psychological Bulletin,* 1956, *53,* 267-293.

Haier, R. J. & Denham, S. A. A summary profile of the non-intellectual correlates of mathematical precocity in boys and girls. In D. P. Keating (Ed.). *Intellectual Talent: Research and Development.* Baltimore, MD: Johns Hopkins University Press, 1976, chap. 11.

Hampton, W. J. How does Japan, Inc. pick its American workers? *Business Week,* 1988, October 3, 84-88.

Handy, R. Y. *Male Sexuality.* Buffalo, NY: Prometheus, 1988.

Hardy, K. R. Social origins of American scientists and scholars. *Science,* 1974, August 9, *185,* 497-506.

Harp, L. Panel blueprint seeks to relate school to work. *Education Week*, 1992, April 15, 1.

Hartmann, H. Towards a concept of mental health. *British Journal of Medical Psychology*, 1960, *33*, 243–248.

Healy, J. M. *Endangered Minds: Why Our Children Don't Think*. New York: Simon & Schuster, 1990.

Heath, D. D. *School size: The effect on adjustment and social contact of high school seniors*. Unpublished doctoral dissertation, University of Pennsylvania, 1971.

Heath, D. H. *Explorations of Maturity: Studies of Mature and Immature College Men*. East Norwalk, CT: Appleton & Lange, 1965.

Heath, D. H. *Growing Up in College: Liberal Education and Maturity*. San Francisco: Jossey-Bass, 1968.

Heath, D. H. Secularization and maturity of religious beliefs. *Journal of Religion and Health*, 1969, *8*, 335–358.

Heath, D. H. *Humanizing Schools: New Directions, New Decisions*. Rochelle Park, NJ: Hayden, 1971.

Heath, D. H. Survival? A bigger school? *Independent School Bulletin*, 1972, May, 9–15.

Heath, D. H. The changing American character: How healthy? Chautauqua, NY: Chautauqua Publications, 1976a.

Heath, D. H. What the enduring effects of higher education tell us about a liberal education. *Journal of Higher Education*, 1976b, *47*, 173–190.

Heath, D. H. Academic predictors of adult maturity and competence. *Journal of Higher Education*, 1977a, *18*, 613–632.

Heath, D. H. *Maturity and Competence: A Transcultural View*. New York: Gardner Press, 1977b.

Heath, D. H. What meaning and effects does fatherhood have for the maturing of professional men? *Merrill-Palmer Quarterly*, 1978, *24*, 265–278.

Heath, D. H. *The Peculiar Mission of a Quaker School*. Pendle Hill Pamphlet no. 225. Wallingford, PA: Pendle Hill, 1979.

Heath, D. H. Wanted: A comprehensive model of healthy development. *Personnel and Guidance Journal*, 1980, *58*, 391–399.

Heath, D. H. A college's ethos: A neglected key to effectiveness and survival. *Liberal Education*, 1981a, *67*, 89–111.

Heath, D. H. *Faculty Burnout, Morale, and Vocational Adaptation.* Boston: National Association of Independent Schools, 1981b.

Heath, D. H. The maturing person. In G. Walsh & D. Shapiro (Eds.). *Beyond Health and Normality.* New York: Van Nostrand Rinehold, 1983, chap. 6.

Heath, D. H. *Fulfilling Lives: Paths to Maturity and Success.* San Francisco: Jossey-Bass, 1991.

Hechinger, F. *Fateful Choices: Healthy Youth for the 21st Century.* East Rutherford, NJ: Putnam Berkley, 1992.

Hedlin, D. & Wolfe, H. The Minnesota Youth Poll. *Quarterly Focus* (Center for Youth Development and Research), 1979, Spring, 5.

Hirsch, E. D. *Cultural Literacy: What Every American Needs to Know.* Boston: Houghton Mifflin, 1987.

Hoge, D. R. *Commitment on Campus: Changes in Religion and Values over Five Decades.* Philadelphia: Westminster Press, 1974.

Holden, C. Creativity and the troubled mind. *Psychology Today,* 1987, April, 9–10.

Holden, C. Briefings: Myths and math. *Science,* 1991, April 19, *252,* 382.

Hook, S. *Education for Modern Man.* New York: Dial Press, 1946.

Howe, H., II. More-of-the-same reform will not achieve both excellence and equity. *Education Week,* 1984, May 23, 24.

Hudson, L. Commentary: Singularity of talent. In S. Messick & Associates. *Individuality in Learning: Implications of Cognitive Styles and Creativity for Human Development.* San Francisco: Jossey-Bass, 1976.

Hunter, M. *A Clinical Theory of Instruction.* Los Angeles: Education Extension, University of California, 1981.

Hunter, M. *Mastery Teaching.* El Sequeno, CA: Tip Publications, 1983.

Hutchins, R. M. *The Higher Learning in America.* New Haven, CT: Yale University Press, 1936.

Hutchins, R. M. *Education for Freedom.* Baton Rouge: Louisiana State University Press, 1943.

Hyman, H. & Wright, C. R. *Education's Lasting Influence on Values.* Chicago: University of Chicago Press, 1979.

Hyman, H. H., Wright, C. R., & Reed, J. S. *The Enduring Effects of Education.* Chicago: University of Chicago Press, 1975.

Inkeles, A. Making men modern: On the causes and consequences of individual change in six developing countries. *American Journal of Sociology*, 1969, 75, 208–225.

Jacob, P. E. *Changing Values in College: An Exploratory Study of the Impact of College Teaching*. New York: HarperCollins, 1957.

Janko, E. Tales of walruses and education, to taste. *Education Week*, 1987, April 22, 32.

Jencks, C., Smith, M., Aciano, H., Bane, M. J., Cohen, D., Gintis, H., Heyns, B., & Michelson, S. *Inequality: A Reassessment of the Effect of Family and Schooling in America*. New York: Basic Books, 1972.

Jennings, L. In teacher poll, minorities show signs of distress. *Education Week*, 1988a, October 5, 1, 23.

Jennings, L. Learning about life: New focus on service as a teaching tool. *Education Week*, 1988b, October 26, 1.

Jennings, W. & Nathan, J. Startling/disturbing research on school program effectiveness. *Phi Delta Kappan*, 1977, 58, 568–572.

Johnson, D. W. & Johnson, R. *Cooperation and Competition: Theory and Research*. Edina, MN: Interaction, 1989.

Karr, A. R. Labor panel urges "cognitive" skills for classrooms. *Wall Street Journal*, 1991, July 3, B3.

Kegel-Flom, P. Predicting unexpected achievement in optometry school. *American Journal of Optometry and Physiological Optics*, 1974, 51, 775–781.

Kelly, E. L. Multiple criteria of medical education and their implications for selection. In E. L. Kelly. *The Appraisal of Applicants to Medical Schools*. Evanston, IL: Association of American Medical Colleges, 1957.

Kilpatrick, J. J. Sex and the high court: A conservative view. *Bangor Daily News*, 1986, July 16, 10.

King, S. H. *Five Lives at Harvard: Personality Change During College*. Cambridge, MA: Harvard University Press, 1973.

Kitchener, K. S. & King, P. M. The reflective judgment model: Ten years of research. In M. L. Commons, C. Armon, L. Kohlberg, F. A. Richards, T. A. Grotzer, & J. Sinnott (Eds.). *Beyond Formal Operations III: Models and Methods in the Study of Adolescent and Adult Thought*. New York: Praeger, 1990.

Kitto, H. D. *The Greeks*. Baltimore, MD: Penguin Books, 1951.

Kleiman, D. Young math experts to face a reckoning. *New York Times,* 1981, July 8, B4.

Kohlberg, L. Moral development and the education of adolescents. In R. F. Purnell (Ed.). *Adolescents and the American High School.* Troy, MO: Holt, Rinehart & Winston, 1970.

Kohlberg, L., Wasserman, R., & Richardson, N. The just community school: The theory and the Cambridge cluster school experiment. In L. Kohlberg (Ed.). *Collected Papers on Moral Development and Moral Education.* Vol 2. Cambridge, MA: Center for Moral Education, Harvard University, 1975.

Kozel, N. J. & Adams, E. H. Epidemiology of drug abuse: An overview. *Science,* 1986, November 21, *234,* 970–974.

Krathwohl, D. R., Bloom, B. S., & Masia, B. B. *Taxonomy of Educational Objectives. Handbook II: Affective Domain.* New York: David McKay, 1964.

Landers, S. Commission, Congress heed APA on AIDS. *APA Monitor,* 1988, August, 25.

Landers, S. High school seniors' illicit drug use down. *APA Monitor,* 1989, May, 33.

Lawton, M. Armed with research, GA. legislator takes aim at plans for consolidation. *Education Week,* 1991a, November 20, 23.

Lawton, M. Many 8th graders spend school day as passive "sponges," study concludes. *Education Week,* 1991b, January 16, 1.

Lawton, M. More than a third of teens surveyed say they have contemplated suicide. *Education Week,* 1991c, April 10, 5.

Lawton, M. Why are children turning to guns? *Education Week,* 1991d, November 6, 14.

Lecky, P. *Self-Consistency: A Theory of Personality.* New York: Island Press, 1945.

Lederer, R. *Anguished English.* Charleston, SC: Wyrick, 1987.

Leestma, R., August, R., George, B., & Peak, L. *U.S. Study of Education in Japan.* Washington, DC: U.S. Department of Education, 1987.

Lehmann, I. J. & Dressel, P. L. *Critical Thinking, Attitudes, and Values in Higher Education.* East Lansing: Michigan State University, 1962.

Levine, A. *When Dreams and Heroes Died: A Portrait of Today's College Student.* San Francisco: Jossey-Bass, 1980.

Levinson, D. J. *The Seasons of a Man's Life.* New York: Knopf, 1978.

Lewis, J. & Nelson, I. The relationship between college grades and three factors of adult achievement. *Educational and Psychological Measurement,* 1983, *43,* 577–580.

Lickona, T. *Educating for Character.* New York: Bantam Books, 1991.

Linn, M. C. & Hyde, J. S. Study: Sexes now do equally well in math and spatial reasoning. *Miami Herald,* 1989, January 17.

Loevinger, J. The meaning and measurement of ego development. *American Psychologist,* 1966, *21,* 195–206.

MacKinnon, D. W. What makes a person creative? *Saturday Review,* 1962, February 10, 15.

Madan, G. William Cory. *Cornhill Magazine,* 1938, July–December.

Marshall, E. School reformers aim at creativity. *Science,* 1986, July 18, *233,* 267–270.

Marston, P. Successful exam schools criticized for "dull" lessons. *Daily Telegraph,* 1989, March 22, 8.

Maslow, A. H. Self-actualizing and beyond. In J.F.T. Bugental (Ed.). *Challenges of Humanistic Psychology.* New York: McGraw-Hill, 1967, chap. 29.

Massey, M. Interest in character education seen growing. ASCD *Update,* 1993, May, *35,* 1, 4–5.

Mathews, J. Jaime Escalante: Tapping the urge to succeed. *Education Week,* 1989, January 11, 31.

McClelland, D. C. Testing for competence rather than for "intelligence." *American Psychologist,* 1973, *28,* 1–14.

McCue, J. D. Influence of medical and premedical education on important personal qualities of physicians. *American Journal of Medicine,* 1985, *78,* 985–989.

McCurdy, H. D. Mass education held genius cure. *New York Times,* 1960, June 12.

McGrath, E. J. *The Graduate School and the Decline of Liberal Education.* New York: Bureau of Publications, Teachers College, Columbia University, 1959.

McKinney, W. J. The recession in American church participation: An analysis of the membership growth, and decline of selected churches with particular attention to external and internal causes, 1965–1975. Unpublished doctoral dissertation, Pennsylvania State University, 1977.

McPherson, R. B., Rinnander, J. A., & Rud, A. G., Jr. To the heart of the mind: Renewal for North Carolina teachers. *Educational Leadership*, 1987, November, 43–48.

Meiklejohn, A. *The Liberal College*. Boston: Marshall Jones, 1920.

Mentkowski, M. Paths to integrity: Educating for personal growth and professional performance. In S. Srivastva & Associates. *Executive Integrity: The Search for High Human Values in Organizational Life*. San Francisco: Jossey-Bass, 1988, chap. 4.

Mentkowski, M. & Doherty, A. *Careering After College*. Final report to the National Institute of Education. Overview and Summary. Milwaukee, WI: Alverno College, 1984.

Mentkowksi, M. & Loacker, G. Assessing and validating the outcomes of college. In P. T. Ewell (Ed.). *Assessing Educational Outcomes*. New Directions for Institutional Research, no. 47. San Francisco: Jossey-Bass, 1985, chap. 4.

Mentkowski, M., Moeser, M., & Strait, M. J. *Using the Perry Scheme of Intellectual and Ethical Development as a College Outcomes Measure: Process and Criteria for Judging Student Performance*. Milwaukee, WI: Office of Research and Evaluation, Alverno College, 1983.

Michigan State Board of Education. *Model Core Curriculum Outcomes: Position Statement*. Working Document. Lansing: Michigan State Board of Education, 1991.

Miller, K. & Moser, G. Moral judgment, personality maturity, and perception of others. Unpublished senior thesis, Haverford College, 1977.

Mirga, T. "Slight" academic gains made by blacks in desegregated schools. *Education Week*, 1983, February 16, 11.

Mirga, T. New federal study links "Protestant ethic" to academic success. *Education Week*, 1986, March 19, 10.

Mischel, W., Shoda, Y., & Rodriguez, M. L. Delay of gratification in children. *Science*, 1989, *244*, 933–938.

Montessori, M. *The Montessori Method*. New York: Frederick Stokes, 1912.

Montessori, M. *The Absorbent Mind*. Madras, India: Kalakshetra Publications, 1949.

Montessori, M. *From Childhood to Adolescence*. (1948) New York: Shocken Books, 1973.

Moses, S. "Educational excellence" goal is unmet. *APA Monitor*, 1991a, February, 40.

Moses, S. Parents' attitudes key to girls' achievement. *APA Monitor*, 1991b, October, 16.

Moses, S. Schools' rough seas due to social factors. *APA Monitor*, 1992, July, 40-41.

Mosher, R. L. & Sprinthall, N. A. Psychological education: A means to promote personal development during adolescence. *Counseling Psychologist*, 1971, 2, 3-82.

Much, N. & Mentkowski, M. *Student Perspectives on Liberal Learning at Alverno College: Justifying Learning as Relevant to Performance in Personal and Professional Roles*. Milwaukee, WI: Office of Research and Evaluation, Alverno College, 1982.

Munneke, G. A. & Bridger-Riley, N. K. Singing those law office blues. *Barrister*, 1981, Fall, 10.

National Assessment on Educational Progress. Dropping Out. *Wall Street Journal*, 1987, March 10, 33.

Neugarten, B. L. & Neugarten, D. A. The changing meanings of age. *Psychology Today*, 1987, May, 29-33.

Newcomb, T. M., Koenig, K. F., Flacks, R., & Warwick, D. P. *Persistence and Change: Bennington College and Its Students, After Twenty-Five Years*. New York: Wiley, 1967.

Newman, J. C. *The Idea of a University, Defined and Illustrated*. (1852) New York: Longmans, Green, 1891.

Niebuhr, R. G. Schools resound with four-letter words. *Wall Street Journal*, 1992, July 8, B4.

96-year-old to receive degree. *Bangor Daily News*, 1988, July 18, 1, 3.

Noddings, N. *Caring: A Feminine Approach to Ethics and Moral Education*. Berkeley: University of California Press, 1984.

North Central Association of Colleges and Schools. *Outcomes Accreditation*. Mt. Pleasant, MI: North Central Association of Colleges and Schools, 1991.

Oden, M. H. The fulfillment of promise: 40 year follow-up of the Terman gifted group. *Genetic Psychological Monographs*, 1968, 77, 3-93.

Office of Educational Research and Improvement. Extracurricular activity participants outperform other students. *Bulletin* (Center for Statistics, U.S. Department of Education), 1986, September, 1–7.

Olney, M. & Peters, R. Intelligence correlates and developmental antecedents of adult maturity and competence. Unpublished senior thesis, Haverford College, 1979.

Olson, L. Foundation outlines plan to rescue nation's "imperiled" urban schools. *Education Week*, 1988a, March 23, 1.

Olson, L. Poll: Teacher job satisfaction coexists with deep concerns. *Education Week*, 1988b, December 5, 5.

Olson, L. Gallup poll finds doubts goals can be met by 2000. *Education Week*, 1990, September 5, 12.

Olson, L. "Supply side" reform or voucher? Charter-school concept takes hold. *Education Week*, 1992, January 15, 1.

Pace, C. *The Undergraduates: A Report of Their Activities and Progress in College in the 1980s.* Los Angeles: Center for the Study of Evaluation, University of California, 1990.

Parelius, A. P. Emerging sex-role attitudes, expectations, and strains among college women. *Journal of Marriage and the Family*, 1975, *37*, 146–153.

Pascarella, E. T. Students' affective development within the college environment. *Journal of Higher Education*, 1985, *56*, 640–663.

Pascarella, E. T., Ethington, C., & Smart, J. The influence of college on humanitarian civic involvement values. *Journal of Higher Education*, 1988, *59*, 412–437.

Pascarella, E. T. & Terenzini, P. T. *How College Affects Students: Findings and Insights from Twenty Years of Research.* San Francisco: Jossey-Bass, 1991.

Pavuk, A. Soviets more hopeful than U.S. youths. *Education Week*, 1987, April 22, 7.

Perry, W. G., Jr. *Forms of Intellectual and Ethical Development During the College Years.* Troy, MO: Holt, Rinehart & Winston, 1970.

Peters, T. J. & Waterman, R. H., Jr. *In Search of Excellence.* New York: HarperCollins, 1982.

Piaget, J. *The Moral Judgment of the Child.* London: Kegan Paul, 1932.

Piaget, J. *The Psychology of Intelligence.* (1947) Orlando, FL: Harcourt Brace Jovanovich, 1950.

Pipho, C. Fixing things or fixing people—the trust factor. *Education Week,* 1988, October 28, 22.

Poincare, H. Mathematical creation. In J. R. Newman (Ed.). *The World of Mathematics.* New York: Simon & Schuster, 1956, chap. 2.

Powell, A. G., Farrar, E., & Cohen, D. K. *The Shopping Mall High School.* Boston: Houghton Mifflin, 1985.

Power, F. C., Higgins, A., & Kohlberg, L. *Lawrence Kohlberg's Approach to Moral Education.* New York: Columbia University Press, 1989.

Prawat, R. S. From individual differences to learning communities—our changing focus. *Educational Leadership,* 1992, April, *49,* 9-13.

Public Broadcast System. Report. 1992, January 2, Miami, Florida.

Ranbom, S. Schooling in Japan. I: The paradox in the pattern; II: High school: Cultural values in conflict; III: Change and constancy. *Education Week,* 1985, February 20 (11-34); February 27 (11-26); March 6 (15-26).

Raushenbush, E. Address to Quaker educators, 1965, Philadelphia.

Regur, N. Japanese colleges urged to curb reliance on entrance exam. *Chronicle of Higher Education,* 1991, January 16, A43.

Reinhold, R. Harvard study calls emotional illness major cause of dropouts. *New York Times,* 1970, October 25, 38.

Rest, J. R. *Development in Judging Moral Issues.* Minneapolis: University of Minnesota Press, 1979.

Rhoads, J. M., Gallemore, J. L., Gianturco, D. T., & Osterhout, S. Motivation, medical admissions, and student performance. *Journal of Medical Education,* 1974, *49,* 1119-1127.

Ricklefs, R. Executives and general public say ethical behavior is declining in U.S. *Wall Street Journal,* 1983, October 31, 33.

Rodman, B. Diverse group urges instruction in democratic values. *Education Week,* 1987, May 27, 5.

Roe, A. *The Making of a Scientist.* New York: Dodd, Mead, 1953.

Rogers, C. R. A theory of therapy, personality, and interpersonal relationships, as developed in the client-centered framework. In S. Koch (Ed.). *Psychology: A Study of a Science.* Vol. 3: *Formu-*

lations of the Person and the Social Context. New York: McGraw-Hill, 1959, 184–256.

Rosenfeld, S. A. Educating for the factories of the future. *Education Week,* 1988, June 22, 48.

Rosenshine, B. & Meister, C. The use of scaffolds for teaching higher-level cognitive strategies. *Educational Leadership,* 1992, April, *49,* 26–33.

Rothman, R. California board seeks more emphasis on values in history texts. *Education Week,* 1987, August 4, 6.

Rothman, R. Middle grades called "powerful" shaper of adolescents. *Education Week,* 1989, June 21, 1.

Rothman, R. Educators focus attention on ways to boost student motivation. *Education Week,* 1990a, November 7, 1, 12.

Rothman, R. In a Massachusetts school, fomenting a "revolution" in time. *Education Week,* February 21, 1990b, 1.

Rothman, R. S.A.T. verbal scores continue slide to lowest level since 1980 and 1981. *Education Week,* 1990c, September 5, 7.

Rothman, R. Students spend little time reading or writing in school, NAEP finds. *Education Week,* 1990d, June 13, 1.

Rothman, R. Study of 8th graders finds 20% at high risk of failure. *Education Week,* August 1, 1990e, 11.

Rothman, R. Psychologist's cross-national studies in math show US's long road to "First in the World." *Education Week,* 1991a, March 13, 6–7.

Rothman, R. Revisionists take aim at gloomy view of schools. *Education Week,* 1991b, November 13, 1.

Rothman, R. Students read little in or out of school, NAEP survey finds. *Education Week,* 1992, June 3, 1.

Rott, M.A.H. *The University Experience: The Third Year: 1966 Freshman Class.* Buffalo: University Research, State University of New York, 1972.

Russell, B. *Education and the Good Life.* New York: Liveright, 1931.

Rutter, M., Maughan, B., Mortimer, P., Oustoon, J., & Smith, A. *Fifteen Thousand Hours.* Cambridge, MA: Harvard University Press, 1979.

Ryan, K. *Don't Smile Until Christmas.* Chicago: University of Chicago Press, 1970.

Samson, G. E., Graue, M. E., Weinstein, T., & Walberg, H. J. Academic and occupational performance: A quantitative synthesis. *American Educational Research Journal*, 1984, *21*, 311–321.

Sanford, N. Developmental status of the entering freshman. In N. Sanford (Ed.). *The American College: A Psychological and Social Interpretation of the Higher Learning*. New York: Wiley, 1962, chap. 6.

Schlechty, P. C. *Schools for the 21st Century: Leadership Imperatives for Educational Reform*. San Francisco: Jossey-Bass, 1991.

Schmidt, P. Despite controversy, consensus grows on the need to teach values in schools. *Education Week*, 1990a, February 7, 1.

Schmidt, P. "Web of factors" said to influence children's views on moral issues. *Education Week*, 1990b, February 7, 1.

Schmidt, P. School-building inventory finds 1 in 8 inadequate. *Education Week*, 1991, November 27, 1.

Segal, S. L. Letter to editor. *Science*, 1987, July 24, *237*, 358.

Self-esteem bill causes blues. *Miami Herald*, 1991, February 7, 5B.

Selman, R. L. *The Growth of Interpersonal Understanding: Developmental and Clinical Analyses*. San Diego, CA: Academic Press, 1980.

Sergiovanni, T. J. *Value Added Leadership: How to Get Extraordinary Results in Schools*. Orlando, FL: Harcourt Brace Jovanovich, 1990.

Sergiovanni, T. J. Why we should seek substitutes for leadership. *Educational Leadership*, 1992, *49*, April, 41–45.

Sevener, D. Students have lost their "thirst for knowledge," study indicates. *Education Week*, 1983, August 17, 8.

Shogren, E. Harassment rampant in U.S. schools. *Bangor Daily News*, 1993, June 2, 7.

Simpson, J. C. Baby boomers have '60s heritage, but charities say they're cheap. *Wall Street Journal*, 1986, September 11, 33.

Sinnott, E. W. The creativeness of life. In H. H. Anderson (Ed.). *Creativity and Its Cultivation*. New York: HarperCollins, 1959, chap. 2.

Sizer, T. R. *Horace's Compromise*. Boston: Houghton Mifflin, 1984.

Sizer, T. R. *Horace's School: Redesigning the American High School*. Boston: Houghton Mifflin, 1992.

Snider, W. Negative peer pressure said to inhibit black student achievement. *Education Week*, 1987, March 25, 1.

Snider, W. Key effects of desegregation policy remain unknown, study contends. *Education Week*, 1989a, April 12, 1.

Snider, W. Known for choice, New York's District 4 offers a complex tale for urban reformers. *Education Week*, 1989b, November 1, 1.

Snider, W. "Personalizing" high schools. *Education Week*, 1989c, March 1, 6-7.

Sparks, D. 13 tips for managing change. *Education Week*, 1992, June 10, 22.

Stanley, J. C. Letter to editor. *Science*, 1988, September 16, *241*, 1414.

Stearns, P. N. Point of view. *Chronicle of Higher Education*, 1991, August 7, A32.

Steen, L. A. A "new agenda" for mathematics education. *Education Week*, 1988, May 11, 28.

Stein, M. I. *Stimulating creativity*. Vol. 1. San Diego, CA: Academic Press, 1974.

Steinberg, L. & Dornbusch, S. M. Negative correlates of part-time employment during adolescence: replication and elaboration. *Developmental Psychology*, 1991, *27*, 304-313.

Steptoe, S. Hassles and red tape destroy joy of the job for many physicians. *Wall Street Journal*, 1987, April 10, 1.

Sternberg, R. J. *The Triarchic Mind*. New York: Viking Penguin, 1988.

Stevenson, H., Azuma, H., & Hakuta, K. *Child Development and Education in Japan*. New York: Freeman, 1986.

Syrkin, M. *Your School, Your Children: A Teacher Looks at What's Wrong with Our Schools*. New York: L. B. Fischer, 1944.

Tavis, C. & Offir, C. *The Longest War: Sex Differences in Perspective*. Orlando, FL: Harcourt Brace Jovanovich, 1977.

Taylor, C. W. & Ellison, R. L. Biographical predictors of scientific performance. *Science*, 1967, March 3, *155*, 1075-1080.

Teen jobs often lead to trouble, study finds. *Miami Herald*, 1992, January 10, 9A.

Teenagers who work: The lessons of after-school employment. *Harvard Educational Letter*, 1986, *2*, #5, 1-3.

Terman, L. M. The discovery and encouragement of exceptional talent. *American Psychologist*, 1954, 9, 221–230.

Thomas, R. *The Search for a Common Learning: General Education 1800–1960.* New York: McGraw-Hill, 1962.

Thompson, K. S. Changes in the values and life-style preferences of university students. *Journal of Higher Education*, 1981, 52, 506–518.

Thorndike, E. L. *Education: A First Book.* New York: Macmillan, 1912.

Tillich, P. Is a science of human values possible. In A. H. Maslow (Ed.). *New Knowledge in Human Values.* New York: HarperCollins, 1959, 189–196.

Tobin, J. J., Wu, D.Y.H., & Davidson, D. H. Preschool education in three cultures. *Education Week*, 1989, September 20, 26.

Torrance, E. P. The importance of falling in love with "something." *Creative Child and Adult Quarterly*, 1983, 8, 72–78.

Travers, N. Jump-starting our schools. *USA Weekend*, 1991, August 23–25, 4.

Trent, J. W. & Medsker, L. L. *Beyond High School.* San Francisco: Jossey-Bass, 1968.

Tugend, A. Suicide's "unanswerable logic." *Education Week*, 1986, June 18, 15–19.

University of Michigan Institute for Social Research. Time with children. *Wall Street Journal*, 1986, October 16, 35.

Vaillant, G. E. Antecedents of healthy adult male adjustment. In D. F. Ricks, A. Thomas, & M. Roff (Eds.). *Life History Research in Psychopathology.* Vol 3. Minneapolis: University of Minnesota Press, 1974, 230–242.

Vaillant, G. E. & Vaillant, C. O. Natural history of male psychological health. X: Work as a predictor of positive mental health. *American Journal of Psychiatry*, 1981, *138*, 1433–1440.

Valedictorian kills mother on graduation morning. *Bangor Daily News*, 1988, June 27, 12.

Van Doren, M. *Liberal Education.* Troy, MO: Holt, Rinehart & Winston, 1943.

Veroff, J., Douvan, E., & Kulka, R. A. *The Inner American: A Self-Portrait from 1957 to 1976.* New York: Basic Books, 1981.

Viadero, D. Minorities' expectations found high. *Education Week,* 1985, March 1, 5.

Viadero, D. Researchers find slight decrease in negative teen-age behavior. *Education Week,* 1986, October 22, 5.

Viadero, D. Apparent link between media coverage and "copycat" suicides worries experts. *Education Week,* 1987a, April 8, 1, 20.

Viadero, D. Schools begin to address problem of "social-skills deficits." *Education Week,* 1987b, February 18, 1, 25.

Viadero, D. L.A. school embraces a West German import. *Education Week,* 1989, November 1, 1.

von Bertalanffy, L. *Problems of Life: An Evaluation of Modern Biological Thought.* New York: Wiley, 1952.

Wall Street Journal, 1991, January 8, C15.

Wallach, M. A. The psychology of talent and graduate education. Paper presented to Conference on Cognitive Styles and Creativity in Higher Education, Montreal, 1972, November.

Walsh, J. U.S.-Japan study aim is educational reform. *Science,* 1987, January 16, *235,* 274–275.

Walsh, M. Key beliefs about TV's ill effects remain unproven, study finds. *Education Week,* 1988, December 7, 1, 19.

Walsh, M. "National schoolhouse" rings in its 2nd generation. *Education Week,* 1989, October 4, 1.

Walsh, M. Students at private schools for blacks post above-average scores, study finds. *Education Week,* 1991, October 16, 10.

Walshe, J. International notes. *Chronicle of Higher Education,* 1990, April 25, A40.

Warren, J. R. & Heist, P. A. Personality attributes of gifted college students. *Science,* 1960, August 5, *132,* 330–337.

Webster, H., Freedman, M. B., & Heist, P. Personality changes in college students. In N. Sanford (Ed.). *The American College: A Psychological and Social Interpretation of Higher Learning.* New York: Wiley, 1962, chap. 24.

Wehrwein, A. C. School size related to test scores, study finds. *Education Week,* 1986, May 14, 9.

Weisman, J. "Latchkey" 8th graders likely to possess emotional "risk factors," study discloses. *Education Week,* 1990, September 19, 6.

Whitehead, A. N. The aims of education. (1916) In A. N. White-head. *The Aims of Education and Other Essays.* New York: Macmillan, 1929a.

Whitehead, A. N. Technical education and its relation to science and literature. (1917) In A. N. Whitehead. *The Aims of Education and Other Essays.* New York: Macmillan, 1929b.

Whitehead, A. N. The rhythmic claims of freedom and discipline. (1923) In A. M. Whitehead. *The Aims of Education and Other Essays.* New York: Macmillan, 1929c.

Whiteley, J. M. *Character Development in College Students. Vol. 1: The Freshman Year.* Schenectady, NY: Character Research Press, 1982.

Whorf, B. L. Science and linguistics. (1940) In E. E. Maccoby, T. M. Newcomb, & E. L. Hartley (Eds.). *Readings in Social Psychology.* (3rd ed.) New York: Holt, 1958, chap. 1.

Widnall, S. E. AAAS presidential lecture: Voices from the pipeline. *Science,* 1988, September 30, *241,* 1740–1745.

Willingham, W. W. Predicting success in graduate education. *Science,* 1974, January 25, *183,* 273–278.

Willingham, W. W., Young, J. W., & Morris, M. M. *Success in College: The Role of Personal Qualities and Academic Ability.* New York: College Entrance Examination Board, 1985.

Willis, S. Educators look to cultivate speaking and listening skills. *ASCD Update,* 1991, June, *33,* 6.

Willis, S. Teaching thinking. *ASCD Update,* 1992, June, 1.

Winkler, K. J. Scholar whose ideas of female psychology stir debate modifies theories, extends studies to young girls. *Chronicle of Higher Education,* 1990, May 23, 1.

Winter, D. G., McClelland, D. C., & Stewart, A. J. *A New Case for the Liberal Arts: Assessing Institutional Goals and Student Development.* San Francisco: Jossey-Bass, 1981.

Wolfe, N. S. *The University Experience: The First Years.* Buffalo: Division of Instructional Services, University of New York, n.d.

Wolfe, N. S. & Claar, J. M. *The University Experience: The Second Year. Interview Study 3: 1966 Freshman Class.* Buffalo: University Research, State University of New York, 1971.

Wynne, E. A. Facts about the character of young Americans. *Character*, 1979, *1*, 1-8.

Yankelovich, D. & Immerwahr, J. The work ethic and economic vitality. Paper presented at the Wharton/Reliance Symposium, 1983, May 1-3.

Index